Recovering Power

GW00535718

Recovering Power

The Conservatives in Opposition since 1867

Edited by

Stuart Ball
School of Historical Studies, University of Leicester

and

Anthony Seldon
Brighton College

palgrave
macmillan

Editorial Matter and Selection © Stuart Ball and Anthony Seldon 2005
Chapters © 1 Stuart Ball, 2 Angus Hawkins, 3 David Steele, 4 David
Steele, 5 Frans Coetzee, 6 David Dutton, 7 Stuart Ball, 8 David
Willetts, 9 Mark Garnett, 10 Dennis Kavanagh, 11 Anthony Seldon
and Peter Snowdon, 2005

All rights reserved. No reproduction, copy or transmission of this
publication may be made without written permission.

No paragraph of this publication may be reproduced, copied or
transmitted save with written permission or in accordance with the
provisions of the Copyright, Designs and Patents Act 1988,
or under the terms of any licence permitting limited copying issued
by the Copyright Licensing Agency,
90 Tottenham Court Road, London W1T 4LP.

Any person who does any unauthorised act in relation to this
publication may be liable to criminal prosecution and civil
claims for damages.

The authors have asserted their rights to be identified as the authors
of this work in accordance with the Copyright, Designs and Patents
Act 1988.

First published 2005 by
PALGRAVE MACMILLAN
Houndmills, Basingstoke, Hampshire RG21 6XS and
175 Fifth Avenue, New York, N.Y. 10010
Companies and representatives throughout the world

PALGRAVE MACMILLAN is the global academic imprint of the
Palgrave Macmillan division of St Martin's Press LLC and of
Palgrave Macmillan Ltd.
Macmillan® is a registered trademark in the United States,
United Kingdom and other countries. Palgrave is a registered
trademark in the European Union and other countries.

ISBN-10   1–4039–3241–7 hardback
ISBN-13   978–1–4039–3241–9 hardback
ISBN-10   1–4039–3242–5 paperback
ISBN-13   978–1–4039–3242–6 paperback

This book is printed on paper suitable for recycling and
made from fully managed and sustained forest sources.

A catalogue record for this book is available from the British Library.

A catalogue record for this book is available from the Library of
Congress.

10   9   8   7   6   5   4   3   2   1
14   13   12   11   10   09   08   07   06   05

Printed and bound in Great Britain by
Antony Rowe Ltd, Chippenham, Wiltshire

Contents

Notes on Contributors

Stuart Ball is Reader in History at the University of Leicester, and the author of *Baldwin and the Conservative Party: The Crisis of 1929–1931* (Yale University Press, 1988), *The Conservative Party and British Politics 1902–1951* (Longman, 1995) and *Winston Churchill* (British Library, 2003), and is editor of *Parliament and Politics in the Age of Baldwin and MacDonald: The Headlam Diaries 1923–1935* (The Historians' Press, 1992) and *Parliament and Politics in the Age of Churchill and Attlee: The Headlam Diaries 1935–1951* (Cambridge University Press, 1999). He has previously edited, with Anthony Seldon, *Conservative Century: The Conservative Party since 1900* (Oxford University Press, 1994) and *The Heath Government 1970–1974: A Reappraisal* (Longman, 1996), and, with Ian Holliday, *Mass Conservatism: The Conservatives and the Public since the 1880s* (Frank Cass, 2002).

Frans Coetzee, who has taught at Yale and George Washington Universities, is the author of *For Party or Country: Nationalism and the Dilemmas of Popular Conservatism in Edwardian England* (Oxford University Press, 1990), and co-editor (with Marilyn Shevin-Coetzee) of *Authority, Identity and the Social History of the Great War* (Berghahn, 1995), *World War I and European Society* (Houghton Mifflin, 1995), and *World War I: A History in Documents* (Oxford University Press, 2002). Together they are preparing a history of the Second World War to be published by Oxford University Press.

David Dutton is Professor of History at the University of Liverpool, and the author of *Austen Chamberlain* (Ross Anderson, 1985), *His Majesty's Loyal Opposition: The Unionist Party in Opposition 1905–1915* (Liverpool University Press, 1992), *Simon: A Political Biography of Sir John Simon* (Aurum, 1992), *Anthony Eden: A Life and Reputation* (Arnold, 1997), *British Politics since 1945: The Rise, Fall and Rebirth of Consensus* (Blackwell, 1997), *The Politics of Diplomacy: Britain and France in the Balkans in the First World War* (Tauris, 1998), *Neville Chamberlain* (Arnold, 2001), and *A History of the Liberal Party in the Twentieth Century* (Palgrave, 2004).

Mark Garnett is Visting Fellow in the Department of Politics at the University of Leicester, and the author of *Principles and Politics in*

Contemporary Britain (Longman, 1996) and *Alport: A Study in Loyalty* (Acumen, 1999), and co-author of *Whatever Happened to the Tories? The Conservative Party since 1945* (Fourth Estate, 1997), *Keith Joseph* (Acumen, 2001) and *Splendid! Splendid!: The Authorized Biography of Willie Whitelaw* (Jonathan Cape, 2002).

Angus Hawkins is a member of the Modern History Faculty at the University of Oxford, Director of International Programmes in the Department of Continuing Education, and a Fellow of Keble College. He is author of *Parliament, Party and the Art of Politics in Britain 1855–1859* (Macmillan, 1987) and *British Party Politics 1852–1886* (Macmillan, 1998), and co-editor of *The Journal of John Wodehouse, first Earl of Kimberley, for 1862–1902* (Royal Historical Society, 1997). He is currently completing a biography of the 14th Earl of Derby, titled *The Forgotten Prime Minister*.

Dennis Kavanagh is Profesor of Politics at the University of Liverpool, and is author of *Thatcherism and British Politics: The End of Consensus?* (Oxford University Press, 1987), *Election Campaigning: The New Marketing of Politics* (Blackwell, 1995), *The Reordering of British Politics: Politics after Thatcher* (Oxford University Press, 1997), *British Politics: Continuities and Change* (Oxford University Press, 4th edition 2000), and co-author of the Nuffield *British General Election* studies since 1974 (Macmillan, 1974–), *The Powers Behind the Prime Minister* (HarperCollins, 1999) and *Consensus Politics from Attlee to Thatcher* (Blackwell, 1989). He is editor of *A Dictionary of Political Biography* (Oxford University Press, 1987), *Electoral Politics* (Oxford University Press, 1992), and co-editor of *Comparative Government and Politics* (Heinemann, 1984), *The Thatcher Effect* (Oxford University Press, 1989) and *The Major Effect* (Macmillan, 1994).

Anthony Seldon is the founding Director of the Institute of Contemporary British History, and Headmaster of Brighton College; he is the author of *Churchill's Indian Summer: The Conservative Government 1951–1955* (Hodder and Stoughton, 1981), *Major: A Political Life* (Weidenfeld & Nicolson, 1997), *Britain under Thatcher* (Longman, 2000), *Blair* (Simon and Schuster, 2004) and co-author, with Dennis Kavanagh, of *The Powers Behind the Prime Minister* (HarperCollins, 1999), and, with Peter Snowdon, of *The Conservative Party: An Illustrated History* (Sutton, 2004). He has previously edited *How Tory Governments Fall: The Tory Party in Power since 1783* (Fontana, 1996); *The Blair Effect* (Little, Brown, 2001); and, with Stuart Ball, *Conservative Century: The Conservative Party since 1900* (Oxford University Press, 1994) and *The Heath Government 1970–1974: A Reappraisal*

(Longman, 1996); with Dennis Kavanagh, *The Thatcher Effect* (Oxford University Press, 1989) and *The Major Effect* (Macmillan, 1994).

Peter Snowdon is co-author, with Anthony Seldon, of *The Conservative Party: An Illustrated History* (Sutton, 2004) and a contributor to the *Political Quarterly* special issue on the Conservative Party.

David Steele was formerly Reader in History at the University of Leeds, and is author of *Irish Land and British Politics: Tenant-Right and Nationality 1865–1870* (Cambridge University Press, 1974), *Palmerston and Liberalism 1855–1865* (Cambridge University Press, 1991) and *Lord Salisbury: A Political Biography* (UCL Press, 1999).

David Willetts has been Conservative MP for Havant since 1992, and is currently shadow Secretary of State for Work and Pensions and Welfare Reform. He is the author of *Mrs Thatcher's Economic Experiment* (Optima, 1989), *Modern Conservatism* (Penguin, 1992), *Why Vote Conservative?* (Penguin, 1997) and *After the Landslide* (Centre for Policy Studies, 1999), and co-author of *Is Conservatism Dead?* (Profile, 1997).

List of Tables and Figures

Tables

Figure

1

Factors in Opposition Performance: The Conservative Experience since 1867

Stuart Ball

The Conservative Party has been in office much more than it has been in opposition, and its public identity and its own self-image are bound up with being a party of government. Between 1867 and the end of 2004, the Conservatives were in office for 86 years and in opposition for 51 years (see Table 1.1 below). Periods of extended dominance led to the Conservatives being seen as the 'natural' party of government, which was to their electoral advantage. The consequence was that they found opposition to be stressful, considering it an aberrant state of affairs rather than part of the normal cycle. However, although sometimes difficult and turbulent, the spells in opposition have been of crucial importance in the history and development of the Conservative Party. The most significant changes in its attitudes, policies and organization have followed from the shock of defeat. The Conservatives' uncomfortable spells in opposition have seen leadership crises, factional strife and intense debate over the Party's future direction. They have also often been the springboard for recovering power, and the foundation for the next spell of political dominance.

The strengths of the Conservative Party have been its adaptability, resilience and desire for power, and these were often most clearly apparent during its periods in opposition. The longevity and success of the Conservative Party has been founded upon its ability to survive setbacks, accommodate to changes in the political, social or economic environment, and maintain its position as the only credible alternative to the government in power. Its experience of opposition can be frustrating, but is rarely sterile. In many cases, the Conservatives have been able to return to power within a comparatively short period. Since 1868, there have been only three spells in opposition that have lasted for more than six years: barely so in 1945–51, and for longer in 1905–15 and after 1997. On some occasions, the Conservatives were back in office either before or as a result of the next general election, and in most others they regained many seats and took a significant step towards recovery. All of the periods in opposition have seen changes of programme and attempts to broaden the Party's appeal, and many have seen reforms and innovations in the organization.

Despite their importance, these periods in opposition have been remarkably neglected. They are, of course, discussed in general histories of the Conservative Party and in biographies of its leading figures, but few have been examined in greater depth.[1] There is no detailed study of any of the nineteenth-century oppositions, of 1924 or of 1964–70, whilst the works on 1945–51 and 1974–79 were published many years ago and had no access to archives.[2] In particular, there has been no systematic or comparative study which has sought to examine this topic as a whole.[3] The present volume is intended to address this gap, and make a fresh contribution to our understanding of both the Conservative Party and the nature of opposition in the British political system. It contains examinations of each period of opposition since the Second Reform Act of 1867, written by experts in the field and based upon primary research. The common themes and patterns which emerge from this are discussed in the remainder of this introductory chapter.

Factors in opposition party performance

The recovery of power by a party in opposition depends upon the interplay of a range of factors. These fall into two main categories: the internal matters, which the opposition party can determine for itself, and the external situation, which it can neither predict nor control. The reason why opposition is frustrating and stressful is that it is the external factors which are the most significant, because they act directly upon public opinion and produce visible changes in the political situation and in the standing and morale of both government and opposition parties. There are seven such factors, and they are likely to be linked and for several to be present rather than just one alone. The first and most fundamental is the performance of the government, as the opportunities for the opposition depend upon it encountering difficulties. The latter can involve a change of Prime Minister (although the 'fresh face' factor can benefit a government, as the Conservatives demonstrated in 1955 and 1992); splits in its ranks, either in cabinet or in the Commons; the adoption of divisive or 'extreme' policies (such as the 'poll tax'); scandals, crises or disasters; a perception of ineffectiveness, incompetence or failed policies in key areas; or a loss of momentum, leading to the feeling that it is 'time for a change'.

Some of these difficulties are likely to be the result of the second factor, which many would regard as the make-or-break aspect of any government's situation. This is the condition of the economy, and in particular prices and incomes, inflation and interest rates, the level of unemployment and the state of industrial relations. The latter point links directly to the third factor, the public's perception of the general 'state of the nation': concerns about 'governability' and social stability, including disorder and crime, public confidence in the legitimacy and effectiveness of political institutions, and changes in social attitudes and personal mores. The fourth factor lies mainly outside the government's control: the effect of international crises and external threats to national security. The fifth factor is often the result of failures in the previous areas, but it adds something further to them: this is a hostile intellectual climate, which is likely to be reflected in much of the media being unsympathetic to the government's objectives and sharply critical of its actions and conduct. The sixth factor is the role of a third party, if this has either a public appeal or holds the balance in the House of Commons, as the Irish Nationalists did in 1885–86, 1892–95 and 1910–14, and the Liberals did in 1923–24, 1929–31 and 1977–79. The final factor is any changes in the electoral system: not only the franchise extensions of 1867, 1884–85 and 1918, but also the redistribution of seats which was part of these Reform Acts and has occurred periodically since (the latter has regularly benefited the Conservative Party, especially in 1885, 1918, 1950 and 1983).

The first five of the above factors combine to shape the overall public view of the effectiveness and utility of the government. The most damaging perception is that the government is at the mercy of events and lacks the ideas or energy to tackle the problems of the day, which are therefore increasing rather than diminishing. This is worse than being unpopular, as that is a state that can be affected by a change of tactics or by opportune events, as the first Thatcher government of 1979–83 demonstrated. It is often linked with a second problem – the length of time that the government has been in office, which gives rise to over-familiarity and impatience, or the 'time for a change' factor. Minor matters erode support and party enthusiasm, as much as any larger ones, and the machine gets lax and complacent. The issue of experience can cut both ways; a party or a Prime Minister may seem to have been around too long, which will weaken their position if they run into other problems. Lack of experience has never prevented the public from electing a party that has been in opposition for a long period, and whose leaders have little or no ministerial experience. When the mood turns against a government, it matters only that a credible opposition exists and that it does not seem to be an even more unpalatable alternative; this was certainly the lesson acted upon by the Labour leadership from the disaster of 1983 to the triumphant return of 1997.

It is these external factors which seem to be the driving force, towing the opposition in their wake. The recovery of unity, support and morale in the opposition flow from the difficulties of the government, rather than causing them in the first instance. The strategy of the opposition is generally shaped by the actions of the government, and it is the government that sets the agenda. The most important things that an opposition party can do are negatives rather than positives, for whilst an opposition cannot win an election by its unaided efforts, it can certainly lose one. The critical objective for an opposition is to put itself in a position from which it can take advantage of the government's problems and weaknesses as they arise, and not let opportunities slip away. The opposition must ensure that it is 'electable': this normally means that it has a credible leader, is united, can put up candidates in most constituencies, and has policies which are not unwelcome to the majority of voters and which have enough coherence and content to be sustainable against attack. Serious flaws in one, and certainly more, of these areas are unlikely to lead to recovering power, even when the government has a poor record or has failed to fulfil expectations.

At a basic level, a party has to recover much of the support that was lost in the previous election, and it may also seek to secure support from new groups in age, gender, class or region. Although it is the external factors that most affect voting intentions, there are five ways in which an opposition party can place itself in the best tactical position. The first of these is 'fresh faces': a new leader or leadership team, and especially the sense of a change of generations. The second is 'cohesion': the maintenance of unity and discipline within the party, which is essential to convey a sense of purpose and effectiveness. The third is 'visibility': a new agenda or a distinctive position, and a distancing from past unpopular policies and their legacy. Here it is important to have an impact upon the political elite and opinion formers, in order to give credibility to revival and reorientation, and for this to be communicated to a wider audience. The fourth element links to this, and is 'efficiency': not just an improved or revived party organization, but the sense that the party is at least master in its own house, and can respond with speed and authority when the need arises. The final element is 'adaptability': a hunger for office, and a pragmatic or unideological approach which gives room to manoeuvre and seize the openings that appear.

These elements combine to shape the public view of the credibility of the opposition, which can be established or reinforced through by-election successes, parliamentary impact or effective propaganda, and for the greatest effect some combination of these. To have an impact and draw support towards itself, the opposition needs to be in tune with the general priorities of the voters who lie between its own invariable supporters and the invariable supporters of the other parties. It needs to identify key aspects of public concern, and to present at the least, effective criticisms of government performance, and possibly credible or even attractive alternative remedies. It needs to develop slogans and a general image that resonate with these concerns, rather than distracting from them or raising the ghosts of past unpopularity and defeat.

A party, or its leaders, can exercise some control over what is said and done in a number of important areas. These combine to create an overall image in the public consciousness, which plays a significant – but not determining – part in the prospects of returning to power. The first and most visible of these areas is the party leadership, and this can have two elements. The action of an opposition party which is most noticed by voters is a change of its leader, although this is not always a positive affair. The new leader may be relatively unknown (perhaps Salisbury, and certainly Bonar Law, Thatcher, Hague and Duncan Smith), and may have a negative impact. The latter could be a matter of a dull or distancing personality (Bonar Law, Heath and Thatcher), or identification with unpopular policies (Bonar Law as a leading proponent of tariff reform, Howard as a cabinet minister under Major and especially his role in implementing the 'poll tax' of the late 1980s). Nevertheless, a change of leader can be beneficial in several ways, especially if a party is seeking to put an unsuccessful or unpopular period in government behind it. It signifies a fresh start of at least some sort, whether of strategy (Bonar Law, Thatcher and Duncan Smith), outlook and background (Bonar Law and Heath), or generation (Salisbury, Heath and Hague). All of these can have their appeal, but if the switch is too extensive there is a danger of losing more than is gained (Salisbury, Thatcher and Hague all aroused concern in this respect).

The second element of change in leadership is in the wider group around the actual leader, as this to a lesser extent also shapes the public image and awareness of what the party stands for. Such changes can be rapid and substantial after a long spell in government, when the retirement of long-serving former ministers brings a change of generation on the front bench as the party enters opposition. This is particularly likely after a major defeat, as the former leaders may be discredited and some will have lost their seats – in 1906, even the Prime Minister and party leader, Balfour, was defeated. There were significant generational changes after the defeats of 1906 (although several figures of the Salisbury era had retired with him in 1902), 1945, 1964 and 1997. This was sometimes obscured by the continuation of the existing leader (Balfour after 1906 and Churchill after 1945), but in all these cases the composition of the Cabinet when the party returned to office was very different from when it had lost power.

Leadership is commonly presented as one of the three main areas in which a party can make changes when in opposition (the others being its policies and its organization). However, there is something of a myth about the Conservative Party's habit of ditching leaders who have led it into defeat, as Table 1.1 demonstrates.

Table 1.1   Periods in Opposition and Changes of Leadership

Period in Opposition				Changes of Leadership	
Date of entering opposition	Date of return to office	Length (years months)	Leader on entering opposition	Date of change (if any)	Leader on return to office, if different
1 Dec. 1868	20 Feb. 1874	5.3	B. Disraeli		
21 Apr. 1880	23 June 1885	5.2	B. Disraeli*	23 June 1885	Lord Salisbury
28 Jan. 1886	25 July 1886	0.6	Lord Salisbury		
11 Aug. 1892	25 June 1895	2.11	Lord Salisbury		
4 Dec. 1905	25 May 1915	9.6	A. Balfour	13 Nov. 1911	A. Bonar Law
22 Jan. 1924	4 Nov. 1924	0.9	S. Baldwin		
4 June 1929	24 Aug. 1931	2.3	S. Baldwin		
26 July 1945	26 Oct. 1951	6.4	W. Churchill		
16 Oct. 1964	19 June 1970	5.8	A. Douglas-Home	2 Aug. 1965	E. Heath
4 Mar. 1974	4 May 1979	5.2	E. Heath	11 Feb. 1975	M. Thatcher
2 May 1997			J. Major	19 June 1997	*unknown***

*   Disraeli had become the Earl of Beaconsfield in 1876.
** John Major was followed as leader by William Hague (19 June 1997), Iain Duncan Smith (13 Sep. 2001), and Michael Howard (6 Nov. 2003).

It is only in the last decade that the pattern has developed of the party leader resigning immediately after an election defeat, as Major did in 1997 and Hague in 2001. Part of the reason for this was the scale of these defeats, and neither Heath in 1974 nor Douglas-Home in 1964 felt the need to resign after losing the poll. In 1964 Douglas-Home had been leader and Prime Minister for just one year, and had managed to reduce what had seemed likely to be a heavy defeat to a very narrow one indeed. He encountered difficulties in opposition, and in 1965 withdrew because of these (as Baldwin also nearly did in 1931). Heath's position after losing office in February 1974 was more contentious, but even so he still led the Conservatives into the next election, although this was mainly because Labour's lack of a majority meant that a dissolution was likely to come soon and the party would be caught at a disadvantage if it was in the midst of a leadership change. In the inter-war period, Baldwin briefly contemplated quitting after the 1923 defeat, and fought off a series of attacks on his position in 1929–31, but he was always able to retain the support of the majority of Conservative MPs. After 1906, Balfour led the Party for nearly six years in opposition, and through two further – though closely related – general elections in January and December 1910, before resigning in 1911. Before this, the need for a new leader had only been due to natural causes, with Disraeli's death in 1881.

Leadership is a key element because it critically affects both a party's public image and the decisions which are taken about the fundamental strategic questions which have to be addressed in any period in opposition. The most significant of these is whether to adopt the 'active' approach of initiating new departures, or the 'reactive' stance of waiting for and exploiting the problems of the government. New policies and directions can have advantages, both in attracting attention and in making a break with the past. However, as with a new leader, they have to be carefully chosen – they may deter as much as attract, and divide as much as unite. There is a particular danger in making commitments to exploit a government difficulty that may be only minor or temporary, as with Bonar Law's statement that the Conservatives would repeal Lloyd George's National Insurance Act of 1911.

If an 'active' strategy is followed, there is also a dilemma over the direction which should be taken: whether to emphasize a distinctively Conservative identity and programme, or to present a consensual image in order to capture the 'middle ground'. The choice for any party is between concentrating upon its core values and expressing the outlook of its most vocal supporters, or giving a higher priority to widening its appeal and social base, even if this means changes in outlook and image. Pragmatism and the hunger for office may promote adaptation to the factors which caused the party to lose power, as in the policy reviews of

1924, 1945–51 and (though more apparently radical) 1975–79. However, as Balfour found in 1906 and Baldwin in 1929–30, an election defeat tilts the balance of strength in the remaining parliamentary party towards the safest seats. The grass-roots membership and MPs from the heartland regions may have little experience of conditions elsewhere, and lack the willingness or need to compromise on cherished objectives.

The danger in the 'active' strategy is that proposals have to be put forward in sufficient detail to be credible, but are then vulnerable to counter-attacks from the government. This leads to an unsatisfactory reversal of roles, as the advantages of being in opposition (flexibility, vagueness, a focus upon general principles and the broad picture) are lost, without gaining the assets of being in government (prestige, patronage and access to civil service and other supporting structures).[4] Churchill was convinced that this was both bad tactics and unnecessary. He strongly favoured making as few commitments as possible and focusing energy on attacking the government, holding the classic view that an opposition's first duty is to oppose, and not to propose. Those who favoured the 'reactive' strategy subscribed, whether consciously or unconsciously, to another basic assumption about the operation of the British political system: the adage that 'oppositions do not win elections, governments lose them'. In other words, it is the actions and performance of the government which determine its fate, and by itself the opposition can do little to affect these matters. It logically follows that the most useful thing an opposition can do is to chip away at the government's morale and popularity, and certainly not to allow it to sidestep its problems by providing either a distraction or an easy target.

Whether the 'active' or the 'reactive' approach was being adopted, there was one further strategic issue that had to be confronted. This was how to respond to measures for which the incoming government could claim a mandate or which were popular, especially when they involved dismantling or reversing the measures of previous Conservative governments. This question was likely to arise from the very beginning of an opposition period, and the response to it could largely predetermine the broader agenda. Thus, in 1868–74 Disraeli did not give any commitment to reverse the early measures of Gladstone's first ministry, whilst on the other hand in 1906–10 the Conservatives used their majority in the House of Lords to wreck or reject a range of Liberal bills – although up to 1909 they were careful not to do so with anything of general appeal. The classic example of accepting changes and looking forwards is the 1945–51 opposition, and this was validated by the subsequent return to power for not just one parliament but three consecutive ones. The problem did not arise to the same extent when in opposition during unsuccessful or minority governments, but the Conservatives accepted the land aspect of Gladstone's Irish policy in the early 1880s and greatly expanded it with measures of their own in 1885, 1887, 1891 and 1896. They continued to use the budgetary device of death duties introduced by the Liberals in 1892–95, and of the graduated levels of income tax in Lloyd George's 'People's Budget' of 1909. Despite any reservations, the measures on race and gender discrimination of the 1964–70 and 1974–79 Labour governments were left in place, as were a range of other social and moral reforms.

The decisions on the basic strategic questions are often strongly contested, and they have been a major source of debate and disunity within the Conservative Party during its periods in opposition in both the nineteenth and twentieth centuries. A key element in this is the interpretations of the reasons for the previous loss of power, and the immediate impact and reactions which have followed defeat. In this context, it is significant that every departure from office since 1868 has been the consequence of defeat in a general election, with the sole exception of 1905 – when electoral defeat was clearly in prospect and followed immediately after. On several occasions, matters were further complicated by differences within the Party over the causes of the defeat or the policies upon which the election had been lost. This happened in 1868 after the Second Reform Act, in 1929 with the moderate economic and social programme, and in 1997 upon the issues of adopting radical 'Thatcherite' policies and of Europe. It was particularly contentious in 1906 over the electoral role of tariff reform, and in 1974 after the 'U-turns' of the Heath government. On the other hand, the task ahead was made simpler, if not necessarily easier, if there was a general consensus upon the reasons for the fall from office. This could still involve self-criticism, as in 1892, 1964 and especially 1923; other defeats were at least partly absolved by attribution to outside factors for which the party was not responsible, as in 1880, 1945 and especially 1885.

The second main area of the internal matters that a party can directly control is its policies. Decisions here are directly affected by the choice between the 'active' or the 'reactive' strategies, as policy matters will be much more important – and possibly contentious – if it is intended to use them as the lever with which to move the rock of public opinion. In any case, a defeated party can hardly rest upon its laurels, especially if they are already withered by age or crushed by popular rejection. Some reappraisal is inevitable, and would occur even if the party had remained in office. There is the natural effect of the passage of time, which brings changing circumstances and unforeseen events, and thereby affects opinions and priorities. The 'reactive' strategy depends upon this process, making the assumption that the difficulties of managing affairs are bound to weaken a government, and that the compromises of office are likely to alienate some of its own supporters and disappoint some of the uncommitted voters. As a pessimistic view of the human condition is a fundamental element in 'natural Conservatism', it is perhaps not surprising that many Conservatives by temperament favoured the 'reactive' strategy. Certainly, it was less in tune with the Conservative mentality to believe – as did the 'whole-hog' tariff reformers in the Edwardian era, or the libertarian right in the 1990s – that a policy or a programme was the vehicle upon which the party would ride back into public favour.[5]

Even so, attention to policy matters is unavoidable, as the incoming government introduces legislation to which the opposition front-bench has to make some response, at least for debating purposes. Purely negative criticism is not, in practice, attainable – for there are implicit choices made by the selection of what to attack, and how to go about doing so. In practice, some indication of a better alternative has to be given, even if it remains shadowy on detail. Otherwise, the government can turn the tables, by alleging that the opposition are bereft of ideas and could achieve no more if they were in office. Furthermore, over a longer period of time a solely critical stance can be a problem for the opposition party itself. The lack of substance may not satisfy its own supporters, or leave a dangerous vacuum in which they will fall out amongst themselves, as happened during parts of the 1905–14 period, in 1929–30, over devolution in 1974–79, and over Europe after 1997. A lack of positive alternatives is also likely to be criticized by normally-supportive newspapers, and so become a problem and distraction. A simply negative 'reactive' strategy may be too partisan for uncommitted voters, who are alienated by narrow tribalistic attitudes – hence the appeal of SDP-Liberal Alliance when it was launched in the early 1980s.

Therefore, whilst criticism of the government and its works will be the first priority of any opposition, there is bound to be a policy-making process running in parallel. Three other factors may encourage this, and determine the importance that is attached to it and the degree of prominence and publicity that it is given. The first of these is the need for distance from the past, to uncouple the party's future fortunes from the legacy of an unpopular record – something that was achieved eventually by Disraeli in 1874, substantially by Churchill in 1951, partially by Heath in 1970 and Thatcher in 1979, but not yet by any of the leaders since 1997. The second need is for distinctiveness from the government, so that the party will be seen as a genuine alternative at the next election and not just as 'more of the same', the 'plague on both houses' feeling that was damaging particularly in the 1964–79 era. Finally, policy changes can be used as a demonstration of vigour and vitality, giving the impression that the opposition party is bursting with answers to the nation's problems, if only it can be given the chance to implement them.

The development of new policies may take a little while to get under way, especially if this is complicated by disputes and inquests over the causes of defeat. There is a natural pause for breath, partly from the physical and mental demands of having been in government and then fighting a general election, and partly to see what will unfold. In this sense there is a natural caution, and in practice the strategy of an opposition is likely to mix reactive 'wait and see' with active 'look at me', and for there to be much more of the former in the initial phases. It may also be that the incoming government puts centre-stage an issue upon which the opposition party already has strong and developed views, which was the case with Irish Home Rule in 1892–93 and 1912–14 (though not when Gladstone first raised it in 1886). Alternative policies were not considered as necessary in the second half of the nineteenth century as they had become by the later decades of the twentieth. Even so, the broad principles that Disraeli set out in two major and lengthy public speeches in 1872 were considered to have given coherence and vigour to the opposition, though they were not delivered until at least half of the parliament had elapsed and the government was visibly faltering.

Between 1906 and 1910, tariff reform was considered to be the focus, but there were constant concerns by its enthusiasts that the pragmatic leadership was not giving it sufficient clarity and emphasis. After the 1910 defeats, there was little development of policy: tariffs were displaced without being repudiated (giving the worst of all worlds), unofficial initiatives in developing answers to Liberal social policy were greeted with suspicion or indifference (the Unionist Social Reform Committee), and everything became bound up in the defence of the Union and the position of Ulster. This aroused passions, but was at best a one-card trick, and with no certainty that it would out-trump the government.[6]

The periods in opposition since the First World War have seen much more emphasis upon policy development, partly as a response to the democratic franchise created in 1918, and partly because the Conservatives are competing for support in that arena with the more ideologically-motivated Labour Party. The two most successful exercises were those of 1924 and 1945–51, and the example of the latter spurred the most extensive review in 1964–70 and the belief in 1974–79 in the value of a defining statement of principles to give intellectual coherence to the Party's position: in 1947 this was *The Industrial Charter*, and in 1976 it was *The Right Approach*.[7] There has been no similar document since 1997, at least not in any public visibility, and no systematic or trumpeted policy review, although certainly there have been plenty of statements, position papers and pamphlets. None of these have made a public impact or lifted the Conservatives' popularity, and there remains an impression that too many areas of policy are dangerous minefields into which the opposition dare not venture, for it has no map with which to avoid blowing itself up.

The last, and perhaps least, of the three main areas that a party can take into its own hands is its organization. It is in many ways the easiest area, because it is normally less contentious than policy, though there can be individuals or even groups of supporters who are unsettled or offended by changes in long-established methods. It takes place mainly out of public view, and is implemented by the salaried officials who are under the executive direction of the party leader, since 1911 through his or her appointee as Party Chairman. There may be some institutional resistance at this level – as with the innovation of the Community Affairs Department at Central Office in 1975 – and more so at local level, where the tradition of constituency autonomy is vigorously defended.[8] Even so, organizational changes are mainly a matter affecting the most loyal elements within the party – Central Office staff, local association chairmen and salaried agents.

A review of the organization is also the most obvious area for action, as deficiencies here are often blamed as a cause of defeat. There is often truth in this, especially when the party has been in office for a lengthy period and the need for efficiency and vitality has been absent for some time. This was certainly the case in 1880 after Gorst's departure as National Agent, in 1906 after the end of the Middleton era at Central Office, in 1945 with the almost complete hibernation of the organization during the Second World War, and in 1964 as the great machine crafted by Woolton began to run out of steam. However, it was much less the case in 1892 when Akers-Douglas as Chief Whip and Middleton as chief organizer were in their prime, in 1923 when the National Union executive committee went out of its way to praise Central Office after the defeat, in 1929 when there was more criticism but the organization was actually at its strongest ever apart from 1947–51, or in 1974 and 1997 when the finger of blame was largely directed elsewhere. Devoting attention to reorganization can also be tempting in another way, as activity here can be substitute for tackling more fundamental and difficult problems in other areas.

Reorganization is the least important of the three areas, because it has the least direct effect upon public opinion. Parties do not pull themselves up by their own bootstraps – if this were so, then returning to power would be a simple exercise indeed. Tackling organization alone will have little impact, unless the government is overwhelmed by a major crisis – and if that should happen, then the opposition will benefit whether or not their party machinery has been improved. Paper restructuring does not of itself attract voluntary workers or bring in donations; it is circumstances in the outside world that do so. In fact, organizational recovery is more a result of revival in a party's fortunes than a cause of it. In many cases, the first response to defeat is apathy and a further falling off in enthusiasm and efficiency. It takes alarm, controversy or adverse conditions to bring back former supporters as well as draw in any new ones. Lord Woolton was credited with much in the recovery after 1945, but his first membership drive in the autumn of 1946 only recovered a part of the pre-war support that had been lost; it was not until after Labour's difficult winter of 1947 that his major fund-raising and recruitment initiatives began to be effective. The role of organizational reforms in the 1945–51 recovery is a powerful element in the heroic myth of that period, but it has much more to do with the return to former allegiance of many middle-class and female working-class voters than with any success in attracting new elements of support.

The period when organizational innovation made the most significant contribution to recovering power was not in 1945–51, but in 1868–74. This was partly because almost nothing existed before the development of the National Union after 1867 and the creation of Conservative Central Office in 1870, and any initiatives would improve upon the existing chaos. It was also the case that in the mid-nineteenth-century electoral system, organization could deliver much greater practical gains. This was firstly in finding candidates to contest seats, an important matter when this was an expensive undertaking, and it was here that Central Office had the most effect. Secondly, the combination of constituency electorates that were often between 2000 and 4000 voters and the importance of the complicated registration system meant that an efficient local organization could significantly shape the outcome before the election was called.

In other periods, organizational changes contributed only at the margins or not at all. The innovation of the Primrose League, founded in 1883, could not prevent defeat in 1885, and victory in 1886 was clearly due to the Liberals' division over Irish Home Rule and lack of support for this policy in many English constituencies. Even where they did take place, organizational changes were not the driving factors in the return to power in 1895, 1924, 1931, 1970 or 1979. The initial reorganization after 1906 actually made matters worse, but the further defeats in 1910 led to the most important changes since the Disraelian foundations of 1867–70. Even so, the creation of the post of Party Chairman in 1911, the restructuring of Central Office, the introduction of new and efficient staff and considerably better funding did not alter the political balance between the government and the opposition. The difficulties in other areas, and especially the lack of an appealing domestic programme, make it at least dubious that the Conservatives would have won a peacetime general election in 1915. Instead, the impact of the First World War brought the Conservatives back into office in the coalition government of May 1915, and by end of the war in 1918 their former rivals, the Liberal Party, had become severely and permanently damaged

The Conservative experience of opposition since 1867

The Conservative Party when in opposition has often been pre-occupied with the internal matters of leadership, policy and organization. This is particularly the case with leadership and strategic direction, which are often bound up together in the choice or retention of the Party leader (as was the case with Salisbury in 1885, Balfour after 1906, Baldwin in the 1920s, Thatcher in 1975, and Hague and Duncan Smith after 1997). These aspects do matter, especially in combining to form and communicate an image to the public at large. A capable party machine, innovative or efficient campaigning methods and good relations with the media will make a difference. So also does the maintenance of unity and discipline within the party, for a factious opposition is unlikely to be effective or to appear an attractive replacement for the government – a problem the Conservatives faced in 1880–85, 1905–10, 1929–31, 1964–70, since 1997, and to some extent in 1974–79. Being in opposition is neither simple nor easy, a problem made worse by the fact that many politicians and commentators assume that it is. There are stresses and pressures, especially from the frustration which develops when there are no clear signs of progress, and tensions and divisions can then emerge. This was a feature of the period 1910–14, in 1930–31, in 1949, in 1968–70 and in the replacement of Duncan Smith in 2003.

The outcomes since 1867 of the Conservative Party's attempts to recover power can be placed in three categories: major successes, modest successes, and failures. There have been five substantial victories, and

Table 1.2 Gains in Seats and Size of Overall Majority on Return to Office

General election	Gain in seats since previous general election	Lead over next largest party	Overall majority
31 Jan. 1874	79	108	48
1 July 1886	69	124	39
13 July 1895	98	234	152
29 Oct. 1924	154	261	209
27 Oct. 1931	210	418	493
25 Oct. 1951	23	26	17
18 June 1970	77	32	20
3 May 1979	62	70	43

Note: The figures for 1886 are for the Conservatives only, and treat the Liberal Unionists as a separate party; if the 77 Liberal Unionists are counted as supporting the Conservatives, their combined overall majority was 116. The figures for 1895 include the Liberal Unionists, as they were now in formal alliance with the Conservatives and represented in the Cabinet. In 1931, the figures for gain in seats and lead over next largest party are for the Conservatives alone, but the overall majority figure is for the National Government as a whole.

it is noticeable that none of these has occurred in the last 70 years. The first, in 1874, is included in this category not so much for the size of the Conservatives' overall majority, which was only 48, or for the number of seats gained in comparison to the previous election, although that was a respectable 79. Rather, it is the fact that any overall majority at all was a huge achievement after almost 30 years of opposition or – rarely and briefly – minority government. The previous Conservative majority had been gained in 1841 by Peel, who then broke the Party apart over the Corn Laws in 1846; Disraeli's victory in 1874 was the first real proof that the rump of the party left after Peel's departure was broadening its appeal. Both this and the other nineteenth-century triumphs, in 1886 and 1895, were based upon two linked factors. The first of these was a feature of elections in this era which dwindled after 1918 and vanished after 1945: a large number of unopposed returns. In 1874, 125 Conservative MPs were returned to Parliament without a challenge; in 1886, it was 118, and in 1895 it was 132; the only other instance with over a hundred unopposed returns was in the following election, in 1900, where there were 163.[9] All four of these high levels were explained by the second factor in these Conservative recoveries – the falling apart of the Liberal Party in the House of Commons into factionalism and apathy. Special factors also applied in the case of the other two landslide recoveries, in 1924 and 1931. In this period the Conservatives benefited from the twin effects of the decline of the Liberal Party and the rise of Labour. These victories were in elections where there was some alarm over Labour's record or intentions, and where the Liberal Party was in disarray and was either putting up many fewer candidates than before (1924) or was in a coalition pact with the Conservatives (1931).

There are three returns to office which, for different reasons, can be placed in the category of narrower victories. The first of these is 1951, when the Party recovered power with the slim, but workable, overall majority in the House of Commons of 17. Given that this represented 111 more seats than the Conservatives held in 1945, it might seem odd to place it in this category. However, the point is that it took two elections to return to office, and whilst it was certainly a significant achievement in a relatively short period – and compares favourably with the record after the other landslide defeats of 1906 and 1997 – it was still a fairly narrow victory, and the Labour Party had a larger total of votes cast in its favour. The other two recoveries in this group have similarities, one of which is that they are in the same decade. The number of seats won back in 1970 was considerable, with 77 gains on the 1966 result. This gave the Conservatives a narrow but sufficient parliamentary majority of 20; for that reason it is in this middle category, even though it is the one occasion on which the Conservatives overturned a large government majority at the next election. In 1979 a similar number of seats gained (62) produced a larger overall majority of 43, but the barrier to be surmounted was much easier, as by the end of the parliament the Labour government was a minority dependent upon a pact with the Liberals to stay in office.

The Conservative Party entered 15 general elections as the opposition, and emerged from eight of them as the next government. This is a fair record, but hardly strong enough to suggest the possession of an innate aptitude or special skills for opposition. If the elections are counted individually, there were seven failures to recover power. In practice, three of these were closely linked to a prior defeat, and were really part of the same political cycle. The general elections of December 1910 and October 1974 are the most obvious examples of this, and 1966 is the other. In the first two cases, neither the personalities, party identities nor public mood had changed much since the previous contest a few months earlier. 1966 saw the working out of the unpopularity and decline of the Conservatives when they left office in 1964 after 13 years of government, and this was even more true of the October 1974 election, which came only eight months after the Heath government had ended in confrontation, crisis and rejection. Even so, a short interval since losing office does not make a return impossible if other circumstances are favourable, as was shown in 1886 (after seven months), 1924 (after 11 months) and 1931 (after two years and five months, about half the length of a parliament). The difference was that in 1966 the government managed its affairs effectively, at least as far as the public perception was concerned, and continued to project the modernizing and meritocratic style that had attracted support in 1964. The Conservatives, on the other hand, not only were still encumbered by the appearance of out-datedness and loss of competence that had harmed them in 1962–64, but also had a leader pushed into retiring and parliamentary disunity over Rhodesia. The new leader, Heath, was certainly a radical break in social background and manner from previous leaders, but he did not have much time to establish himself. Whilst there was an extensive policy exercise, it suffered from the blunderbuss effect – a horde of small shots, but little that really dented the target.

Having set these three cases aside, there remain four failures to recover power after more or less a full parliament in opposition: 1885, January 1910, 1950 and 2001. Of these, the position in 1885 is complicated, and in the literal sense it is actually an election in which a Conservative government loses office, rather than a Conservative opposition failing to recover it. The previous general election in 1880 had seen the defeat of Disraeli's government and the installation of the Liberals, with Gladstone taking the office of Prime Minister for the second time. However, the customary pattern of Liberal disintegration in the later part of a parliament emerged again, and in June 1885 the Liberals resigned after a losing a relatively unimportant vote in the Commons, glad to escape the burdens and frustrations of office. The recent passage of the Third Reform Act, the Liberals' one major domestic measure, meant that a general election was politically impossible on the old franchise, but the new electoral registers would not be ready until November. In these circumstances, Lord Salisbury accepted the invitation to form a minority Conservative government, known as the 'Caretaker Government' as its duration was only to last the few months until the election in November. The Conservatives therefore contested the 1885 election as the government in office, though in reality their position gave them very little power and for over five years during the parliament they had been the party in opposition.

The other complication in assessing 1885 is that the electoral system had changed greatly since the previous contest. The Third Reform Act not only extended the franchise in the county seats (a Liberal measure specifically intended to undercut the Conservatives in their stronger areas), but also radically redrew the electoral map of Britain by moving towards single-member constituencies of roughly equal population size, whilst the 1883 Corrupt Practices Act changed the way in which elections were fought. It is therefore difficult to compare the 1885 performance with that of 1880 or the previous recovery of 1874. Given the circumstances against them in 1885, the Conservatives' net gain of 12 seats was not such a dismal outcome as it might seem, and there were particularly encouraging signs of electoral advance in the larger towns and in the key regions of Lancashire and London. Although it was only 11 seats more, as far as real progress is concerned the outcome in 1885 is in a different league from that of 2001. Nevertheless, the immediate result when the new parliament met in January 1886 was that the Liberals, with Irish Nationalist support now that Gladstone had declared for Home Rule, voted the Salisbury administration out and Gladstone became Prime Minister for the third time.

The remaining cases of failure, significantly, are the parliaments which followed the three massive defeats of the twentieth century in 1906, 1945 and 1997. On none of these occasions, despite having had at least four years in which to restore their fortunes, did the Conservatives win the next general election. The best result was in 1950, with 88 seats regained and – more importantly – the government's overall majority reduced to only six. Not only was this small enough to rule out any major new legislation from the government and make a further full term almost impossible, but there was also the comfort that the Cabinet were clearly exhausted both physically and politically, in visible contrast to the reinvigorated and confident opposition. Whilst there had been something of a crisis of confidence in 1949 due to the failure to make any by-election gains, the extent of the ground made up in the 1950 election was more than enough to calm the Party's nerves and give it encouragement and purpose. It was followed by one of the most effective opposition periods as far as tactics and policy were concerned, with a disciplined Party making full use of its parliamentary opportunities and an important public commitment on housing, a major issue of the day on which the government had under-performed. In the earlier case of the January 1910 election, although the Conservatives won back 116 seats and drew almost level with the Liberal Party in the House of Commons, in the sense that really matters they remained a long way short of recovering office. This was because as long as the Liberals retained the support of the Irish Nationalists, who had 82 seats, and to a lesser extent the new Labour Party, which had 40, their parliamentary position was unassailable. As they had also broken the power of the House of Lords to prevent bills being passed, and were beholden to the Irish to bring in a Home Rule bill, the Conservatives after January 1910 could only contemplate utter frustration, and not surprisingly some of them cast round for any methods that could be used against the government.

The 2001 result was unarguably the worst of all in electoral terms and for party morale; there was nothing to take encouragement from at all, and the loss of some seats to the Liberal Democrats was a worrying complication. Based on the experience of not only 1906, 1945 and 1966, but also 1924, 1931, 1959 and 1983, it had been assumed that any sweeping victory depended upon temporary factors, some of which were bound to have diminished by the next election. It was therefore thought to be almost a law of political gravity that some inroads would be made upon a government majority which was by nature ephemeral, and by the time of the next election somewhat unreal. The question was only how extensive the opposition's recovery of its former territory would be, not whether it would occur at all. So, when it did fail to happen, the shock and dismay were all the greater, especially as the electoral mountain of Labour's 1997 majority still remained to be climbed. It had already been accepted by most observers, whatever the Conservative front-bench felt required to say for the sake of maintaining confidence and motivation, that a landslide victory like 1997 would take more than one parliament to overturn. This view was based on what happened after 1906, 1945 and 1983, although it discounted 1966 as less of a victory and ignored the 1924 example as somehow not applicable (despite the parallels frequently made with the Edwardian era). It now seemed that this slow process of erosion still all lay ahead, and that it could no longer be taken for granted. However, a consideration of some other examples of opposition fortunes would deprecate the view that this was a novel and unprecedented departure. Despite all the economic and political problems of the Heath government, in February 1974 the Labour Party only recovered 13 seats, and in 1987 it did not do much better with 20 gains. In 1955 and 1959 the Labour opposition actually lost ground to the government, ending up with 107 seats less than the Conservatives. The closest parallel is with the Liberals in 1900; suffering from even more parliamentary disunity and paralysis in leadership and policy-making than Labour in the 1950s, they won only six more seats than in their landslide defeat of 1895.

There is a myth of recovery in opposition to which the Conservative Party particularly subscribes, being still in thrall to the heroic image of 1945–51. In reality, a much more common pattern is the metaphor of climbing a mountain that is too large to be tackled in a single stage. Only once since 1900 have the Conservatives returned to office against a government in possession of a workable majority – and that was under

Heath in 1970, after the most forgotten and derided of the opposition periods. The victories of 1924, 1931 (as part of a coalition) and 1979 were all over minority governments, and Labour's majority of six in 1950–51 was clearly unsustainable. The only other examples are all in the very different party and electoral environment of the nineteenth century. In 1874, 1886 and 1895 Liberal majorities were replaced by Conservative ones, but in all three cases the unity of the Liberals had collapsed and they had suffered parliamentary defeat before resigning office; in that sense, whatever the apparent numbers, they no longer possessed a workable majority.

Table 1.3   Electoral Recovery at the Next General Election

Date of election defeat	Date of next election	Interval (years months)	Change in no. of seats	Change in % vote	Return to office?
17 Nov. 1868	31 Jan. 1874	5.2	+ 79	+ 5.5	YES
31 Mar. 1880	24 Nov. 1885	5.8	+ 12	+ 1.5	NO*
24 Nov. 1885	1 July 1886	0.7	+ 144	+ 7.9	YES
4 July 1892	13 July 1895	3.0	+ 98	+ 2.1	YES
12 Jan. 1906	15 Jan. 1910	4.10	+ 116	+ 3.4	NO
6 Dec. 1923	29 Oct. 1924	0.11	+ 154	+ 8.8	YES
30 May 1929	27 Oct. 1931	2.5	+ 210	+ 16.9	YES**
5 July 1945	23 Feb. 1950	4.7	+ 88	+ 3.9	NO
15 Oct. 1964	31 Mar. 1966	1.5	– 51	– 2.4	NO
28 Feb. 1974	10 Oct. 1974	0.7	– 20	– 2.1	NO
1 May 1997	7 June 2001	4.1	+ 1	+ 0.4	NO

*   The Conservative Party returned to office in June 1885 due to the resignation of the Liberal government, but were defeated in the election in November 1885.
**   The Conservative Party joined the National Government on 24 August 1931.

Note: This table considers the outcome of the first general election to be held after the Conservative Party enters opposition, whatever the interval; this is not necessarily the occasion at which the Conservatives return to power. The comparison of seats is with the previous election defeat, and does not take into acount any by-election gains that have been made since then.

In all of the opposition periods, the economic fortunes of the government were important, but – unless dire – they were not alone a guarantee of opposition success. This was a less significant factor before 1914, as governments then were not regarded as having primary responsibility for this area. A link could be made if there were government actions which could be portrayed as unsettling for trading conditions or business confidence, as Gladstone successfully suggested when assaulting the Disraeli ministry before the 1880 election, but in general it was not the sharpest weapon in an opposition's armoury. It was not a main element in the Conservatives' return to power in 1874 or 1886, and played a slightly different role in 1895. There was depression in this period, and it was the time of particular concern over the erosion of British markets by competition from rising industrial powers, and in particular from Germany. More of a problem for the 1892–95 Liberal government was the effects of the employers' counter-offensive against the trade union gains of the late 1880s, with the formation of employers' federations and the resulting lockouts and strikes. The disappointment of some Liberal trade unionist support with the government's failure to act in this area was one of the factors in Liberal disunity and low morale by 1895, as well as impelling some towards the creation of the Independent Labour Party and the supporting of separate parliamentary representation.[10] In the opposite way, the economic growth and general prosperity from 1905 to 1914 did not help the Conservative opposition – especially in 1908–10, when it undermined the case for their radical proposal of tariff reform.

The state of the economy was not a factor in the short Labour government of 1924, but became critical in their second term of 1929–31. The depression and the steep rises in unemployment broke the government – immediately in August 1931 on the issue of the budget deficit that had developed, but before that the ministry's confidence had crumbled, its supporters were plunged in gloom and its popular support was ebbing away. The slump was also a powerful force impelling the Conservatives to unity and focused activity in 1931, and it helped considerably to overcome the internal party conflict of the previous two years. Oppositions reaped the best harvest when economic difficulties were apparent over a longer period, even where they were balanced by other factors – such as low unemployment – or popular measures in other areas. This was the case in 1945–51, 1964–70 and 1974–79, especially when in all these cases it was accompanied by the visible 'failure' (politically, as it could help in economic terms) of devaluation. Where Conservative governments encountered similar problems, as in 1874–80, 1924–29, 1961–64, 1972–74 and 1990–95, they also were defeated at the next election. It has been a critical problem for the Conservatives since 1997 that the Blair government's economic record, under Gordon Brown's careful stewardship, has not yet presented the opposition with any real opportunities.

Even where it is important, the economic situation has acted through and in parallel with another major factor – the impression of government competence and effectiveness. Certainly, economic problems are the greatest eroder of a government's standing, especially if it takes unpopular steps without achieving an improvement that is apparent in people's everyday experience. This was the case with the austerity measures of 1945–51, with the prices and incomes policies of 1966–70 and 1974–79, and the abandoned attempt to tackle industrial disputes with the *In Place of Strife* White Paper of 1969. A similar impression of the government being ineffective and out of touch played a major part in the Conservative defeats of 1929, 1964, 1974 and 1997. Just as damaging – and often occurring at the same time – were the effects of scandals and of disunity in the government or its parliamentary support.

The different outcomes of the periods in opposition which followed the four major defeats confirm the view that it is the interplay of the economic situation, government performance and opposition viability that determines the outcome. The two most successful results, in 1950 and 1970, were in the periods with the most economic difficulties and against governments that did not seem able to address them. In 1950 the Conservatives had a more popular leader, had engaged in a more substantial re-orientation of policy and image, and had a better resourced organization and a much larger membership than was the case in 1970. However, they perhaps also had a much greater legacy of popular antipathy to overcome than was the case after 1964, and the Labour government had a stronger record elsewhere (especially with the introduction of the welfare state). These points may account for the relatively similar scale of recovery, although the baseline in 1945 of 210 MPs and 39.6 per cent of the vote was considerably lower than the 253 MPs and 41.0 per cent poll in 1966. The contrast in factors becomes clearer when the other two periods are considered. The economic climate was favourable to the government in 1997–2001 and 1906–January 1910, and in both periods the Conservative opposition remained identified with unpopular policies and internal disunity. There was some variation between the two periods in the performance of the government, but the Liberals recovered from the ineffectiveness of their first three years with the introduction of old age pensions in 1908 and the 'People's Budget' in 1909, and secured an election on issues that rallied their own supporters. The Blair government was much more in command of the situation in 1997–2001 and, although disappointing some sections of active Labour supporters, its pragmatism may have been rewarded in the lack of opposition success in 2001.

This analysis suggests that whilst hard times and government failure may be essential in providing the key, the lock will only turn completely and the door open if the opposition have oiled the machinery; that is, if they have made themselves appear a reasonable alternative. The opposition do not have to be loved: if the government are sufficiently disliked, it will be enough that they are at least the lesser evil – which explains the pattern of opinion polling and the result in 1970. Therefore, although an opposition's internal activities will not by themselves lift it back into office, they play a significant role in facilitating this process. In the case of the Conservatives, the opposition periods have often been particularly significant in bringing about changes in the Party's programme and general outlook, and in its organizational structures. The opposition periods which saw critical definitions of the Conservative Party's identity, programme or future direction were 1868–74, with Disraeli's statement of principles in 1872; 1886, with the adoption of Unionism (by no means inevitable, as some of the leaders had been toying with making common cause with the Irish only a few months before) and the alliance with the Liberal Unionists; 1905–10, in that Balfour officially adopted tariff reform as the 'first constructive work' of the party; 1924, with Baldwin's 'New Conservatism'; and 1929–31, with the readoption of a full 'free hand' tariff policy and, at the last minute, the making of the National Government. One of the most significant was 1945–51, with the acceptance of the mixed economy, planning, Keynesian demand management, new roles for the state, and the provision of welfare and social security. The other period of significant re-orientation came after Thatcher's election as leader, in 1975–79. However, this tends to be accorded more significance in hindsight than was really the case, as electoral caution and the lack of enthusiasm of some of the shadow cabinet meant that the scope for radical change was restricted.

Several periods are absent from this list. No new direction was needed in 1892–95: the Liberal government focused upon the same issues as before, and the Conservatives did not need to debate their reaction to them. There were plenty of efforts to develop policies in 1964–70, but this was almost a way of avoiding tackling the more fundamental questions, as the process lost sight of the wood for the trees. Finally, there were three periods when the Conservatives badly needed to reinvent themselves, but they made almost no progress. These are 1880–85, 1910–14 and since 1997. All three were affected by problems of leadership, and saw difficult changes of leader; they were also largely sterile on new policies, and apart from simply negative attacks on the government they had nothing with which to catch the public eye. It is not a coincidence that two of these periods (1880–85 and 1997–2001) account for the two smallest increases in the number of Conservative seats. The final one was interrupted by the outbreak of the First World War, but given the lack of any alternative to the Liberals' domestic policy and land campaign, and the fact that the situation in Ireland after Home Rule was enacted would not necessarily make the Conservatives' support for Ulster a mainland vote-winner, it is hard to see that there was a prospect of overhauling the margin that Irish and Labour support gave the Liberals, even if there had been organizational improvements and by-election successes.

The other respect in which the periods in opposition were crucial in changing the Conservative Party was in its organization, both inside and outside Parliament. The foundations of the national organization were laid by Disraeli in 1868–74, particularly with the creation of the Central Office. This established a permanent and professional administrative headquarters, answerable to the Party leader but providing important services to the constituencies. Although it was technically founded in November 1867, shortly before the Conservatives lost office, it was also in the period from 1870 to 1874 that the National Union was expanded into a truly national federation of local constituency associations, with over 400 branches established by 1874. The next period in opposition saw the founding in 1883 of the most popular and influential mass Conservative organization of the late-Victorian and Edwardian age: the Primrose League. Named in memory of Disraeli, it was an auxiliary rather than a part of the formal party machine, and by 1886 it had 1200 branches and approaching a quarter of a million members. This parliament also saw the appointment, not long before the temporary return to office in the 'Caretaker Government' of 1885, of the skilful Principal Agent who shaped the party organization for almost 20 years, 'Captain' Middleton.

In 1911, after the third successive defeat, the leadership initiated major organizational changes which set the broad structure that has remained in place ever since. Two key posts were created, one of Party Treasurer and the other of Chairman of the Party Organization, setting an experienced parliamentarian in administrative charge of the Central Office. It was accompanied by a complete reorganization of the office itself, an expansion of its staff, an increase in its funding, and the creation of new and professional links with the media. The most important addition to the bureaucracy created in 1911 came during another spell in opposition, with the creation of the Conservative Research Department in 1929. That spell in opposition also saw the most ambitious growth of the party's self-education wing, with the opening of the Bonar Law Memorial College at Ashridge, Hertfordshire, in 1930. Indeed, the only significant development between 1870 and 1945 that was during a period in office was the establishment of women's organizations in the period after 1918, prompted by the extension of the franchise.

The most famous organizational changes of all took place in the wake of the 1945 defeat, and their impact was strengthened by the marketing skills and revitalizing role of Lord Woolton as Party Chairman, although Woolton himself made few changes in the structure. The new developments were more the work of, or associated with, R.A. Butler, and some of them grew out of the wartime policy committees. As well as the revival of the Conservative Research Department under Butler's leadership, there was the establishment of the Advisory Committee on Policy and, as both a consultation and an opinion-forming mechanism, the Conservative Political Centre (also overseen by Butler). In the mass party, this was the period of the famous Maxwell-Fyfe Committee reforms of 1948–49, which strictly limited financial contributions from MPs to their local associations, in order to stimulate the latter into fund-raising activity and to ensure a fairer and more meritocratic process of candidate selection.[11] Finally, this period saw the replacement of the inter-war youth movement, the Junior Imperial League (which had been quite successful in the 1920s and 1930s, but became moribund during the war) with the launch of the Young Conservatives in July 1946.

The next two periods of opposition saw less fundamental or lasting changes, with committees of inquiry into specific aspects and mainly managerial changes of departmental boundaries at Central Office. One of the more important innovations, though it did not last, was the creation of the Community Affairs Department at Central Office in 1975, with the specific brief of reaching groups of voters where Conservative support was weak, by using new methods.[12] At the end of that opposition period, although it was not announced until after the 1979 election, the separate existence of the Conservative Research Department came to an end, and ever since its role has been subsumed within the Central Office. The development with the greatest impact in 1975–79 was not strictly speaking an innovation, as the Party had used advertising agencies before, but the partnership which developed with Saatchis in this period was of a new closeness and significance, and has lodged in the Party's consciousness alongside the Woolton/Maxwell-Fyfe era as a model of how an opposition can recover ground. Finally, there have been radical and extensive changes since entering opposition in 1997: not only in leadership selection (discussed below), but in the reshaping of the National Union and the creation of a new managerial structure in the Party Board, announced in the *Fresh Future* proposals in February 1998.[13]

Almost all of the most important developments in parliamentary organization and leadership selection also took place during periods in opposition. The first of these was the introduction of the permanent subject committees in 1924; the second was more gradual, but it was in the post-war parliament of 1945–51 that the unofficial backbench organization of the 'Private Members (1922) Committee' became more recognized and influential, acquiring representation on party bodies such as the new Advisory Committee on Policy and becoming a forum that was regularly addressed by the Party leader.[14] The 1922 Committee assumed an even more central role when the first formal procedure for selecting the Leader of the Party was introduced in 1965, when the Conservatives were once more in opposition. The most significant revisions to these rules have also occurred whilst out of office: the provision for challenges to an incumbent leader was introduced in 1975, and the final choice between the two candidates most favoured by the MPs was given to the grass-roots membership under Hague, and used for the first time on his resignation in 2001.

The spells out of power have frequently reshaped, and very often relaunched, the Conservative Party. They have contributed crucially to its development, its electoral victories and its lengthy periods of government and political dominance. Although they are the minority in timespan, remove the periods of opposition from the history of the Conservative Party and it would, in every sense of the term, cease to be.

Notes

1. D. Dutton, *His Majesty's Loyal Opposition: The Unionist Party in Opposition 1905–1915* (Liverpool: Liverpool University Press, 1992); S. Ball, *Baldwin and the Conservative Party: The Crisis of 1929–1931* (New Haven and London: Yale University Press, 1988); and for 1997–2001, M. Garnett and P. Lynch (eds), *The Conservatives in Crisis* (Manchester: Manchester University Press, 2003).
2. L. Johnman, 'The Conservative Party in opposition 1964–1970', in R. Coopey, S. Fielding and N. Tiratsoo (eds), *The Wilson Governments 1964–1970* (London: Pinter, 1993), 184–206; J.D. Hoffman, *The Conservative Party in Opposition 1945–1951* (London: MacGibbon and Kee, 1964); R. Behrens, *The Conservative Party from Heath to Thatcher: Policies and Politics 1974–1979* (Farnborough: Saxon House, 1980).
3. There is a brief comparative discussion of a shorter period: S. Ball, 'The Conservatives in opposition, 1906–1979: a comparative analysis', in Garnett and Lynch, *The Conservatives in Crisis*, 7–28.
4. R.A. Butler, *The Art of the Possible* (Hamish Hamilton: London, 1971), 135.
5. Lord H. Cecil, *Conservatism* (London: Williams and Norgate, 1912), 9–10; Q. Hogg, *The Case for Conservatism* (Harmondsworth: Penguin, 1947), 11–12.

6. For a critical view of the Conservative Party's position in 1914, see S. Ball, *The Conservative Party and British Politics 1902–1951* (London: Longman, 1995), 55–56; E.H.H. Green, *The Crisis of Conservatism: The Politics, Economics and Ideology of the British Conservative Party 1880–1914* (London: Routledge, 1995), 297–306.

7. *The Industrial Charter* (London: Conservative Central Office, 1947); *The Right Approach* (London: Conservative Central Office, 1976).

8. A. Rowe, 'The Community Affairs Department 1975–79', in S. Ball and I. Holliday (eds), *Mass Conservatism: The Conservatives and the Public since the 1880s* (London: Frank Cass, 2002), 200–17; D.J. Wilson, 'Constituency Party autonomy and central control', *Political Studies*, 21 (1973), 167–74.

9. Whilst there were 91 unopposed Conservative returns in the election defeat of 1868, only 436 Conservative candidates stood and the Liberals also enjoyed a considerable number of unopposed returns – as had been usual in pre-1867 elections.

10. See D. Powell, 'The Liberal Ministries and Labour 1892–1895', *History*, 68 (1983), and D. Howell, *British Workers and the Independent Labour Party 1888–1906* (Manchester: Manchester University Press, 1983).

11. *Committee on Party Organization, Interim Report*, 2 Sep. 1948 (London: Conservative Central Office, 1948).

12. Rowe, 'Community Affairs Department 1975–79', 200–17.

13. For the development of the party organization in the Disraelian age, see E.J. Feuchtwanger, *Disraeli, Democracy and the Tory Party* (London: Oxford University Press, 1968); for the Primrose League, see M. Pugh, *The Tories and the People 1880–1935* (Oxford: Blackwell, 1985); for the twentieth century up to the early 1990s, see S. Ball, 'The national and regional Party structure', and S. Ball, 'Local Conservatism and the evolution of the Party organization', in A. Seldon and S. Ball (eds), *Conservative Century: The Conservative Party since 1900* (Oxford: Oxford University Press, 1994), 169–220, 261–311; for developments since 1997, see R. Kelly, 'Organizational reform and the extra-parliamentary party', in Garnett and Lynch, *The Conservatives in Crisis*, 82–106.

14. S. Ball, 'The 1922 Committee: the formative years 1922–45', *Parliamentary History*, 9 (1990), 153, 155–6. Churchill was the first Party leader to address meetings regularly; his predecessors had been hosted at formal dinners, but those were occasions for celebration rather than debate.

2
The Disraelian Achievement: 1868–1874

Angus Hawkins

A crushing electoral defeat, failure in the face of their opponent's progressive moral agenda, and subsequent condemnation as a party incapable of government; this was the ruin that confronted Conservatives in December 1868. They had suffered a historic humiliation at the hands of a charismatic Liberal leader. In November 1871 *The Times* loftily pronounced a Conservative recovery of power to be impossible. 'The leaders of the party do not believe in it. The country gives them no confidence. The majority is against them. All the forces of the time are strained in an opposite direction.'[1] The popular embrace of the progressive Liberal agenda of political, economic and social reform, promising a more meritocratic and efficient society, had seemingly rendered the Conservatives marginal, irrelevant and unelectable.

The 64-year-old Conservative leader Benjamin Disraeli was all too familiar with the miseries of enfeebled opposition. 'There are few positions', he wrote in 1852, 'less inspiriting than that of the leader of a discomfited party.'[2] Recrimination and rancorous blame inevitably form the bitter diet of a vulnerable failed leadership.

A disheartened opposition will be querulous and captious. A discouraged multitude will have no future; too depressed to indulge in a large and often hopeful horizon of contemplation, they busy themselves in peevish detail, and by a natural train of sentiment associate their own condition of ill-luck, incapacity and failure with the most responsible member of their confederation.[3]

Leading a dejected and demoralized opposition was a thankless task. A defeated party quickly descends into chronic self-recrimination with failure promptly attributed to incapable leadership. Yet, within six years, Disraeli oversaw the debilitating collapse of William Gladstone's Liberal government. In 1874 the Conservatives recovered office with their largest Commons majority for 33 years. Emerging from their slough of malignant despond, the Party once again occupied the sun-lit uplands of parliamentary power. The commanding Commons majority of 106 MPs that the Liberals enjoyed in 1868, was transformed, in 1874, into a Conservative Commons majority of 52 MPs. This, the *Spectator* observed, was 'Conservative reaction with a vengeance!'[4] As Disraeli commented in his 1847 novel *Tancred*, 'a majority is always the best repartee'.

How was this triumph achieved? In truth, of course, Disraeli's great victory was the confluence of various restorative processes that combined in 1874 to deliver an electoral triumph. Some of these factors Disraeli and the Conservative Party controlled, others they did not. Some were intentional, others were contingent. But all came together to create a tide in the affairs of the Conservative Party which, taken at the flood, led on to fortune.

'Time is the great physician', Disraeli observed in his 1837 novel *Henrietta Temple*. Most tellingly after 1868, the Conservatives saw the once powerful momentum of moral Liberal reform gradually falter, then collapse, under the unrelenting pressure of government. In office, Liberals discovered their incompatible differences. A powerful progressive sense of collective purpose, which had galvanized Whigs, Liberals and radicals in 1868, was gradually eroded by the day to day challenges, the inconvenient details and the unforeseen crises of executive government. For the Conservatives, patience brought its own reward. Gladstone's personal priorities and those areas of government in which he was most closely involved were Ireland and retrenchment, which had formed the main issues in his 1868 campaign. The cry of Irish disestablishment had played well in the Celtic fringe (Ireland, Scotland and Wales) and had attracted the support of Dissenters. In 1869 he personally drove forward the legislation disestablishing and disendowing the Church of Ireland. An Irish Land Act followed in 1870 giving tenants an interest in any improvements they carried out to the property, compensation for disturbance while rent was paid, and the possibility of purchasing the land with state aid, if 20 per cent of the purchase price was laid down by the tenant. After 1870, however, Ireland became an increasingly divisive issue for Liberals. Anxiety about the power of the Catholic Church in

Ireland and fear of civil disorder increased. This growing unease was exacerbated by the 1870 Vatican Council. Dissenters had no particular sympathy for Irish Catholics and the Irish Land Act appeared to set uncomfortable precedents for legislative interference with the rights of property. When Gladstone introduced an Irish University bill in 1873, establishing a federal structure under which Anglican, Catholic and Presbyterian colleges could come together, supported by Trinity College's endowment, Liberals became deeply divided.

The cry of retrenchment and greater government efficiency, which had also formed a prominent part of Gladstone's 1868 Liberal campaign, suffered a similar fate after 1869. Reductions in military spending and the introduction of competitive examinations for entry into the civil service promised cheaper and more meritocratic government. Between 1868 and 1873 Gladstone's ministry cut £4 million from defence expenditure. But the outbreak of the Franco-Prussian War in 1870 forced unexpected and unwelcome defence spending on the Liberal Cabinet. The disastrous capsizing of the Royal Navy's new iron-clad warship, *HMS Captain*, on its maiden voyage in September 1870 (with the loss of 450 crew and observers), appeared an embarrassing illustration of the country's vulnerability. The payment of £3.25 million to the United States in 1872, as compensation for building the *Alabama* for the Confederate navy during the American Civil War, also threw Liberal financial calculations into disarray. The unpopularity and incompetency of Robert Lowe, as Chancellor of the Exchequer, proved equally damaging. Following allegations of Treasury ineptitude, for example over the supervision of Post Office Savings Bank funds, Gladstone was forced to remove Lowe from the Exchequer in 1873. The maladroit Lowe, Gladstone concluded, had proved 'wretchedly deficient'.[5] Gladstone regarded government finance, an area in which he had established a formidable personal reputation for technical mastery during the 1850s and 1860s, as his political trump card. But when an increasingly beleaguered Gladstone played this card in 1874, by proposing the abolition of the income tax, it proved a busted flush.

Other aspects of Liberal government after 1868, in which Gladstone was less directly concerned, also stirred up bitter controversy. The 1870 Education Act disquieted radicals, alarmed Dissenters, failed to satisfy Anglicans, and produced resistance to paying for working-class education out of local rates. The 1872 Licensing Act, regulating public houses and their opening hours, alienated the brewing interest. Legislation extending political entitlements, the municipal franchise in 1869; the election of school boards and married women's property in 1870; the protection of trade union funds in 1871; and the introduction of the secret ballot for parliamentary elections in 1872, all generated different sources of opposition. In 1868 the Liberals, under Gladstone's charismatic leadership, had swept into office fired by a progressive moral agenda offering efficient and meritocratic reform, removal of the social and political barriers represented by Anglican exclusivity and, in the extension of political entitlements, the encouragement of individual civic responsibility. After 1872 all facets of this progressive agenda were proving controversial and divisive. In March 1873 a disconsolate Gladstone privately acknowledged that there was 'no *cause*' or 'great public object on which the Liberal Party are agreed and combined'.[6]

Patiently observing increasing ministerial discomfort, as the euphoria of progressive reform gave way to disillusionment, and avoiding initiatives which might provide the Liberal Party with any renewed sense of cohesion, was a Conservative opposition strategy with a long pedigree. In opposition to Lord Melbourne and Lord John Russell's Whig government from 1835 to 1841, Sir Robert Peel consistently supported moderate ministerial proposals against radical attack. After 1846, Lord Derby urged 'masterly inactivity' in opposition, so that Whig, Liberal and radical differences might be brought to the fore. In November 1855, despite his temperamental predilection for action, even Disraeli conceded that 'silence and inertia appear to me to be our wisest course'.[7] This strategy of 'killing with kindness' was calculated to affirm that the disagreements of moderate Liberals with their radical colleagues were greater than their quarrels with the Conservatives.[8] The aim of what Derby called 'armed neutrality' was to encourage centrist realignment.[9] So might Whigs and moderate Liberals, unsettled by radical enthusiasms, be drawn into the Conservative fold. In 1860–61 it led to the covert 'truce of parties', through which Derby and the Conservatives aided the Liberal prime minister Lord Palmerston in suppressing Gladstonian and radical proposals. In 1866 'armed neutrality' encouraged the revolt of Whig and moderate Liberal 'Adullamites' against Russell and Gladstone's plans for parliamentary Reform.

'Masterly inactivity', however, did more than encourage the adhesion of disenchanted opponents. It allowed the Conservative opposition to maintain a patriotic stance by avoiding factiousness. In giving the Queen's ministers 'a fair trial' and by abstaining from selfish party manoeuvre, Conservatives might refute damaging accusations of disloyalty. Only once, when in opposition between 1832 and 1868, did the Conservative Party oust their opponents from office by a direct and concerted attack – in August 1841 when Peel won a motion of no confidence against

Melbourne's tottering ministry. In 1852, 1855, 1858 and 1866 Whig-Liberal governments were removed from office by hostile censure issuing from their own side of the Commons. In 1852 and 1866 it was the revolt of Whigs and moderate Liberals that prompted the ejection of the government. In 1855 and 1858 it was radical initiatives that provoked the removal of Whig-Liberal ministers from office. On each occasion the Conservatives supported those critics of the government who were condemning their own front bench. On each occasion the Conservatives exploited their opponent's divisions, rather than assailing a Whig-Liberal government with hostile initiatives of their own. They supported, but did not instigate, attacks on Whig-Liberal administrations.

Underlying this opposition strategy of 'masterly inactivity' was the conviction that a progressive alliance of Whigs, Liberals and radicals was an inherently unstable association. In opposition to the Aberdeen coalition from 1853 to 1855, Derby declared it 'difficult to imagine how a government can go on formed of such discordant materials as that which Aberdeen has brought together'. [10] Similarly, in opposition to Palmerston's second government, Derby believed the alliance of Whigs, Liberals and radicals brought together in the Willis's Rooms in June 1859 was a fragile party combination surely destined to fracture in office. A 'patience policy', described by Derby's confidant Lord Malmesbury as keeping the 'cripples on their legs', was calculated to cleave the Liberal Party along the natural grain of Whig, Liberal and radical differences.[11] Vindication of this belief came in 1866 when, following Palmerston's death, the Willis's Rooms alliance fell apart over parliamentary Reform. Cautious Whigs, moderate Liberals and enthusiastic radicals, Derby maintained, could never be harmonious ministerial colleagues when confronted with framing and seeing through progressive legislation.

When, therefore, in 1872 Disraeli advocated a Conservative opposition strategy of 'utmost reserve and quietness', he drew on a well-established tradition.[12] By refraining from opposition for opposition's sake, accusations of factiousness could be refuted, the observance of patriotic duty maintained, and fundamental Liberal differences emphasized. Disraeli, a colleague noted in May 1870, 'looks forward to Gladstone becoming useless to the radicals and a disruption. Gives two years or more.'[13] Disraeli knew that shared animosity cements party affiliation as firmly as common principles. Avoiding giving the Liberals the cohesive convenience of unity in response to Conservative attack denied Whigs, Liberals and radicals the refuge of a shared antipathy. At the same time, the Conservative's claim to disinterested loyalty, both to the national interest and the Crown, preserved a statesmanlike shunning of cynical party manoeuvre. The premature exploitation of their opponent's weakness was to be avoided.

In March 1873 Gladstone resigned from office, following a Commons defeat on the second reading of his government's Irish University bill by three votes. A total of 38 Whigs, English radicals and Irish Liberals opposed the measure, and 22 Irish Liberals abstained from the vote. Gladstone insisted to Queen Victoria that Disraeli be asked to form a ministry. But Disraeli refused to release Gladstone from his predicament. Over the following days the Queen invited Disraeli to form a government three times. On each occasion Disraeli declined. His thinking was simple and sound. The Conservatives should not seem over eager to seize office, when a prolonged Liberal tenure in power would only exacerbate existing ministerial divisions. For the Conservatives to take office, without a Commons majority, would only create the favourable circumstances for Liberals to unite in opposition; a short-lived Conservative tenure of power on sufferance soon giving way to a prolonged resumption of opposition. The diligent country gentleman Sir Stafford Northcote, Disraeli's lieutenant and Gladstone's former private secretary, was convinced that the Liberal Party was rapidly disintegrating. Only precipitancy on the part of the Conservatives could prevent it. Moreover, taking office before a dissolution of Parliament, Disraeli commented, was 'a delusion and a snare'.[14] Northcote confirmed Disraeli's judgement. Convinced that time was required to mature the fast ripening Conservative feeling in the country, Northcote agreed that the 'hallucinations' which had attached a great mass of moderate opinion to the Liberal cause were dissipating.

[Gladstone] has expended the impetuous force which brought him into office, and is now brought face to face with new, or rather old, difficulties which he can hardly surmount without alienating one or other wing of his party. If he goes with the Extreme section, a large body of his moderate supporters will rank themselves with the Conservatives: if he quarrels with the Extreme section, they will become the opposition, while the conduct of affairs will fall to the acknowledged Conservatives, who will obtain the support of the moderate Liberals. But if we appeal to the country before the breach in Liberal ranks is fully made, and before the policy of the Extreme men is fully developed, we shall consolidate them; the Extreme men will hold back a little, the moderates advance a little, and there will be more confusion and confiscation.[15]

While, to the general approval of his supporters, Disraeli held his nerve, an angry Gladstone was denied the comfort of opposition. On 16 March 1873, Gladstone limped back into office. As the Liberal minister Lord Kimberley noted in his journal: 'we can hardly hope to escape discredit', and their faces 'looked very gloomy' when they found themselves again in a Cabinet.[16] A deadly contagion of languor and indiscipline infected the Liberal Cabinet during the 1873 parliamentary session. Between May 1873 and January 1874 ten Liberal seats were lost to the Conservatives at by-elections. Finally, on 24 January 1874, Gladstone suddenly announced, to the surprise of many of his ministerial colleagues, an immediate dissolution of Parliament. Conservative patience was subsequently rewarded with the electoral collapse of the Liberal Party as, following the polling, 352 Conservative MPs looked across the chamber at 242 Liberal and 58 Irish Home Rule MPs. On the hustings Liberal candidates had largely avoided making any pledges as to the future, but preferred to present their legislative achievements since 1868. However, this proved a deeply contentious legacy. Following Disraeli's example of six years before, on 17 February 1874 Gladstone resigned as Prime Minister before meeting the new Parliament. The constitutional inference was clear; it was the verdict of the electorate, not the vote of the Commons, that now decided who should govern.

The collapse of the Liberals' collective sense of progressive purpose was clearly the primary external factor in Conservative political recovery between 1868 and 1874. Doing little brought much gain. Yet, at the same time, an opposition pose of 'utmost reserve and quiet' placed significant strain on the Conservative Party internally. Outward repose did not reflect an inner peace. Indeed, the stresses produced by deliberate inactivity often exacerbated those tensions born of humiliating electoral defeat in 1868. Routed parties inevitably turn on their failed leadership. Maintaining party unity in the cause of placid inaction seriously tested the Conservatives' own collective sense of purpose between 1868 and 1874.

In 1868 Disraeli was the resourceful Commons leader who, the previous year, had dexterously conjured a far-reaching English Reform Act out of the disarray of the Liberal opposition. Conservative backbench mistrust of the exotic Disraeli was momentarily submerged in the exaltation of a progressive triumph over the Whigs as the self-declared monopolists of enlightened reform. No longer could Liberals define Toryism as mistrust of the people, tempered only by fear. The rehabilitation of the Conservatives as a moderate party, capable of delivering responsible reform, owed as much to the long-term aspirations of the ageing Lord Derby, Conservative leader from 1846 to 1868, as to the brilliant short-term tactics of Disraeli in 1867. But with Derby a rapidly fading parliamentary presence, Disraeli immediately fashioned the 1867 Reform Act into the celebratory proof of his own success in 'educating' the Conservative Party. The Conservatives, Disraeli claimed to an Edinburgh audience on 29 October 1867, had settled a vexed question which a divided Liberal Party had proved unable to resolve. The 1867 Reform Act, he declared, was a comprehensive settlement founded upon the clear principles of household suffrage and the personal payment of taxes; principles in harmony with the manners and customs of the English people. This, Disraeli pronounced, demonstrated the Conservatives' dedication to the authentic interests of the nation, as opposed to the cosmopolitan and sectional impositions of Liberalism. This presentation of the Conservatives as a party in tune with historic English manners and customs, combating cosmopolitan Liberalism, sounded a consistent note in Disraeli's subsequent rhetoric.

However, Disraeli's direct appeal to a popular audience at Edinburgh was a rare event. The 1867 Reform Act created a popular arena in which Disraeli was strikingly reluctant to perform. He disliked extra-parliamentary forays, feeling much more at home in familiar Westminster, the intimate setting of salons in St James's and London's cosy Clubland. The enfranchisement of respectable working men, moreover, drew on his long-held belief in social paternalism, rather than intimating any new vision of a 'Tory democracy'. In November 1867 Disraeli regarded the establishment of the National Union of Conservative and Constitutional Associations with wary suspicion. The masses, in his view, should continue to give their allegiance to the nation's traditional ruling elite. They should not be encouraged to organize themselves, except within the social hierarchy defined by land, Church and aristocracy. Kept at arm's length by Disraeli, the NUCCA was not enlisted as a ready means of galvanizing working-class Conservatives in the 1868 election.

Immediately after the 1868 defeat, Disraeli's leadership was perilously insecure; old suspicions of him being a cynical and exotic adventurer, without morals or principles, quickly resurfaced. Meanwhile, literature, philosophy and history, rather than politics, occupied his own thoughts and the publication of his novel *Lothair*, in May 1870, did little to disperse mistrust. Colourful romance and social satire dressed his tale of the spiritual questionings of a young aristocrat with an accomplished literary polish that could not, despite the novel's serious tone, disguise a lack of intellectual depth. Disraeli's former confidant the 15th Earl of Derby, who had succeeded to the title in 1869 following the death of his father, the long-serving Conservative leader, caught the response of many readers. The novel, Derby observed, exhibited an 'almost childish love of what is gorgeous and striking; the same oriental turn of mind that inclines my friend like most of his race, to take pleasure in striking exhibitions of colour'.[17] Deep doubts and simmering hostility to Disraeli's leadership increased. When Lord Malmesbury, the elder Derby's faithful lieutenant, declined to continue as Conservative leader in the Lords for the 1869 session, a number of peers looked to the young Lord Salisbury as a cure for Disraelian ills. Since entering Parliament as Lord Robert Cecil and MP for Stamford in 1853, Salisbury (elevated to the Lords in 1868) had been a bitter and prominent critic of Disraeli's leadership. Disraeli's Conservative convictions, Salisbury declared in his journalism, were an accident of his career. In March 1867 Salisbury (as Lord Cranborne) had resigned from the Conservative Cabinet in disgust at Disraeli's course on parliamentary Reform. In an article in the October 1869 *Quarterly Review* he again vented his visceral dislike of Disraeli and the ignominious capitulation to democracy that he represented. Salisbury's succession, which was supported by the Dukes of Marlborough and Richmond, would have made Disraeli's position as party leader impossible. Disraeli staved off this humiliation by securing the appointment of the pragmatic Ulsterman and lawyer Lord Cairns as leader in the Lords. But this proved a short-lived solution. Although a close associate of Disraeli, Cairns, a strong low-church adherent possessed of a robust intellect, proved ineffective in marshalling Lords' opposition to Irish disestablishment. By November 1869 a dispirited Cairns was wearily indicating his wish to resign.

Following the elder Derby's death in October 1869, his eldest son, the 15th earl, emerged as an obvious replacement for Disraeli. The credentials of the young Derby, who was 22 years Disraeli's junior, were impressive; proven talent, a conscientious intelligence, and an aristocratic lineage were compelling qualifications. Since the 1850s many, including Malmesbury, had seen the young Derby as the man to supersede Disraeli. But Derby's temperamental aversion to narrow Toryism, a wish to preserve his political freedom of action, and an inclination to 'assume a neutral position for the time, waiting events', caused him to hold back.[18] This proved crucial for Disraeli. Derby's distaste for the leadership left overall command of the Party in Disraeli's hands. There were no credible alternatives. The Duke of Richmond, who posed no threat to Disraeli's overall authority, assumed the leadership of the Conservatives in the Lords. This was despite the strong High Churchman and vocal anti-Disraeli peer Lord Carnarvon again pressing Salisbury's claim.

In January 1872 another ebullition of anti-Disraeli feeling occasioned a small private meeting of prominent Conservatives at Burghley House.

Some members of the last Conservative Cabinet were joined by a few representative backbenchers and Gerard Noel, the Commons Chief Whip. At the gathering Cairns floated once again the name of Derby as a replacement for Disraeli. Of those present, only Lord John Manners and Sir Stafford Northcote defended Disraeli. But Derby's continued aversion to assuming command of the Party stripped the Burghley House conversation of reality. Disraeli's leadership just barely survived, hanging by the thread of Derby's reticence.

During the early months of 1872 Disraeli's thoughts finally shifted from literature and philosophy to the state of Conservative politics. Disraeli, Cairns reported to Richmond, was no longer 'down in the mouth and rather repelling meetings to concert plans, etc'. Instead, Disraeli now believed that 'things are looking up, and awakening himself, he turns round and insists that every one else is asleep'.[19] The collapse of Liberal consensus and Disraeli's continued, if precarious, grip on the Conservative leadership, prepared the ground for a recharged definition of a compelling Conservative – or rather anti-Liberal – party identity. 'With words we govern men', Disraeli once observed.[20] In 1872 his resonant words provided the Conservatives with a potent language about themselves that rekindled their partisan intent. This achievement proved Disraeli's lasting legacy to his party. He had little interest in mundane legislative detail. Rather, it was the broad sweep of Conservative aspiration, captured in the evocative phrases of his vibrant rhetoric, that fired his literary imagination. Language was the pliable medium of his art and his own career his most compelling creation. Much in what he said was not new. But the occasion and the moment were significant. Since 1868 Disraeli had resisted repeated demands to address directly the party faithful in Lancashire. In April 1872 he finally relented. Speaking for three and a half hours to a packed loyal Conservative audience of 6000 in the Free Trade Hall, Manchester, he was received with rapturous enthusiasm; despite the oppressive heat of the Hall and the fact that his voice was often inaudible to many of his listeners. The rarity of the event gave his performance even greater significance. On 24 June, with a more concise address, he spoke at the Crystal Palace to the National Union of Conservative and Constitutional Associations. At both events he delineated the broader horizons of Conservative thinking as a restorative antidote to the restless, divisive and cosmopolitan doctrines of wearied Liberalism.

At Manchester, Disraeli's generalized propositions reaffirmed that the purpose of the Conservative Party was to maintain the constitution. The monarchy, as a symbol of national unity and source of political wisdom, the Lords, representing the responsibilities of territorial property, and the Church of England, providing a civilizing moral authority, together embodied those historic institutions which Conservatives were dedicated to defend. If there was little that was novel in this message, recent republican attacks on the reclusive Queen Victoria and increasingly militant Nonconformist demands for disestablishment gave the cry a renewed force. At the Crystal Palace Disraeli also roused the Party to defence of the Empire. By persistent and subtle means, often for narrow reasons of economy, the Liberals had sought to dissolve Britain's relations with her colonies. Disraeli did not call for imperialist expansion. But he did firmly bring Britain's imperial ties with her existing 'white colonies', Australia, New Zealand and Canada, into the historic framework of national institutions which Conservatives should commit themselves to protect. Alongside subversion of the Empire, Disraeli also set inept bungling and humiliating failure in foreign policy as part of the Liberal government's record. Instead of Liberal pusillanimity, Disraeli called for the firm and decisive promotion of Britain's honour and prestige in the world. The nation's attitude towards Europe, he declared, should be a policy of proud reserve. Such Conservative principles, he concluded, were the authentic expression of the people's Conservative (used 'in its purest and loftiest sense') sensibilities.

> I mean that the people of England, and especially the working classes of England, are proud of belonging to a great Country, and wish to maintain its greatness – that they are proud of belonging to an Imperial Country, and are resolved to maintain, if they can, their Empire – that they believe on the whole, that the greatness and empire of England are to be attributed to the ancient institutions of the land.[21]

Patriotic pride, dutiful care for the nation's historic institutions, and the integration of newly enfranchised voters within an organic social vision of the country's authentic aspirations were ideas calculated both to flatter working men and to reassure the upwardly mobile middle classes. Liberal legislation allowed the Conservatives to present themselves to the middle classes as the party committed to protecting property and the freedom of contract. To working men, the Conservatives pointed out that labour would be the first victim of any disturbance of trade and capital. This was a passable pastiche of Palmerstonianism.

All this was familiar, if timely, in 1872; the novel, if somewhat vague, element which Disraeli introduced into Conservative policy was 'social reform' – the suggestion that the provision of healthy habitation, unadulterated food, the reduction of industrial working hours and the regulation of urban sanitation were legitimate objects of party policy. *'Sanitas sanitatum, omnia sanitas.'*[22] The alchemy of Disraeli's rhetoric was to transform the base metal of mundane 'social reform' into the gold of party triumph. Prior to 1872, social legislation was seen as a useful, if rather dull, area of national concern conventionally outside the parameters of partisan debate. The very term 'social reform' remained an awkward innovation during the 1870s. Some talked of measures of social amelioration or social improvement, and some simply referred to miscellaneous, as opposed to political, legislation. Social questions, it was implied, should be considered apart from party feeling. Nor was the argument for measures of social improvement an entirely new element in Disraeli's own thinking. His 1845 novel *Sybil, or the Two Nations* addressed what was called 'the condition of England' question. In December 1864 he had declared that the health of the working classes was crucial to the greatness, liberty and wealth of the nation.

A curious and brief episode in 1871, dubbed the 'New Social Movement', revealed elements within the Conservative Party sympathetic to, if hesitant about, such legislative concerns. Encouraged by the progressive Conservative MP Sir John Pakington, who in the 1850s had championed the cause of working-class education, tentative private discussions were initiated between individual Conservatives (Carnarvon, Salisbury, Northcote, Lord John Manners, Gathorne Hardy, Cairns and Pakington himself) and labour leaders, such as Robert Applegarth, George Howell (Secretary of the Reform League), George Potter and R.M. Latham (Chairman of the Labour Representation League). Discussion focused on improved working-class housing, reduced working hours, better education and the provision of unadulterated food. Pakington's public elaboration of these ideas, in a speech to the Social Science Congress at Leeds in October 1871, however, caused much consternation among discomforted Conservatives privately sympathetic to such proposals. Pakington's public pronouncements had caught too many Conservatives unawares. But his proposals also suggested a potentially powerful basis of popular appeal. The Conservative daily, the *Standard*, welcomed greatly-needed social reform as a diversion from factious contests and artificial attempts at needless political and constitutional change.

What was new in 1872 was Disraeli's official inclusion of 'social reform' in his substantiation of the Conservatives' claim to be a truly national party. Just as he asserted, rather idiosyncratically, that his 1867 Reform Act had restored the working classes' ancient political entitlements, swept away by the Whigs in 1832, which in turn had caused the rise of Chartism, so his call for 'social reform' showed the Conservatives attending to the material conditions of the working classes, and affirmed their claim to be the party of the nation. By providing the Conservatives with a renewed collective purpose, his Manchester and Crystal Palace speeches transformed Disraeli from being a political liability into an inspiring leader. Even Salisbury, by 1873, was no longer publicly pillorying him. The Party began to turn from internecine strife to consolidated attack.

Alongside Disraeli's rhetorical pronouncements, others tended to Conservative constituency organization. This proved the final crucial element in Conservative recovery after 1868. By 1874 approximately 60 per cent of all English and Welsh constituencies had some kind of active Conservative Association operating within them. While monitoring the electoral register, distributing pamphlets and holding meetings, these Associations also provided a social and cultural focus for party supporters. In April 1870 the Lancastrian John Gorst, barrister and former MP for Cambridge, succeeded Markham Spofforth as principal Conservative Party agent. From his office in 6 Victoria Street, Spofforth had concentrated his organizational efforts on the English counties, the traditional heartland of Conservative electoral support. Loyal, industrious, but on occasion given to misjudgement, Spofforth's vision of party activity had proved debilitatingly limited. By contrast, Gorst had gained a reputation for his work with the London and Westminster Conservative Association, attending to those new artisan voters created by the 1867 Reform Act. After April 1870 Gorst saw future electoral success as crucially dependent upon the marshalling of Conservative votes in the boroughs. As he observed to the Conservative Chief Whip, Gerald Noel, in September 1870: 'We are generally strong in the counties and weak in the boroughs, and we shall never attain stable political power until the boroughs are conquered.'[23] Immediately Gorst began gathering detailed electoral intelligence on the English borough constituencies with a view to driving Conservative inroads into urban areas of Liberal support. This proved the critical organizational counterpart to Disraeli's rhetorical courting of urban electors.

In 1870, Gorst set up the Central Conservative Office at 53 Parliament Street, Westminster. The following year Gorst and his assistant J.C. Keith-Falconer became joint honorary secretaries of the National Union and moved the organization's headquarters to the Central Conservative Office. A conference of the Conservative Registration Society at the Westminster Palace Hotel, London, on 24 June 1872 pressed forward Gorst's agenda. Links between the Party leadership and provincial associations were strengthened. The identification of possible candidates for future elections was formalized and their suitability for particular constituencies carefully considered. At the same time, Gorst and his staff encouraged constituency committees to work more closely with local working-men's associations and to maintain a close scrutiny of electoral registers. In February 1873 Gorst informed Disraeli that 69 new Conservative Associations had been established in England and Wales. For good measure, the Central Press Board was purchased by the Party to publish articles and electoral literature for the use of local associations. Between May 1873 and January 1874 ten by-elections were won by the Conservatives, on each occasion Liberal candidates being defeated. One of these losses occurred in Gladstone's own constituency of Greenwich; the other sitting Liberal member for Greenwich, Sir David Salomons, having died. Likewise, the Conservative V.F. Stanford ended long-standing Liberal representation in Shaftesbury in August 1873, with the support of the dowager Marchioness of Westminster, who, in the name of Whig principles, wished to protect Anglicanism and the monarchy.

An increasingly confident Disraeli, upon his installation as Lord Rector of Glasgow University in November 1873, denounced the Liberal urge for perpetual change and the harassment of historic interests. The country, he declared, yearned for tranquillity. The nation was exhausted by unrelenting reform and wished for quiet good government. Gladstone's career of 'plundering and blundering', he privately observed, was coming to a close.[24] At Glasgow Disraeli also portrayed Europe as convulsed by an epic conflict between atheism and ultramontane usurpation. As the 'national party', Disraeli continued, the Conservatives would ensure that Britain played a 'noble part' in this struggle by 'taking a firm stand upon the principles of the Reformation', which for 300 years had been 'the source of our greatness and glory'. Britain must 'leave off mumbling the dry bones of political economy, and munching the remainder biscuit of an effete Liberalism'. An elated Disraeli reported that he received 'the greatest reception ever offered to a public man'.[25] Derby judged Disraeli's Glasgow speech 'to be "the best thing" you "ever did" – "the most concise and the best sustained"'.[26]

In December 1873 Disraeli was in good spirits, but he remained committed to observing imminent Liberal collapse, rather than actively seizing power. Noel's severe illness prompted a crisis in the Whip's office, which led to Taylor being recruited as a temporary replacement. Noel's assistant Sir William Dyke eventually succeeded Taylor in 1874. This strengthened Disraeli's preference for vigilant inaction, as Liberal squabbles incapacitated the Liberal front-bench. Gladstone then surprised everyone by suddenly announcing a dissolution of Parliament in January 1874. The fate of his government was to be submitted to the judgement of the electorate. While many Conservatives were startled by Gladstone's unexpected decision, Derby was sanguine. 'To the Conservatives, I see no loss in this sudden summons: they are confident, well organized, and have been long preparing . . . On the whole I incline to think Gladstone has made a mistake.'[27]

Both Disraeli and Gorst remained cautious in their expectations of the forthcoming general election. Gorst predicted a narrow Conservative majority of three MPs. Disraeli 'did not seem either sanguine or eager, as to the result: he seems to think the majority either way will be narrow, but not to expect that we shall win'.[28] Neither anticipated an overwhelming Conservative triumph. In his hastily composed election address Disraeli reiterated his established themes, deprecating the 'incessant and harassing legislation' of the past five years.[29] What followed, however, stunned and delighted the Conservative leadership. One after another urban bastion of Liberal support swung over to the Conservatives. On 6 February an elated Cairns wrote to Disraeli: 'I lose my breath at Manchester, Brighton, Nottingham, Marylebone and Westminster! and I may have some further shocks of an agreeable kind from the City and Metropolitan boroughs for which we are waiting.'[30] Further London seats were won in Chelsea, Greenwich, Southwark and Tower Hamlets. Successes in Guildford, Andover and Kidderminster followed. While they made virtually a clean sweep of the Home Counties, further north the Conservatives also won significant victories in Manchester, Oldham, Stalybridge, Warrington and Wigan. Victories in the English counties and mainly southern larger English boroughs, strengthened by the solidity of loyal Conservative support in Lancashire, delivered a stunning electoral success. The new Parliament of 1874 gave the Conservatives a commanding Commons majority of 52 MPs. This was, indeed, Conservative reaction with a vengeance. From being a marginal and defeated party in 1868, the Conservatives returned to power six years later on a resurgent wave of electoral triumph.

How was this recovery of power achieved? The most important factors, the exhaustion of Gladstonian reform and the reaction of popular opinion against Liberal zeal, were contingent advantages encouraged by patient Conservative restraint. Vigilant reserve allowed external forces to do the opposition's work for them. By 1872 the progressive moral consensus that had galvanized Liberal support in 1868 was fracturing. The demands of office were prising apart Whig, Liberal and radical opinion, as divisive disillusionment slowly contaminated the early elation that had surrounded Gladstone's charismatic leadership. Meanwhile, in the country, employers became alarmed by the growing strength of trades unions; the brewing interest were dismayed by Liberal legislation and temperance campaigns; foreign events such as the Paris Commune and insurrection in Spain suggested excessive reform might escalate into revolution; the assault on Anglican entitlements appeared to threaten Britain's Protestant heritage, as anxiety about ultramontane Catholicism mounted; the 1870 Irish Land Act seemed to set a precedent for legislative interference in the rights of property; narrow economy appeared to render Britain militarily vulnerable; and sectarian animosity was roused by the Liberal's 1870 Education Act. As popular support for the Liberal government ebbed away, the tide of middle-class and suburban opinion flowed towards the Conservatives. While doing little, the opposition gathered to themselves those disenchanted by persistent Liberal exertion.

The third important factor in the Conservative recovery after 1868 was the abating of internecine strife within the Conservative Party after 1872. This was less due to the strength of Disraeli's authority, which remained precarious and vulnerable. Rather, it was the difficulties raised by his two main rivals, the acerbic and sceptical Salisbury and the punctilious and reticent Derby, that saved Disraeli's position. It was anticipated that neither Derby nor Salisbury could work harmoniously together. Neither did Derby, at the critical juncture, wish to assume the leadership himself. Salisbury alone was unacceptable to more progressive Conservatives. Others, such as Cairns, Carnarvon and Hardy, were not credible challengers. These considerations enabled Disraeli to survive the intrigues intended to displace him. After 1872, plots to remove Disraeli gave way to more concerted action to replace their opponents in office, once the Liberal alliance was irretrievably split by the divisive demands of government.

The fourth most important factor in Conservative recovery after 1868 was the revitalized sense of collective purpose Disraeli gave the Party in his Manchester and Crystal Palace speeches of 1872. Disraeli established the anti-Liberal credentials of the Conservatives as a patriotic national party committed to defence of the constitution, to preservation of the Empire, and to improving the material conditions of the working classes. Safeguarding the monarchy, the aristocracy, the Anglican Church and the Imperial ties with Britain's 'white colonies', as the historic manifestations of national greatness, were the antidote for Liberal penny-pinching, narrow rationality and cosmopolitan principles. Social reform was the reassuring remedy for ceaseless political and institutional innovation. Loyalty and religious reverence, Disraeli claimed, were as necessary to a heroic tradition as reason. Upon a free aristocracy and the health and knowledge of the multitude were built the durability and vitality of a great nation. This, in turn, he presented as the key to the restoration of Britain's power and prestige abroad. British civilization stood as the 'ornament and honour of the world'. Disraeli's timeless abstractions gave Conservatives a resonate language about themselves that caricatured Liberalism as a desiccated doctrine, under which the historic roots of British achievement had withered.

The final factor in the Conservative recovery after 1868 was the more efficient party organization established by Gorst after 1870. Following the 1874 general election the myth emerged that it was Gorst almost single-handedly who had delivered the Conservative electoral triumph. This retrospective assertion was misleading for a number of reasons. First, the effectiveness of party organization was crucially dependent upon those more significant factors described above. Without the collapse of the Liberal moral agenda, a shift in popular opinion towards the Conservatives, the eventual abatement of querulous self-recrimination within the Conservative leadership, and the compelling reassertion of Conservative purpose by Disraeli in 1872, more efficient party organization would have counted for far less. Secondly, such a myth discounts the genuine achievements of Gorst's predecessors, such as Sir William Jolliffe in the 1850s and Markham Spofforth in the 1860s. Gorst's success owed a debt to those who had gone before him. Thirdly, the extent of the Conservative triumph in 1874 surprised even Gorst himself. He did not predict or anticipate an electoral landslide. In 1868 the Liberals had polled 42 per cent of all registered votes; the Conservatives gained 31.56 per cent of votes cast in the general election. In 1874 the Liberals gained 36.24 per cent of votes cast and the Conservatives polled 36.53 per cent of all registered votes. This represented an electoral swing away from the Liberals towards the Conservatives in 1874 of 5 per cent.[31] The concentration of Conservative votes in the English counties and the larger English boroughs produced a commanding Commons majority. But it was also true that the erosion of the Liberal vote overall exceeded the Conservative gain – Liberal weakness, as much as Conservative strength, secured Disraeli his success. In Ireland, for example, 58 Irish Home Rule candidates took seats from mainly Liberal MPs. In 1868 the Liberals had won 65 Irish seats: in 1874 they won only 17 seats. In itself, more efficient party organization, rather than create electoral success, could only channel more effectively those movements in voting opinion prompted by other considerations. Gorst's exertions could not guarantee an electoral landslide. But they did enable the Conservatives to take greater benefit of the advantages they otherwise enjoyed.

Politics, like chess, is an adversarial activity in which one's own decisions are informed by the moves of your opponent. Moreover, like chess, those moves anticipated but never played can be as important as what actually occurs. Conservative success in 1874 was primarily due to the foundering of the Liberals' progressive resolve and the increasing disenchantment of many voters with a constant cascade of contentious legislative reform. To these voters Disraeli offered calm repose and quiet government, upholding the welfare and prestige of the nation. Factious internal intrigue was ultimately contained. Electoral organization was attended to and the tempting precipitous seizure of power resisted. Patient vigilance fulfilled the dictum that Disraeli had penned in his novel *Sybil*, that everything eventually comes to men who can remain 'firm and calm'.

Notes

1. *The Times*, 20 Nov. 1871, cit. W.F. Monypenny and G.E. Buckle, *The Life of Benjamin Disraeli, Earl of Beaconsfield* (London: John Murray, 1910–20), vol. 5, 171.
2. B. Disraeli, *Lord George Bentinck* (London: John Murray, 1852), 10.
3. Ibid., 11.
4. *The Spectator*, 7 Feb. 1874, cit. R. Shannon, *The Age of Disraeli, 1868–1881: The Rise of Democracy* (London: Longman, 1992), 177.
5. Gladstone to Granville, 9 Sep. 1873, cit. A. Ramm (ed.), *The Gladstone–Granville Correspondence* (Cambridge: Camden Classic Reprints, vol. 5, Royal Historical Society, 1998), 407.
6. H.C.G. Matthew (ed.), *The Gladstone Diaries, Volume 8: July 1871–December 1874* (Oxford: Clarendon Press, 1982), 299.
7. Disraeli to Sir William Jolliffe, 7 Nov. 1855, Somerset Record Office, Hylton MSS, C/2165.
8. J. Vincent (ed.), *Disraeli, Derby and the Conservative Party: Journals and Memoirs of Edward Henry, Lord Stanley, 1849–1869* (Hassocks: Harvester Press, 1978), 92.
9. Derby to Spencer Walpole, 30 Jan. 1853, Liverpool Record Office, Derby MSS, 920 DER(14) 182/1.
10. Derby to Liddell, 4 Jan. 1853, Derby MSS, 920 DER(14) 182/1.
11. Earl of Malmesbury, *Memoirs of an Ex-Minister* (London: Longman, 1884), vol. 2, 215.
12. Monypenny and Buckle, *Disraeli*, vol. 5, 103.
13. N.E. Johnson (ed.), *The Diary of Gathorne Hardy, Later Lord Cranbrook, 1866–1892: Political Selections* (Oxford: Clarendon Press, 1981), 115.
14. Ibid., 173.
15. Northcote to Disraeli, 14 Mar. 1873, British Library, Iddesleigh MSS, 50016, f. 144.

16. A. Hawkins and J. Powell (eds), *The Journal of John Wodehouse, First Earl of Kimberley for 1862–1902* (Cambridge: Camden Fifth Series, vol. 9, Royal Historical Society, 1997), 275.

17. J. Vincent (ed.), *A Selection from the Diaries of Edward Henry Stanley, 15th Earl of Derby (1820–1893) between September 1869 and March 1878* (London: Camden Fifth Series, vol. 4, Royal Historical Society, 1994), 61.

18. Ibid., 38.

19. Cairns to Richmond, 23 Jan. 1872, cit. E.J. Feuchtwanger, *Disraeli Democracy and the Tory Party* (Oxford: Clarendon Press, 1968), 11.

20. B. Disraeli, *Contarini Fleming* (London: John Murray, 1832), part 1, chapter 21.

21. For Disraeli's Crystal Palace address, see T.E. Kebbel (ed.), *Selected Speeches of the late Earl of Beaconsfield* (London: Longman, 1882), vol. 2, 555–613.

22. A much-quoted observation by the French scholar Giles Ménage (1613–1692), used by Disraeli in his speech at the Free Trade Hall, Manchester, 3 Apr. 1872.

23. Gorst to Noel, 22 Sep. 1870, Bodleian Library, Hughenden MSS, B/XXI/N/120a.

24. Disraeli to Grey de Wilton, 3 Oct. 1873, cit. Monypenny and Buckle, *Disraeli*, vol. 5, 262.

25. Monypenny and Buckle, *Disraeli*, vol. 5, 267, 267–8.

26. Corry to Disraeli, 4 Dec. 1873, Hughenden MSS, B/XX/Co/92.

27. Vincent, *Derby Diaries 1869–1878*, 159.

28. Ibid., 160.

29. Shannon, *The Age of Disraeli*, 173.

30. Cairns to Disraeli, 6 Feb. 1874, Hughenden MSS, B/XX/Ca/110.

31. See J.P.D. Dunbabin, 'Parliamentary elections in Great Britain, 1868–1900: a psephological note', *English Historical Review*, 81 (1966), 82–99.

3
A New Style and Content: 1880–1885 and 1886

David Steele

The context

Over these few years a new Conservative Party emerged, much more purposeful and effective, to the undisguised dismay of Gladstone, then at the height of his powers and his fame. The third Marquess of Salisbury, whose direction of British foreign policy for most of the last quarter of the nineteenth century was, and is, admired, is not always given his due for the political transformation on the home front. If the reading of his character in several modern authorities is to be accepted, it is difficult to understand how someone with his deficiencies could have risen to lead his party and to head three administrations between 1885 and 1902.[1] He was, we are told, 'inept at all but the most intimate or the most impersonal relations'. As a reactionary, and apparently he was at heart never anything else, 'his political persona was largely a function of his fears and antipathies'.[2] It is a strange judgement on a man whose intellectual distinction and ability to handle the shifting realities were almost universally recognized by his opponents. In their view, he had by the mid-1880s 'recreated a Conservative party that is a living, disciplined organization with living principles'.[3] What follows here is an extended commentary on that specimen of the tributes he attracted. The nature of his undoubted achievement has to be set in a context that may require some exegesis.

In Victorian England practical politics excluded an unintelligent resistance to change. Erskine May's *Constitutional History of England*, an influential work from its publication in 1861, accounted for the surprising spectacle of aristocratic leadership in a steadily more industrial and urban society by the readiness of landed politicians to adopt the 'progressive' policies that were necessary for their continued primacy.[4] Not less important to the historical perspective is the complexity and absence of rigidity in the contemporary class structure, well described by a Prime Minister, the fourteenth Earl of Derby, whose great possessions and hereditary influence were concentrated in Lancashire. In his experience of one of the most economically advanced and densely populated areas of the kingdom, he said in a speech of 1863 'two people would probably not agree whether they belonged to the higher, or higher-middle, to the lower-middle, or the lower class'.[5] If this was a politic exaggeration, it was nearer the truth than the crude theory of necessarily antagonistic classes formulated by a German Jewish exile in London, of whom few people in England had then heard. In general use long before Marx had come to this country, the language of class had been employed to express the aspirations and discontents of interests identified by themselves and by others with social classes: Palmerston took class collaboration to the length of claiming to be a working man himself, to the good-natured amusement of Glaswegian artisans.[6] The Liberal broad church, with adherents ranging from Whigs as conservative as any Tory in most respects to outspoken radicals, owed its regular majorities to the realization all round that change was unstoppable, and beneficial when evolutionary. '... [T]he Church and the Aristocracy are great realities', wrote Cobden to John Bright in 1859, 'which will last for your life and your sons' [lives]. To ignore them or despise them is equally incompatible with the part which I think you have the ambition to play.'[7]

Famously stigmatized by J.S. Mill as 'the stupidest party',[8] the Tories followed where Whigs and Canningites had led in the greatest political crisis of the century over the first reform bill. A socially unifying rhetoric was the stock in trade of both parties. At no time, it should be pointed out, was Salisbury an exception to this; the clash with Derby and Disraeli over household suffrage in 1866–67 was a question of tactics and timing. At one moment Salisbury seems to have considered joining the Liberals in his disgust with the Tory leadership. What that exhaustively discussed episode did was to establish him as the conscience of the Party, proof against the temptation to perform a political somersault for the sake of office. 'You have at least been faithful found' said his friend, the historian Dean Milman, calling him 'the Abdiel of Conservatism' after the seraph in *Paradise Lost* who stood alone against the hosts of Lucifer.[9] Salisbury lived up to that role when he moved to the Lords, where he played a leading part in resisting the controversial legislation of Gladstone's first ministry. The usual consensus on strategy between the parties had given the conduct of opposition, by one side or the other, an air of unreality, more often than not. Contemporaries saw quite clearly what J.M. Cornford terms 'the parliamentary conspiracy ... [with] wide areas of agreement and common assumption'. Evident in the Commons, the propensity for shadow-boxing was stronger in the Lords. Palmerston's unsuccessful attempt to introduce life peers – later taken up by Salisbury, also in vain – was intended to revive a chamber which to a peer in his cabinet felt like 'the Palace of the Dead'.[10] When Salisbury entered the Lords, he took every chance that presented itself to make the Upper House an instrument of principled opposition to an exceptionally powerful Prime Minister backed by a large Commons majority.

Each year from 1869 to 1872 Salisbury rebelled against his party's leadership in the Lords, arguing, as he was to do in the 1880s and 1890s, that endangered interests must fight every inch of the way against ill judged and sometimes predatory reforms – the Irish church, Irish land, university tests and ballot acts. If these measures were not greatly changed by the spirited attacks to which Tory peers rallied contrary to the advice of their official leaders, Lord Cairns and the Duke of Richmond, Salisbury added considerably to his standing and imbued the Lords with a sense of their continuing importance as a piece of constitutional machinery. Determined to prevent the reduction of the House to a 'purely decorative' place in the constitution, he set forth a doctrine with a very long life: the peers should give way on 'those great and rare occasions on which the national mind has fully declared itself'; but only a government mandated by the voters to enact a specific measure could summon the House to yield. Even then he reserved to the Lords an indeterminate right to amend the legislation, one which they exercised freely at his instance in opposition to successive Gladstone ministries. Salisbury coupled this coherent updated theory of the peers' freedom with a candid admission that the composition of the House as well as its rationale needed attention. 'We belong too much to one class', he told his order, '... with respect to a large number of questions we are all too much of one mind.' A middle-class element, judiciously selected, would do the Chamber nothing but good. But unless the Lords, reformed or not, displayed the political courage he embodied, they would deserve to die of inanition, as was quite widely predicted.[11] In practice, Salisbury and his followers regularly had to submit to the combination of resolute Liberal governments and apprehensive Tory front-benchers in both Houses. Nevertheless, he and they demonstrated that Toryism had a backbone, and that intelligent conservatism, with a small 'c', was not a Disraelian monopoly.

Salisbury and the future of Toryism

'Drab' and 'cynical' are two epithets recently applied to Salisbury; their use conveys an impression of his personality and politics that is hard to dispel.[12] It is not well founded in fact, and reflects the unspoken assumption that to be an authentic Conservative is to sin against the light. Salisbury brought to the most fraught situations a light touch which relieved the tensions created by the 'wild elephant mood' in which he sometimes set about offending Liberal bills. There is among the Duke of Richmond's papers a delightful letter from the end of the 1872 session when Salisbury was holding the fort for colleagues who had mostly dispersed for the recess. 'I delivered your firman', he wrote to his long-suffering leader, '(first pressing it reverently to my forehead): but I regret to say ... a majority could not be got together ... All your faithful servants have fled ... I ... only I, remain, and I shall get up a quarrel with somebody unless you speedily come back.'[13] After the Tory victory in 1874, delivered by Gladstone's mistakes rather than Disraeli's generalship, the rebel was very nearly left out of the ministry. The new premier's resentment of someone who had damned him as a 'Jew adventurer' was reinforced by the misgivings of the cautious mediocrities who collect at the top of political parties. Salisbury's inclusion was to be justified by his record at the India Office and the Foreign Office and above all by the qualities he displayed inside and outside the Cabinet during the Eastern crisis of 1876–78, which earned him the respect of his chief and the admiration of the Liberal opposition. People soon saw him as Disraeli's political heir; the story circulated that the older man had intended to name him as such on his death bed. But the Tories were not ready for Salisbury: the Party leadership went into commission between the leaders in the two Houses. The Commons had Sir Stafford Northcote, who led for the government in that House after Disraeli promoted himself to the Lords in 1876. In the Lords it was with a certain reluctance that Richmond waived his claim to resume the leadership which had been his before Disraeli took a peerage. If Northcote was wholly unconvincing as the Tory answer to Gladstone, the distrust of Salisbury with his history of rebellion and aversion to compromise was too strong for him to emerge as the undisputed leader of the Party. Pending a Tory government, whose head the monarch would choose, after the customary soundings, the Tories laboured under the increasingly obvious disadvantage of a divided leadership, split by arrangement between two men with even less in common than was at first thought.[14]

Salisbury's uneasy relationship with Northcote, somebody unsuited by temperament and conviction to restore the self-confidence of a party badly beaten at the polls, was only part of Disraeli's legacy. The onset of the late Victorian depression, the discredit of military setbacks in Africa and Asia and – a factor to which considerable importance was attached at the time – clerical discontent with the Public Worship Regulation Act of 1874 constituted a sufficient explanation of electoral defeat.[15] But Salisbury shared the feeling that Gladstone's personal triumph in the election had deeper causes.[16] Disraeli's populism had been superficial, and never intended to be anything else, while his brand of rhetoric tended to bombast. His open letter to the Duke of Marlborough, which did duty as an election manifesto in 1880, struck a very old friend and former cabinet colleague, the fifteenth Earl of Derby, as 'absurd if addressed to educated men, but not ill-adapted to be read in public houses'.[17] The friendship which replaced Salisbury's old detestation of Disraeli had not changed his estimate of that extraordinary figure as a politician, one whose 'only fixed principle was that the party must on no account be broken up'.[18] Among the sharpest critics of the Party as Disraeli left it was Canon Nathaniel Woodard, founder of the eponymous schools. An unsung hero of middle-class Toryism, he was one of several clergymen to whom Salisbury listened and opened his mind on politics. 'The Tories … at present', Woodard reflected in 1881, 'have no policy, and are too selfish to create one. The inertness of matter at the Creation was not more complete than is the hypostasis of selfishness in landowners.' It would be a miracle, he went on, if Salisbury succeeded in making anything of his own class.[19]

Given its disturbing uncertainties, the future in politics lay with those on the lower levels of the social pyramid. 'My one remedy for all this', Woodard told Salisbury '… is to secure "the *Lower* Middle Classes"', by which he meant the amorphous mass hard to separate from artisans at one end and from business and professional men at the other.[20] The social foundations of Nonconformity were to be found here, but so too were the urban conquests and reconquests of resurgent Anglicanism in the Victorian age. By 1884, or earlier, Salisbury had worked out a theory of electoral behaviour which incorporated such advice as Woodard's and determined his tactics in the conclusive trial of his abilities as a leader of the opposition, that is, in the long drawn-out crises over the third and fourth instalment of nineteenth-century parliamentary Reform. He did not believe that a large majority of the English population was politically rootless. The attachment to the Church of so many millions – evident from the statistics of Sunday school attendance and of marriages in church rather than from the late Victorian samples of regular attendance at places of worship – defined, very roughly, the predominant conservatism, always with a small 'c', of the country.[21] For his part, Gladstone thought the hard core of the support he enjoyed was 'religious liberalism (so to call it) and ... little else'. From Salisbury's angle of vision, Nonconformity was 'permanent Radicalism', assisted by a few anti-clericals of the Continental type and contained with growing difficulty by the Liberal aristocracy whose decline and 'party lukewarmness' Gladstone never ceased to lament.[22] The fear that haunted Salisbury during the crisis of 1884 and the approach to it was that although floating voters and the permanent adherents of Liberalism did not, in his view, amount to a majority of the electorate, a flawed redistribution of seats might quite easily hand power to the Liberals for a generation.

Salisbury's computations had revealed to him the reality of the Tories' crushing defeat in 1880. If between 2000 and 3000 electors, comprising the margin of victory in 63 seats, had voted the other way, that would have been enough to give his party an absolute majority of 1 in the Commons.[23] It was the possibility of another such result that decided Salisbury to surprise and outflank Gladstone in the negotiations between the parties over redistribution in 1884 by adopting a position close to the Chartist demand for parity in the size of constituency electorates. Echoing his friend Gladstone, Lord Acton saw the dissolution of Toryism in this radical move,[24] and Salisbury's loyal colleague, Lord Cranbrook, thought it 'a revolution':[25] but, as the 1885 election showed, it had transformed Tory prospects in the big towns. Gladstone ought not to have been disconcerted by Salisbury's boldness: the existing distribution of seats, with or without enlargement of the electorate, was plainly too favourable to the Liberals. As leader of the party of innovation, Gladstone had long exploited Tory fears in the belief that he might safely pretend to be more radical than he really was. He had, in fact, rather more confidence than Salisbury in the innate moderation of 'the English people' – the Celtic fringe was omitted from the scope of this generalization – and complained chiefly of their excessive deference to wealth and its pervasive influence.[26] The certainty that Gladstone – who was, as he continued to insist, a traditionalist at heart, yet without being a Tory – could afford to make play with appeals to class feeling against the House of Lords explains his tactics in the stand-off between the Houses in 1884.[27] Salisbury countered by calling his bluff, having satisfied himself that to do so was not to incur an unacceptable risk. Lord Derby, one of the diarists in the Liberal Cabinet, deemed the Prime Minister's express and implied threats of serious unrest 'skilful though unscrupulous', but noted that there was no groundswell of opinion to float a popular agitation, and that a crude index of working-class prosperity, savings bank deposits, provided confirmation that the benefits of falling prices outweighed the hardships inflicted by the prevailing depression.[28] If Gladstone did succeed in frightening a number on both sides, Salisbury's nerve held.

In the last year of Disraeli's leadership, between defeat in April 1880 and his death in April 1881, gloom and defiance characterized his utterances in private and public. The Party was 'a sinking ship',[29] and he exaggerated the significance of the mild encroachment on landlord rights in the Ground Game Act of 1880, which the Lords sensibly passed.[30] However, his mood bespoke a general unease about the spread of subversive ideas on the Continent and in these islands. It should not be forgotten that the 1880s saw a social revolution in Ireland, to which the Compensation for Disturbance Bill thrown out by the Lords in the summer of 1880 was an initial concession. The Land League responded to that disappointment by intensifying its campaign of violence and intimidation. Derby, not yet a member of the Liberal Cabinet, surmised that it suited the government to let 'a moderate degree of terror' build up the pressure on Irish landlords while the 1881 Land Bill, which involved a substantial transfer of rights to their tenants, was in preparation.[31] Against the background of events in Germany and Russia, Bismarck's outlawing of the Social Democrats and the ruthless terrorism of the Narodniks, culminating in the assassination of Alexander II in March 1881, the Irish situation was deeply disturbing.[32] Letters and diaries tell of the 'strange ... dread of something vague' which surfaced in the conversations at dinner tables: 'it reminds me of what one has read of as heralding ... great revolutions' mused Lord Carnarvon in May 1881. In an English context a Russian, or an Irish, revolution might seem improbable, but everywhere Carnarvon found acute anxiety at the 'onward march of extreme radicalism'.[33] Yet John Morley put the number of Liberal MPs classifiable as advanced or extreme radicals, with whom he had a good deal in common, at no more than 25 after the election.[34] The real cause for alarm was the nature of Gladstone's politics: Tories and Whiggish Liberals believed it lay in his power to make the Liberal Party serve radical ends alien to its historic character.

Gladstone, fair trade and empire

'Party is the team that draws the coach':[35] Gladstone's dictum was irrefutable, notwithstanding the speculation in the 1880s that the two-party system was likely to break up into smaller groups on the contemporary French pattern.[36] But party organization in the centre and in the constituencies was still in its infancy: the parties rested on their respective traditions, reinvigorated and expanded by changing circumstances.[37] A continuous process of adaptation called for skills that were in short supply. Gladstone was, by any standards, a supremely gifted communicator, reaching his peak in the Midlothian campaign of 1879–80. Then and for the long remainder of his career, he presented a fascinating paradox, identifying or seeming to identify with the crowds at his meetings but returning to base at the seat of Lord Rosebery or another landed magnate.[38] Over the six years to 1886 his views evolved in a radical direction, and not only on Home Rule for Ireland. His Boswell, Edward Hamilton, discerned what escaped others, the political affinity between Gladstone and Chamberlain, obscured by their conflicting personalities and later separation.[39] Salisbury saw this rather earlier than most, although it puzzled him that 'so coarse a revolutionist as Chamberlain should have Gladstone for his jackal'.[40] As became clear in 1885 to 1886, it was the Prime Minister, and not his Brummagem colleague, who took Liberalism forward. 'My practice', said Gladstone in December 1883, 'has been to leave behind those who cannot keep up with me', and Chamberlain was among those so left.[41]

'Fair Trade + Parnell + Church + Chamberlain': reviewing the results of the 1885 election, which deprived his party of their majority, Gladstone ascribed the setback to this cocktail made up of discontents and mistakes exploited by Salisbury and the Tories in the course of offensives mounted year after year since the Liberals swept them out of office.[42] Their main attack could only take the form of platform oratory: 'the only weapon we have – and we must go on plugging away', Salisbury told Northcote in 1882.[43] By the following year Salisbury had established himself as an orator to rival Gladstone and Chamberlain. The content of his speeches might be unpalatable: there could be no doubting their impact. He was, Liberals said respectfully, 'a really good fighting man'.[44] His mockery of Gladstone's earnest performance in this line did not disguise the fact that he had been learning from a master. 'Power', Salisbury advised a son at the start of a political career, 'is more and more leaving Parliament and going to the platform.'[45] From a Liberal point of view nothing was more revealing of the change that came over England since the mid-century than this Tory commitment to mass politics. As was to be expected, Salisbury soon overshadowed Northcote, whose conscientious addresses had none of Salisbury's 'fight and invective' and little of his ability to sketch credible alternative policies to those of a government, while retaining the freedom of manoeuvre valued by oppositions.[46] Without deliberately seeking to undermine Northcote's position, he was remedying the obvious weakness of the dual leadership: the want of a 'central figure of a party in the Commons to which constituencies are wont to look, if their confidence is asked for that party'.[47]

Northcote was still less satisfactory at Westminster than on the stump. Bi-partisan by nature, this West Country baronet had once been Gladstone's private secretary: it was harder for him than for most others to stand up to the greatest parliamentarian of the day. He was also conscious of being at a social disadvantage in relations with Salisbury: not a rich man, he had no equivalent of the peer's town house in Arlington Street; Lady Northcote had neither the means nor the personality to match Lady Salisbury as a political hostess.[48] The attitude of the Prime Minister compounded Northcote's woes: Gladstone was not at all grateful for his opposite number's conciliatory bearing. He held him responsible for the appearance of an independent opposition on the back benches centred on the 'Fourth Party' of Lord Randolph Churchill, Sir John Gorst, Sir Henry Drummond Wolff and Salisbury's nephew, A.J. Balfour.[49] They openly looked on Salisbury as the destined chief of the whole party: he insisted on his obligations to Northcote, whose leadership he shored up as best he could.[50] But his aggressive opposition in the Lords had much in common with that of the 'Fourth Party', who went to the length of abetting the obstruction practised by Parnell's nationalists. Gladstone complained to those around him of such Tory methods, which, according to him, overstepped the limits of constitutional resistance to a government's measures. It was, he said in a letter the gist of which was to be conveyed to Northcote, 'one of my primary duties', to sustain him, not surprisingly when it seemed to Balfour that his leader in the Commons really did dislike upsetting the Treasury bench.[51] At the same time, and in private, Gladstone repeatedly criticized Northcote's 'flabby weakness' towards his MPs.[52]

The Gladstonian ideal of a Tory opposition was expounded to a Whig duke in September 1885, when Liberal divisions had led to Salisbury's reluctant formation of a minority administration. The Tories were 'destitute ... of a respectable Conservatism', and quite unlike their predecessors under Sir Robert Peel, who of course included Gladstone himself. The offence of Salisbury and his party was the exploitation of 'popular passion and excitement', self-defeating because it only supplied '*a new point of departure*' for the radical wing of Liberalism.[53] Looked at dispassionately, Gladstone's real objection was to the successful promotion of policies which were, or threatened to be, as popular as those in his armoury. Salisbury had not been wholly wrong when in 1880 he feared that Gladstone might be disposed to encourage 'a serious war of classes'.[54] Two years afterwards the Liberal Prime Minister drafted a short and hostile analysis of the weak points in his opponents' defences: 'Causes tending to help the Conservative Party and give it at least an occasional preponderance through a minority of the nation'. The Tories had more money to fight elections and more of the powerful influence deriving from the concentration of landownership in relatively few hands. They had the backing of great vested interests drawing their strength from 'privilege or ... artfully constructed monopoly in the Army, the Law, the Clergy'. Finally, Westminster and Whitehall were susceptible to the insidious attraction, in many forms, of the 'wealthy and leisured class' in the capital. These are notes for Gladstone's personal use: they show that the critical references to class in the speeches were not mere rhetoric. As he saw it, inherited riches and power were hard to justify unless they were put at the service of the permanent Liberal government which, with 'occasional' intervals of Tory rule, represented the natural order of things.[55]

This was what the Tories were up against: Gladstone with his immense prestige and ability to unite the disparate elements of Liberalism represented, both actually and potentially, a far greater menace than Chamberlain, who was a deeply divisive figure. Salisbury was to tell the Queen in 1886 that with the all important exception of Gladstone 'the forces of subversion have no very dangerous champion'.[56] The best way to defeat the 'Grand Old Man' was to beat him at his own game, by stirring up feeling on issues which the Liberals did not like to have discussed in emotive language, if at all. As always in that age, protectionism, revived under the name of 'Fair Trade', was bound up with Empire. England's isolation as a free-trading nation had been a matter of pride during mid-Victorian prosperity, and was still so seen by industries capable of meeting foreign competition that had the advantage of rising tariff barriers. In the last quarter of the century, agriculture was hardest hit by North American imports but the recession stretching from the 1870s to the 1890s did not spare the industrial heartlands of England. Leeds is a case in point. There, as in some other towns, local Toryism evinced a stubborn fondness for protection. W. St James Wheelhouse, the barrister and municipal politician who sat for Leeds, was a persistent sceptic with regard to free trade: he resurrected the idea of an imperial customs union, aired by Disraeli in his Crystal Palace speech of 1872 and dropped as not being practical politics. While Wheelhouse's successor, the Leeds leather manufacturer and future cabinet minister, W.L. Jackson, was not an enthusiast for 'Fair Trade', he told the Commons that he could not ignore a petition signed by 25,000 people in the constituency. The prospective imposition of a 400 per cent duty on nine-tenths of leather exports to France had evidently persuaded him that without retaliatory tariffs, or at least the power to impose them, in such a situation, 'we should find ourselves left behind in the commercial race'. He mentioned the troubles of Leeds engineering employers, 'some of the most eminent ... in England', with the protectionism written into the French patent law.[57]

In this context, Salisbury took up the idea of retaliation from the beginning of the 1880s, but left himself plenty of room to repudiate charges of abandoning free trade and with it free food. A candidate's protectionist sympathies might be a winning card to play, and not only in an agricultural by-election, as in carrying North Leicestershire for the Tories in September 1881. 'Has not fortune given us a weapon which never could have been anticipated in the combination of farmers and manufacturers on this question?' wrote Lord Carnarvon to Salisbury. The latter, however, had already warned his friend about the risk of alienating the '"Literary Class"' in whom it was then their common aim to develop a friendlier attitude to the Party.[58] There was, Salisbury firmly believed, 'a mass of Conservative thought at the bottom of men's minds', which was not to be reached by identifying Toryism with the unthinking protectionism of a previous generation.[59] Instead, he called over the next few years for a critical re-examination of the comparative merits of free and fair trade. When the time was ripe, he used the issue to serve notice on Gladstone and Chamberlain that such a question lent itself to exploitation as easily as the confrontation between Lords and Commons. It was 'mere derision' to talk of parliamentary reform to the unemployed in a long-running recession. They were people for whom 'prosperity or depression means the difference ... between a life of hope and a life of despair'. Against that background he was able to put into perspective accusations that the Tories were only 'protectionists in disguise'.[60]

The attractions of 'Fair Trade' increased those of an expanding empire, and more particularly of some sort of economic union with the colonies of settlement, whose impressive growth was as much an inspiration to contemporary imperialism as was the Raj in India. 'We must now go in for a Greater Britain' – that is, Canada and the other self-governing territories – 'and a Great Empire', observed the businessman and leading Tory politician W.H. Smith in 1882.[61] It was easier to take this stance because the distinction that Gladstone perceived between 'Jingoism' – imperial adventures of which he disapproved – and the legitimate assertion of English interests, by force if necessary, could not be demonstrated to the satisfaction of others. 'Jingoism' had its adherents in the Liberal ranks. Chamberlain, for one, confessed to being 'a little Jingo' at the time; perhaps too much so, he added, for the kind of public opinion he was courting.[62] Salisbury himself hardly qualified as a Jingo. His preferred definition of empire was the old Palmerstonian one: the 'civilizing influence' of informal empire rather than conquest.[63] He was thus well placed to criticize the execution of Gladstone's Egyptian policy, arguing that Arabi Pasha's nationalist uprising against foreign domination might have been prevented by a more resolute and a more understanding attitude on the part of England. While Gladstone rejoiced, privately and publicly, at the victory of Tel-el-Kebir, Salisbury asked whether the bombardment of Alexandria, the destruction of the Egyptian army, the treatment of the Khedive and finally, the loss of the Sudan to the Mahdi was 'a process ... likely to leave our name imprinted on ... [Egyptian] minds ... with affection and respect'. The resulting form of indirect rule, from which he foresaw that it would be extremely difficult to withdraw, was naturally complicated by the Egyptians' enduring resentment. Thus he took the gloss off Gladstone's imperial triumph.[64]

In the last, most often quoted article he wrote for the *Quarterly Review* (October 1883) – ominously entitled 'Disintegration' – Salisbury was really criticizing the wishful thinking apparent in Gladstone's policies, almost everywhere abroad and in Ireland. The Gladstonian reliance on the Concert of Europe in Great Power politics seemed perilously unrealistic to him, and in going back to the Foreign Office in 1885 he substituted close co-operation with Bismarck's Germany.[65] He was similarly scathing about the government's handling of the Disraelian legacies in the world beyond Europe. As a member of the Tory Cabinet, he had not been in favour of advancing deep into Afghanistan or into the Boer republic of the Transvaal; nor did he want to see the problems of the Sudan added to those which England had to face in Egypt proper. Intervention, however, created obligations: to friends and clients among Afghan and Sudanese tribesmen, and to the helpless African majority in the Transvaal and its region who had believed in assurances of England's protection against their enemies. Gladstone discovered genuine national feeling to which a Liberal government must bow in the Afghans, Boers and the Mahdi's followers. Salisbury pointed to the hundreds of thousands of Africans handed over to the tender mercies of the Transvaal by agreements that were 'really in the interest of slavery'. When Gladstone asserted that the Sudanese were 'a people rightly struggling to be free', Salisbury retorted, to amused cheers, 'My impression ... is that the Sudanese are struggling for abridging the liberty of other people in the shape of the slave trade.' Loss of face, moreover, involved loss of power. Acquiescence in the defeat at Majuba, the failure to retain Kandahar, and at least a part of the Sudan after the humiliating failure to rescue General Gordon: these reverses diminished the 'military and political credit' of the country the world over. As a direct consequence, other nations had little time for England's representations about higher tariffs and her practical exclusion from large tracts of Africa and Asia. The fall in her international standing registered in 'that heightening of tariffs ... that closing of markets'. This refrain in Salisbury's speeches was so well received in the industrial areas that he was emboldened to hint, on the eve of taking office in 1885, that enlarging the internal market of the British Isles to include the colonies was not only desirable but compatible with the principle of free trade.[66]

Taking the fight to the enemy

Weakness and the acceptance of defeat beyond Europe encouraged Parnell, allied with Fenians and the agrarian Ribbonmen, to step up his demands on the Gladstone ministry.[67] This theme of Salisbury's touched a painful nerve in the body politic. Although sweeping concessions in the land legislation of 1881–82 and two stringent Coercion Acts contained the unrest that had fast been making Ireland ungovernable, it was plain that with the extension of household suffrage to Ireland in the anticipated reform bill, Parnell's party would win a commanding majority of Irish seats.[68] Then, said Gladstone privately in February 1882, 'an Irish Parliament would be irresistible. They could ... make their own terms.'[69] While Salisbury did his best in the Lords to modify the land bills, the looming confrontation between England and Ireland and their future constitutional relationship were matters he treated with circumspection. After the assassination of Lord Frederick Cavendish in May 1882, Carnarvon thought any government would have to choose between 'Irish independence or very stern repression'; there was no *via media*.[70] The hints of impending Home Rule of some kind that Gladstone dropped from early 1882 onwards were intentionally hard to interpret. Most ministers, the Liberal Chief Whip, Lord Richard Grosvenor, was saying in March that year, expected civil war in Ireland to follow the election of a nationalist majority of her MPs.[71] Gladstone's elucidation of his remarks in the Commons – he explained that Home Rule would not affect the supremacy of the Westminster Parliament – was greeted with incredulity by political friends and enemies. 'If he really believes this he is the only man in England who does so', commented Derby.[72] In this atmosphere there was a general reluctance to bring on the crisis prematurely, but the tension generated influenced the reception of

Chamberlain's attacks on English institutions and notably those on the Established Church.

The legislative invasion of Irish landlords' rights inevitably excited fears for property on the other side of the water. With reason, for Gladstone was talking privately about a statutory English tenant right resembling that in the 1881 Irish Land Act.[73] So apprehensive were Tory MPs and peers of provoking Gladstone that they shrank from using their party's position in the Upper House to insist on amendments to the Irish land bills. The Duke of Argyll, who had resigned from the Cabinet over the 1881 Bill, besought Salisbury not to tempt Gladstone into dissolving on the measure: 'The town feeling is hostile to us – the farmers are not to be trusted. Gladstone's personal authority rules many minds.'[74] When Salisbury nevertheless courted a dissolution in 1882, on the bill writing off most of the arrears of rent owed by 130,000 small Irish tenants, his Lords majority first professed their eagerness to fight and then melted away. The controlled outburst with which he relieved his feelings in the chamber left his followers experiencing, as one of them said, the sensations of 'whipped hounds'. On the platform shortly afterwards he pointed to the superiority of the American supreme court to the Lords as a means of defending democracy against itself, that is, against an all powerful Prime Minister and his Commons majority. Admiration for the American political system at its strongest continued to feature in his speeches.[75] At the height of the battles over the 1884 Reform Bill, he said of the United States senate: 'I wish we could institute it in this country – marvellous in its efficiency and strength.'[76] These were not the reflections of a Tory traditionalist fighting blindly against change.

Apparently convinced that Salisbury wanted to see the Lords disappear, freeing him to re-enter the Commons, Gladstone fastened on a supposed indiscretion to that effect by Lady Salisbury, turning it to account with worried Tory peers and equally alarmed Liberals. 'Salisbury (who naturally rules the roost) does not care if the House of Lords is thrown into the cauldron along with other materials', the Prime Minister concluded after speeches and demonstrations had raised the political temperature. Gladstone did care: he wanted to carry the reform bill on his terms, but he was sincere when he protested to the Queen, whom he had succeeded in alarming, 'organic change in the Lords ... I hate – and ... I am making all this fuss to avoid'.[77] An examination of their correspondence and pronouncements leaves little doubt who, Gladstone or Salisbury, was the bolder of the two. Liberal efforts to detach Tory peers from Salisbury's uncompromising position met with limited success, while Chamberlain and the radicals eagerly welcomed the Tories' readiness to divide borough constituencies and to aim for a rough equality between electorates. This element in his cabinet and party took Gladstone with them, complaining that the scheme was 'too radical for him'.[78] Chamberlain mistakenly believed these advances were bound to work in the Liberals' favour, but Salisbury was quickly seen to have come out the winner from a bruising encounter. So clear was Gladstone's discomfiture that Liberal MPs spoke of Salisbury's 'dictation': it was 'perfectly sickening', remarked an influential backbencher. The victor was to ask Alfred Austin of the *Standard*, a trusted contact with the 'Literary Class', not to refer to the premier's 'submission', which was 'a little too strong'.[79]

By then Tory spirits had risen sharply since 1882, when Northcote described the Party's MPs as 'thoroughly demoralized'.[80] The scourge of his Commons leadership, Churchill, who began by calling for Salisbury to be regarded as the Tories' single head, went on to try conclusions with him in a bid to take over the mass party organization, such as it was. Churchill's brilliance in parliamentary debate and on the platform did not compensate for his obvious failings.[81] His 'Tory Democracy' was the invention of an incorrigible *frondeur*, of someone, according to a shrewd observer, 'for whom politics is a burlesque'.[82] Employing a mixture of firmness and flattery, Salisbury induced Churchill to settle for a place in the Party's inner councils. This he was able to do because Churchill, then and subsequently, acknowledged his personal ascendancy as a fellow-combatant in the war between the parties, as his master in the manoeuvres within their own party, and, above all, as a creative political mind.[83] 'Conservative policy', said *The Times* in 1883 of Salisbury's speeches, 'is no longer a mere string of negations'.[84] 'Fair Trade' won many urban and rural votes, and deprived free trade of its iconic status. These voters were not much interested in the fate of the Irish landlords, but they were not indifferent to Salisbury's suggestion that the Gladstonian Land Acts had jeopardized property in general. He was not addressing rootless proletarians but men of small property whose bourgeois values permeated the mass of the population. There was no need to remind him that the respectable working-class, and indeed those lower down, were 'the most conservative section of the community'. Like their betters, plebeian Tories assumed, however inarticulately, a religious sanction behind the existing order; they also understood instinctively the Burkean idea of change that Salisbury expounded to them without a trace of condescension: 'nothing is static, nothing is permanent in this world … but let there be changes worked by the slow process of persuasion, by the natural growth of institutions'.[85]

Among these changes were social reforms that extended the reach of the state. He constantly adverted to 'the great mission which the next generation have to perform, to make the conditions of life more tolerable to all'. There was no question 'so overwhelming in its magnitude as ... relations between the well-to-do and the poor'. But he had to tread very carefully in questioning so powerful an orthodoxy as *laissez-faire* economics. When he singled out slum housing for detached, and penetrating, analysis in the newly founded Conservative *National Review* (November 1883) he gave the impression of having radical intentions which he did not see his way to enacting in an acceptable fashion.[86] The Gladstonian reaction was to dismiss this essay in social politics as the Tories' 'only cry'.[87] Liberals also underestimated his revival of the time-honoured warning, 'the Church in danger'. He took the gloves off in setting about the political Dissenters whom he intensely disliked. They had gone too far in throwing the mantle of toleration over the secularist MP Charles Bradlaugh, whom the Commons refused a seat until 1886: 'there is an old proverb, "You may know a man by his associates", and infidels are always Liberals'. Wesleyans, however, the largest of the sects, were to be applauded as 'good patriots and good Christians', not least because they contained a sizeable Tory element. Such intemperate attacks paid an electoral dividend in 1885: the Dissenters who often formed a dominant minority in the towns were none too popular with their fellow-citizens and the unashamed militancy of urban Anglicans in the Tory interest resulted in a wave of successes in parliamentary and municipal politics.[88]

For five years Salisbury invited his mixed but of course half-educated admirers to think through with him the policies which, ultimately, they would determine. In his recension of Toryism the unforgivable sin was to set class against class, as Gladstone was capable of doing when he thought circumstances justified recourse to that expedient. Like other realistic men of the right, then and since, Salisbury saw that only the people could resist abuse of power by a democratized legislature. 'I do not think it is to be deplored', he announced at Liverpool in 1882, as he castigated the Liberal record, '[that] the direct action of the people is superseding the indirect action of its representatives'.[89] It should be remembered that there had always been a populist strain in Toryism, the rediscovery of which delighted traditionalists like Lord John Manners.[90] Salisbury did not at first expect much of the Primrose League founded in 1883, but its astonishing growth, with membership rising from under a thousand in 1884 to 200,000 in 1885 and a million in 1891, took place in the context of Salisbury's popularization of Toryism.[91] He contrasted the League with Tory MPs and the party machine. 'If I may say so without irreverence', he told it in May 1886, 'you are rather the preaching friars of the message than the regular clergy attached to each district.'[92] The metaphor was apt: the Primrose League did for Toryism what St Francis and St Dominic had done for the medieval Church. It was largely owing to this agency, writes the League's historian, that 'no other political party approached as closely to a party of social integration before 1900'. Toryism had always resembled a political church: the Salisburyian counter-reformation opened it to new realities. It was indicative of the change when in 1887 the League passed the first of its recurring resolutions in favour of women's suffrage.[93]

Salisbury more than once employed another historical analogy to describe the necessary involvement of the Party with the people. Tories were to engage in political warfare in the spirit of British infantry closing with the enemy at Inkerman, the 'soldier's battle' of the Crimean campaign.[94] Chamberlain played into Salisbury's hands by his 'violent' language,[95] by seeming to force the pace of change, in his 'Unauthorized Programme' of 1883–85 as a whole, and especially by trying to bring forward the general national debate on disestablishment anticipated in the not too distant future. 'Socialism was in the air', said Chamberlain in 1883,[96] but 'the complete social revolution' of which he talked in London society had as its goal an Americanized and not a Socialist England. Breaking up the great estates and class distinctions down, class warfare directed against the landed interest was what he meant when he dismayed fellow-guests by saying 'none of us in the upper classes had any idea what was coming – a new world'.[97] Industrialists, and rentiers such as he had himself become when he retired from business to enter politics, had nothing to fear from him. The 'socialism' of his programme was akin to Salisbury's, concerned with housing and education, as well as the allotments and small holdings which he was soon driven to expect as no more than a good landlord would provide.[98] The famous 'three acres and a cow', taken literally by newly-enfranchised agricultural labourers, delivered a number of habitually Tory county seats to the Liberals in 1885: but Chamberlain's colleagues, like Salisbury, foresaw that the inevitable realization of how little was really possible, or intended, would count against the Liberals next time, as it did in the 1886 election.[99] It was the borough returns that mattered in 1885: there, his Liberal critics noted, he had a 'tremendous fall'.[100]

Chamberlain's 'urban cow', as he termed it, was free elementary education, for which, he admitted, the borough voters showed little enthusiasm.[101] His notorious 'ransom' speech of July 1885, in which he enquired what property would pay in higher taxes for its continued security, dogged him throughout the election campaign. 'I am not a communist', he protested, 'although some people will have it that I am.'[102] He attempted to compensate for increasing moderation in that direction by making more of disestablishment, to which 500 Liberal candidates had pledged themselves with widely varying degrees of ambiguity. Gladstone himself had hinted in his manifesto that disestablishment's time was coming. Salisbury seized on the admission of leading Liberals that Gladstone and Chamberlain had stirred up 'a sleeping lion' in raising a question of tremendous import. The Tories would sacrifice 'every other consideration that governs us' to save the Church whose fall, on the Continental precedents, must open the floodgates to irreligion. 'I do not believe', he declared, '... if properly appealed to, the people are against us.'[103] He was right: it quickly emerged that too many Nonconformists, and not only the Wesleyans, did not like the idea of a lay state, now that the more irritating aspects of Anglican privilege had been legislated away. The 1885 election left Chamberlain looking like an unconvincing bogeyman.[104] The year before his overt threats of disorder if the Lords stood their ground over the reform bill had failed to impress Salisbury, although Gladstone let it be known that he took them seriously. While their setbacks of 1885 in the English counties, and a net gain of only two seats in Scotland and Wales, restricted the Tories' electoral revival to very modest proportions, they were stronger than the final returns suggested. There were good reasons for this unexpected strength: under Salisbury the Party had demonstrated that it was fit to govern and much less of a prey to internal disagreements than the Gladstone ministry. But the 'continued rhetorical battle'[105] of a campaign that really began in the summer of 1885 had by mutual consent kept the great question of the day in the background: what would a commitment to Irish Home Rule do to the Liberals, and to the Tories?

Office and the return to opposition, 1885–86

Salisbury's aims as the opposition's effective leader were to keep the Tories together, and to present them as a party of government, while educating the public, and moderate Liberals in particular, about the dangers, in which he really believed, from the new radicalism. There were complaints about the detachment that was in fact one of his strengths. He spent many months abroad, coolly withdrawing to the Continent for much of the recess in 1884 when the Liberals were trying to raise the political temperature over the reform bill: but his letters show that he was quite aware of what was happening at home. Not that he was optimistic about the future in the long or the short term. In the short term Gladstone and Gladstonianism remained extremely strong. In the long term England could not be immune to the advance of the left in Germany and France. There were moments when he doubted his fitness to lead a great party. Yet intellectual conviction and temperament saved him from the defeatism rife among Tories in the early 1880s, and still widespread in the middle of the decade. Change was inevitable: radical change, falling short of revolution in an English setting, was not. He hesitated over taking office in June 1885 because the position of a minority administration, pending the introduction of a new and expanded electoral register in the autumn, might only serve to rally the temporarily disunited Liberals. In the end he yielded to the representations of the Queen, resolutely and unintelligently anti-Gladstonian, and to those of colleagues, Northcote included, naturally eager for office. Once he had obtained assurances, indispensable to a government's survival, from the Liberals about ways and means, he signalled his determination to show that not withstanding the Party's weakness in the Commons, Tories could both develop the policies they had been airing, and respond with constructive boldness to the need for a settlement of the Irish question.[106]

The Tories' seven months in office were in a sense hard to distinguish from the opposition they had experienced since 1880, and to which they returned in January to July 1886. Gladstone was, and continued to be, the most popular politician in the country when he resigned in June 1885, following a narrow defeat on his budget's unpopular increases in the beer and spirits duties, brought about by Liberal abstentions in the face of a Tory–Irish combination. The Cabinet were, however, so deeply divided by their disagreements, above all on Ireland, and by the tension between Hartington and Chamberlain, personifying, respectively, the Whig and radical wings of Liberalism, that resignation came as a relief to many, if not most, of its members. The incoming Salisbury ministry appointed a royal commission on the prevailing depression – that is, to explore the case for some departure from free trade – and enacted a housing bill, from which the Liberals excised the discounted sale of Crown sites for working-class dwellings. That provision Gladstone described as 'one of the very worst pieces of socialism that has yet come into our view'.[107] There was general approval of Salisbury's own performance at the Foreign Office, held with the premiership. Churchill at the India Office made an unexpectedly good impression, although managing him was one of the heaviest prime ministerial burdens; while Northcote, at Churchill's insistence, went to the Lords with the title of First Lord of the Treasury and few of the responsibilities of the post. Overhanging the government's brief life, however, was the question of Home Rule. Salisbury wanted to discover whether some form of autonomy could be devised that was acceptable to the Irish nationalists and to Englishmen. The investigation, entrusted to Carnarvon as the Irish viceroy, convinced ministers, with the partial exception of Carnarvon himself, that they could not proceed.[108]

'We are come to the break-up of the Liberal Party', said Gladstone in July 1885.[109] To carry Home Rule, with Parnell's support, was the last and greatest of the imperatives of his political life. Already estranged from the majority of Liberal peers by his Irish land legislation, he rightly believed that he had a firmer hold on his middle- and working-class adherents. He hoped to limit the damage to his party by backing a Tory Home Rule bill that satisfied the nationalists, and he intimated as much to Salisbury. The latter had made it clear to Carnarvon that he had no intention of playing the part of Sir Robert Peel in the repeal of the Corn Laws.[110] But Salisbury's keynote speech at Newport in October 1885 had contained an explicit, encouraging response to Parnell's suggestion in a speech only days before that a mutually acceptable Anglo-Irish relationship might resemble the dual monarchy of Austro-Hungary. This passage supported Gladstone's belief that it was indeed time for a large measure of Irish self-rule within the Empire.[111] The mood of the Cabinet and Party, and Salisbury's own assessment of the political situation on both sides of the Irish Sea, ruled out a Tory commitment to Home Rule. When the Salisbury government fell at the end of January 1886, its Irish policy consisted of a return to the coercion they had let drop the previous summer; a second instalment, to follow the 1885 Land Purchase Act, of public finance enabling tenants to buy out their landlords; and a prospect of local government reform more or less in line with that being discussed for England. Liberals who, reluctantly in many cases, went with Gladstone on Home Rule, came to recognize over the next few months that 'the only alternative policy – because the only real alternative government – is that of Salisbury'.[112]

As early as November 1885, Chamberlain predicted a Tory majority if Gladstone regained power after the impending election, and then dissolved on Home Rule, as he was to do, when his party split.[113] Chamberlain was being driven towards what became the Unionist alliance by the conviction he shared with Salisbury: that a Dublin parliament must lead to separation, unless the United Kingdom were to adopt an American-style federal constitution complete with a supreme court to uphold the authority of the centre and protect individual liberties. 'I am not going to swallow separation with my eyes shut', he wrote in

December, although he made the attempt as a member of the third Gladstone ministry between February and March 1886.[114] Co-operation with the Tories thereafter was less difficult than it seemed at first sight: Salisbury's Newport speech had set out his credentials as a reformer and a democrat. At Newport Salisbury bade farewell to the politics of the past: in the new era, he said, 'all must be professional politicians'.[115] The speech was the most important of all his years at the head of the Party. It wove into Conservative policy strands of Gladstonian populism, Disraelian imperialism and the social radicalism of Chamberlain. 'In short, he picks out of Mr G[ladstone]'s political pudding the best plums', they conceded in the Liberal camp.[116] Salisbury added a vigorous defence of the Church against disestablishment and unfair competition for her educational effort from the better funded Board schools. Few major speeches can have had such a favourable reception all round: had Salisbury been the reactionary of legend, he would not have enjoyed that widespread approval for his distillation of Tory and Liberal politics, without which Unionism, born of the divisions over Home Rule, could hardly have fused Toryism, Whiggish or moderate Liberalism, and Brummagem radicalism, as it succeeded in doing by 1895 under Salisbury's leadership.

'Who sups with the Devil must have a long spoon. A game of chess with Gladstone is nervous work', remarked Salisbury as the jockeying for position over Home Rule reached its end in the last days of 1885.[117] There is little evidence to support the theory that Gladstone decided for Home Rule as the means of recovering the control of his party which had been slipping away to Chamberlain and Hartington, focuses for radical and conservative discontent within Liberalism. To the extent that such a shift had begun to take place, it was due to Gladstone's frequent references to a longed-for retirement; otherwise his leadership was unchallengeable. He saw Home Rule as a measure of justice transcending party politics. So did Hartington and Chamberlain, who put their principled objections to his policy before Liberal unity.[118] They had no choice but to work with Salisbury against Gladstone's bill: and he did everything in his power to secure their political survival. From April 1886 they had his promise that if and when Gladstone appealed to the electorate against the parliamentary resistance, they could look to the Tories not to contest their seats. The Tory Party's organization had considerably improved under Salisbury's eye, but only his personal authority induced Tories in the constituencies to observe the compact that lay behind the defeat of Home Rule in June by 30 votes. In return, although they declined to form a coalition in which Salisbury was willing to serve under Hartington, the dissident Liberals with 77 seats had 'a moral claim' to their aid for the purely Tory administration that took office in July.[119] It was the intention of Hartington and Chamberlain to rejoin the main body of the Liberals once the aged Gladstone had left the scene, and in 1887 they entered into abortive negotiations to do so while he was still at the helm.

The campaign of 1886 was remarkable for the intensity of the debate and the partial breakdown of the conventions covering political exchanges. Tories and rebel Liberals insisted that the Empire was in mortal danger: the concession of self-rule to Irish nationalists, England's bitterest enemies, would be interpreted everywhere as a sure sign that a great nation was ceasing to believe in herself. While Gladstone dwelt on the compelling righteousness of his policy, many Liberals preferred to emphasize, on and off the platform, the limited nature of the constitutional proposals, falling short as they did of the autonomy enjoyed by the settler colonies. Gladstone appealed to the masses against wealth and rank: 'fuel to the flames. That unfortunate "class" allusion has been fixed upon with avidity', wrote a depressed admirer.[120] Salisbury also played with fire, telling the voters of Leeds that the anarchy predicted for Ireland under Home Rule would flood the larger island with Celtic immigrants driving 'more British workmen down to the terrible level ... known in economics [as] ... the starvation point'.[121] The Tory leader endorsed Churchill's earlier suggestion in Belfast that Protestant Ulster's resistance was 'unlikely to remain within the lines of ... constitutional action'. Why, asked Salisbury, should not the Ulstermen prepare to defend themselves against foes bent on suppressing 'any independent and free life' in Ireland? The undeniable overlap between constitutional and revolutionary nationalism and between political action and agrarian violence had created the atmosphere in which it was possible for Salisbury to use such language, depicting the Celtic (and Catholic) Irish as 'habituated to the use of knives and slugs' and quite unfit for the ordered freedom of more advanced peoples. His rhetoric expressed rather than inspired the feeling that led the royal commander-in-chief, the Duke of Cambridge, to say openly in society that if the Ulstermen rose against Home Rule, the army would refuse to put down the rebellion.[122]

But the central force of this election, as of the entire period since the 1867 Reform Act, was Gladstone himself, of whom Salisbury said, choosing his words carefully, that while he was 'not dishonest ... his assurances cannot be trusted'.[123] This was the price Gladstone paid for what he modestly called his one 'striking gift', of responding to and moulding events and not showing his hand until he was ready.[124] The historian Lecky, a contemporary, summed him up as 'an honest man with a dishonest mind'.[125] Chamberlain, whom Gladstone brought on within the Party, distrusted him; Hartington, whom he regarded as his successor, distrusted him even more strongly. The Salisbury of 1886, someone whom the political nation viewed quite differently from the Salisbury of 1880, had his critics, and many of them, but he did not, at that time or later, excite anything like the same distrust. Hartington, whose integrity and courage were instrumental in defeating Home Rule, gave Salisbury's Tories a better character than he thought his own party deserved: 'they do unprincipled things but are not animated with Liberal hatred to property' – and not only that of Irish landlords; Gladstone's resort to the language of class warfare was too much for him.[126] Salisburyian Toryism throve on Gladstonian ambiguity.

Notes

1. I am grateful to the owners and custodians of the MSS on which I have drawn for this chapter, and in particular to Mr Robin Harcourt Williams at Hatfield House. Any student of Conservative politics in this period must acknowledge his debt to, among other scholars: R. Blake, *The Conservative Party from Peel to Churchill* (London: Eyre and Spottiswoode, 1970), R.T. Shannon, *The Age of Salisbury: Unionism and Empire* (London: Longmans, 1996), P. Marsh, *The Discipline of Popular Government: Lord Salisbury's Domestic Statecraft 1881–1902* (Brighton: Harvester Press, 1978) and the indispensable H. Pelling, *Social Geography of British Elections 1885–1910* (Aldershot: Gregg Revivals, 1994). The central figure of Lord Salisbury – the subject of his daughter Lady Gwendolen Cecil's unfinished classic, *Life of Robert, Marquis of Salisbury* (London: Hodder and Stoughton, 4 vols, 1929–32) – was oddly neglected for many decades: there are now, besides Marsh's book, the studies by A. Roberts, *Salisbury. Victorian Titan* (London: Weidenfeld and Nicolson, 1999), D. Steele, *Lord Salisbury. A Political Biography* (London: UCL Press, 1999) and M. Bentley's iconoclastic *Lord Salisbury's World: Conservative Environments in Late-Victorian Britain* (Cambridge: Cambridge University Press, 2001).
2. P. Smith (ed.), *Lord Salisbury on Politics: A Selection from his Articles in the Quarterly Review, 1860–1883* (Cambridge: Cambridge University Press, 1972), 97, 105.
3. Sir Robert Morier to Salisbury, 29 Feb. 1886, H[atfield] H[ouse] M[uniments] /3M [3rd Marquess] /E; subsequently cited as HHM/3M.
4. Sir T. Erskine May, *The Constitutional History of England since the Accession of George the Third, 1760–1830* (London: Longmans Green and Co., 3rd edn, 3 vols, 1871), vol. 1, 165.
5. *The Times*, 12 Oct. 1863.
6. A. Briggs, 'The language of "Class" in early nineteenth century England', in M.W. Flinn and T.C. Smout, *Essays in Social History* (Oxford: Oxford University Press, 1974); *The Times*, 1 Apr. 1863; and see E.D. Steele, *Palmerston and Liberalism, 1855–1865* (Cambridge: Cambridge University Press, 1991), esp. 205–14.

7. Cobden to Bright, 29 Dec. 1859, in J. Morley, *The Life of Richard Cobden* (London: T. Fisher Unwin, Jubilee edn, 2 vols, 1896), vol. 2, 350.
8. J.S. Mill, *Utilitarianism, Liberty, and Representative Government* (London: J.M. Dent and Sons, 1954), 261, n. 1.
9. Steele, *Lord Salisbury*, 56–7.
10. J.M. Cornford, 'The parliamentary foundations of the Hotel Cecil', in R. Robson (ed.), *Ideas and Institutions of Victorian Britain* (London: G. Bell and Sons, 1967), 272; Steele, *Palmerston and Liberalism*, 226.
11. Steele, *Lord Salisbury*, 65–73; quotations from 70 and 66.
12. C. Matthew, 'Gladstone and the University of Oxford', *Oxford Magazine* (Second Week, Michaelmas Term, 1999), 6.
13. Steele, *Lord Salisbury*, 71.
14. Ibid., 53; Lady John Manners to Salisbury, 19 Apr. 1881, HHM/3M/E.
15. T.O. Lloyd, *The General Election of 1880* (Oxford: Oxford University Press, 1968).
16. Marsh, *Discipline of Popular Government*, 6; Salisbury to Lady John Manners, 18 Apr. 1880, HHM/3M/D; R. Harcourt Williams (ed.), *Salisbury–Balfour Correspondence: Letters exchanged between the Third Marquess of Salisbury and his nephew Arthur James Balfour, 1869–1892* (Ware: Hertfordshire Record Society, 1988), 40.
17. Diary of the 15th Earl of Derby, 13 Mar. 1880, Liverpool Record Office, Derby MSS, 920 DER (15); subsequently cited as Derby diary.
18. Harcourt Williams, *Salisbury–Balfour Correspondence*, 41–2.
19. J. Otter, *Nathaniel Woodard: A Memoir of his Life* (London: John Lane, The Bodley Head, 1925), 302.
20. Woodard to Salisbury, 9 Nov. 1881, HHM/3M/H.
21. Salisbury to the Rev. Malcolm MacColl, 11 July 1884, in G.W.E. Russell (ed.), *Malcolm MacColl: Memoirs and Correspondence* (London: Smith, Elder and Co., 1914), 92–3.
22. Gladstone to Granville, 19 May 1877, in A. Ramm (ed.), *The Political Correspondence of Mr Gladstone and Lord Granville, 1876–1886* (Oxford: Clarendon Press, 2 vols, 1962), 40.
23. Salisbury to Lord Carnarvon, 25 Mar. 1882, British Library, Carnarvon MSS, 60759.
24. H. Paul (ed.), *Letters of Lord Acton to Mary ... Gladstone* (London: George Allen, 1904), 192.
25. Nancy E. Johnson (ed.), *The Diary of Gathorne Hardy, later Lord Cranbrook, 1866–1892: Political Selections* (Oxford: Clarendon Press, 1981), 546, 3 Dec. 1884; subsequently cited as *Cranbrook Diary*.
26. M.R.D. Foot and H.C.G. Matthew (eds), *The Gladstone Diaries with Cabinet Minutes and Prime-Ministerial Correspondence* (Oxford: Clarendon Press, 14 vols, 1968–94), vol. 11, 655; afterwards cited as *Gladstone Diaries*.
27. A. Jones, *The Politics of Reform* (Cambridge: Cambridge University Press, 1972).
28. Derby diary, 29 June 1884.
29. Harcourt Williams, *Salisbury–Balfour Correspondence*, 39.
30. Salisbury to Lady John Manners, 13 June 1880, HHM/3M/D.
31. Derby diary, 17 Dec. 1886.
32. *Cranbrook Diary*, 470, 14 Mar. 1881.

33. Carnarvon diary, 11 May 1881, Carnarvon MSS, 60916.
34. Derby diary, 7 Apr. 1880.
35. Gladstone to Lord Hartington, 10 Oct. 1884, in *Gladstone Diaries*, vol. 11, 217.
36. Salisbury to T.H.S. Escott, 1 Nov. 1882, British Library, Escott MSS, 58780.
37. The extensive modern literature on these topics rests on the foundations laid by H.J. Hanham, *Elections and Party Management: Politics in the Time of Disraeli and Gladstone* (London: Longmans, new impression, 1964) and E.J. Feuchtwanger, *Disraeli, Derby and the Tory Party* (Oxford: Clarendon Press, 1968).
38. A.J.P. Taylor, *The Trouble Makers: Dissent over Foreign Policy* (London: Hamish Hamilton, 1957), 70.
39. Unpublished diaries of Sir E.W. Hamilton, 14 Sep. 1885, British Library, Sir Edward Hamilton MSS, 48641.
40. Steele, *Lord Salisbury*, 145.
41. D.W.R. Bahlman (ed.), *The Diary of Sir Edward Walter Hamilton, 1880–1885* (Oxford: Clarendon Press, 2 vols, 1972), vol. 2, 517; subsequently cited as Bahlman, *Hamilton Diary*. Chamberlain's thinking is examined in P. Marsh, *Joseph Chamberlain: Entrepreneur in Politics* (New Haven and London: Yale University Press, 1994).
42. Gladstone to Lord Richard Grosvenor, Liberal Chief Whip, 27 Nov. 1885, in *Gladstone Diaries*, vol. 11, 436.
43. Salisbury to Northcote, 17 Oct. 1882, British Library, Iddesleigh MSS, 50020.
44. Bahlman, *Hamilton Diary*, vol. 2, 417, 3 Apr. 1883.
45. Steele, *Lord Salisbury*, 142.
46. Bahlman, *Hamilton Diary*, vol. 2, 697, 4 Oct. 1884.
47. Harcourt Williams, *Salisbury–Balfour Correspondence*, 51.
48. Northcote's diary, 28 Apr. 1880, Iddesleigh MSS, 50063 B.
49. R.F. Foster, *Lord Randolph Churchill. A Political Life* (Oxford: Oxford University Press, 1982), chs 3–5.
50. Steele, *Lord Salisbury*, 157–9, 172–3.
51. Gladstone to A.E. West, 24 June 1882, in *Gladstone Diaries*, vol. 10, 287; ibid., Introduction, clxxiii–iv; Harcourt Williams, *Salisbury–Balfour Correspondence*, 49–50.
52. Gladstone to the Duke of Argyll, 31 Aug. 1884, in *Gladstone Diaries*, vol. 11, 201.
53. Gladstone to Argyll, 30 Sep. 1885, in *Gladstone Diaries*, vol. 11, 408–9. The emphasis is Gladstone's.
54. Harcourt Williams, *Salisbury–Balfour Correspondence*, 40.
55. Memorandum, 14 Aug. 1882, in *Gladstone Diaries*, vol. 10, 312.
56. Salisbury to the Queen, 31 Jan. 1886, in G.E. Buckle (ed.), *The Letters of Queen Victoria* (London: John Murray, 3rd ser., 3 vols, 1930–02), vol. 1, 34.
57. E.D. Steele, 'Imperialism and Leeds politics', in D. Fraser (ed.), *A History of Modern Leeds* (Manchester: Manchester University Press, 1980), 345.
58. Carnarvon to Salisbury, 19 Sep. 1881, Carnarvon MSS, 60762.
59. Steele, *Lord Salisbury*, 149.
60. H.W. Lucy (ed.), *Speeches of the Marquis of Salisbury* (London: George Routledge and Sons, 1885), 166–8.

61. W.H. Smith to Sir Richard Cross, 18 Dec. 1882, British Library, Cross MSS, 51268. *Greater Britain* was the title of Sir Charles Dilke's enormously influential book, first published in 1868, on the Anglo-Saxon race and its global expansion.
62. Chamberlain to Escott, 3 Dec. 1883, Escott MSS, 58777.
63. Steele, *Lord Salisbury*, 140.
64. Ibid., 153; and see E.D. Steele, 'Britain and Egypt, 1882–1914', in K.M. Wilson (ed.), *Imperialism and Nationalism in the Middle East. The Anglo-Egyptian Experience, 1882–1982* (London: Mansell Publishing, 1983), 10–13.
65. D. Steele, 'The place of Germany in Salisbury's foreign policy, 1878–1902', in A.M. Birke, M. Brechtken and A. Searle (eds), *An Anglo-German Dialogue: The Munich Lectures on the History of International Relations* (Munich: K.G. Saur, 2000).
66. Steele, *Lord Salisbury*, 150–6; quotations from 151 and 156.
67. For the interaction of English and Irish politics, see Matthew's introductory essay in the *Gladstone Diaries*, vol. 10, cx–clxi, with its references to recent scholarship.
68. Derby diary, 19 Feb. 1881.
69. Ibid., 28 Feb. 1882.
70. Carnarvon diary, 7 May 1882, Carnarvon MSS, 60918.
71. Derby diary, 13 Mar. 1882.
72. Ibid., 18 Feb. 1882.
73. Northcote to Edward Gibson MP, 23 Dec. 1880, House of Lords Record Office, Ashbourne MSS, Box B71/10; *Gladstone Diaries*, vol. 11, 656.
74. Argyll to Salisbury, 15 Aug. 1881, HHM/3M/E.
75. Steele, *Lord Salisbury*, 168–9.
76. Lucy, *Speeches of the Marquis of Salisbury*, 118.
77. Steele, *Lord Salisbury*, 161.
78. Diary of Lord Carlingford (Lord President), 31 Oct. 1884, British Library, Carlingford MSS, 63692.
79. Steele, *Lord Salisbury*, 164–5.
80. Northcote to Salisbury, 10 Aug. 1882, HHM/3M/E.
81. Foster, *Lord Randolph Churchill*, chs 4 and 5.
82. Bahlman, *Hamilton Diary*, vol. 1, 181, 2 Nov. 1881.
83. Cecil, *Life of Robert Marquis of Salisbury*, vol. 3, 335–6.
84. *The Times*, 31 Mar. 1883.
85. Steele, *Lord Salisbury*, 146–7.
86. Ibid., 147–8.
87. Bahlman, *Hamilton Diary*, vol. 2, 500, 9 Nov. 1883.
88. Steele, *Lord Salisbury*, 146; Gladstone to Lord Richard Grosvenor, 27 Nov. 1885, in *Gladstone Diaries*, vol. 11, 436.
89. Steele, *Lord Salisbury*, 149.
90. Ibid.
91. M. Pugh, *The Tories and the People, 1880–1935* (Oxford: Blackwell, 1985).
92. Steele, *Lord Salisbury*, 232.
93. Pugh, *The Tories and the People*, 42, 59.
94. *The Times*, 22 May 1889.
95. Ibid., 17 Apr. 1884.

96. Chamberlain to Edward Russell, 22 Jan. 1884, Birmingham University Library, Joseph Chamberlain MSS, JC5/62/4.
97. Steele, *Lord Salisbury*, 146–7.
98. Chamberlain to Russell, 22 Jan. 1884, Joseph Chamberlain MSS, JC5/62/4; C.W. Boyd (ed.), *Mr Chamberlain's Speeches* (London: Constable and Co., 2 vols, 1914), vol. 1, 190–1.
99. Lord Spencer to Lord Hartington, 3 Oct. 1885, in P. Gordon (ed.), *The Red Earl. The Papers of the Fifth Earl Spencer, 1835–1910* (Northampton: Northamptonshire Record Society, 2 vols, 1981, 1986), vol. 2, 79–80; Lucy, *Speeches of the Marquis of Salisbury*, 193–7; Buckle, *Letters of Queen Victoria*, 2nd ser., vol. 1, 34.
100. Unpublished diaries of Sir E.W. Hamilton, 8 Dec. 1885, Sir Edward Hamilton MSS, 48642.
101. Chamberlain to Henry Labouchere MP, 4 Dec. 1885, Joseph Chamberlain MSS, JC5/50/41.
102. Boyd, *Mr Chamberlain's Speeches*, 169.
103. Steele, *Lord Salisbury*, 194.
104. Marsh, *Joseph Chamberlain*, 185.
105. Derby diary, 16 Oct. 1885.
106. Steele, *Lord Salisbury*, 144–5, 172.
107. *Gladstone Diaries*, vol. 11, 380.
108. Steele, *Lord Salisbury*, 173–4, 183–91.
109. E.D. Steele, 'Gladstone and Ireland', *Irish Historical Studies*, vol. 17, no. 65 (1970), 60.
110. Steele, *Lord Salisbury*, 185.
111. Lucy, *Speeches of the Marquis of Salisbury*, 183–5; 'I imagine Salisbury is going to propose Home Rule ... At least he said so at Newport', wrote Sir Henry Ponsonby, the Queen's private secretary, to his wife, 7 Jan. 1886, in A. Ponsonby, *Henry Ponsonby: His Life from his Letters* (London: Macmillan, 1942), 205–6.
112. Sir William Harcourt MP to Chamberlain, 30 May 1886, Joseph Chamberlain MSS, JC5/38/52.
113. Chamberlain to Labouchere, 27 Dec. 1885, ibid., JC5/50/56.
114. Chamberlain to Labouchere, 26, 27 Dec. 1885, ibid., JC5/50/53, 56.
115. Steele, *Lord Salisbury*, 175.
116. Ibid., 177.
117. Salisbury to Churchill, 26 Dec. 1885, Cambridge University Library, Churchill MSS, RCHL 1/10/1213a.
118. P. Jackson, *The Last of the Whigs. A Political Biography of Lord Hartington, later Eighth Duke of Devonshire (1833–1908)* (London and Toronto: Associated University Presses, 1994), 254–61, makes a good case for rejecting the interpretation of the 1886 crisis in A.B. Cooke and John Vincent, *The Governing Passion. Cabinet Government and Party Politics in Britain, 1885–86* (Brighton: Harvester Press, 1974).
119. Derby diary, 22 July 1886.
120. Unpublished diaries of Sir E.W. Hamilton, 6 May 1886, Sir Edward Hamilton MSS, 48643.
121. *The Times*, 19 June 1886.
122. Steele, *Lord Salisbury*, 200.

123. Ibid.
124. J. Morley, *The Life of William Ewart Gladstone* (London: Macmillan, new edn, 2 vols, 1906), vol. 2, 874–5.
125. W.E.H. Lecky, *Democracy and Liberty* (London: Longmans, Green and Co., new edn, 2 vols, 1908), vol. 1, xxvi.
126. Lord Rosebery's journal, 24 Sep. 1887, in the Marquess of Crewe, *Lord Rosebery* (London: John Murray, 2 vols, 1931), vol. 1, 303.

4
Opposition from Strength: 1892–1895

David Steele

Class in late Victorian politics[1]

The note of class conflict that Gladstone sounded in the 1886 election, while maintaining that his motive was to remove a cause of social division, recurs in his continuing exhortations to his party and the public. He contended that the outcome of the election – a Tory and Liberal Unionist majority of 116 – concealed the magnitude of the support that Home Rule commanded in the British electorate. The disarray into which his party had been thrown by splitting only weeks before the poll sent the number of uncontested seats up to more than 150, excluding Ireland, compared with 22 in 1885; of these, 118 returned opponents of Home Rule. Yet in those that saw a fight the aggregate Unionist vote exceeded that of the Gladstonians by a mere 76,000.[2] The moral victory, the 'Grand Old Man' proceeded to argue, lay with him. An analysis of the voting by class demonstrated, to his satisfaction, that 95 per cent of Liberal working-class electors in Britain had opted for Home Rule against 20 per cent of Liberals defined as 'employers, or [those] who are socially in a position to draw with them the votes of others'. 'Independent working men', he implied, were likely to be Liberals; by them he meant those whose skills and wages raised them above their fellows, the 'labour aristocracy' of Marx and the historians. This 'very great inequality among classes' as a moral factor in favour of Home Rule was something that Gladstone kept before the public. England, he conceded, had rejected Home Rule as decisively as Scotland and Wales had supported it: and he set himself to convert her.[3] By-election results for 1887 strongly suggested that he was on course to succeed with his condemnation of the 'leisured ... educated ... wealthy ... titled classes' that reached a crescendo in the 1892 general election; when he portrayed Home Rule as 'a labour question ... for the Irish are the most needy and the most suffering'.[4] What was more, the struggle for Irish self-government and against the coercive legislation enacted to check legitimate agitation and the violence to which it regrettably gave rise, was 'blocking the way' for urgently required reforms in Britain.[5]

The 1892 election disappointed the Liberals and vindicated Salisbury's tactics in persisting with the popular Toryism that Gladstone so disliked. An English majority for Home Rule eluded the latter, leaving his last ministry dependent upon the Irish nationalists for its survival. The tone of Gladstone's references to class might be disturbing, but even the advanced programme adopted by the National Liberal Federation's Newcastle conference in 1891 contained little to develop the social dimension of Liberalism. Irish Home Rule came first, naturally, but thereafter the emphasis was on disestablishment in Wales and Scotland, and the enforcement of temperance by local option; the priorities of the Dissenting activists on whom the Party relied heavily in the localities.[6] Gladstone complained of his uphill task in persuading 'the democratic majority' that they did not have to defer to 'a hierarchy of classes and establishments savouring in part of feudal times and principles', but, as ever, he shrank from any serious interference with the laws of the market beyond that embodied in extant legislation.[7] By contrast, the Tory manifesto over Salisbury's signature stated simply that the working class was strong enough to get, after discussion, whatever 'they generally believe will conduce to their welfare ... No party will have the power ... of refusing to listen to their unanimous wish.' The document lists free education, elective county councils and state intervention in the West of Ireland to alleviate chronic distress as the most significant reforms for many years, and promises attention to the problems of poverty and to those of industrial relations against a background of strikes and agitation for a statutory eight-hour day. Indeed, Salisbury may be said to have invited what he privately called Gladstone's 'revolutionary appeal to the jealousy of the poor' by the boldness with which, in continuation of earlier speeches, his campaign oratory addressed the worst tension between capital and labour since the 1840s.[8]

Salisbury's important speech at Hastings in May 1892 at the start of the election campaign, characterized the labour unrest of the day as 'social war ... nothing but war', and put forward government arbitration as a sensible remedy, reasonably confident that the unions would see it in that light.[9] His frank recognition of working-class power, actual and latent, was based on a better understanding of class relations than Gladstone chose to display when engaged in trying to frighten the upper and middle classes into accepting his policies, and above all Home Rule. Of the three independent labour candidates returned in 1892 – Keir Hardie and John Burns in London, and Havelock Wilson in Middlesbrough – Burns and Wilson quickly assumed a Liberal identity in line with that of the 'Lib-Labs' elected in recent years, mainly from mining constituencies.[10] Strikes, and the violence incidental to them, failed to develop the kind of class consciousness desired by the very few people in the country who wished to emulate German social democracy and the Communard tradition in France. In the epic dock strike of 1889, an aristocratic observer who had gone down to the East End in the expectation of witnessing raw hostility was amused and relieved by what he found. The attitude of the police on duty was distinctly relaxed. Neither Burns nor Ben Tillett, the dockers' leader, alluded to Socialism in their exhortations: 'it was simply the statement of a bargain ... Nothing about rich men grinding the poor, or property being robbery.' Burns described how he had put some strike-breakers to flight by marching 50 pickets past the dock gates 'to the bloody and awe-inspiring strains of "We won't go home till morning"'. 'Altogether ... rather impressive', the visitor concluded.[11] In the circumstances, Salisbury was not afraid to look on such trials of strength between employers and their workforces as quite legitimate, however worrying. 'It is only natural', he told the Conservative National Union conference, 'that all who take part in making the profit are as anxious to get as large a slice of it for themselves as they can.'[12]

In his classic *Social Geography of British Elections, 1885–1910*, Henry Pelling had some difficulty in explaining to his readers the formidable phenomenon of the Tory working man. His predilections are apparent in a comment on the success enjoyed by a metropolitan banker, Seymour King, as the long-serving member for the constituency of Kingston-upon-Hull Central, where in 1892 and 1895 he saw off a 'Lib-Lab' challenge. King 'knew just how to win working class votes. He talked vaguely of "social reform", denounced the immigration of foreign paupers, and maintained his adherence to ... Free Trade.' There was, as Pelling recognized in this passage and elsewhere in his study, more to popular Toryism than xenophobia – a term he employed – and the natural self-interest of voters attracted to protection or in the case of Hull, nervous of it.[13] The talk of social reform was not mere verbiage: it had borne, and was to bear, some fruit. Nor were the adverse reactions to alien, largely Jewish, immigration prompted solely by prejudice. As for protection *versus* free trade, everybody realized that it was a vital issue, in town and country, with profound implications for the Empire and its standing in the world. The election addresses of Tory and Unionist candidates reflected these concerns. They also reflected the attachment to the Established Church and its social values that lay at the heart of popular Toryism.[14] While Salisbury fully appreciated the importance of tying Chamberlain and his regional influence across the West Midlands into the Unionist alliance, he declined to accept the radical's unqualified claim to have imposed the 'Unauthorized Programme' and its mind-set upon the Tories: his own Newport speech of October 1885 was evidence to the contrary.[15] The thinking of Salisbury and Chamberlain converged because neither man shared, at least to the same extent, Gladstone's obstinate belief, whatever he might say in public under pressure of circumstances, that 'it is not by the State that man can be regenerated and the terrible woes of this darkened world effectually dealt with'.[16] Finally, Gladstonian Liberalism and the Unionist allies both sought to benefit from the perception that *they* were the patriotic choice, although Gladstone's insistence upon the second Home Rule Bill gave his opponents the edge in that respect. As Leader of the Opposition in 1892–95, Salisbury worked upon these methods, professing 'a Conservatism which had little need of assistance from Joseph Chamberlain to find expression at the polling booths'.[17]

Policies for power

The old Tory hope of consolidating a natural conservative majority in England by detaching the Whigs or so-called moderates from the Liberals was realized in 1886 and again in 1892, when Salisbury lost his overall lead to a seemingly inevitable reaction against a government too long in office. It was no mean achievement to hold on to England, given Gladstone's skilful presentation of himself and his party as wedded, like the Tories and Liberal Unionists, to tradition as well as progress. While most of the Liberal peers had deserted him, the social composition of his MPs showed that he retained the allegiance of a substantial minority of the classes that could afford to sit unpaid in the Commons and bear all or a large part of the costs of fighting an election.[18] Both sides in politics felt, however, that they must anticipate the demands which the working class, for all its reassuring conservatism, would surely make on property, and which a small number of them were beginning to formulate. The Newcastle programme's bias towards the aims of Nonconformist activists masked a growing belief on their side that the Liberals were not going to recover lost ground unless they ceased to appear 'as ... defenders of fiscal privileges and exemptions of the wealthy which are universally condemned',[19] that is, as supporters of the regressive system of taxation shaped by Peel and Gladstone a generation before, and passionately upheld by the latter ever since. The words quoted are those of Sir William Harcourt, no radical but the heir to an ancient estate, whose introduction of death duties Gladstone deplored – 'by far the most Radical measure of my lifetime'.[20] Anxious not to let the Liberals overtake the Unionist alliance in the field of social reform, Chamberlain pressed Salisbury to devote his spell in opposition to a programme to be announced when they met Parliament after losing the 1892 election.[21]

Salisbury's discouraging response to detailed suggestions from his colleague is often cited as proof that he had no enthusiasm for this aspect of contemporary politics: 'I fear these social questions are destined to break up our party ... why incur the danger, before the necessity has arrived', and when Home Rule remained a danger?[22] Reluctance to force the pace should not be understood to mean that he was really averse to change of a kind with which he had been at pains to associate Toryism. He had pointed out to Chamberlain's Tory critics that the Newport speech foreshadowed everything done by the government of 1886–92 at the supposed instigation of Birmingham radicalism.[23] Chamberlain himself needed no reminder of the inherent divisiveness of social legislation that was not carefully drafted. By 1894 he was predicting an exodus of 'wealth, intelligence and moderation' from the Liberals as, after Gladstone, that party yielded to pressure from the newly formed Independent Labour Party (ILP) and a more politically assertive Trades Union Congress (TUC).[24] This was not an entirely welcome prospect to him: he read far more into the collectivism of the ILP and the TUC than it contained, and tried to communicate his alarm to Salisbury and Hartington, now the Duke of Devonshire. The propaganda of the nascent English left, emerging in the resolutions of the two principal organizations involved, 'means confiscation of workmen's savings and houses'.[25] Tories and Liberal Unionists had to counter this ideological threat by asking 'the working class to choose with their eyes open between revolution and social reform', a package of measures which, taken together, were to underpin capitalism with the beginnings of what became the welfare state.[26] Where Salisbury was concerned, he was preaching to the converted: the language the Tory leader used in redefining the obligations of the state and society is not easily forgotten, once disinterred from the faded newsprint.

'What we need above all in this country is peace and a close attention to the terrible social problems that beset us', Salisbury advised the Primrose League in April 1894. Internal peace, 'between classes', was not less important than the avoidance of war in an increasingly dangerous world.[27] Within the 'Great Depression' that spanned the last quarter of the century, the limited recovery of the later 1880s had petered out, dispelling hopes that the economy's rate of growth would restore unemployment and under-employment to mid-Victorian levels. Coupled with the recurrence of strikes on a large scale, it was a position that filled Salisbury, speaking in June 1894, with 'uneasiness and anxiety ... We do not believe that the salvation of the people is to be worked out by something which apart from bloodshed does not differ from permanent civil war.'[28] But his nerves were stronger and his insight truer than Chamberlain's: Socialists who aspired to common ownership of the means of production were indeed 'enemies of the human race', but there was another version of Socialism to which he gave his blessing before the assembled delegates of the National Union. 'To use the machinery of the state for ... objects in which the community generally is agreed ... in that socialism ... I can see no harm at all.' The Post Office was obviously better run by government, and perhaps the railways too, although that was more doubtful. Going on to the familiar plight of those driven upon the Poor Law in old age, he asked Tories to think hard about some state provision to relieve such 'terrible individual and social suffering', against which the poorest could not be expected to safeguard themselves under the prevailing economic system.[29] Chamberlain's advocacy of old age pensions, it may be noted, ended for the time being, with the reflection that it would be 'prudent' to see how public opinion evolved. On this and related questions – among them working-class housing, industrial arbitration, and immigration – Salisbury was moving forward at an accelerated pace the new Toryism that owed much to his grasp of the possible.[30]

Leading elements in the Tory Party realized the value to the upper and middle classes of a 'progressive' image in respect of social reform. A.J. Balfour and his brother Gerald are examples at party conferences and in their industrial constituencies; Leeds Liberals were concerned at Gerald's ability to attract a crowded audience for his views on capitalism and the workers.[31] But it was their uncle Salisbury who set the tone. On the one hand, he induced Chamberlain to accept that it would be unwise to commit their supporters, and especially Tories, to a full and formal programme of social measures, more than was easily digestible in the run up to the next election. On the other, Chamberlain agreed that they should continue to make the social policies they favoured known through their speeches.[32] Salisbury had, however, brought in a bill on one of the topics discussed with his ally. Legislation to check the mainly Jewish immigration from Eastern Europe, which had undoubtedly had an adverse effect on employment and housing in London and several provincial cities, had been prepared in government at the end of the 1880s. The influx was seen as subverting the homogeneity of a nation that had resisted the only previous substantial alien immigration in race and religion, and had confined its permanent legacy to usually well-defined Irish districts. There was also concern about abuse of the country's traditions of free entry and asylum by foreign revolutionaries. The Liberal government relied on statistics that understated the problem. 'I prefer', said Salisbury drily, 'figures ... that have not been sweated.' He insisted on the 'clear and special right' to exclude both economic migrants and extremists. The numbers of the former oppressed the ratepayer as well as the wage earner, often the same person: 'We have a right to say that our poor rate and our social system is for ourselves.'[33]

Salisbury was no more successful with his attempted measure than Palmerston had been with the Conspiracy to Murder Bill in the middle of the century; a second reading was all he could secure. He quoted Rosebery on the undesirability of poverty-stricken immigration: but the ingrained liberalism of Gladstonians and their separated brethren on the opposition benches were too much for Salisbury.[34] Chamberlain, who had registered the Jewish community's enmity to the bill, thought it was not worth many votes.[35] There was nevertheless a political reward in the places affected: popular feeling against a sizeable alien presence was not transient. Salisbury had identified the Tories as the party that cared about the impact of immigration on those most exposed to its disadvantages. Whether immigration, housing or another aspect of the larger social question, came into play, it was clear what they had to do. 'Our mission ...', he declared in a speech to Conservative and Unionist candidates on Harcourt's budget, 'is to try to diminish in some degree the misery of those who belong to the same race as ourselves.'[36] When Chamberlain commended the decision to make immigration an issue as 'valuable to us for strategic purposes', it was a clinical assessment of a move which to the man who made it was not only a tactic in the political game.[37] Salisbury's achievement in demonstrating a degree of emotional sympathy with the 'people', comparable with that for which Gladstone was, and is, celebrated, has hardly been recognized. The reports of Tory MPs show how the Aliens Bill helped to reinforce the impression that the Tories, quite as much as Chamberlain's radical Unionists, had a genuine affinity with the working class.[38]

Liberals did what they could to weaken that impression. Salisbury did not fall into the trap of using the Lords' obsolete power of rejecting money bills to frustrate the introduction of death duties, which lifted the duty payable on settled estates from as little as 1 or 2 per cent to a maximum of 8. 'The richer classes', he observed, 'are the natural prey of the Chancellor of the Exchequer'; money was needed for the increased naval expenditure almost universally seen as imperative in the worrying international situation of the time. The higher, and more rigid, taxation was therefore 'an injustice which may be excused for serious need'. His preferred alternative was to tax the unearned increment when property was sold or leased, but he did not advertise it. He had little to say about the whole matter, in contrast to those Unionists, and notably Devonshire, who demanded a bigger fleet and objected to paying the price.[39] Salisbury's resistance in the Lords to the Liberal Employers' Liability Bill, dropped as a result, seemed to offer more hope of discrediting him with working-class voters; MPs in industrial seats were alarmed. But his refusal to sacrifice existing schemes of compensation, to which some of the workers affected were attached, went with a promise, duly honoured, of more widely drawn legislation.[40]

Disappointed again, the Liberals tried to exploit Salisbury's continuing flirtation with protection. He guarded himself against a frontal attack by the categorical statement at Trowbridge in May 1894 that protection was 'dead and cannot be revived'. Ahead of Gladstone's retirement Harcourt was saying that, without him, only the urban fear of seeing free trade repudiated could save the governing party from defeat at the polls. At the same time protection was winning friends year by year: Salisbury followed his ambiguous declaration for free trade by describing the harm it had done to English agriculture since the 1870s, forcing labourers off the land into overcrowded slums; a 'great economical blunder which ... has deeply tinged with misery the lives of ... hundreds of thousands of the least powerful, least defended of our population'. They were not the words of someone who regarded free trade as set in stone. He had impressed it upon the party organizers that a movement for the return of protection must come '*from below*' – with judicious encouragement that was not inconsistent, to his mind, with affirmations of support for free trade.[41] The 'tariff war' that almost all civilized countries waged on England and on each other, he informed the Primrose League a month after the Trowbridge speech, diminished employment throughout the economy. The message was inescapable: 'what is called the social question' could not be solved without the erection of English tariff barriers. To the extent that Harcourt's budget, the subject of this speech, was a resort to class-based politics, Salisbury's use of protection made it doubtfully relevant to the condition of the poor in a recession which it seemed would never end.[42]

The human costs of nineteenth-century capitalism were as shocking to Salisbury as they were to any of its assailants. A supposedly non-political address on the spiritual needs of East London just before the 1895 election might be cited to illustrate his pessimism and detachment, in reality, from the tasks of social reform awaiting a government with the necessary political will. It was now undeniable that the paternalism of landlords and employers, which had softened the impact of industrialization, was passing. In the sprawling industrial districts along the Thames impersonal limited companies had displaced 'the old type of individual whose conscience can be appealed to, and whose liberality can, therefore, be counted upon'. He implored the owners of capital to remember that their comfortable lives rested on working people in such areas, out of sight and frequently out of mind, as a consequence of the residential segregation that had grown up over half a century and more. He asked businessmen and investors, 'as patriots', not to forget that working-class deprivation, and consciousness of neglect, must tell upon the confidence and security of an industrial nation.[43] Read with other speeches that throw light on his social thinking, this one shows how he breathed new life into clichés about the place of religion in a class society. There was still general agreement on the role of Christian belief and practice, denominational antagonisms notwithstanding, in making society work without the smouldering class warfare apparently inseparable from any stage of industrial growth in great Continental states. 'It is due to the religious customs of the country that the avarice of the capitalist has been kept in check', said the president of the 1892 Trades Union Congress. In that context, trade unions and the infant Labour movement, in which convinced Christians figured prominently, were unwilling to embrace the Marxist doctrine of the class struggle preached by Hyndman's Social Democratic Federation from the mid-1880s.[44] Salisbury's Christian politics differed from Gladstone's better-known variety in the much greater awareness he displayed of the limitations of orthodox economic theory, which the 'Grand Old Man'. was always disposed to invest with something like scriptural authority. Working-class voters did not fail to notice the contrast, as Gladstone had been quick to see that they would.

It is impossible to agree – in the light of what Salisbury said on the platform and of what he, with Chamberlain, managed to do after the Unionist victory in 1895 – that 'the policy implications of Salisburyian Conservatism were quietist'. To say that the strategy was 'to *control* and not to practise popular politics' is to make a distinction that does not hold water.[45] No alternative existed to practising that kind of politics, which had been evolving at least since Palmerston's day.[46] Popular politics is by its nature combative, and the distaste for the fray imputed to Salisbury was no more evident now than it had been when he was a parliamentary rebel in either House. Posterity tends to depict him as fastidious and reserved; a misleading portrait even of the private man.[47] In his lifetime he was famous for the 'blazing indiscretions' in his speeches and for the vigour with which he set about his foes. His outspokenness during this last period in opposition was extraordinary and struck many as reckless. It reflected the strength of his personal position and that of the Unionists; the strength, too, of convictions which he could now afford to state without much fear of alienating voters in the middle. The tide was running against the Liberals during their three years in government. It was clear from the outcome of the 1892 election that Gladstone's preoccupation with Home Rule had hurt his party. But the '*British*' issues which he saw at once would have to be given more prominence were those preferred by the Nonconformist-dominated National Liberal Federation.[48] The social issues about which Tories and Unionists were talking purposefully were mainly represented among the Liberal ministry's bills by employers' liability. The extension of local democracy with the creation of district and parish councils was not controversial, except in so far as the second was intended to reduce clerical influence over villagers. Salisbury mocked the Liberals' implausible attempt to portray the legislation as 'emancipating the rural classes from the terrible despotism of the squire and the parson'.[49]

Welsh disestablishment overshadowed those bills, despite the tussles they occasioned between the Houses.[50] While Anglicans were a minority in the principality, their dioceses had always formed an integral part of the Church of England. For militant Nonconformists the attack on the Church in Wales was preliminary to a final assault upon the Establishment. Gladstone's successor Rosebery, and many other Liberals, put the best face they could upon this instalment of the Newcastle programme, asserting that the excision of Wales would not materially affect the English Church, 'which was like a rock, much stronger than some years ago'.[51] As he confessed to the Queen, Rosebery was a prisoner of his Gladstonian inheritance, of which the programme was a part; were he to go back on a commitment to its principal demands on the leadership, 'the only result would be that he and not the measures would disappear'.[52] Although Chamberlain and Nonconformist Unionists, mindful of past pledges, left the defence of the Welsh Church to the Tories – Chamberlain indeed cast a second reading vote against the Church – Salisbury counter-attacked with every expectation of being able to drive Liberals off the high moral ground which they assumed was theirs by right. Even statistically, the case for Welsh disestablishment was weaker than it had been made to seem. Arguing with Gladstone that it met the 'national or quasi-national' claims of Wales did not enthuse English opinion. Regarded as a blow against what the agnostic John Morley, Gladstone's closest colleague, had joined in calling 'religious privilege ... that great question', the bill introduced in 1895 found the public in England largely indifferent to statements, not endorsed by Gladstone, that the principle of establishment was everywhere wrong and outdated. Englishmen might not care for the clericalism of High Churchmen, but Gladstone calculated that perhaps three-quarters of them owned to 'some kind of membership' of the Church; she satisfied their religious needs, and she was not so closely associated as Nonconformity with the desire to curb popular pleasures.[53]

Salisbury had no hesitation in stigmatizing the 'Puritanical hypocrisy' of Nonconformity as the driving force behind the temperance lobby. He was equally scathing about its motives in attacking the Welsh Church: 'Nothing seems to me more repulsive than that those who are stripping a man by the wayside should assure him that they do it from a Christian love of his soul.' The political pressure for disestablishment and disendowment was inspired by rancour, above all by 'the passion of jealousy ... which can leave nothing behind it but ... perpetual conflict and unsatisfied revenge'. It was not too highly coloured a description of the bitterness excited by the feud between church and chapel, especially in Wales. The participation of Morley and secular radicals of his type in the warfare justified Salisbury's reference to 'those who wish no good ... to the Christian religion'. Such displays of righteous anger by the Church's friends were tempered by a certain unreality about the fighting over the Welsh Church: if disestablishment passed the Commons, the Lords were sure to kill it, and to do so with impunity, given the public mood outside Wales. In conferences with the primate, Archbishop Benson, and other prelates, Salisbury guided the mobilization of clergy and laity against the bill, finally introduced in the last months of the Rosebery government.[54] The Church's enemies were at a disadvantage, and they knew it. In this favourable climate for her friends, Salisbury addressed a graver question for the Church in England and Wales: the future of her schools, denied rate aid and harassed by an unsympathetic bureaucracy. Their difficulties raised the prospect that the undenominational religious teaching of the Board schools might become the norm, 'a patent compressible religion', he had always held, characterized by 'essential insincerity'. This one of his policies for power was potentially divisive, of the Church herself and of Unionism, as events proved in 1896–97 and again in 1902. For the time being, however, Salisbury's aggressiveness towards a failing government made good sense in view of its demonstrable success in the last confrontation with Gladstone over the Home Rule Bill of 1893.[55]

The defeat of Home Rule

The election of 1895 was disastrous for the Liberals, the worst result for either of the great parties since 1832, and a triumph for conservatism, whether spelt with a capital or a small 'c'. All the ILP's 28 candidates were defeated, as were the four put up by the Marxist SDF; a bare 1 per cent of the total vote went to the Socialists. It was a vindication of Salisbury's insistence that Tories and Unionists were responsive to the plight of the poor and the vulnerable and stood ready to alleviate them through a legitimate form of 'Socialism'. So complete was the Unionist victory in this respect that it impeded the social legislation of the final Salisbury administration. If England had proved so resistant to infection by the virulent Socialism gaining ground on the Continent, why was it necessary to press on with radical initiatives? The left was to rise from its ashes: Gladstonian Liberalism had had its day; it was insufficiently progressive, and bound by its dated ideology to policies that must weaken the cohesion of the United Kingdom and her international standing. John Morley, whose intimacy with Gladstone did not blind him to a revered chief's defects, had begged Rosebery as far back as 1891 to 'make yourself the exponent and the leader of a practicable socialism'.[56] Salisbury filled that role: and Morley lost his seat at Newcastle in 1895 to a Unionist helped by the intervention of a Labour candidate who polled more than 2000 votes. Harcourt, on the other hand, succumbed at Derby to a clerical offensive which, according to him, provided all the ammunition one could possibly want against a state Church whose adherents resorted to every kind of misrepresentation.[57] The fact was that Liberal leaders entered the election conscious of having let the Unionists, and Salisbury in particular, dictate the issues on which it was fought.

Without the 'organ voice'[58] of Gladstone to rally them, the demoralized Liberals failed to put up candidates in a third of more than 400 seats won by the Unionists, who had less than half that number of unopposed returns three years previously. Rosebery was privately reconciled to a crushing reverse: 'I do not complain, for I see matter for congratulation in what had occurred to the patriot, though not perhaps to the politician.'[59] Harcourt, who shared the leadership of the Party with Lord Kimberley after Rosebery stepped down in 1896, had viewed the coming election with 'philosophic indifference', ahead of his discomfiture at Derby,[60] and said afterwards that his aim in politics was to support Salisbury personally and keep the Unionist government in power. He saw in the Tory the only 'real check … on imperialism'.[61] This puts Salisbury's opposition to Home Rule in perspective. The daemon of imperialism which he tried to guide and contain was, he said later, a reaction to the defeatism implicit in the policy of Home Rule: 'That it was which Mr Gladstone stumbled against and aroused and challenged its wrath.'[62] The feelings of insecurity and resentment that Irish nationalism produced in the ruling nation tended to erode the moderation and willingness to compromise on which Salisbury's stewardship of a global empire was based. The domestic consequences of giving in to the nationalists had also to be taken into account. The Lords would go down 'like a ninepin' before it if and when there was a solid Commons majority, bent on reforming the Upper House to get Home Rule through: and the shock was likely to spread to other parts of the English constitution: 'You cannot have a revolution on limited liability', he remarked.[63] But he made a greater impression with other aspects of the perennial Irish question.

'A crazy and rickety Republic: Ireland', the end result that Salisbury predicted for Gladstone's second Home Rule Bill of 1893, if it passed, would furnish hostile states with a base from which their cruisers could prey on England's sea lanes, intercepting vital food supplies. Yielding to Irish nationalism must do something more dangerous still and weaken the English people's imperial will: 'The taste for surrender spreads like contagion in the spirit of the country which has admitted the fatal germ'; subject races like those of India, restrained by awe as much as by force would follow where the Celtic Irish had led. Salisbury went beyond this restatement of his arguments against Home Rule when he defined 'the real Irish question' in the starkly racial and religious terms which the Irish themselves employed. Rosebery said 'he would rather cut his arm off than do what Lord Salisbury was going to do'. Nothing like the language Salisbury proceeded to use had been, or was to be, heard from an ex-premier on the Irish question.[64] What was more, he visited Ulster to give his sanction to the formidable resistance that was being organized in the half-Protestant province. He had spoken earlier of Archbishops Walsh and Croke, pre-eminent nationalist prelates, as bent on erecting 'an ultra-clerical state', the creation of which England, being 'the Protestant nation of the world', must oppose. Now, at Londonderry, he denounced the settler population's hereditary enemies as licensed to harry them by 'the old charter printed in letters of blood in Irish history', with the help of 'a lamentably disciplined corps of Celtic priests animated … by … old traditional hatred'. Lady Salisbury had to defend her husband to the Queen, no friend of the Irish. His wife claimed that the speeches in Belfast and Londonderry had calmed the fears of the Protestants. They had learnt at first hand that they had 'powerful friends' in England. She was probably right: John Morley, the Irish Secretary, realized that the Protestant Ulstermen would never submit peacefully to nationalist rule; he was afraid to outlaw their preparations for rebellion and 'perhaps set a match to an explosion'.[65]

It was really British opinion that Salisbury wanted to rouse, and he was confident of success. Internecine strife between Parnellites and anti-Parnellites had undermined the nationalist cause with its best friends across the Irish Sea. Salisbury was sure of his ground: he reflected that the best weapon to counter Irish separatism was not available to him: the fullest use of democracy through that unEnglish device, the referendum.[66] Along the western seaboard of Britain, where the inhabitants were more sensitive to the real or supposed threat to national security from an independent Ireland, and wherever immigration had built up a sizeable Celtic Irish presence disliked by the native working class, Salisbury's rhetoric was warmly appreciated. In the industrial west of Scotland the Unionist alliance captured nine of the 13 burgh constituencies in 1895, compared with three in 1892. Even in Wales, where Liberals worked disestablishment for all it was worth, their opponents' representation rose from three seats to nine, out of 34.[67] A full-blooded assault on the Celtic Irish complemented Salisbury's concern for the working class in an unending recession, as it seemed, and his references to foreign policy. The French embassy noted as 'one of the most mordant that the ex-prime minister has delivered' his speech at Cardiff in November 1893: in it he dwelt on the perilous instability of heavily armed Continental powers with grave internal problems.[68] Gladstone's objections to higher naval estimates were all of a piece with his wilful blindness to the risks inherent in Home Rule.

The last battle of the period over Home Rule was really won and lost outside Westminster. The almost ridiculous margin by which the Lords threw out the bill of 1893 – 419 to 41 – did not provide the expected impetus for Lords reform, which left the public unmoved. The Liberals had to concede that the House spoke for the democracy;[69] on succeeding Gladstone Rosebery wasted no time in announcing that the consent of England, 'the predominant member' of the Union, was indispensable to any future Home Rule bill, as was the good behaviour of its beneficiaries in Ireland.[70] One of a good many Liberal politicians who had never been an enthusiast for Irish self-government, Rosebery was in effect admitting that Salisbury had seen off the question which for Gladstone and devout

Gladstonians defined their Liberalism. The 'Grand Old Man' had argued for years that the denial of this manifest justice to Ireland would have the understandable effect of radicalizing English and British politics, beyond the point which he thought safe: the inevitable result of the unequal division in the propertied classes for and against Home Rule.[71] Salisbury countered by redoubling his appeals to the innate conservatism of the English majority, and of a minority of the Scots and Welsh, irrespective of class. Without Gladstone's energizing power Home Rule was a liability for the Liberals, and felt as such. With Salisbury's leadership, still underrated today, Tories and Unionists made the transition to a mass party, controlled as such parties always are from above, but successful because it adapted the class co-operation of preceding generations to a fully fledged representative democracy in a mature industrial society. Another age might usefully study his approach, at once spirited and conservative, to the eternal predicament of being in opposition.

Notes

1. Readers are referred to the first note of the preceding chapter for acknowledgements and a brief list of standard works on the Conservative Party and its leadership during the period.
2. W.E. Gladstone, *The Irish Question* (London: John Murray, 1886), 27. See also W.C. Lubenow, *Parliamentary Politics and the Home Rule Crisis. The British House of Commons in 1886* (Oxford: Clarendon Press, 1988), ch. 7. Gladstone omitted the electors in uncontested seats from his calculations, *The Times*, 31 July 1886.
3. Gladstone, *The Irish Question*, 25–7, 33–43.
4. F.W. Hirst, 'Mr Gladstone and Home Rule', in W. Reid (ed.), *The Life of William Ewart Gladstone* (London: Cassell and Co., 1899), 722; H. Pelling, *Social Geography of British Elections 1885–1910*, (Aldershot: Gregg Revivals, 1994), 415.
5. Hirst in Reid, *Gladstone*, 711–2.
6. E.D. Steele, 'Gladstone and Ireland', *Irish Historical Studies*, 17, no. 65 (1970), 59.
7. M.R.D. Foot and H.C.G. Matthew (eds), *The Gladstone Diaries with Cabinet Minutes and Prime Ministerial Correspondence* (Oxford: Clarendon Press, 14 vols, 1968–94), vol. 12, xlvii; afterwards cited as *Gladstone Diaries*.
8. D. Steele, *Lord Salisbury. A Political Biography* (London: UCL Press, 1999), 275.
9. *The Times*, 19 May 1892.
10. Pelling, *Social Geography of British Elections*, 53, 329–30.
11. Stephen Gwynn, *The Letters and Friendships of Sir Cecil Spring-Rice. A Record* (London: Constable and Co., 1929), 98–9.
12. *The Times*, 27 Nov. 1889.
13. Pelling, *Social Geography of British Elections*, 296, 424–6.

14. Steele, *Lord Salisbury*, chs 9 and 12.
15. Salisbury to Chamberlain, 22 June 1892, Birmingham University Library, Joseph Chamberlain MSS, JC5/67/117; Salisbury to Sir H.H. Howorth MP, 3 Dec. 1891, H[atfield] H[ouse] M[uniments]/3M [3rd Marquess]/C7; subsequently cited as HHM/3M.
16. Gladstone to G.W.E. Russell MP, 6 Mar. 1894, in *Gladstone Diaries*, vol. 12, 395–6.
17. Pelling, *Social Geography of British Elections*, 287.
18. Lubenow, *Parliamentary Politics and the Home Rule Crisis*, 286, 317–9.
19. Harcourt to Lord Rosebery, 4 Apr. 1894, in A.G. Gardiner, *The Life of Sir William Harcourt* (London: Constable and Co., 2 vols, 1933), vol. 2, 283–7.
20. *Gladstone Diaries*, vol. 13, 416.
21. P. Marsh, *Joseph Chamberlain: Entrepreneur in Politics* (New Haven and London: Yale University Press, 1994), 344.
22. R. Harcourt Williams, *Salisbury–Balfour Correspondence. Letters exchanged between the Third Marquess of Salisbury and his nephew, Arthur James Balfour 1869–1892* (Ware: Hertfordshire Record Society, 1988), 430.
23. Salisbury to Howorth, 3 Dec. 1891, HHM/3M/C7.
24. Chamberlain's memorandum, 13 Nov. 1894, Chatsworth, 8th Duke of Devonshire MSS, 340. 2588.
25. Chamberlain to Devonshire, 13 Nov. 1894, ibid., 340. 2587.
26. Chamberlain to Salisbury, 29 Oct. 1894, Joseph Chamberlain MSS, JC5/67/21.
27. *The Times*, 20 Apr. 1894.
28. Ibid., 9 June 1894.
29. Ibid., 31 Oct. 1894.
30. Memorandum with Chamberlain to Salisbury, 29 Oct. 1894, Joseph Chamberlain MSS, JC5/67/21; Marsh, *Joseph Chamberlain*, 349–52.
31. E.H.H. Green, *The Crisis of Conservatism. The Politics, Economics and Ideology of the British Conservative Party, 1880–1914* (London and New York: Routledge, 1996), 130; E.D. Steele, 'Leeds and Victorian Politics', *University of Leeds Review*, 17, no. 20 (1974), 281.
32. Memorandum with Salisbury to Chamberlain, 9 Nov., Chamberlain to Salisbury, 15 Nov. 1894, Joseph Chamberlain MSS, JC5/67/ 22, 24.
33. Steele, *Lord Salisbury*, 290–1.
34. Ibid.
35. Memorandum with Chamberlain to Salisbury, 29 Oct. 1894, Joseph Chamberlain MSS, JC5/67/21.
36. *The Times*, 9 June 1894.
37. Memorandum with Chamberlain to Salisbury, 29 Oct. 1894, Joseph Chamberlain MSS, JC5/67/21.
38. Steele, *Lord Salisbury*, 291.
39. *The Times*, 9 June 1894; Steele, *Lord Salisbury*, 298–9.
40. Ibid., 279–82, 302–4.
41. Ibid., 297–9.
42. *The Times*, 9 June 1894.
43. Steele, *Lord Salisbury*, 299.
44. J. Harris, *Private Lives, Public Spirit. Britain 1870–1914* (London: Penguin Books, 1993), 158–9.

45. Green, *Crisis of Conservatism*, 125–7.
46. D. Steele, 'Gladstone and Palmerston, 1855–1865', in P.J. Jagger (ed.), *Gladstone, Politics and Religion* (London: Macmillan, 1985).
47. Lady Gwendolen Cecil, 'Lord Salisbury in Private Life', in Lord Blake and H. Cecil (eds), *Salisbury. The Man and his Policies* (London: Macmillan, 1987).
48. Gladstone to Harcourt, 14 July 1892, *Gladstone Diaries*, vol. 13, 42–3.
49. Steele, *Lord Salisbury*, 292.
50. P.M.H. Bell, *Disestablishment in Ireland and Wales* (London: SPCK for the Church Historical Society, 1969).
51. The Queen's journal, 10 Mar. 1894, in G.E. Buckle (ed.), *The Letters of Queen Victoria* (London: John Murray, 2nd ser., 3 vols, 1930–02), vol. 2, 380.
52. Rosebery to the Queen, 14 May 1894, ibid., 399–400.
53. Steele, *Lord Salisbury*, 294.
54. Ibid., 293–5.
55. Ibid., 295–6, 309–10, 370–2.
56. D.A. Hamer, *John Morley: Liberal Intellectual in Politics* (Oxford: Clarendon Press, 1968), 294.
57. Harcourt to Gladstone, 16 July 1895, in Gardiner, *Harcourt*, vol. 2, 371.
58. Hirst in Reid, *Gladstone*, 732–3.
59. Steele, *Lord Salisbury*, 300.
60. Hamer, *John Morley*, 303–4.
61. Steele, *Lord Salisbury*, 317.
62. *The Times*, 19 May 1899.
63. Steele, *Lord Salisbury*, 278.
64. Ibid., 288–9.
65. Ibid., 276, 288–9.
66. Ibid., 288.
67. Pelling, *Social Geography of British Elections*, 163, 401.
68. Steele, *Lord Salisbury*, 285–6; Pelling, *Social Geography of British Elections*, ch. 12 records how in Lancastrian constituencies the Unionists successfully exploited an imperial question that was a cause of local concern: the Indian cotton duties increased in 1894.
69. Hamer, *John Morley*, 283–4.
70. *House of Lords Debates*, 4th ser., 22, col. 32, 12 Mar. 1894.
71. For example, Gladstone to the Queen, 28 Oct. 1892, *Gladstone Diaries*, vol. 13, 122–6.

5
Faction and Failure: 1905–1910

Frans Coetzee

When Arthur Balfour's Conservative government left office in December 1905, it was the last to do so in anticipation, rather than as a consequence, of electoral defeat.[1] The Conservatives could look back on an enviable political record, having won three of the previous four general elections and having governed for 17 of the past 20 years. Few, if any, members looked to the immediate future with any expectation of comparable success. Balfour clung to the hope that after his resignation, his successor, Sir Henry Campbell-Bannerman, and the notoriously fractious Liberals might prove unable to form an administration. But his hopes were dashed, and when the electorate went to the polls in January 1906, it was the Conservative campaign that was hobbled by division and discord.

Most Conservatives expected that they would be defeated, and fairly decisively at that. 'We shall get hideously beaten', thought the former Secretary for India, but even he could not have anticipated the magnitude of the Liberal triumph.[2] On the first day, the Liberals gained 13 seats in Lancashire alone, and when the final returns were in, the Conservatives had been reduced to a mere 157 seats, or around just a quarter of the new Parliament.[3] Electoral defeat could, in certain circumstances, be construed as a blessing in disguise, as Winston Churchill was reminded when his wife sought to console him after the debacle of 1945. Often it took the sting of rejection to provide the impetus for an otherwise complacent party to 'clean house', make way for younger, energetic members, refashion its image and message, and reform its electoral organization. Some reassurance might be drawn from parallels with military disasters, for examples could be found of armies stung by reverses on the battlefield which subsequently reflected, rebuilt and rebounded to ultimate victory (such as the Prussian recovery after Jena in 1806).[4]

A century later, however, serious challenges faced the Conservative Party if it was to stage a comparable revival. The first imperative, as John Ramsden has observed, was for the Party 'to construct an explanation of the disaster ... consistent both with the facts and collective self-respect'.[5] If the Conservatives could diagnose the sources of their electoral collapse, they could settle upon a prescription for recovery. But the attempt to come to terms with defeat only cast a brighter light on the fractures within the Party whose prominence and persistence would stymie its return to power.

Several factors in the defeat were readily conceded by prominent Conservatives. The swing of the electoral pendulum was bound to tell against the Party, its movement fuelled by the varied grievances accumulated during the Party's long tenure in power. Voters increasingly irritated by, or indifferent to, the maddeningly familiar Conservative governments would inevitably, it was assumed, turn for relief to the rival Liberals. Party organization, grown complacent from previous victories, or rusty from disuse in constituencies with unopposed candidacies, was another tempting target. These were perennial challenges faced by any government seeking re-election, and the Conservatives could reasonably expect to be their beneficiary at the next election.

In 1906, however, the verdict could not be so simple. In a searching assessment of the fiasco, E.B. Iwan-Muller, editor of the *Daily Telegraph*, reminded Balfour that 'never in the history of electioneering had a party to fight so many and so heterogeneous confederates as did the Unionists at the late election'.[6] There were, according to Iwan-Muller, the 'permanent' liabilities which Balfour's administration, like any seeking re-election, had faced, but more significant were the 'special' influences which led to its demolition at the polls. The lack of effective platform speakers hindered the Party's ability to broadcast its message and would prove a recurring problem in future elections. 'Chinese slavery' (the resort to indentured Chinese labour to rebuild South Africa in the wake of the Boer War, under often deplorable conditions) made the Conservative government appear to condone racism and oppression. The Balfour government's reform of secondary schools embodied in the 1902 Education Act antagonized Nonconformist ratepayers, who objected to subsidizing Anglican schools, making the Conservatives appear heavy-handed and unresponsive in matters of conscience. Neither such imperial nor religious issues were novel, and the Conservatives might entertain the hope that these questions would gradually fade from prominence and lose their power to mobilize Liberal opposition.

Yet, as Iwan-Muller and other commentators emphasized, two other issues simply could not be wished away. Whatever the electoral purchase of Disraeli's claim to embrace the Tory working-man in the 1870s, or of 'beer barrel politics' and the robust defence of popular pleasures against coercive Nonconformist moralists in the two subsequent decades, by 1906 the Conservative appeal to labour had lost its direction.[7] Trade union members could look to the Party for little sympathy and even less assistance in the face of pressure from employers. The Taff Vale Judgment of 1901 was only the most visible sign of the deteriorating legal position of organized labour. Likewise, neither the Conservative leadership nor local party elites were receptive to the idea of working-men as candidates, and even more publicized ventures after 1906, like the Trade Union Tariff Reform Association, barely got off the ground.[8] An aspect of the Party's inheritance from the Third Marquis of Salisbury's successful administrations was the determination to tame democracy, to 'discipline' popular government, and trust that attentive exploitation of the registration provisions of the franchise could dampen anti-Conservative turnout. Hence the notion, so influential in the historiography of this topic, that Conservative success rested on 'negative hegemony'.[9]

In 1906 any such expectations were highly unrealistic. Campbell-Bannerman timed the election to take advantage of a fresh register, but, far more ominously, the Liberals had concluded an electoral agreement in 1903 (the 'MacDonald–Gladstone pact') with the nascent Labour Party. The resulting 'Progressive Alliance' curtailed debilitating three-cornered contests (in which the progressive vote might be split) and ensured the more effective disposition of resources and concentration of the anti-Conservative vote. This fact, as much as any of the varied 'special' causes, explained the Liberal landslide as well as the return of 29 Labour members, whose sudden appearance struck many startled Conservatives as a thunderbolt from the heavens.

If the Conservatives' adversaries were now more united than ever, Tory ranks were more deeply fractured than at any point over the past half-century. After the divisive experience of Peel's repudiation of the Corn Laws in 1846, protectionist tariffs were widely assumed to be, as Disraeli put it, 'dead and damned'. The issue had percolated thereafter, especially during the 1880s with the Fair Trade movement, which had been a response to Britain's relative economic decline in the face of agricultural depression and the inability of the manufacturing sector to retain its former supremacy against buoyant rivals like Germany and the United States.

It was the experience of the Boer War that had helped bring the issue of 'tariff reform' to a boil. The difficulty British forces encountered in defeating two distant, thinly-settled republics did not bode well for the nation's prospects against more populous, heavily-armed neighbours.[10] Only by drawing upon the resources and loyalty of a cohesive empire could Britain assure its security and prosperity. When, in May 1903, Joseph Chamberlain called upon his colleagues to embrace tariffs and imperial preference, it was that prospect of a united Greater Britain that he had in mind. Moreover, tariff reformers suggested, by sustaining more secure employment and subsidizing ameliorative social reform, their policy could dampen the potential discontent of the working class.

Chamberlain's vision attracted many adherents within the Conservative Party, who felt they finally had a great, constructive cause to work for, and some hurled themselves with quasi-religious fervour into a crusade.[11] Familiar advocates of protection, like Henry Chaplin of the agricultural interest, or Sir Howard Vincent of the Sheffield metal trades, welcomed the new initiative. But, despite the new geo-political imperatives to which protectionism might now be harnessed, tariff reform repelled many in the Party, including some of its most senior figures.[12] Free trade was for many an article of faith, and to tamper with it raised the spectre of special interests and corruption. More troubling to many observers, Chamberlain's stated emphasis on preferential remissions of duties on colonial imports (thereby to tighten economic bonds within the Empire) would entail taxing imported wheat and other foodstuffs, raising the cost of living. The working class would absorb a disproportionate share of the burden, and free traders were quick to pillory the 'food taxes' which would leave potentially vulnerable working families no alternative but an insufficient 'little loaf'.

Conservative critics of Chamberlain's proposals, then, argued that the electoral costs of tariffs were all too tangible and imminent, and the benefits too vague and distant. Between mid-1903 and late 1905 the battle-lines were drawn, both between the parties and within the Conservative Party. The decision in the internecine party struggle would turn on the attitude of the Prime Minister, A.J. Balfour, and the response of the Party's centre, or 'ballast', to whatever lead he provided. Well aware of Peel's precedent and unwilling to consign a shattered party to decades in the political wilderness, Balfour instinctively sought a moderate, even ambiguous, position that would alienate the fewest possible number. Yet he shared the protectionists' doubts over the equity and efficacy of adhering to free trade in an increasingly protectionist world, and he strove to articulate a retaliationist alternative that might reconcile the warring factions.[13] Accordingly, when Balfour led his party into the 1906 general election he did so, many believed, as a lukewarm tariff reformer. However, although his opaque comments made tariff reformers doubt his commitment, they did little to assuage the fears of free traders that they could still find shelter within the Party.

Little wonder, then, that in the wake of that electoral disaster attention turned immediately to the question of leadership and to whether Balfour was the man to guide the Conservatives to reclaiming power. How did he propose to lead the opposition, and how did he propose to deal with the Party's most controversial policy, tariff reform? The two questions were intimately related, for Balfour clung to the belief that the opposition's duty was a negative one, to oppose, harass, and delay the government, rather than to expose itself by offering grand, positive alternatives which would only invite rebuttal and condemnation in return.

Given the decimated Conservative remnant in the Commons, the most influential instrument for opposition rested on the Party's secure hereditary majority in the Lords. Shortly after the defeat, Balfour hinted at this strategy by announcing that his party 'should still control, whether in power or opposition, the destinies of this great Empire'.[14] He intended that the Lords' powers should be exercised with tact and discretion. The Lords would let pass unimpeded such legislation as enjoyed widespread popular support, but would reject or mutilate measures that were geared toward narrower, sectional interests. Such tactical victories would raise Conservative morale, frustrate their opponents and curb the efforts of the Liberals to sustain their majority with special favours for particular groups. The key to all this, of course, lay in tact and discretion: if the Lords appeared to act immoderately and in an uncompromisingly partisan manner, the Liberals were likely to seek retribution by mobilizing on the constitutional question. At risk would be the Lords' veto power, the status and privilege of the peerage, and even the Union with Ireland.

Tact and discretion, in turn, depended on the balance of power within the Party, which itself reflected the progress of tariff reform. In the immediate aftermath of the 1906 general election, there was no absolute consensus whether a repudiation of tariffs or a stronger commitment to them would have improved the Party's electoral performance.[15] Prominent free traders and tariff reformers alike had gone down to defeat, and even Balfour himself suffered the ignominy of losing his seat in the Commons until another safe haven could be found. The Party's more ardent spirits hoped that the dynamic Joseph Chamberlain would take advantage of Balfour's predicament to challenge him for the leadership and provide Conservatives with the ruthless, combative direction they had so sorely lacked.[16]

In retrospect, a leadership switch at this juncture would have been unlikely unless Balfour lost his nerve. Despite his undoubted talent and drive, Chamberlain alienated as many members as he inspired through his authoritarian personality, naked ambition, Radical heritage, Unitarian faith and Liberal Unionist allegiance. During early February 1906, Chamberlain and Balfour circled one another warily, with the former calling for a party meeting to elicit an unambiguous endorsement of tariff reform and imperial preference, and, by implication, at a minimum, to censure Balfour's tepid protectionism and indifferent performance. In the end, Balfour retained his position because many MPs, already shocked by the recent election, were reluctant to exacerbate the situation with the turmoil of a controversial change of leadership. A compromise was patched up, sealed by an exchange of letters between the principals on 14 February 1906 (the so-called 'Valentine compact') in which they agreed that 'fiscal reform is, and must remain, the first constructive work' of the Party.[17] Balfour would retain his position, but his future leeway would be constrained by his commitments and enforced by the clear predominance of tariff reformers within his party. Even when Joseph Chamberlain suffered a debilitating stroke in July 1906, which effectively ended any chance of his ever contesting the leadership (or of playing anything but a consultative role in politics), Balfour's preference to maintain an Olympian detachment from the daily fray would not insulate him from the growing discontent within the party that would lead to his eventual replacement.

That would not occur until 1911; from the perspective of 1906, the Party, having temporarily resolved questions of leadership and policy, could look forward again to the task of recovering the ground it had so recently lost. Surprisingly, after such dramatic failure, the party organization underwent little in the way of reform (far more sweeping changes would be instituted in 1911). A specifically constituted organization committee achieved little, and the principal change was a further separation between Central Office and the National Union, leading to 'less centralisation and more amateurism'.[18] But that weakness was less readily apparent over the next three years, in part because the real struggles would be fought elsewhere.

Balfour led a spirited opposition in the Commons on issues that interested him, such as education and defence policy, and even critics grudgingly conceded that in such instances his dazzling parliamentary skills were put to effective use. The House of Lords let a Trades Disputes Bill pass without difficulty (afraid for the moment of risking any further wrath from the trade unions), but made mincemeat of the government's efforts to pass legislation reforming education and licensing. By 1908, the Conservative opposition was taking its toll: discontent built within the Progressive Alliance over the government's apparent inability to translate its popular support and overwhelming majority in the Commons into a correspondingly impressive legislative programme. Passage in 1908 of old age pensions (something Joseph Chamberlain had once hoped that tariff revenue would enable a Conservative administration to introduce) helped somewhat to buoy Liberal supporters, but it was clear that they faced stiff challenges ahead.

For one thing, the Conservatives were beginning to get traction from tariff reform. An economic downturn in 1907–08 lent some credence to pessimists who warned that Britain's prosperity was at risk, and earned at least a hearing for those who pointed to unimpeded foreign competition as the most visible manifestation of the threat. With the exception of a handful of vocal, talented free traders (principally Balfour's relatives, Lords Hugh and Robert Cecil) the Party was committed to tariff reform, and outwardly presented a more unified face than in the run-up to the previous election. The weight of the party machinery was thrown behind tariff reformers; or perhaps more accurately, free traders could expect no assistance, and Tariff Reform Leaguers no obstruction, from Central Office or the Party's leadership.[19]

The Tariff Reform League itself had evolved into an effective vehicle for mobilizing local voters and enforcing conformity on the fiscal issue (one reason, perhaps, why vocal tariff reformers did not push harder to modernize the party organization). Balfour proved only too willing to wash his hands of troublesome local disputes by asserting the autonomy of local Conservative associations to adopt their own candidates and to acquiesce when the Tariff Reform League secured the repudiation or withdrawal of candidates who refused to accept the tariff policy.[20] Very public instances where sitting Conservative MPs were either overthrown by their associations (T.G. Bowles at Norwood in April 1908) or severely circumscribed in their independence (Lord Robert Cecil in Marylebone in March 1908) were sufficient to make the point, one re-emphasized in January 1909 by the *Morning Post*'s 'blacklist' of Unionist free traders who, whatever their service to the Party, could not expect any official support in the coming campaign if they persisted in their heretical opposition to tariffs. It was widely believed that the paper's editor, Fabian Ware, printed his accusatory article only after close consultation with Percival Hughes (Principal Agent) and Acland-Hood (Chief Whip).[21]

By-election results also suggested that the tide was beginning to flow in the Conservatives' favour. Ardent tariff reformers won at Mid-Devon in January 1908 and at Worcester the following month (in the latter case, it was Edward Goulding, Joseph Chamberlain's 'man Friday', who headed the poll).[22] Even the spectacular victory of the independent Socialist candidate Victor Grayson in Colne Valley could be interpreted as a welcome crack in the Progressive Alliance, raising the prospect that the Liberal government was losing support and that consequently Labour or independent candidates might be emboldened to oppose sitting members and divide the progressive vote.

The re-emergence of the naval issue early in 1909 heralded further difficulties for the government. Introduction of the swift, heavily-armed battleship HMS *Dreadnought* in 1905, followed shortly by additional ships of the same type, had given Britain a qualitative advantage over her naval rivals, but at the cost of rendering obsolete the many ships upon which her traditional quantitative superiority had rested. It did not take long for other nations, such as Germany, to introduce similar ships, and the Admiralty and the navalist press worried that if rivals built such 'Dreadnoughts' at a faster pace, Britain's seemingly slender naval lead would disappear. The potential consequences were too terrible to contemplate: an island nation vulnerable to invasion (of which some spectacular fictional examples fed popular anxieties) or susceptible to blockade and starvation.[23] By March 1909, Britain faced a full-blown naval scare. Suspicions mounted that the German naval building programme was accelerating, while British preparations that only recently had seemed prudent (scaling back plans given the cost of these huge ships and the fact that much of the Russian fleet had been destroyed by the Japanese) now appeared perilously inadequate. Conservatives pilloried Asquith's government for a cavalier and parsimonious approach to national defence, and the return of the Conservative candidate at the Croydon by-election with a greatly increased majority suggested the Party could run effectively on the naval issue.[24]

Superficially, then, the Conservative recovery seemed to be well under way, whilst its Liberal opponents appeared fumbling and indecisive. The House of Lords had effectively disrupted much of the government's legislative programme. The Party seemed relatively united, and could campaign on the government's inability to provide for national security or prosperity. Navalists deplored the malign influence of Liberal 'Little Englanders' who lacked the vision or will to grasp how Britain might survive in a Darwinian world of power politics. Tariff reformers echoed those charges in condemning free traders who, obviously stymied by the dilemma of simultaneously funding social reform and military construction, would surely deny the gravity of the situation and ignore the protectionist solution that alone could provide the revenue adequate to the escalating responsibilities of the state.

Moreover, in the allegedly 'stupid party' (J.S. Mill's formulation), there was evidence of intellectual regeneration, as a younger generation grappled with the Party's future role under changing circumstances. Many of their views found expression in a collection of essays published in 1908, entitled *The New Order*, which sought to discuss contemporary issues such as collectivism, conscription and social reform 'in a spirit consistent with Unionist traditions, and at the same time without hostility to reasonable innovation'.[25] Nevertheless, upon closer inspection, such discussions revealed that the Party's new-found unity did not run deep. Although many Conservatives shared Balfour's limited conception of the role of opposition, and understood a Conservative government to be concerned first and foremost with resisting change rather than promoting it, a significant contingent of the Party's younger and more vocal members disagreed. Often described as 'Radical Conservatives', these men were sometimes hard to categorize as a homogeneous bloc and they often differed on tactical questions.[26] But they shared a sense that the nation stood at a dangerous crossroads; at risk, they believed, was a precious heritage, whose essentials included traditional institutions (such as the monarchy or the Anglican Church) and imperial possessions, an ordered society that revered (or at least tolerated) some measure of hierarchy, one that therefore repudiated class antagonism, accepted inequality and accorded respect to the notion of lineage.

To secure these familiar Conservative ends, however, radicals within the Party were willing to contemplate bolder, far-reaching means. In particular, they were willing to embrace more direct, popular appeals to a working-class electorate and to promote an expanded role for the state to modernize British society, whether through the application of social reform, protectionist and preferential tariffs, or (in some cases) compulsory military service. Radical Conservatives were impatient with their more traditionalist colleagues, whose timidity and inertia they believed would ultimately imperil the nation they sought to preserve. Likewise, Radical Conservatives trained much of their fire on the more advanced, radical wing of the Progressive Alliance, arguing that its Socialist brand of collectivism would cause disaster by bankrupting the state, sapping individual self-reliance and any entrepreneurial spirit, and neglecting the national defence. George Wyndham underlined the gravity of the situation by depicting it as the contest between the proponents of two ideals 'fighting to the finish':[27]

> 1. Imperialism which demands Unity at Home between classes, and Unity throughout the Empire; and which *prescribes* Fiscal Reform to secure both.
> 2. Insular Socialism, and Class Antagonism ...
> Between these two ideals a great battle will be fought. I do not know which will win. If ... Imperialism wins, we shall go on and be a great Empire. If Socialism wins we shall cease to be. The rich will be plundered. The poor will suffer. We shall perish with Babylon, Rome and Constantinople.

These assumptions help to explain why the tone of Edwardian political debate was often so bitter, why even parliamentary decorum within the House of Commons fell victim (on one memorable occasion a lachrymose Asquith was shouted down without a hearing, and Balfour's eventual successor, Andrew Bonar Law, warned his adversary of his need to appear 'very vicious').[28]

Such bitterness was not confined to debates between parties, however, as frustration mounted within the Conservative Party over the intolerant stance of Radical Conservatives. Lord Salisbury (the son of the former Prime Minister), one of the Party's more eloquent moderates, lamented the 'violent nature of the changes proposed', and admitted that 'the whole of [his] Conservative training revolts against the catastrophical theory of politics'.[29] Tariff reform was 'an effort to drive the Conservative elements of our society into a policy of far-reaching change . . . not put forward as a moderate but a revolutionary new departure'.[30] Lord Cawdor, who hewed to the Balfourite centre of the Party, brooded that 'Joe [Chamberlain and, by extension, tariff reform extremists] considers things [such as education and the Church] as "dust in the balance" which we consider to be of much importance . . . possibly he would put Home Rule in his dust heap too.' Then, peering into the uncertain future, Cawdor ventured, 'We may have to face throwing out some government Bill in the Lords, thereby forcing an election on a definite issue, and we ought not to be hampered if such an occasion arises, by Tariff Reform.'[31]

As predictions go, this one would prove pretty accurate. Not only was the post-1906 (or post-Valentine compact) unity of the Party rather tenuous and apt to fracture under pressure, but the Liberal government proved itself more adept at recovering the political initiative than

Cawdor's colleagues could have anticipated. When Campbell-Bannerman retired in 1908, his successor as Prime Minister, H.H. Asquith, took the opportunity to fashion a talented cabinet, one highlighted by David Lloyd George at the Exchequer and Winston Churchill at the Board of Trade. Already committed by early 1909 to an ambitious and expensive programme of social reform (notably the old age pensions enacted the previous year, but also the prospect of unemployment insurance in the near future), Asquith's government was challenged to find additional sources of revenue sufficient to sustain increased naval construction while at the same time renouncing the tariff duties touted by the opposition as a potential solution to escalating budget deficits. The 'New Liberals' were far removed from their Gladstonian predecessors' conception of a limited, 'night-watchman' state, and opted for redistributive taxation as the centrepiece of future financial policy.[32] The budget Lloyd George introduced in April 1909 was obviously provocative, for it contained a super-tax on large incomes, increases in death and licensing duties, and, most ominously, provisions for land valuation. It appeared calculated to spare the modest, heavily Liberal sectors of the electorate and to levy its harshest burdens directly upon the Conservatives' traditional sources of support, especially the landed peerage.[33] Cynics suspected that Lloyd George had cunningly laid a trap, hoping to goad an infuriated House of Lords into ignoring political precedent and rejecting a money bill. The subsequent election could then be fought on constitutional grounds congenial to Liberal sympathies, as the 'peers versus the people'. In fact, the Liberals could not presume conclusively that events would follow this scenario, but nonetheless Lloyd George's budget was a tactical masterstroke that did much to revive his party's morale.

By contrast, it left the Conservatives impaled on the horns of a dilemma: to reject the budget in the Lords was to lay that institution open to ridicule, reform, condemnation or worse, yet to concede was to accept that the Liberals had effectively refuted the Conservatives' persistent refrain that tariff reform was the only solution to the inadequacy of free trade finance. Tensions escalated over the summer as the budget wound its way toward a constitutional confrontation. Liberal ministers justified the overall equity of the 'People's Budget's provisions and poured scorn on the idle rich who would pay a larger share of their unearned income as a result. Conservatives responded by decrying its confiscatory, Socialistic thrust and questioned whether the electorate would possibly have given their blessing to such piracy if they had known in 1906 what schemes the Liberals would entertain. In the end, the Conservative leadership opted for rejection, deciding that it could not shrink from a challenge and alienate those who were responding favourably to the Party's renewed sense of purpose and self-confidence. In early November, despite strenuous Conservative opposition, the budget easily passed the Commons given the commanding Liberal majority there; on 30 November 1909 the equally commanding Conservative majority in the Lords threw it out by a vote of 350 to 75.

Once again, the Liberals preferred to hold the general election on a fresh register, meaning that polling would have to wait until January 1910. This time around the Conservative armoury was much better stocked. In the campaign, tariff reform did double duty, so to speak, for it was touted both as industrial protection to secure greater employment in otherwise vulnerable industries ('Tariff reform means work for all', ran the daily slogan in R.D. Blumenfeld's *Daily Express*) and as an antidote to predatory Socialism that would transfer the burden of taxation ('England expects that every foreigner shall pay his duty', as the Tariff Reform League put it). What initially had been envisioned as a bold, constructive initiative that would recast the Conservatives as a party of resurgent imperialism *and* innovative social reform was now, nearly a decade later, translated into a defensive posture to protect the prerogatives of land and wealth.

Other issues inevitably took a back seat. 'The Liberals shout "budget" and we shout "tariff"', complained Lord Milner, 'and the question is who shouts the loudest. It is horrid.'[34] The Conservatives pressed their adversaries on the question of naval supremacy and doubted whether the Liberals possessed either the resolve or the resources to preserve Britain's accepted margin of safety at sea, the 'two power standard'. The peerage defended its rejection of the budget as an action consistent with its role as a constitutional watchdog. That decision, the reasoning went, strengthened democracy by affording the electorate an opportunity to be consulted on what, after all, might be regarded as a flagrant violation of acceptable, sane budgetary policy. The Conservative campaign also manifested a strong undercurrent of masculine nationalist sentiment, whereby Balfour's and Lansdowne's party stood firm in robust, principled defiance of the fissiparous maliciousness of a Progressive Alliance cobbled together from sectional interests and (Celtic) fringe groups. The intemperate editor of the *National Review*, Leo Maxse, fulminated against the sight of his beloved England being 'governed by Scotsmen, kicked by Irishmen, and plundered by Welshmen'.[35] The electoral calculus indicated that if the election were close, Asquith would govern only by dint of Irish votes, and Conservatives muttered darkly about what shameful backroom deals would inevitably result.

During the early stages of the campaign, it was the Liberals who possessed the momentum, generated by Lloyd George's devastating critiques of a selfish, lazy peerage, and accentuated by the inept efforts to defend themselves of peers lacking any sense of perspective or intellectual distinction. But the long interval between dissolution and the onset of polling afforded the Conservatives an opportunity to catch up, and they nearly did so. As the votes were counted, the results afforded satisfaction and disappointment alike to each side. The combination of the intense campaign, bitter partisan invective, and fresh electoral register produced extremely high voter turnout, in fact the highest recorded for any British general election (86.7 per cent). However, a popular mandate was harder to discern, for the returns amounted to a stalemate.[36] The Conservatives made such significant inroads in the Liberal ranks that the two parties were now evenly matched in the Commons. They gained 116 seats and reclaimed their dominant position in English constituencies, an impressive achievement given the disaster that had befallen them just four years before. Yet, to the dismay of ardent tariff reformers who had persuaded themselves that victory was now within their grasp, they were unable to dislodge the Liberal government. Asquith, Lloyd George and Churchill could content themselves with having retained power and thereby having 'won' a referendum on the 'People's Budget'.[37] The great Liberal majority was gone, never to return, and the Cabinet's room to manoeuvre would now be constrained by the dependence on Irish (82) and Labour (40) votes to retain office.

That tactical situation ensured that, whatever the energies expended by all the participants, the election of January 1910 had not settled much of anything. The budget would pass, although the Irish Nationalists raised objections to some of its provisions (notably whiskey duties), and the House of Lords duly acquiesced. The peerage, though, was now firmly in the political cross hairs. Liberal and Irish Nationalist politicians alike shared a frustration with the Lords as the principal obstacle to further legislation, even where they differed on future legislative priorities. The Irish party's leader, John Redmond, made clear to Asquith the price for his continued support: the immediate abolition of the veto powers of the upper chamber and the introduction of a measure of Irish Home Rule. Salisbury's fears were coming to pass, and it was readily apparent that a second election was in the offing to address the issue.

Conservative proposals to reform the House of Lords and modify its composition had never been taken too seriously by the Party and, by mid-1910, were manifestly inadequate to the gravity of the situation. Many observers suspected that Asquith would seek from the King a pledge to use the royal prerogative, if necessary, to secure a constitutional settlement in which the upper chamber's powers were curtailed to that of delay rather than absolute rejection. The death of Edward VII in May 1910 impelled both sides to seek a breathing space and to meet in conference to resolve major differences and avoid thrusting Edward's inexperienced successor, George V, into a partisan maelstrom. Creative spirits from either side even floated the dramatic idea of a national coalition that could enact key desiderata of the Radical Conservatives (such as tariffs and conscription), but at the cost of policies on which most Conservatives could not compromise (such as Home Rule). The proposal was, as John Ramsden rightly observes, 'a desperate attempt to reconcile the irreconcilable', and the entire conference collapsed on 10 November.[38]

The way was now clear for a second election to be held during December 1910. The Conservatives had made up enough ground in the January election that many hoped that one additional push would bring the Party back into power. Realistically, however, little had changed during the intervening few months, and the Party was not in a position to defeat many of the Irish or Labour MPs upon whom the Liberal parliamentary majority rested. Balfour remained the leader, and Central Office bore a familiar face as well, so the only arena for innovation lay in terms of policy. Willingness to concede reform of the House of Lords was not by itself a compelling case to elect a Conservative administration, and vituperative attacks on the Irish Nationalists (and on Redmond who, having returned from raising funds among Irish-Americans, was denounced as the 'dollar dictator') could not dramatically improve the Party's appeal. A significant change in image could only involve tariff reform. As frustration mounted within the Party at the fact that victory seemed so near yet beyond reach, the image of Sisyphus struggling up the electoral hill, straining for the finish line but impeded by his boulder (food taxes), seemed cruelly apt. The prospect of shelving the food taxes, whilst it alarmed those for whom colonial preference and the imperial implications were paramount, attracted moderates who believed that the Party could win many marginal (i.e., predominantly working-class) seats if it were no longer handicapped by popular fears that tariffs would increase the cost of living. Lancashire, the traditional 'cockpit of Victorian elections', was the focus of such a strategy, and prominent MPs from constituencies there (such as Bonar Law) and journalists (J.L. Garvin of *The Observer*) provided the impetus. 'Since it is impossible that we can win upon this issue [food taxes] why should we be handicapped by it', Garvin wondered, '... in a way that endangers – the Second Chamber – the Constitution – the Union itself?'[39]

This late, desperate search for votes crystallized in the form of a referendum, an idea discussed during the abortive constitutional conference as a way of settling heated questions without subjecting the parties (and the nation) to persistent upheaval. The Lords cloaked their rejection of the Lloyd George budget in referendal language, and on the eve of the December election Balfour now found himself urged to follow in a similar vein. He could shed the liability of food taxes for the immediate campaign by pledging to postpone the introduction of tariff reform (and thereby severing the Party's fortunes from its acknowledged first constructive policy). On 29 November 1910, in a packed Royal Albert Hall, Balfour told an expectant audience that he had 'not the least objection to submit the principles of Tariff Reform to Referendum'.[40]

'That's won the election', shouted an enthusiast in the crowd. Sadly for Balfour, the man was mistaken. He hoped to gain some tactical leverage by challenging the Liberals to state their willingness to follow suit and submit Home Rule to a referendum, but they refused to take the bait. Whole-hoggers within his own party seethed at the retreat, and all the familiar doubts about Balfour's integrity, toughness and capacity to lead resurfaced. 'It is unpardonable', declared Leo Maxse; 'Balfour must go, or Tariff Reform will go – that is the alternative.'[41]

The majority of the Conservative Party would have been willing to overlook such doubts if Balfour had led them to victory in December 1910; instead, he earned the dubious distinction of having presided over three successive electoral defeats. Although a number of seats changed hands by small majorities, the results confirmed those of the previous January.[42] The Party remained condemned to opposition, with a leader temperamentally unsuited to the bruising fray in the future and compromised by his vacillations in the past. As for policy, it was all too clear that the Party no longer spoke with a single voice, and if defence of the Union could elicit order and unity from what had lapsed into a bewildering programmatic cacophony, the means to promote that policy were now at risk. Balfour's strategy to dictate the direction of representative government by resorting to hereditary means lay in ruins, and his party would be nearly bereft of constitutional weapons with which to protect the Union with Ireland. Maxse was correct: Balfour would go, choosing to resign in November 1911 (though given his active role in promoting Balfour's departure, Maxse's prediction was something of a self-fulfilling prophecy). The Party faced an uncertain future, and, given its tumultuous experience of four frustrating years of opposition, would do so without the emphasis upon continuity in leadership, policy, personnel and organization that had proven reassuring in the past.

Much evidence, therefore, appears to confirm a pessimistic appraisal of the Party's position at the end of 1910. If one defines successful political recovery as the return to office at the next available opportunity (or after a fairly short interval of opposition), then the Conservative recovery after 1906 was limited indeed. What troubled some 'wirepullers' was the fact that the Party's significant increase in votes polled, while undeniably impressive in absolute terms, was insufficient in relation to the opposition. Conservative organizers seemed to have reached a threshold of support which they could not breach, and there was no immediate prospect of improvement. The 'other' side noticed as well; in an influential article, J.A. Hobson drew attention to the elections of 1910 as having signalled the electoral division of Britain into two nations.[43] Conservative strategists, especially those who instinctively thought of the polity in English terms, deplored the Liberal reliance upon an 'illegitimate' minority cobbled together from sectional and regional 'fringe' interests, which inevitably would neglect the nation's welfare. The result was an increasingly bitter frustration with the course of politics, and a dangerous advertised willingness to skirt the constitution that would leave Bonar Law's party in a precarious situation on the eve of the Great War.

Prominent historians of the Edwardian situation, such as Neal Blewett and E.H.H. Green, have reinforced this sense that the Conservative Party was confronted with an obstacle it was nearly powerless to overcome: the Progressive Alliance of Liberals and Labour, further fortified by Irish Nationalist support.[44] Past Conservative success had owed more, these scholars suggest, to the failures and division of the Tories' opponents, than to intrinsic achievement on their part. Green, for example, notes that 'the Conservatives' opponents ..., for once, got something right', and goes on to argue that 'Rather than speaking of the failures of Conservatism in the Edwardian period it is perhaps more accurate to speak of the success of Liberalism, the Progressive Alliance, and Irish Nationalism.'[45] On this reading, the best hope for the Conservative recovery lay not in their own efforts, but in patient inertia, a 'wait and see' attitude, until Asquith's government splintered of its own accord. Although on one level this view may illustrate what eventually happened, on another it runs the risk of assigning the Party too passive a role in its own resurgence and of consigning seeds of change at the grass-roots to historiographical oblivion.

After all, the Conservative Party's difficulties during the Edwardian era went deeper than the fact its political adversaries formed an unprecedented united front. In that transitional period, the Party responded hesitantly to varied challenges whose only similarity lay in their severity: the declining electoral influence of aristocratic paternalism, the advent of class-based mass politics, and the nation's growing political and economic vulnerability, all of which sharpened the debate over the state's deepening responsibilities and fiscal needs. These posed questions for which the answers of Disraeli and the Third Marquis of Salisbury were now inadequate. And yet, however slowly or reluctantly, the party of Balfour and Bonar Law began the task of reorienting itself toward the demands of the new century.

It may require strong magnification to discern much evidence of recovery before the First World War, but some signs are there. During its period of opposition, the Party in the Commons underwent a needed generational change. Many elderly fixtures left their positions of influence as the normal toll taken by advancing age or infirmity was magnified by defeat at the polls and/or ostracization over the tariff issue. Devonshire, Ritchie, Arnold-Forster, Joseph Chamberlain were replaced by younger, able men (Bonar Law, F.E. Smith, Baldwin, MacNeill, Amery) who would find the way clear to a faster ascent. The example of organizations like the Tariff Reform League indicated ways in which the Party might move more aggressively to mobilize voters, court business and other propertied interests, and solicit funds. It is no accident that tariff reformers figured prominently in the successful efforts to reform party organization in 1911.[46] In the constituencies too, one could find evidence of the growing recognition that more professional administration of local party organization was both desirable and possible. There were clear signs of recovery in local politics, from the spectacular successes in the 1907 London County Council elections to the increasing effectiveness of Conservative-dominated local ratepayers' associations, which were often able to marshal significant numbers of voters (including Liberals) against Labour municipal candidates or 'Socialistic' extravagant spending. Although historians disagree about the significance of municipal politics for parliamentary elections, it is possible that the loyalties engendered by these 'reactionary vanguards' marked early fissures in the Progressive Alliance.[47]

Ideologically, too, there were signs of ferment. Many in the Party, of course, were only too happy to fight on familiar ground (the Union, Empire, privilege and the landed interest) and their discomfort with alternate terrain only accentuated the somewhat fratricidal tenor of Conservative politics – which, in turn, delayed the Party's recovery. However, if the Conservatives were to poise themselves to exploit the eventual division of their opponents to the fullest, they would need to do more than return to stale themes. Ross McKibbin has shown how effectively during the inter-war period the Conservative Party aligned itself with the 'public interest' against selfish, sectional ones.[48] That definition, and by extension the Party's improved performance in the inter-war period, did not emerge from thin air; it drew upon a language of anti-Socialism forged in the heat of municipal politics and the budget controversy, and then tempered in the crucible of war.

The overall impression of the Conservatives' fractious spell of opposition from 1906 to 1910 is one of deepening frustration, at both modest opportunities squandered and – more seriously – the diminished leeway for electoral triumph. That this dismal picture would deteriorate further before it improved is undeniable, but so too are the glimmers of recovery visible in the margins.

Notes

1. Although during this period the Unionist and Liberal Unionist Parties were formally distinct, they co-operated closely enough to warrant describing their collective action as that of the Conservative Party.
2. St. John Brodrick to Selborne, 24 Nov. 1905, Bodleian Library, Selborne MSS, 2/118, quoted in D. Dutton, *'His Majesty's Loyal Opposition': The Unionist Party in Opposition 1905–1915* (Liverpool: Liverpool University Press, 1992), 14.
3. The Conservatives polled 43.6 per cent of the vote, so their abysmal showing was exaggerated by the first-past-the-post electoral system. It is likely, however, that the apparent stability in the absolute number of Conservative votes cast concealed significant abstentions, and was, in any case, dwarfed by a major increase in Liberal turnout: N. Blewett, *The Peers, the Parties and the People: The General Elections of 1910* (London: Macmillan, 1972), 36–7; A.K. Russell, *Liberal Landslide: The General Election of 1906* (Newton Abbot: David and Charles, 1973).
4. G. Andreopoulos and H. Selesky (eds), *The Aftermath of Defeat* (New Haven: Yale University Press, 1996).
5. J. Ramsden, *The Age of Balfour and Baldwin 1902–1940* (London: Longman, 1978), 23.
6. Iwan-Muller to Balfour, 13 Feb. 1906, British Library, Balfour MSS, 49796, ff.115–59.
7. J. Lawrence, 'Class and Gender in the making of urban Toryism, 1880–1914', *English Historical Review*, 108 (1993), 629–52; E.H.H. Green, *The Crisis of Conservatism: The Politics, Economics and Ideology of the British Conservative Party, 1880–1914* (London: Routledge, 1995), 120–44.
8. K.D. Brown, 'The Trade Union Tariff Reform Association, 1904–1913', *Journal of British Studies*, 9 (1970), 141–53.
9. Blewett, *Peers*, 20–3; J. Cornford, 'The transformation of Conservatism in the late nineteenth century', *Victorian Studies*, 7 (1963), 35–66; P. Marsh, *The*

Discipline of Popular Government: Lord Salisbury's Domestic Statecraft 1881–1902 (Brighton: Harvester, 1978).

10. A. Friedberg, *The Weary Titan: Britain and the Experience of Relative Decline, 1895–1905* (Princeton: Princeton University Press, 1988); G.R. Searle, *The Quest for National Efficiency* (Oxford: Blackwell, 1971).

11. For example, Leo Amery compared the impact of Chamberlain's speech to Luther's actions at Wittenberg: L.S. Amery, *My Political Life*, 3 vols (London: Hutchinson, 1953–55), vol. 1, 236. See also A. Sykes, *Tariff Reform in British Politics, 1903–1913* (Oxford: Oxford University Press, 1979); J. Amery, *Joseph Chamberlain and the Tariff Reform Campaign* (London: Macmillan, 1969).

12. The Duke of Devonshire was but one of several prominent cabinet members who would leave Balfour's government over the issue, while other Unionist free traders (notably Winston Churchill) felt compelled to cross the floor to the opposition benches. Their troubles are chronicled in R. Rempel, *Unionists Divided: Arthur Balfour and the Unionist Free Traders* (Newton Abbot: David and Charles, 1972).

13. E.H.H. Green, *Ideologies of Conservatism* (Oxford: Oxford University Press, 2002), 18–41.

14. Dutton, *Loyal Opposition*, 69.

15. Estimates varied as to the exact relative strength of tariff reformers and free traders within the Party, but one influential calculation by *The Times* divided MPs as follows: 109 Chamberlainites, 32 Balfourites, 11 Free Fooders, and 5 unclassified. But even if the specific figures are subject to revision, the overall preponderance of tariff reformers within the shrunken post-1906 party is undeniable. Perhaps most interesting in the electoral post-mortems was Balfour's attempt to deny the deleterious impact of the controversy over tariff reform; Campbell-Bannerman, he thought, was 'a mere cork, dancing on a torrent which he cannot control' and the Liberal landslide 'a faint echo of the same movement which has produced massacres in St. Petersburg, riots in Vienna, and Socialist processions in Berlin'. Balfour to Knollys (copy), 17 Jan. 1906, Balfour MSS, 49685.

16. Dutton, *Loyal Opposition*, 19–32; D. Dutton, 'Unionist Politics and the aftermath of the general election of 1906: a reassessment', *Historical Journal*, 22 (1979), 861–76.

17. Balfour to Joseph Chamberlain, 14 Feb. 1906, quoted in Sykes, *Tariff Reform*, 110–11.

18. Ramsden, *Balfour and Baldwin*, 26; R.B. Jones, 'Balfour's reform of party organisation', *Bulletin of the Institute for Historical Research*, 38 (1965), 94–101.

19. Sykes, *Tariff Reform*, 176–82; F. Coetzee, *For Party or Country: Nationalism and the Dilemmas of Popular Conservatism in Edwardian England* (New York: Oxford University Press, 1990), 85–94.

20. Balfour to Sandars (copy), 5 Apr. 1907, Balfour MSS, 49765, ff.46–51.

21. E. Goulding to Bonar Law, 25 Jan. 1909, House of Lords Record Office, Bonar Law MSS, 18/5/87.

22. Blewett, *Peers*, 66; J. Collings to J. Chamberlain, 8 Nov. 1908, Birmingham University Library, Joseph Chamberlain MSS, JC 22/44.

23. A.J.A. Morris, *The Scaremongers: The Advocacy of War and Rearmament, 1896–1914* (London: Routledge, 1984); Coetzee, *For Party or Country*, 72–85, 108–115.

24. Coetzee, *For Party or Country*, 109–110; F. Coetzee, 'Villa Toryism reconsidered: Conservatism and suburban sensibilities in late-Victorian Croydon', in E.H.H. Green (ed.), *An Age of Transition: British Politics, 1880–1914* (Edinburgh: Edinburgh University Press, 1997), 42–3.
25. Lord Malmesbury (ed.), *The New Order: Studies in Unionist Policy* (London: Francis Griffiths, 1908), 4–5.
26. Green, *Crisis of Conservatism*; G.R. Searle, 'Critics of Edwardian society: the case of the Radical Right,' in A. O'Day (ed.), *The Edwardian Age* (London: Macmillan, 1979), 79–96; Searle, 'The "Revolt from the Right" in Edwardian Britain', in P. Kennedy and A.J. Nicholls (eds), *Nationalist and Racialist Movements in Britain and Germany before 1914* (London: Macmillan, 1981), 21–39.
27. Wyndham to his father, 24 Jan. 1906, quoted in Sykes, *Tariff Reform*, 116. In a similar vein, Wyndham proposed that only 'socialists and imperialists are living men; the others are old women and senile professors. Let them clear out of the ring for what would be a fight to the finish.' See K. Brown, 'The Anti-Socialist Union', in K. Brown (ed.), *Essays in Anti-Labour History* (London: Macmillan, 1974), 236.
28. Ramsden, *Balfour and Baldwin*, 67.
29. Salisbury to Selborne, 10 Aug. 1904, Selborne MSS, 5 ff.88–91.
30. Salisbury to Selborne, 25 Feb. 1906, Selborne MSS, 5 ff.128–37.
31. Cawdor to Balfour, 8 Feb. 1906, Balfour MSS, 49709 f.27.
32. H.V. Emy, 'The impact of financial policy on English party politics before 1914', *Historical Journal*, 15 (1972), 103–31; P.F. Clarke, *Lancashire and the New Liberalism* (Cambridge: Cambridge University Press, 1971).
33. B.K. Murray, *The People's Budget 1909/10* (Oxford: Oxford University Press, 1980).
34. Milner to Lord Roberts (copy), 24 Nov. 1909, Bodleian Library, Milner MSS, 15, f.188.
35. Morris, *Scaremongers*, 227.
36. The Conservatives won 273 seats on 46.9 per cent of the vote, the Liberals 275 seats with 43.2 per cent of the vote.
37. As Churchill put it, with his characteristic sense of history, the results that, while acceptable, fell short of crushing victory, amounted to 'Wagram, not Austerlitz'; Blewett, *Peers*, 141.
38. Ramsden, *Balfour and Baldwin*, 35.
39. Garvin to J.S. Sandars, 14 Nov. 1910, Balfour MSS 49795, ff.145–8.
40. *The Times*, 30 Nov. 1910.
41. Maxse to Goulding, 10 Dec. 1910, House of Lords Record Office, Wargrave MSS, WA/3/2.
42. The Conservatives and Liberals each won 272 seats (with 46.3 per cent and 43.8 per cent of the vote respectively), while Labour returned 42 MPs (with 7.2 per cent of the vote) and the Irish Nationalists 84 (with 2.5 per cent).
43. J.A. Hobson, 'The general election: a sociological interpretation', *Sociological Review*, 3 (1910), 105–17.
44. Blewett, *Peers*; Green, *Crisis of Conservatism*.
45. Green, *Crisis of Conservatism*, 309–10.
46. Ramsden, *Balfour and Baldwin*, 56–62; Interim Report of the Unionist Organization Committee [Apr. 1911], Wiltshire Record Office, Long MSS, 450/13; Index of Proceedings to 31 March 1911, Long MSS, 450/12.

47. Coetzee, 'Villa Toryism', 44–5; C. Cook, 'Labour and the downfall of the Liberal Party 1906–1914', in C. Cook and A. Sked (eds), *Crisis and Controversy: Essays in Honour of A.J.P. Taylor* (London: Macmillan, 1976), 38–65; D.M. Tanner, 'Elections, statistics and the rise of the Labour Party, 1906–1931', *Historical Journal*, 34 (1991), 893–908; Tanner, *Political Change and the Labour Party 1900–1918* (Cambridge: Cambridge University Press, 1990), 124–8.

48. R. McKibbin, *The Ideologies of Class* (Oxford: Oxford University Press, 1990), 259–93.

6
Conservatism in Crisis: 1910–1915

David Dutton

'I think that our election here has cleared the air', wrote the Liberal Prime Minister, Herbert Asquith, as the dust settled on the contest of December 1910. It had 'made the way fairly plain, if not exactly smooth'.[1] It is doubtful if many Conservatives[2] shared this analysis. The high hopes of January now seemed a distant memory, and the Party had failed once more to recover the reins of power. Balfour's pledge to submit the central policy of tariff reform to a referendum had not only failed to win over any significant number of new voters, but had also served to reopen deep wounds within the Party over this issue, while placing a renewed question-mark over Balfour's commitment to the policy itself. Conservatives now entered upon a new and even more turbulent period of opposition which was only transformed by the outbreak of European war in the summer of 1914.

Much of the historical analysis of the years 1911–14 has been written in the context of a 'crisis of Conservatism'. Though the word 'crisis' is among the most overused of the historian's vocabulary, the case for its deployment in this context is strong. Thus for Geoffrey Searle, the Party was 'in a parlous state' on the eve of the Great War, its fundamental weakness 'an inability to win elections'.[3] It was not that the Party had done particularly badly in the two contests of 1910. The complete destruction of the Liberal government's independent parliamentary majority just four years after the landslide of 1906 was no small achievement. There were now as many Conservative MPs in the House of Commons as Liberals. But the very fact that the Conservative position remained essentially unchanged between January and December and that it was secured on a high turn-out and with a higher aggregate of the popular vote than the Party had ever before gained in the constitution created by the Third Reform Act of 1884 suggested that the Conservative vote had peaked. Moreover, it had peaked at a level which could still not return the Party to power because of the Liberals' alliance with Labour and the Irish Nationalists.[4] Such a situation engendered a mood of frustration and helplessness within Conservative ranks, especially as the Liberal government now proceeded to use its continued control of the House of Commons to undermine the powers of the upper chamber and destroy the Union of Britain and Ireland. That feeling of helplessness in its turn encouraged the growth of extremism.

Thus the crisis of Conservatism went deeper than merely a pattern of electoral defeat. Before the outbreak of war the Party 'found it difficult to establish a consensus on any major issue; the Party's disagreements led to the resignation of one leader and the threatened resignation of his successor'.[5] According to Alan Sykes, the crisis was both 'ideological and institutional' and 'was precipitated by the emergence on the right of the party of groups which distrusted, and in 1911 defied, the official party leadership which they thought had proved ineffectual in preventing steady national decline'.[6] Larry Witherell writes in similar vein of a dysfunctional party. 'This dysfunction pushed a new generation of Conservatives towards a political aggressiveness, or radical conservatism, with which the Party was unaccustomed. It even provoked near cannibalistic behaviour in certain quarters of the Party.'[7]

Following a third successive electoral defeat all three of the traditional butts of an opposition party's discontent – leadership, policy and organization – would eventually be subjected to renewed critical examination. Organization was the easiest and most immediate cat to kick. Frustrated Conservatives had as yet no other scapegoat upon which to vent their spleen, apart from Balfour himself – a development for which the majority were still unready. Though the leader had studiously avoided giving attention to this matter after Joseph Chamberlain's enforced removal from front-line politics in the summer of 1906, the jolting shock of two further setbacks at the polls was hard to ignore. What had happened at Southampton was illustrative of the depth of the problem and of the amateurishness of the Central Office. As the local agent noted:

> When I arrived here last Monday fortnight the place was absolutely naked as far as organization was concerned. No agent had been here since last March, not a single voter had been canvassed, all the old returns had been burnt or destroyed, the local association was heavily

in debt, the Ward Committees might as well have been non-existent and a paralysing apathy pervaded the whole Party in the Borough. That was the situation which the Central Office had invited me to step into at *about a fortnight before the poll!*[8]

Walter Long was first off the mark in trying to stir Balfour into action. Why, he wondered, had the efforts of the leadership not been rewarded with success at the polls? 'Chiefly', he suggested, 'because in the great majority of constituencies the organization – for which, after all, the Central Office must be in the main responsible – was either non-existent or deplorable.'[9] At the beginning of 1911 Long sent Balfour a petition signed by a large number of Conservative MPs calling for a formal inquiry, while Comyn-Platt, prominent in the earlier Confederacy, was busy marshalling backbench opinion in favour of a 'thorough cleansing of the Augean Stables'.[10] With pressure also coming from Lords Curzon, Salisbury and Derby, Balfour was obliged to capitulate. A Unionist Organization Committee was set up in February. Balfour entrusted the chairmanship of the inquiry to Aretas Akers-Douglas, a respected former Chief Whip. Membership reflected a wide cross-section of the Party's interest groups, but the presence of Lord Willoughby de Broke indicated a desire to create confidence among 'the younger and more ardent members' of the Party's radical right wing.[11]

After a thorough investigation involving 43 meetings, the interviewing of 103 witnesses and the receipt of written testimony from 289 others, the committee produced an interim report containing its major recommendations in April. The most important reforms related to the position of the Chief Whip and that of the National Union. The former was now freed of what had become an impossibly heavy burden. Relieved of his responsibility for the management of the Party in the country, the Chief Whip was left to concentrate on his parliamentary duties. Organization, finance and the provision of literature and speakers became the responsibility of a revamped Central Office headed by a new official, the Chairman of the Party, who would enjoy a status equivalent to that of a cabinet minister. The new post was given to the youthful Arthur Steel-Maitland, a Birmingham MP but a Conservative rather than a Chamberlainite Liberal Unionist. Meanwhile it was agreed that reforms initiated in 1906 which, in the supposed interests of 'democratization', had created a system of divided control between the Central Office and the National Union should be reversed. The National Union found its wings neatly clipped. It would abandon its pretensions to a policy-making role and revert to being a body whose limited function was to educate and report the views of the rank and file.

The whole operation was completed with a minimum of spilt blood. Acland-Hood, the existing Chief Whip, was inevitably the leading casualty. Despite rumours that he would be retained in the post of Party Treasurer, Hood interpreted the report as an indictment of his performance over the past decade and determined to withdraw from public life. He was replaced as Chief Whip by Lord Balcarres, while Lord Farquhar emerged as the new Treasurer. Steel-Maitland quickly embarked on a thorough overhaul of the Central Office which before long involved the replacement of most of the existing senior staff. William Jenkins, district agent for the Midlands Liberal Unionists, became chief organizing agent; John Boraston, formerly the Liberal Unionist Council's chief agent, was appointed the Conservatives' Principal Agent in 1912; and Malcolm Fraser, a former newspaper editor, took over the press bureau and was soon engaged in negotiating over the future of *The Globe*. Fraser's appointment reflected a clear recognition of the importance of the press in the age of mass politics as the most important way for the Party to engage with the majority of the population.

Overall, the reforms enacted in and after 1911 made for a considerable strengthening of the Party apparatus. In particular, the reduction in the Chief Whip's responsibilities and the creation of the office of Chairman were important long-term steps in the modernization of the Party's organizational structure. Whatever the Party's other problems, the machine which existed at the outbreak of war was more efficient than had existed for a generation. The reforms of 1911 would not on their own carry the Party back to power, but they formed the basis of Conservatism's long-term organizational superiority over its rivals which would characterize the twentieth century as a whole.

The question of the party leadership posed altogether more difficult problems. In theory, the organizational reforms of 1911 strengthened Balfour's hand. The administrative changes confirmed his control over the Party apparatus through subordinates, including the Chairman, who would be nominated by himself. At the same time the encroachments of the extra-parliamentary National Union had been curbed. In practice, however, Balfour's position never fully recovered from what was after all the third successive defeat sustained under his leadership in December 1910, especially as the Party had fought that election under his chosen referendum pledge. His very record stood, it seemed, as eloquent testimony to the failings of his style of leadership. 'I meet no one', declared Joseph Lawrence, the former MP and committed tariff reformer, 'who forgives

him his bad tactics.'[12] Leo Maxse of the *National Review* was of the same
mind: 'we are led by a tactician without convictions or enthusiasm who
can only be got to espouse any cause under pressure'.[13] Yet the majority
of leading Conservatives were probably still willing to give their leader
the benefit of the doubt, at least until he had had the opportunity to
show his mettle in response to the government's Parliament bill.

Characteristically, Balfour failed to respond to the challenge. As far
as his critics were concerned, especially those on the Party's right, he
was as unable as ever to reply to the government's plans with the sort of
hard-hitting and uncompromising opposition for which they longed. In
June Maxse complained that the Party had so far mounted a 'lamentable
fight' and that Balfour constantly behaved as if he were in league with the
government, appearing to block any serious resistance to the Parliament
bill.[14] In fact, Balfour's major failing, as so often in the past, lay in his
inability to take his followers along the reasoned paths which his own
mind had travelled. Aware that the government was in deadly earnest
in its readiness to create as many Liberal peers as were necessary to force
the government's measure through the House of Lords, Balfour decided
that the best course was to pursue a line which left the Conservatives
with as much power as possible within the upper chamber. In the last
resort this meant acquiescing in a legislative limitation of the Lords'
powers rather than fighting an heroic but ultimately futile battle which
would only lead to a permanent Liberal majority in the house of peers.
However, Balfour's failure to take his party with him led by the summer
of 1911 to internal party divisions as bitter as any that had been seen
since Joseph Chamberlain launched his tariff reform crusade in 1903. The
leader's opponents interpreted his tactical surrender to the government
as a sacrifice of principle. Ominously, the summer witnessed a further
growth of splinter groups, working largely outside official party channels
but often numbering shadow cabinet members among their adherents.
The most important of these was the Halsbury Club, set up under the
nominal leadership of the aged former Lord Chancellor, Lord Halsbury,
with the declared aim of keeping alive the spirit of the no-surrender group
who had wished to oppose the Parliament bill to the finish. Without
declaring its overt hostility to the leadership, the club provided a cover
for the continuing activities of an anti-Balfour faction.

Balfour only added to his problems by the ineptitude of his own
behaviour. Absent from London between the 3 and 7 August, he departed
for his Continental holiday even before the final vote in the House of
Lords on the Parliament bill had been taken. On his return to Westminster
he found it difficult to recapture his earlier enthusiasm for the political

fray. Meanwhile, the anti-Balfour campaign in the *National Review* reached its climax in October when the leader was unequivocally blamed for the destruction of the constitution. By the beginning of that month, however, he had already decided to resign and his decision was made public in early November. Balfour seems to have been particularly influenced by an 'extraordinary letter' received from Walter Long, 'my *professed* friend and upholder'.[15] Long pulled few punches:

> I have only written thus strongly to you from a deep sense of duty, and because I am convinced that unless prompt and determined steps are taken to grapple with the situation, not only will you find yourself with very few followers, but our Party will, as a result of your leadership, be hopelessly broken up, and cease to be the great instrument for public good which it has always hitherto been, and which it must continue to be if the safety of the country is to be secured.[16]

Though Balfour cited his age, his indifferent health and the length of his parliamentary service in justifying his decision to retire, it is difficult to escape the conclusion that the Conservative Party had driven its own leader from office.

The appointment of a new leader gave hope that the divisions which had scarred Balfour's stewardship could at last be repaired. But the choice of a successor was no easy matter with the parliamentary Party fairly evenly divided between the claims of Austen Chamberlain, the somewhat inadequate inheritor of his father's radical agenda and in any case a Liberal Unionist rather than a Conservative, and Walter Long, representative of the more traditional landowning class within the Conservative fold, but by no means distinguished by the eminence of his intellect. In the event, the two candidates, in the hope of avoiding a damaging contest, both agreed to stand down, making way for the unanimous election of Andrew Bonar Law, 'a Presbyterian of Canadian origin who had spent most of his life in business in Glasgow'.[17] While the society hostess, Lady Londonderry, despaired that a Glasgow merchant should now lead the party of English gentlemen, more astute observers would have agreed with Lloyd George that 'the Conservatives have done a wise thing for once. They have selected the very best man – the only man.'[18]

While at one level there appeared to be something accidental about Law's elevation, at another the Conservatives had made a conscious decision to renounce Balfour's style of leadership. At a time when the Party believed it needed martial qualities in its leader, Law was ready to offer what Balfour had so patently lacked. As his latest biographer has put it:

> Bonar Law's hard-hitting style was intended to bruise those opponents who had humbled Balfour and who held so many, if not all, of the parliamentary cards. It was also intended to unite the sometimes fractious Tories around a single battle standard, and to give heart to those whose frustration had perhaps contributed to make his predecessor's leadership impossible.[19]

But leadership was now inseparable from the third item on the agenda of a frustrated and fractious opposition, party policy. On the one hand the issue of tariff reform remained unresolved. On the other the Parliament Act – dubbed by Law the 'Home Rule in Disguise Bill' – had, by removing the veto power of the House of Lords, opened up the possibility of a renewed attempt on the part of the Liberal government to grant Home Rule to Ireland. Indeed, the government's on-going dependence on the Irish Nationalist group of MPs transformed a possibility into a certainty.

The question of tariff reform was almost inevitably the first policy issue to confront the new Party leader. The status of the referendum pledge of November 1910 in relation to future elections would have required clarification even had Balfour retained the leadership. True Chamberlainite believers continued to argue that Balfour's luke-warm support for tariff reform, epitomized in his November pronouncement, was the main reason why the Party remained on the opposition benches. They took comfort from Law's past record and calculated that the Party would now take a more decisive stance in favour of tariffs than at any time before. But Law was a politician to his finger-tips and his failure, standing as a committed tariff reformer, to take the seat of North-West Manchester at the last general election had convinced him that it was in practice the political rather than the economic arguments relating to tariffs which were decisive. Not surprisingly, the new leader was subjected to a barrage of conflicting advice from the Party's opposing factions. But Law was determined to move cautiously and, though the shadow cabinet decided in March 1912 that food taxes should remain a plank in the Party's programme and that the referendum pledge should be dropped, this decision was not made public and Law remained open to evidence of the political impact of the revised policy. His feeling at this time was that any proposal to abandon food duties or submit them to a referendum would provoke another deep split in the Party's ranks at precisely the time that unity was the imperative necessity in advance of the even more serious challenge of Home Rule. So it was not until 14 November that Lord Lansdowne, the Conservative leader in the upper chamber, used a speech at the Albert Hall to announce the repudiation of Balfour's referendum pledge.

Law had miscalculated. Despite his belief that the balance of party advantage lay in placating the Chamberlainite wing, by the end of 1912 the number of Conservative MPs still unswervingly committed to the full programme of tariff reform was relatively small. So by making the shadow cabinet's decision public, Law and Lansdowne risked fermenting precisely the sort of schism which that decision had been designed to forestall. Majority opinion in the Party now took the view that the full policy of Imperial Preference, which was bound to include food taxes, imposed an insuperable electoral hurdle. The outcry was led by the local party in Lancashire and its leader, Lord Derby, 'perhaps the last great aristocrat more powerful for what he was than what he did'.[20] Law's attempts to find common ground only made matters worse. Speaking at Ashton-under-Lyne in December, the leader now seemed to limit food taxes to wheat, meat and possibly dairy produce, while shifting the onus for their imposition upon the will of the Dominions. Without significantly allaying the fears of men such as Derby, Law had managed to alarm whole-hearted tariff reformers as well. Over the next few weeks he reached the conclusion that the policy agreed by the shadow cabinet in March would have to be changed once more, but doubted whether such a modification would be possible under the leadership of himself and Lansdowne. His inclination was to call a party meeting and resign.

But few Conservatives had the stomach for a further leadership contest, not least in view of the stern parliamentary battles which lay ahead. A divided party would be quite unable to defend the Union. As Balcarres put it, 'we are not only in danger of losing our leaders, but equally of losing the Union, the Welsh Church and Tariff Reform into the bargain'.[21] Furthermore, it was by no means clear who could possibly take over from Law in this situation:

> if he goes, there is no leader who can possibly take his place, for Lansdowne, Austen, Walter Long, Wyndham and Carson are all in the same boat and if they were to consent to accept the choice of leadership when their leader had resigned it on a question to which they gave their approval, I do not see how they can have any influence in the country or with their party.[22]

In the circumstances, Conservative MPs rallied round the leadership and produced a round-robin memorial urging Law to postpone food duties but stay at the helm of the Party. Law, persuaded of his own indispensability, agreed that a future Conservative government would delay the imposition of food taxes until approval had been received at a second general election. In effect the whole policy of tariff reform had been placed on the legislative back-burner.

A major split had been avoided, but the fact that it was the Party's radical wing which had been obliged to give way indicated a significant change in the internal balance of forces since 1910. The desire to recover power and the belief that food taxes posed a huge impediment to this objective had ultimately proved compelling. But many lamented the effective loss of the one constructive policy with which Conservatives might compete with their Liberal and Socialist opponents for the support of the British working class. At the end of 1913 Page Croft remained convinced that 'unless our leaders can inspire all candidates to place the Tariff in the forefront ... our working-class supporters will go over to the Labour Party'.[23] The debate thus simmered on, but most Conservatives concluded that it would be a mistake to run unnecessary risks by provoking any group into further disruptive action, especially in view of the need to regroup in the face of the government's proposed Home Rule legislation. The same reasoning prevented any significant long-term damage to Law's own position. The Party needed its leader if it was to have any hope of thwarting the government's intentions.

The focus of political debate now moved remorselessly towards the issue of Ireland and the Union. In a sense, therefore, the opposition enjoyed the luxury of a political battle on its own ground and terms. The coalition of Conservatives and Liberal Unionists owed its very existence to the split which occurred within the Liberal ranks when Gladstone had first attempted to introduce Home Rule in 1886. Indeed, if Unionists as a body could not now unite in defence of the existing constitutional arrangement of the United Kingdom, there was really nothing to keep the Party intact. Walter Long went so far as to declare that the Union was 'the greatest cause ever committed to the care of mortal man'.[24]

But the Party was less in control of the political agenda than this might imply. The government was firmly committed to Home Rule, not least because of its dependence on the Irish Nationalists for its very survival; the House of Lords could not now throw out the government's bill as it had done in 1893; and the terms of the Parliament act ensured with an eerily predictable precision that the government's bill, first introduced in April 1912, would make its way on to the statute book by the summer of 1914. The law now dictated that a bill would become an act, despite being rejected by the Lords, providing it was passed by the Commons in three successive sessions and providing at least two years had elapsed between the bill's second reading in the first session and its third reading in the third session. The opposition would do everything in its power to defeat Home Rule and it enjoyed some minor successes. In November 1912, for example, Sir Frederick Banbury moved a surprise amendment to a financial resolution in the bill which led to a government defeat by 22 votes. At the end of the day, however, the chances of beating the bill by conventional means were limited. Thus, while the defence of the Union offered Conservatives the hope of an internal unity that had been largely missing during the years of opposition so far, it was by no means clear what, in the last resort, they could do to stop the government in its tracks. Some of the extreme measures which the Party now adopted, or at least considered, are only explicable when its fundamental impotence is appreciated.

Conservative extremism also needs to be explained in terms of the genuine intensity of feeling aroused by the plans of the Asquith government. This was in no sense a case of ritualized opposition for opposition's sake. At a time of acute concern over Britain's future as an imperial nation, Conservatives believed that to lose control over Ireland would be the first, but certainly not the last, step in the collapse of the Empire. As Edward Carson, since 1910 the leader of the Irish Unionists in the House of Commons, explained:

> If you tell your Empire in India, in Egypt and all over the world that you have not got the men, the money, the pluck, the inclination and the backing to restore order in a country within twenty miles of your own shore, you may as well begin to abandon the attempt to make British rule prevail throughout the Empire at all.[25]

Furthermore, the government's legislation was, in Conservative eyes, particularly ill-timed. On the one hand, the Liberals had failed, at either general election in 1910, to secure a clear mandate from the electorate for the introduction of Home Rule. On the other, the Parliament act had left the constitution in a state of suspension. Its pre-amble contained the unredeemed promise of a reformed and more representative second chamber as the concomitant of the ending of the Lords' veto. In such a situation, Conservatives believed, no further constitutional legislation should be introduced. That such legislation was now being put forward reflected only a 'corrupt bargain' between the government and the Irish

Nationalists. Such thinking led Austen Chamberlain, not usually prone to intemperate language, to enquire 'what moral right has the government to claim obedience to legislation of this character passed in this way? A conspiracy hatched in secret, nurtured in fraud and trickery by which you snatched support from the electors.'[26] Indeed, for some of those on the Party's right, wearied by the long years of Balfour's elegant sophistry, the potential for unbridled passion contained in a campaign in defence of the Union was its greatest attraction. 'The real value of the Home Rule struggle', declared Willoughby de Broke, 'will be to stiffen the sinews; warm up the blood, and show all the enemies of England at home and abroad that they still have to reckon with the old spirit.'[27]

The Conservative campaign against Home Rule, and specifically Law's leadership of it, have been variously assessed. For some critics Law was pushed by extremists in his own ranks into dangerously unconstitutional waters. In a famous address at Blenheim Palace in July 1912 he declared that, if the government went ahead with its proposed legislation, he could 'imagine no length of resistance to which Ulster can go in which I should not be prepared to support them and in which … they would not be supported by the over-whelming majority of the British people'. As Robert Blake remarked, Law 'was in effect saying that the passing of Home Rule into law by a parliamentary majority was not decisive, that the men of Ulster had a right to resist by force and that, if they did so, they would have the Unionist Party of England whole-heartedly behind them'.[28] In addition, Law suggested to the King that he was not automatically obliged to give the Royal Assent to the government's bill and, in the early months of 1914, toyed with the idea of amending the Army Annual Act, which gave the government formal legal authority over the armed forces of the Crown. A somewhat different interpretation sees Law engaged in a high-stakes game of bluff, maintaining an extreme position and in the last resort eschewing compromise in the belief that Asquith would be forced into a general election rather than risk the civil war which would result from the coercion of Ulster or the imposition of Home Rule.[29] 'He was using unconstitutional means to secure a constitutional end.'[30] But other writers have stressed that, behind an extremist façade, Law was prepared to compromise and that such a compromise would be based on the separate treatment of Ulster or some part of it. 'Much of his leadership', writes John Ramsden, 'was … a form of pragmatic extremism, extreme action and the threat of more extreme action to come, but used in the cause of more limited objectives.'[31]

The most balanced assessment remains that Law's preferred option was to force an election which would give the British people the chance to reject Home Rule. But if the Union could not be preserved intact, he had a genuine fall-back position based on exclusion, even though this risked alienating uncompromising Unionists, especially those from the south and west of Ireland. The notion that Law entered secret discussions with Asquith, determined to avoid a compromise, is excessively Machiavellian. A letter to Lansdowne well explains his thinking. Though it might be possible to force an election by making the conduct of parliamentary business impossible, the consequences would be 'appalling' and would 'destroy perhaps for a generation our whole Parliamentary institutions. These considerations, which I do not think exaggerated, make me feel that if it is possible to secure a settlement by consent we ought to secure it even if it should be a settlement which we dislike.'[32]

While defence of the Union had promised to be the unifying cause which would bind all Conservatives together after the divisions over tariff reform, the reality was somewhat different. Once the possibility of compromise entered the Party's vocabulary, its full range of conflicting views became apparent. Some hint of this emerged as early as June 1912 when the Liberal MP, Agar-Robartes, moved an amendment to exclude the four counties of Antrim, Armagh, Londonderry and Down from the jurisdiction of the proposed Dublin parliament. From around the same time some sections of the Party championed an alternative approach to the Irish conundrum based on variations of federalism, devolution or 'home rule all round'. But others feared that any deviation from an unqualified defence of the Union spelt disaster and viewed the Asquith–Law talks in the autumn of 1913 and the abortive Buckingham Palace conference of July 1914 with suspicion and alarm. 'I fear the worst', wrote Balcarres on learning of the conference: 'another terrible split, a fresh change of leaders, a dissolution while we are in the throes of internal dispute, another long period under the harrow. The outlook is hateful.'[33] To the extent that Law himself was wary of a compromise, it was because of the way it might be received by his own party. His tactics risked breaching the unity which the re-emergence of Ireland as a political issue had briefly secured.

In trying to create a situation in which the government would be forced to hold an election, Law clearly believed that it would be fought on an issue upon which his party could emerge victorious. Conservative leaders argued that the evidence of by-elections showed that the majority of the electorate backed the Party's stance on the Union. But it seems unlikely that a commitment to resist Home Rule could ever have developed into the sort of constructive policy which might wed a significant part of the mass electorate to the Party's cause. Opposition to Home Rule was a step 'to political dominance, but not part of the social war that now holds the people's mind'.[34] But the Party was slow to adopt a more constructive agenda. It is true that a Unionist Social Reform Committee was set up in February 1911 with the aim of drawing up specific proposals for social and economic reforms. It proved to be the first Conservative attempt 'to address systematically the role of the State in a mature economy'. Its ideas 'anticipated the Conservative statist thought of the inter-war years and Macmillan era'.[35]

However, these ideas never permeated the heart of the pre-war Party. Divided Conservative responses to the Liberal government's National Insurance Bill of 1911 well illustrate the Party's problems. To begin with, Conservatives were keen to avoid the impression of opposition to a measure of social reform and, from the front bench, Austen Chamberlain even suggested that the issue should not become a matter of inter-party dispute. But, in the face of mounting unease from business interests and evidence also of working-class concern, the Conservative stance became more ambiguous. In early 1912, Law pledged a future Conservative government to repeal the legislation, an unfortunate statement only partially corrected by a subsequent letter to the press. In part, the Irish preoccupation provides an explanation for such confusion. 'At present', declared Law, 'my mind is so filled with the dangers in front of us in connection with Home Rule that, till that question is settled, I have hardly interest enough to argue any other.'[36] More fundamentally, the Conservative leadership doubted whether social issues offered a profitable line to pursue. According to Long, 'the Radical party has been so active and has foreshadowed such an attractive programme that in fact there is nothing to offer, except of the wildest description'.[37] Thus, as E.H.H. Green justly concludes:

> By allowing Radical Conservatives to develop their ideas Law left open the possibility of a more positive approach to the mass electorate, but by refusing to endorse their programme he reassured quietists that he would not embark on any 'adventures' that would offend the party's core support.[38]

Analysis

Unlike the other periods considered in this volume, the years of opposition which ended in May 1915 did not culminate in victory at the polls. The Conservatives returned to government, not because of the expressed wish of the electorate, but following the invitation of the

Liberal Prime Minister, Herbert Asquith, offered for reasons which remain highly disputed, to join a wartime coalition. This situation leaves the historian with two vital, but ultimately unanswerable, questions. First, how near were the Conservatives to recovering power when the outbreak of European war in August 1914 distorted the whole pattern of domestic politics? Or, to put the question in a different form, how good were the Party's prospects of victory in the general election due to be held in the normal course of events before the end of 1915? And second, what had been the contribution of the Party's own efforts to whatever recovery in its fortunes may be discerned in the last years of peace?

Historians have long speculated on the likely outcome of a general election held in 1914 or 1915, most usually because of its perceived importance as an indicator of the state of health of the Liberal Party in the on-going debate over that body's ultimate decline. In the absence of a national contest between December 1910 and December 1918, available evidence from local politics and parliamentary by-elections has been subjected to intense, sometimes microscopic, examination. Yet the picture remains somewhat unclear. What can be said with certainty is that Conservative by-election gains since 1910 had left them comfortably the largest single party in the House of Commons. By the outbreak of war Conservative MPs outnumbered their Liberal opponents by 288 to 260, leaving the government more dependent than ever upon its parliamentary alliance with Labour and the Irish Nationalists. In only one by-election during 1914 was there a small decrease in the Conservative vote compared with 1910, and this was in a constituency complicated by a three-cornered contest. A similar picture may be discerned from municipal elections, where the Conservatives had made substantial gains, largely at Liberal expense. By 1913, 'the Conservatives had rarely been stronger in the councils of the land, or indeed more poised for success in a forthcoming General Election'.[39] Such evidence has led one historian to conclude that 'what was at work was not so much "the Strange Death of Liberal England" as "the Strange Revival of Tory England"' and that the most likely electoral outcome 'was not apocalyptic, merely a Conservative triumph in the general election scheduled for 1915'.[40]

Others, however, have taken a far gloomier view. For E.H.H. Green the 'crisis of Conservatism' was as deep in 1914 as it had ever been, with Bonar Law no more successful than his predecessor in resolving the Party's difficulties. 'The Party was still electorally weak and likely to grow weaker with the abolition of plural voting', a reform being actively prepared by the Liberal government.[41] Certainly, many leading Conservatives lacked confidence in their party's prospects, not least as a result of their own failure to focus on vote-winning issues. Many were privately anticipating a fourth successive electoral defeat, an eventuality which could have destroyed the Party's credibility as a party of government. According to William Hayes Fisher, first elected for Fulham in 1885,

> there are a number of seats in London which will depend on the turn-over of just a few hundred votes, and however strongly we may endeavour to force the electors to vote on the Home Rule issue only, they will not be deterred from supporting a candidate who promises them speedy relief from a position of financial injustice, while the other candidate refuses to recognize in his addresses or in his speeches that they have any grievances for which any remedy can be found.[42]

In like vein the Party Chairman warned of the consequences of the failure of Conservatives to grasp the nettle of social reform:

> If we do nothing for the people in the ways immediately touching their lives, while the Radicals and Socialists profess to do all, then the masses as a whole … will gallop to socialism as hard as they can. It will be a rush, a stampede …. We may see the Social Revolution carried out through the ballot-box with appalling rapidity and ease.[43]

Austen Chamberlain, saddened by the relegation of the policy of tariff reform to the back-burner of Conservative politics, commented in March 1913:

> The fact is I think our present position illogical and indefensible, our recent history cowardly and disgraceful, our prospects of winning poor, and our prospects if we do win, alarming; I say to myself that it would be better that we should be beaten again and learn in that fiery trial to find faith and courage and leadership such as may deserve victory first and be able to use it afterwards.[44]

Significantly, a retrospective assessment drawn up by the Central Office in 1916 produced a pessimistic analysis of the Party's pre-war prospects. At best, it was suggested, the Conservatives might have secured a majority of 12 in a general election held late in 1914. More probably, however, the government would have delayed going to the polls until the abolition of plural voting had been secured, a situation in which the Liberal Party, it was estimated, would have won a majority of about 40 over the Conservatives in a spring 1915 election.[45]

Furthermore, it may well be that the slump in the government's fortunes had already passed its nadir by 1914. The Liberals suffered a markedly lower swing against them after November 1912, and recent writers have stressed that the New Liberalism was far from being an exhausted force by 1914. The government and in particular Lloyd George were beginning to embark upon a second wave of radical reforms. The new focus of the Chancellor's attention was the land, and his proposals included establishing security of tenure for tenant farmers and creating Wage Boards to set minimum wages for agricultural workers. Like so much else these schemes, launched in the autumn of 1913, fell victim to the changed priorities of the war years. But 'most of the signs that are available suggest that the land campaign had every chance of success when war intervened to transform the political landscape'.[46] Certainly, the evidence suggests that the government's second wind had the effect of placing the opposition on the back foot as far as the forthcoming election was concerned, particularly in English rural constituencies, two-thirds of which were in Conservative hands. The Party responded slowly and without conviction to Lloyd George's proposals. Its difficulty was to come up with a counter-policy which would alleviate the condition of the rural working class without alienating traditional support among the landowning community. In June 1914 Steel-Maitland privately conceded that his party had completely lost the initiative on the land question and that its prospects for the coming autumn looked extremely unpromising.[47]

Closer examination of the by-elections of the period 1911–14 suggests that the most salient element of the pre-war electoral battleground was less the run of Conservative victories than the on-going relationship between the Liberal and Labour Parties. Some of the Conservative gains were in straight fights, but Labour intervened in 11 formerly safe Liberal constituencies, causing five seats to be lost to the Conservatives. C.P. Scott, editor of the *Manchester Guardian*, was quite clear about the conclusion to be drawn: 'As a result of three-cornered contests, it is quite possible that while Liberalism and Labour are snapping and snarling at each other the Conservative dog may run away with the bone.'[48] Speaking at Ladybank in April 1914 Asquith himself pointed out that all but one of the Liberals' losses over the past two years had been the result of what he called a split in the forces of progress. Indeed, when Conservative candidates took seats on a minority vote, Liberals were inclined to respond that the combined 'Progressive' vote was proof that, while the government's candidate had been beaten, its policies had not. It seems probable, therefore, that the outcome of the next general election would have been determined by the development of relations between the Liberal and Labour Parties, rather than by the performance of the Conservatives. The possibility or otherwise of the re-creation of the sort of electoral arrangement between the forces of the left which had stood them in such good stead over the three previous general elections has been vigorously debated between historians of the Liberal and Labour Parties, but falls outside the scope of the present study. It does however underline the point, germane to the whole Edwardian era, that electorally this period is more about the success of Liberalism and of the Progressive Alliance than it is about the failure of Conservatism. Even at its lowest point in 1906 the Conservative Party still managed to secure 43.6 per cent of the popular vote. In the post-war era, when Labour and the Liberals went their separate ways, the Conservatives were able to achieve a very comfortable victory in 1922 on just 38.2 per cent of the vote.

Although the Conservatives faced an uncertain future at the outbreak of war in 1914, it is probably going too far to suggest that the conflict against the Kaiser's Germany played a 'significant role in saving the Conservative Party from disintegration'.[49] That said, key problems remained unresolved. The last years of peace offered few signs that the Party had really come to terms with the demands of governing a mass democracy. Despite some evidence of Conservative elements that were progressive and constructive, it was only in defence of the Union, an issue which probably excited considerably less passion among voters than it did among Conservative politicians, that the Party had really emerged as a potent force in national politics. Even if it had been successful at the polls in 1914 or 1915, a single general election victory would not have provided conclusive evidence that Conservatism's long-term future was assured. This is particularly apparent in the context of the partial electorate which existed before 1918. The total of those entitled to vote in 1910 stood at just under 7.7 million, a mere 28 per cent of the adult population. Notwithstanding what did happen in the very different circumstances which existed after the war, it is an open question how many of the disenfranchised – all women and up to 40 per cent of adult men – would have felt themselves drawn to the sort of Conservatism on offer in the pre-war era.

The coming of war transformed the situation. The change was apparent at the very outbreak of hostilities. While the Liberal government hesitated, at least before the German violation of Belgian neutrality, to plunge the country into conflict, Conservatives were in no doubt where their duty lay. As Law and Lansdowne told Asquith on 2 August, 'any hesitation now in supporting France and Russia would be fatal to the honour and to the future security of the United Kingdom'.[50] As the conflict progressed, Conservatives experienced fewer difficulties than did at least a substantial minority of the Liberal Party in accommodating the demands of total warfare. Resulting Liberal divisions were bound to work to the advantage of their political opponents. War also offered Conservatives a new opportunity to display their Disraelian credentials as the champions of patriotism and nationalism. At the same time, pre-war difficulties could be put to one side in the greater national interest. 'I have no party', insisted Henry Page Croft, 'until Europe has been saved from the piracy of the German nations.'[51]

Nonetheless, the Conservatives' position was not an easy one. One possibility was an immediate coalition, but Law set his face against such a development. Yet if the Conservatives did not join the government, they could scarcely carry on the functions of an opposition as if nothing had changed. The Irish problem illustrated this dilemma. To begin with, Conservatives could not bring themselves to believe that the government would continue with such a controversial measure as Home Rule. However, when attempts to agree upon a compromise proved abortive, Asquith went ahead with his bill. Home Rule was enacted, without an accompanying Amending bill to deal with Ulster, though its operation was suspended for the duration of the war. The challenge for Conservatives was to show their disgust without incurring charges of a lack of patriotism by shattering the political truce. At the end of the day, whatever the government did over Ireland, the opposition felt bound to continue to offer general support for the war effort. In what could be no more than a theatrical gesture, Conservative MPs made their feelings known by walking out of the Commons chamber, resembling, in Asquith's words, 'a lot of prosaic and for the most part middle-aged gentlemen trying to look like early French revolutionists in the Tennis Court'.[52]

Even without a formal coalition, some leading Conservatives moved close to the seat of power. Balfour, a long-standing member of the Committee of Imperial Defence, was invited to join the War Council which Asquith set up in November 1914, while Austen Chamberlain and Lord St. Aldwyn, as surviving former Conservative Chancellors of the Exchequer, took up semi-official posts at the Treasury. Such arrangements were a mixed blessing and Law and Lansdowne, anxious that the government should not take undue advantage of the opposition's enforced good behaviour, tried, not always convincingly, to draw a distinction between co-operating with the administration and having any responsibility for its policies. By the beginning of 1915 many Conservatives, frustrated by the evidence of military stalemate, began to conclude that 'patriotic' opposition amounted in practice to no opposition.

Out of a desire to find ways of criticizing the government, a group of Conservative MPs led by Basil Peto, Ernest Pollock and W.A.S. Hewins came together at the end of January to form the Unionist Business Committee. Their aim was to encourage a more vigorous prosecution of the war effort than had been seen hitherto. By March Churchill sensed that a group of Conservatives around Law were now ready to revive party conflict at the earliest opportunity.[53] That opportunity was not long in coming. As the government became beset by crises at the Admiralty and over the supply of munitions on the Western Front, backbench Conservatives were ready to recreate the sort of parliamentary battleground that had existed until July 1914. If, however, it was the Conservatives who now, in May 1915, *forced* their way into a coalition government, the reaction of many of the Party leadership to the recovery of power was curiously unenthusiastic. 'I am very uneasy', recorded Walter Long, 'as always because I believe these brutes will best us, take the kernel, give us the husks, plus the responsibility. Feeling as strongly as I do I can't contemplate a coalition without grave anxiety.'[54] For Curzon, coalition was 'long expected' but 'much dreaded'.[55] However, it was probably Austen Chamberlain who came closest to capturing the prevailing mood:

> God knows each one of us would willingly avoid the fearful responsibility; but the responsibility of refusing is even greater than that of accepting, and in fact we have no choice … we cannot shirk this job because we don't like it or because we think the risks to ourselves too great.[56]

At all events, the Conservative Party was back in government. True, that government would be headed until the end of the war and beyond by successive Liberal premiers and it would be a further seven years before the Party, standing alone, would be victorious at a general election. Nonetheless, by the end of 1916 it was the parliamentary Conservative Party upon which the government largely rested and by the end of hostilities there was little doubt that it was Conservative policies and values which had prevailed in the prosecution of the war. The post-war era opened up new and promising prospects for Conservatism, projecting itself now as a bulwark against the advance of the Socialist left and profiting from an irreparable breach in the forces of Progressivism. The Party had finally emerged from the bleakest period of opposition it was to experience in the entire twentieth century, albeit by the most unexpected and unpredictable of routes.

Notes

1. S. Koss, *Asquith* (London: Allen Lane, 1976), 126.
2. The word 'Conservative' is used throughout this chapter rather than the more accurate 'Unionist' which denotes the increasingly close alliance between Conservatives and Liberal Unionists.
3. G.R. Searle, 'Critics of Edwardian society: the case of the Radical Right', in A. O'Day (ed.), *The Edwardian Age* (London: Macmillan, 1979), 79.
4. E.H.H. Green, *The Crisis of Conservatism: The Politics, Economics and Ideology of the British Conservative Party 1880–1914* (London: Routledge, 1995), 136.
5. Ibid., 270.
6. A. Sykes, 'The Radical Right and the crisis of Conservatism before the First World War', *Historical Journal*, 26 (1983), 661.
7. L. Witherell, *Rebel on the Right: Henry Page Croft and the Crisis of British Conservatism, 1903–14* (Newark: University of Delaware Press, 1997), 18.
8. G. Armstrong to J.P. Hughes, 9 Dec. 1910, Wiltshire Record Office, Long MSS, 449/21.
9. J. Kendle, *Walter Long, Ireland and the Union 1905–1920* (Montreal: McGill – Queen's University Press, 1992), 61.
10. Comyn-Platt to Long, Jan. 1911, Long MSS, 449/17.
11. Balfour to Douglas, 17 Jan. 1911, Kent Record Office, Douglas MSS, c. 22/21.
12. Lawrence to A. Chamberlain, 14 Dec. 1910, University of Birmingham Library, Austen Chamberlain MSS, AC 8/7/23.
13. Maxse to Law, 29 Sep. 1910, House of Lords Record Office, Bonar Law MSS, BL 18/6/124.
14. Maxse to Steel-Maitland, 15 June 1911, Scottish Record Office, Steel-Maitland MSS, GD 193/151/3.
15. Note by Short, Oct. 1911, Bodleian Library, Oxford, Sandars MSS, c. 764/113; memorandum by Sandars, 8 Nov. 1911, British Library, Balfour MSS, Add. MS 49767.
16. C. Petrie, *Walter Long and his Times* (London: Hutchinson, 1936), 165–7.
17. R. Blake, *The Unknown Prime Minister: The Life and Times of Andrew Bonar Law* (London: Eyre and Spottiswoode, 1955), 86.
18. J. Vincent (ed.), *The Crawford Papers* (Manchester: Manchester University Press, 1984), 247; J.M. McEwen (ed.), *The Riddell Diaries* (London: Athlone Press, 1986), 27.
19. R.J.Q. Adams, *Bonar Law* (Stanford: Stanford University Press, 1999), 72.
20. Ibid., 86.
21. Vincent (ed.), *Crawford Papers*, 298.
22. H. Gwynne to L. Amery, 7 Jan. 1913, Amery MSS, D45.
23. Page Croft to Law, 8 Nov. 1913, Law MSS, BL 30/4/17.
24. *The Times*, 30 Aug. 1906.
25. B. Bond, *British Military Policy between the Two World Wars* (Oxford: Clarendon Press, 1980), 18.
26. J. Smith, *The Tories and Ireland 1910–1914* (Dublin: Irish Academic Press, 2000), 55.
27. Sykes, 'Radical Right', 671.
28. Blake, *Unknown Prime Minister*, 130.

29. Smith, *Tories and Ireland*; J. Smith, 'Bluff, bluster and brinkmanship: Andrew Bonar Law and the Third Home Rule Bill', *Historical Journal*, 36 (1993), 161–78.
30. S. Evans, 'The Conservatives and the redefinition of Unionism, 1912–21', *Twentieth Century British History*, 9 (1998), 13.
31. J. Ramsden, *The Age of Balfour and Baldwin 1902–1940* (London: Longman, 1978), 67.
32. Law to Lansdowne, 8 Oct. 1913, Law MSS, BL 30/5/68.
33. Vincent (ed.), *Crawford Papers*, 340.
34. K. Feiling, *Toryism: A Political Dialogue* (London: G. Bell and Sons, 1913), 8.
35. Green, *Crisis*, 287.
36. *The Times*, 22 Nov. 1913.
37. Long to Law, 8 Aug. 1912, Law MSS, BL 27/1/28.
38. Green, *Crisis*, 294.
39. C. Cook, 'Labour and the downfall of the Liberal Party, 1906–14', in A. Sked and C. Cook (eds), *Crisis and Controversy: Essays in Honour of A.J.P. Taylor* (London: Macmillan, 1976), 63.
40. W.L. Arnstein, 'Edwardian politics: turbulent spring or Indian summer?' in O'Day (ed.), *Edwardian Age*, 78.
41. Green, *Crisis*, 309.
42. Hayes Fisher to Lansdowne, 16 Dec. 1913, Long MSS, 947/441.
43. Note by Steel-Maitland, n.d., Steel-Maitland MSS, GD 193/80/5.
44. A. Chamberlain, *Politics from Inside: An Epistolary Chronicle 1906–1914* (London: Cassell, 1936), 534.
45. Green, *Crisis*, 269.
46. I. Packer, *Lloyd George, Liberalism and the Land: The Land Issue and Party Politics in England, 1906–1914* (Woodbridge: Boydell Press, 2001), 194.
47. Steel-Maitland to Law, 23 June 1914, Law MSS, BL 39/4/40.
48. A. Hetherington, *The Guardian Years* (London: Chatto and Windus, 1981), 326.
49. Green, *Crisis*, 333.
50. C. Petrie, *The Life and Letters of the Right Hon. Sir Austen Chamberlain*, vol. 1 (London: Cassell, 1939), 373.
51. Witherell, *Rebel*, 207.
52. H.H. Asquith, *Memories and Reflections 1852–1927*, vol. 1 (London: Cassell, 1928), 33.
53. M. Gilbert, *Winston S. Churchill*, vol. 3, companion part 1 (London: Heinemann, 1972), 652–3.
54. Kendle, *Long*, 91.
55. C. Hazlehurst, *Politicians at War, July 1914 to May 1915* (London: Jonathan Cape, 1971), 286.
56. Chamberlain to Law, 17 May 1915, Law MSS, BL 37/2/37.

7
Democracy and the Rise of Labour: 1924 and 1929–1931

Stuart Ball

The Conservative Party was in opposition for only two short periods during the three decades from 1915 to 1945. The two occasions had much in common: both were during minority Labour governments, and both were comparatively short – nine months in 1924, and 25 months in 1929–31. In both cases, the Conservatives had lost a general election which their leaders had been hopeful of winning, and they entered opposition in some disarray. There were disagreements over policy, presentation and leadership, and for much of these sojourns in opposition the Conservatives were preoccupied with internal factionalism and crises. During both periods, there were threats to the position of the leader of the Party, Stanley Baldwin. Finally, the issues and concerns of both periods were very similar: what attitude to adopt towards the minority Labour government, how to appeal to the new 'democracy' of adult suffrage, what position to take on the critical issue of protectionist tariffs, and what relationship – if any – to have with the Liberal Party, which held the balance in the House of Commons. The first two sections of this chapter discuss the context and development of each of the opposition periods in turn, and the final section deals with them together in a comparative analysis.

The first Labour government, January to November 1924

Three factors shaped the politics of the early 1920s: the rise of the Labour Party, the troubles of the Liberal Party and the legacy for the Conservative

Party of the overthrow of the Lloyd George Coalition in 1922. The latter had marked a decisive change in the Conservatives' leadership and strategy, but both were still in contention during the following two years. Nearly all of the Conservative cabinet ministers had supported continuing the coalition in October 1922, and the revolt from below which this provoked had swept them out of office along with Lloyd George. Apart from the new Prime Minister, Bonar Law, and the Foreign Secretary, Lord Curzon, the Cabinet of the purely Conservative ministry which replaced the Coalition were inexperienced and relatively unknown. The ousted pro-coalition Conservative leaders waited in the wings, confident still of their own superiority and indispensability, and anticipating blunders that would lead to their recall on their own terms. Leadership was not the only significant change in 1922: instead of an anti-Socialist alliance with the Liberals, the Conservatives had opted to set their own course and stand on their own merits.[1] This had important implications for their attitude to the other parties, as it involved accepting the advance of Labour to the position of being the major opposing party and potential alternative government. The Conservatives would benefit from such a polarization, but it meant that the Liberal Party was now a distraction which they wished to see eliminated as a significant force. However, the swift progress of the Labour Party worried many Conservatives, and periods of stress and difficulty produced renewed speculation about a return to coalitionism. So long as the former coalitionists could provide an alternative leadership and strategy, Conservative politics would remain in an unstable condition.

These were the predominant themes during the turbulent events of 1922–24, both before and after the Labour Party took office for the very first time.[2] On becoming Prime Minister after the fall of the Coalition, Bonar Law immediately called a general election which was held in November 1922. Although they gained only 38.5 per cent of the votes cast, the Conservatives won 344 seats and secured a comfortable majority in the House of Commons. With 142 seats, and 29.7 per cent of the vote, the Labour Party took the position of the official Opposition, a significant rise in status. The Liberals were handicapped by the continuing split and hostility between the Lloyd George (former Coalition) and Asquith (anti-Coalition) wings. The followers of Lloyd George were reduced to 53 MPs whilst the Asquithians increased to 62, but more significant was the relegation of the Liberals as a whole to the position of the third party. The Bonar Law government faced challenges abroad in the Ruhr crisis and at home, where the stagnant economy and Labour's attacks upon capitalism made the issue of unemployment the focus of attention. In

May 1923 terminal illness forced Bonar Law to resign the premiership. The government had managed competently enough, and Conservative MPs neither desired nor felt the need to turn to the former coalitionists, who remained aloof and detached. The choice of successor therefore lay within the existing Cabinet; there was widespread support amongst ministers and MPs for the Chancellor of the Exchequer, Stanley Baldwin, who became Prime Minister on 22 May despite his relative inexperience.

What followed only a few months later took everyone by surprise, and seemed to prove the dangers of a novice leader. At the Conservative Party conference on 25 October 1923, Baldwin announced that in his view only protective tariffs could reduce the level of unemployment; because Bonar Law had pledged in 1922 that these would not be introduced in this parliament, the Prime Minister's declaration made a fresh election an immediate prospect. It seems that Baldwin had intended to wait until the spring for this, but the mounting speculation rapidly made such a delay impossible. Baldwin announced the dissolution of Parliament on 13 November, and polling day was fixed for the minimum legal interval on 6 December. The Conservatives were unprepared, and the election was a confused affair. The policy was vague, many candidates were unclear or unenthusiastic, and the Party was soon on the defensive.[3] The best thing that could be said was that Baldwin managed to hold his cabinet together, despite the presence of an anti-tariff minority. Raising the old tariff cry also brought Austen Chamberlain and the former coalition ministers back into the fold, without any concessions being made to them. However, it was also the one issue with the power to reunite and revitalize the Liberal Party, and its electoral disadvantages remained. The Liberal and Labour Parties returned to the pre-war charge that it meant 'food taxes' and a rise in living costs for the ordinary household. The election results produced an unstable position: the Conservatives remained the largest single party with 258 MPs, but they had a net loss of 88 seats and no longer had a governing majority. The tariff policy had clearly been rejected and the two free trade parties had gained seats, with Labour now having 191 MPs and the Liberals not so far behind with 158.

The first issue that faced Baldwin and the Cabinet after the results were apparent was whether to resign at once, or to meet Parliament. The latter would involve staying in office for over a month, as the new session would not begin until after the Christmas recess, in mid-January 1924. On the day after the election results were declared a dejected Baldwin considered resignation, and there followed a few days of intrigue revolving around replacing him with another leader who would be willing and able to make a pact with the Liberals and forestall the dangerous prospect of Labour in power.[4] Not surprisingly, the former coalition leaders Austen Chamberlain and Lord Birkenhead were prominent in this, but it also involved the influential Earl of Derby and some cabinet ministers who were aware that Baldwin might quit.[5] In fact, neither prospect lasted through the weekend. Baldwin decided to stay in office and meet Parliament, forcing the Liberals to side openly with Labour.[6] The coalitionist plots evaporated: Derby was half-hearted, and the most credible replacement for Baldwin, the former Conservative Prime Minister A.J. Balfour, refused to take part.[7] Significantly, Balfour considered that Baldwin had established his position with the public during the campaign and, despite failing to win, had become the Party's strongest electoral asset.[8] Even the rumour of a coalitionist coup was enough to produce a rally of support for Baldwin amongst ministers and MPs, and to mute the criticism from those who had lost their seats.[9]

The moment of greatest danger to Baldwin's leadership had swiftly passed. It was clear that he remained the most acceptable leader, and that his continued presence was seen by the majority as a guarantee of the Party's independence and integrity.[10] On the following Tuesday, 11 December, the Cabinet met for the first time since the election, and decided unanimously for Baldwin's strategy of remaining in office and meeting Parliament. This decision had several consequences, and determined the events of the new few weeks. It confirmed that the government would meet the new House of Commons without changing its leadership or policy. With Baldwin as Prime Minister, there would be no negotiations with either the official Liberal leader, Asquith, or his rival, Lloyd George. This left the Liberals with no option but to combine with Labour and defeat the government when Parliament met, and Asquith announced this decision on 18 December. The Liberals would therefore be responsible for propelling Labour into office and would bear the blame for any alarm or failures that followed. Baldwin was much calmer about the prospect of a Labour ministry than were most Conservatives, as he had confidence in the moderation of the Labour leadership and the idealism and patriotism of their supporters.[11] He believed that any backstairs deals to keep Labour out would offend the public's notion of fair play, provoke class antagonism and lead to a backlash in Labour's favour that would soon give them a governing majority.[12] Although it was mainly a case of making the best of a bad job, Baldwin's argument that a Labour government could hardly be tried under safer circumstances offered some consolation and reassurance. The initial panic over the prospect of a Labour government abated during the Christmas recess, and by the time the new Parliament met in mid-January the politicians, press and public had become accustomed to the idea. The Conservative Cabinet presented a Royal Address that was still committed to the tariff policy, giving the Liberals no room to manoeuvre.[13] In the debate on the Address in the House of Commons they supported a free trade amendment moved by the Labour Party, and the government was defeated by 72 votes on 17 January 1924. Baldwin resigned on the next day, and Ramsay Macdonald took office as Prime Minister of the first Labour government.

The Conservatives entered opposition calmer and more united than would have appeared possible immediately after the election, but there were still problems of leadership and policy that had to be resolved. The ending of the rift that had existed since the fall of Lloyd George in 1922 was accomplished without great difficulty, as this was not a situation in which the Conservatives could afford the luxury of internal dissension – or one in which it would be tolerated by MPs and the local constituencies. With the Liberal Party reunited under Asquith and committed to free trade, the Conservative ex-coalitionists had no alternative but to accept Baldwin's leadership and return on his terms. This made it possible for him to bring them back without losing any of his existing cabinet, and Austen Chamberlain, Balfour, Birkenhead and Lord Crawford were invited to attend the first meeting of the shadow cabinet on 7 February.[14] This gathering then took the crucial decision about the Party's economic policy, also with little controversy.[15] There was almost no support for continuing with the full tariff programme, and it was decided to return to Bonar Law's pledge that if a Conservative government was returned at the next election there would be no move to protectionism.[16] All that the Party would propose was the extension of the moderate and limited Safeguarding of Industries Act. This gave some shelter to specific industries which could demonstrate that they were facing subsidized or unfair foreign competition; it was far removed from a general tariff and, as it did not apply to imports of food or raw materials, it was not vulnerable to the 'food tax' charge.

The uniting of the leadership and dropping of the unsuccessful tariff programme defused the remaining criticism within the Party.[17] The influential region of Lancashire had been most discomfited by the 1923 tariff policy, and there was a possibility that its meeting on 9 February might pass a damaging vote of censure. Instead, partly under Lord Derby's guidance, this was replaced with a milder resolution, and afterwards the press were specifically briefed 'that it should on no account be looked upon as a vote of censure on the leaders of the party'.[18] A meeting of the parliamentary party had already been summoned for 11 February, at the Hotel Cecil in London; this was the most important forum, because only a meeting of MPs could remove or install the Party leader. Various strategies had been considered, and it was settled that – as the leader in office – Baldwin would chair the meeting. It was also now clear that he would seek a vote of confidence and be willing to continue as leader, and that there was no serious alternative candidate.[19] As at several other points in his career, at the critical moment Baldwin produced a masterful speech, moving his audience and changing the agenda to his own favoured themes. After a brief justification of the election, he accepted that 'the country as a whole did decide in a sense hostile to our main proposal', and therefore the general tariff would have to be set aside until there was some 'clear evidence' that public opinion had altered. The most important and powerful part of the speech came later, focusing not upon policy but on the moral vision which Baldwin communicated so well, and upon which his authority as leader was founded. He openly acknowledged the sincerity and idealism which motivated the supporters of the Labour Party to work tirelessly in order to achieve a better future. In response, he called upon Conservatives to match this selflessness and altruism, for 'it is a spirit which can only be beaten by a similar spirit in our Party'. This speech began the process of establishing over the following months what came to be called the 'New Conservatism' of moderate reformism, class conciliation and social harmony.[20] It was an appealing combination, especially to many former Liberal supporters, and it was reinforced by further speeches which Baldwin gave during the summer months.

The Hotel Cecil party meeting resolved the questions of leadership and policy. The vote of confidence after Baldwin's speech was symbolically moved by Balfour and seconded by Austen Chamberlain, and carried unanimously.[21] The most difficult and divisive matters had now been cleared out of the way and, as Lord Derby wrote in mid-February, 'The only thing now is to go on quietly, get our organization right and get the Party together again.'[22] However, Winston Churchill's candidacy in the Westminster Abbey by-election in March 1924 caused a further brief disruption. One of the most prominent and capable Liberal ministers in the Lloyd George Coalition, Churchill had been emphasizing anti-Socialism and moving towards the Conservatives for several years. The Conservative coalitionists were keen to bring him into the Party, but many others regarded him with reserve and even hostility. Churchill's intervention in the by-election as an 'Independent Anti-Socialist' candidate – in competition with an official Conservative – threatened to reopen disunity in public. With some difficulty, Baldwin was able to restrain both sides and keep a balance during the campaign.[23] This was one of the safest Conservative seats in the country and the other parties had only a marginal presence; perhaps fortunately, the official Conservative secured victory, with Churchill only 43 votes behind. The campaign had shown Churchill's effectiveness but the result had not damaged the party, and passions cooled. With Baldwin's approval, Central Office helped Churchill to find a constituency, and in September he was adopted by the safe seat of Epping in Essex, although he was still not formally a Conservative.[24]

After this distraction, the dominant tone of the remainder of the period in opposition was one of purpose and confidence.[25] The Conservatives made effective progress in four main areas: the containing of the Labour government, the exploitation of Liberal disunity, the strengthening of their own organization and the developing of a new programme that was moderate and attractive. The minority position of the government and its dependence upon a Liberal Party that split three ways on many important votes – some for the government, some against and some absent – gave a wealth of opportunities to a united and cohesive opposition party. The Conservatives had leaders and senior backbenchers with experience of the more difficult task of opposing the Liberal governments of 1906 to 1914, and the whips were adept in the tactics that delay legislation and harass the governing party. However, this had to be pursued with some care. For several reasons, there was no wish to remove the government too quickly.[26] It was important that Labour be seen to have a fair chance, whilst a very short spell in office would most likely be followed by a minority Liberal government rather than a general election. The Conservatives also needed time to develop new policies and prepare their organization; not long after Labour took office, the constituencies were advised to prepare for an election in November. Finally, it would be necessary to wait for a suitable issue upon which Labour could be defeated without gaining public support, and which if possible would also place the Liberals at a disadvantage.[27]

The tone that was adopted towards the Labour government in Parliament was one of fairness and moderation, especially on the part of Baldwin.[28] The government was accepted as legitimately in power, and entitled to the privileges and respect which went with that position. Where it might err, at least in the initial honeymoon period, this was put down to inexperience and the honesty of its intentions were not called into question. This attitude – which could shade into the patronizing – was generally displayed by the front bench and, on the whole, by backbenchers as well, in formal debates and at question time. However, in parallel with this, but with much less public visibility, the whips and backbenchers were making use of procedural devices and delaying tactics to obstruct or amend Labour legislation, especially at the committee stage. The government had to abandon several bills, but did succeed in some areas where they could rely upon Liberal support or where a confrontation on the issue would have been to the Conservatives' disadvantage. In the first category was the reaffirmation of free trade by the abolition of the McKenna duties, a wartime protectionist expedient, and the repeal of the Safeguarding of Industry Act; in the second was the Housing Act overseen by Labour's Minister of Health, John Wheatley. Neville Chamberlain, who had been responsible for the previous measure on housing in 1923, considered 'we shall do no good by futile opposition', and, whilst criticizing aspects of Wheatley's measure, took a moderate and constructive tone in the debates.[29] Baldwin's campaign of public speeches during the summer months continued to display tolerance and fair-mindedness, increasing the attractiveness of his brand of Conservatism to Liberal and even Labour supporters. However, this was complemented by the more partisan and critical line taken by other front-benchers, by MPs and candidates in the constituencies, and by the more overtly anti-Socialist line of the propaganda produced by Conservative Central Office.

This period in opposition saw some innovations which were to become permanent features of the parliamentary party. The first of these was a range of policy committees, 14 of which were established in February 1924. Apart from one on parliamentary procedure, they each covered the field of a government department, such as agriculture, education or foreign affairs. The scheme had been devised by the Chief Whip, Bolton Eyres-Monsell, and the committees were chaired by the appropriate minister from the previous government, so they were firmly under the direction of the leadership.[30] Their membership consisted of backbenchers knowledgeable or interested in the field, but the regular meetings – usually weekly when Parliament was sitting – became open to all Conservative MPs who wished to attend. The committees were given two important tasks: shadowing the particular department and preparing proposals in their area for a new party programme. They were effective in both respects, and their work occupied the energies of MPs which might otherwise have taken more divisive directions. When the Conservatives returned to office in 1924 the committees were continued, and began to elect their own chairmen and officers from their backbench members; they have existed in this form ever since, acting as an important channel of communication between the party leaders and their followers.[31]

The second development of the period did not have official parentage, but was similar in that its utility to the whips made it acceptable and permanent. The '1922 Committee' had been founded in April 1923 as an educative group for MPs newly-elected in 1922, but in the wake of the 1923 defeat it began to develop into a forum for all Conservative MPs. What made it different was that it was a loyalist rather than a critical body, and the whips were closely involved in its evolution. The 1922 Committee was still unofficial and existed alongside rather than above the policy committees, but it began to have a co-ordinating role, with MPs giving reports on the work of the other bodies. It provided another useful and private link between leaders and followers, and after 1924 it continued to expand and acquire more important functions.[32]

The third initiative lapsed when the Conservatives returned to power, but was recreated in the permanent form of the Conservative Research Department during the next period in opposition after 1929. This was the creation of a Secretariat to support and co-ordinate the policy review, with its officials acting as secretaries to the policy committees. The secretariat was essentially a substitute for the civil service advice that was no longer available in opposition. It was headed by Lancelot Storr, who had served as Baldwin's secretary whilst he was Prime Minister, and it shared space at Central Office with the leader's personal staff. The policy committees worked swiftly, and their proposals were summarized by Neville Chamberlain in the pamphlet *Looking Ahead: Unionist Principles and Aims*, which was published on 20 June 1924. The detail of this was less important than the fact that it established a fresh image which was in tune with the 'New Conservatism' and gave the Party credibility and confidence. The new outlook was reinforced by a series of speeches from Baldwin, and its content and tone were reflected in the election manifesto a few months later.

Although in defeat it often served as a handy excuse and whipping-boy, the Party organization had not been blamed in 1923. Instead, the executive committee of the National Union declared that the work of the Central Office staff had been 'extraordinarily good' and the literature produced 'the best ever known'.[33] Major reorganization was not considered necessary and the Party Chairman, Stanley Jackson, remained in his post. The one change was the replacement of Sir Reginald Hall as Principal Agent, the senior professional post in the Party machine. A former Admiral and a sitting MP, he had been appointed in March 1923, but the problems of running the campaign whilst trying to defend his own seat had shown this experiment to be a failure. Hall lacked the knowledge and personal skills needed in the post, and was removed in February 1924.[34] His replacement, Herbert Blain, a successful businessman and the author of the standard textbook on office management, was expected to increase the efficiency of the Party machine. The Central Office publicity and propaganda department was expanded under a new head, the former MI5 officer Joseph Ball, and the Party was able to produce much larger numbers of leaflets and posters for the next election. In general, the period from 1922 to 1925 saw an increasing sophistication and professionalism within the Party organization at both national and local levels. The membership expanded considerably – especially in the women's branches – and larger numbers of trained and full-time local agents were employed.[35] In many of the Conservative seats that had been lost in 1923, the setback led to an overhaul of the local association and a higher level of activity.[36]

The Party was therefore well-placed to take the offensive after the summer recess, and two issues had emerged which provided excellent opportunities to do so. The first of these was the treaty the government had negotiated with Soviet Russia, which included a controversial loan. The second was the decision to drop the prosecution for sedition of the editor of the Communist newspaper *Workers' Weekly*, J.R. Campbell. Both of these allowed the Conservatives to play the 'red card' to full effect, and left the Liberals embarrassed and exposed. When it became clear that the Liberals would oppose the Russian treaty and support an inquiry into the Campbell Case, MacDonald decided to treat both matters as votes of confidence. The debate on the Campbell affair came first, and Baldwin left the Liberals with no avenue of retreat by announcing that the Conservatives would support their call for a select committee. On 8 October the Liberal motion was carried by 364 votes to 199, and MacDonald resigned and secured a dissolution of Parliament.

The Conservative Party was by now ready and eager for the contest, and confidence was high. The chairman of the Manchester Conservative organization noted: 'our people are as keen to fight now, as they were slack at the last election', and Baldwin told his mother on 12 October that 'our party is in good heart and we have an excellent list of candidates. I hope you will worry as little as I do!'[37] During the campaign, the Conservatives had the twin benefits of Baldwin's enhanced popular appeal and the clearly-established position of being the only credible anti-Socialist party.[38] These were reflected in the three main elements in their campaign: the claim that only the Conservatives could provide stability in government, the positive appeal of the moderate and constructive policies in the Party programme, and the negative attack on Socialism.[39] One part of the latter was to cast doubt upon Labour's moderation, and the 'Zinoviev letter', which was published in the press four days before the poll, seemed to underline this. The origins and authenticity of the document were unclear, but it supposedly contained instructions from Moscow to British Communists to take over the Labour Party from within. Whilst Baldwin avoided partisanship in his speeches, other Conservative leaders and local candidates were unrestrained in their 'anti-red' rhetoric. However, just as significant in the outcome was the disarray of the Liberals, who fielded only 339 candidates compared to over 500 for both the other parties. Where Liberal candidates did stand they did badly, and where they did not it was the Conservatives who benefited most. The result of the poll on 29 October 1924 was a landslide Conservative victory, with 412 MPs elected and a 46.8 per cent share of the vote. The Labour Party lost only a little ground, reduced from 191 to 151 MPs, and slightly increased their share of the vote. It was the Liberals who were shipwrecked, reduced by almost three-quarters from 158 MPs to a mere 40, and only 17.8 per cent of the votes. The Conservatives returned to power in a commanding position, and in a more clearly polarized political system with only two main governing parties.

The second Labour government, June 1929 to August 1931

The political context at the end of the 1920s had not changed greatly from that of 1924. By 1929, the Labour Party had strengthened its position as the main alternative to the Conservatives, and the decline of the Liberal Party was more apparent. The Conservative Party had benefited from a secure period in government from 1924 to 1929, but was still troubled by rumours of intrigues aimed at reviving the coalition alliance with Lloyd George. The 1929 general election was held under the most 'normal' circumstances of any during the inter-war period, with no crisis or coalition pact between parties. It was called by Baldwin as the end of the parliament approached and the three main parties contested it independently, with each of them fielding over 500 candidates. The reappearance of Liberal nominees in seats which they had not contested in 1924 drew votes away from the Conservatives, although in nearly every case it was Labour who benefited. Polling took place on 30 May, and for the first time Labour became the largest single party in the House of Commons, with 287 MPs. The Conservatives lost many seats, especially in the industrial areas, and were reduced to 260 MPs, whilst Lloyd George's great attempt to revive the Liberal Party failed, with only a small increase from 40 to 59 MPs.

It was clear that this outcome meant a second term in office for the Labour Party, but the Conservatives still had the tactical choice between resigning immediately or waiting to meet the new Parliament. In comparison to 1923, there was little alarm over the prospect of Labour forming a government, and less to be gained by forcing the Liberals publicly to support them. Baldwin was more concerned to avoid any impression of unfairness or of clinging to office, telling the King's private secretary on 2 June that 'he accepts his defeat and, if he resigns, the Democracy in an equally British spirit will take off their hats to him as a good sportsman'.[40] On 3 June the Conservative Cabinet agreed on resignation, and two days later Ramsay MacDonald formed the second minority Labour government.

Although the Liberals once again held the balance in a hung parliament, the situation was significantly different from the aftermath of the 1923 election. Labour would not need active Liberal support in order to stay in office, and Liberal MPs could abstain or even – if they were careful not to go too far – oppose the government without bringing it down. The strategic options for the Conservatives had diminished, as they could only block a measure or defeat the government if at least half of the Liberal MPs voted with them and the other half abstained. This was very unlikely, for two reasons. The outlook of the Liberals on many issues was much closer to that of Labour, and the fundamental divide in British politics was still that between free trade and protection. Even though the Conservatives' manifesto in 1929 had renewed the pledge not to introduce a general tariff in the next Parliament, it remained their long-term objective and the Liberals would be deeply reluctant to help the Conservatives recover power. The certainty of some Liberal MPs – and some of the Labour Cabinet – in the continuing merits of free trade began to erode under the impact of the world recession and mounting unemployment, but this did not happen until the later part of 1930 and in 1931. However, by that time the second reason for the Liberals to keep Labour in office had become even stronger: their reluctance to face a general election. With the great effort of revival having failed in 1929, the Liberals soon reverted to factionalism and disunity, and their organization again decayed. As the economic position worsened in 1930, it was clear that their public support was shrinking and an election would result in the loss of most of their seats; just as turkeys do not vote for Christmas, the Liberals had no wish to hasten their own demise. However, this left them little option but to give dogged support to a government that both they and the public saw as failing, a position which further diminished their credibility and support.

Equally, there was little desire in the Conservative ranks for any dealings with the Liberals. Many MPs and ex-MPs were bitter about their intervention and tactics in the 1929 election, and they were suspicious and hostile towards any suggestions from the former coalitionists in the shadow cabinet – principally Winston Churchill and Austen Chamberlain – of negotiating with Lloyd George.[41] The Liberals were seen as Labour's allies, and on the few occasions that they opposed the government – such as over the Coal Bill in February 1930 – they were a broken reed. The Conservatives were determined to return to power on their own terms, without any hampering obligations. This was particularly the case as far as tariff policy was concerned, and any arrangements with Liberals had to be based upon their acceptance of this. However, by the spring of 1931 some Liberal MPs were willing to move in this direction, impelled by the twin pressures of the deteriorating economic position and their dwindling prospects of re-election. This loose grouping was given credibility by the leadership of Sir John Simon, who began giving public hints of his growing agnosticism over free trade in March 1931. Negotiations followed for a pact under which Conservative candidates would not stand against Simon's followers if they endorsed the need for an emergency tariff and voted with the Conservatives to eject the government from office. Slow but steady progress was made, and on 26 June 1931 Simon took the symbolic step of resigning the Liberal whip. When Parliament rose for the summer recess a few weeks later, the Conservatives had every prospect of being able to muster sufficient votes to defeat the government when the new session opened in the autumn; they were anticipating victory in the general election that would follow, and the return to power of a purely Conservative administration.

However, during the first two years of the Labour government the Conservative Party was distracted by internal dissensions, and its effectiveness as an opposition was much reduced.[42] At first, attention was focused on the tariff issue, but this developed into a direct assault upon Baldwin's leadership. Tariff policy had been a source of contention even before the 1929 election. In August 1928 Baldwin had ruled out the extension of safeguarding duties to the iron and steel industry, considering this too close to introducing a general tariff, in violation of his pledge of 1924. A substantial number of Conservative MPs wanted a more assertive policy, and were unhappy at the continuation of the 'no tariff' pledge in 1929. Defeat on that strategy reopened the question of what fiscal policy the Party should adopt, whilst at the same time the balance of opinion within the parliamentary party had shifted. The protectionist MPs often sat for safe seats and so after the election they made up a larger proportion of the parliamentary party, whilst the numbers of the more cautious MPs from the marginal seats in the industrial regions had been much reduced. Even so, the majority of Conservative MPs were pragmatic rather than committed protectionists, and were mainly concerned to find a position that was workable and had the maximum of public support.[43]

The situation within the parliamentary party was therefore fluid, and would alter with changes in the economic situation, in public opinion, or in the degree of pressure mounted by the protectionists. The latter came from four different elements. First, there was a minority in the shadow cabinet – principally Leo Amery and Neville Chamberlain – who were keen to adopt a bolder policy. Second, many of the backbench MPs were in favour of a tariff policy, on manufactured goods at least. Third, there was considerable support for protection in the constituency associations of the safer Conservative seats and in the agricultural areas, which were suffering from prolonged depression. Finally, there was a new element which raised the temperature and turned it from a debate over policy into a battle for the soul of the party – the intervention of the 'press lords'. Lord Beaverbrook and Lord Rothermere were maverick figures who were influential because of the size of their newspapers' circulation: Beaverbrook's main title, the *Daily Express*, sold 1.69 million copies daily in 1930, and Rothermere's *Daily Mail* sold 1.84 million. Beaverbrook had been a Conservative MP from 1910 to 1916 and a close friend of Bonar Law; he was seen as sincere in his views but impulsive and misguided in his tactics. Certainly, the partnership with Rothermere did not help his cause – the other press lord sometimes supported Lloyd George and had never formally been a Conservative, and he was regarded as hostile by most of the Party. However, during the serious internal party crisis which developed during the press lords' public campaign, their strongest asset was not their popular newspapers. Their power came from the fact that they were articulating what the grass-roots membership in the Conservative stronghold areas of the south, the suburbs and the rural seats wanted.[44] In the opinion of the editor of the staunchly Tory newspaper, the *Morning Post*, the press lords' real strength was that their policy was 'endorsed secretly or openly by 85% of the Conservative Party'.[45]

Baldwin had good reasons for resisting the protectionist pressure, even though this risked his own position. For much of the period, tariffs were divisive in Conservative politics, with divergent views within the shadow cabinet and, in the country, between grass-roots opinion in the north and the south. Baldwin was primarily concerned to maintain unity and took a median position; as he remarked to a senior backbencher, 'I must try and keep as many of my people with me as I can!'[46] However, this problem diminished during 1930, as the free trade group within the Cabinet declined in weight and conviction, and the impact of slump caused the industrial areas to look more favourably upon tariffs. Baldwin's second reason was the recognition that a general election could come with very little warning, and he was determined not to be caught with an unpopular policy that would be an easy target for Liberal and Labour attacks. Until the end of 1929 at least, there were signs that Labour had gained popularity, and there was a concern that MacDonald might dissolve Parliament and ask for an outright majority. This possibility receded as the government's failure to grapple with unemployment became more apparent, but it was replaced by the prospect that the government might suddenly collapse or be defeated over a measure the Liberals could not accept, as nearly happened with the Coal Bill in February 1930. Most of all, Baldwin knew that the Conservatives could only return to power by recovering the lost marginals, which were mainly in the midland and northern urban areas. Public opinion here was resistant to the lure of protection, and only moved slowly towards it as the depression deepened in 1930. Baldwin's need to keep in step with this meant that he could not satisfy the demands for a stronger policy that came most vigorously from the MPs and associations in the safer southern seats.

The problem with Baldwin's strategy was that it made him look hesitant and reluctant, moving only when under pressure; combined with his style in opposition, it gave the impression of weak leadership. Baldwin did not find opposition congenial and did not wish to take a partisan line on every question; such conduct was contrary to his outlook, as well as inconsistent with his public image. He was also a variable performer in the House of Commons during this period, and his poor performances outnumbered his successes. The result was frustration amongst his colleagues and a corroding sense of lack of grip and missed opportunities, such as over the London Naval Treaty in May 1930. Baldwin put much of his effort into speaking outside Parliament, but the value of this was less visible to the MPs at Westminster. After initial attempts at co-operation, the press lords concluded that Baldwin would never adopt tariffs with vigour or enthusiasm, and that his removal was an essential prerequisite for success. However, any declaration of open warfare upon the leader from outside the Conservative Party produced an immediate rally to him, as it changed the debate from the acceptable area of policy into the dubious one of personality.

In the immediate aftermath of the 1929 defeat, protectionism was too dangerous a liability to be considered. In July the shadow cabinet reaffirmed the no-tariff pledge, and postponed any reconsideration into the indefinite future. Beaverbrook began his 'Empire Crusade' campaign in his newspapers shortly after, advocating a 'whole-hog' protectionist policy which included preference for Empire produce and duties on food and raw materials imported from elsewhere. This was presented under the slogan 'Empire Free Trade', but from the outset food taxes were fundamental to his policy. In the by-election at Twickenham the Conservative candidate was pressed into adopting Beaverbrook's programme, and official recognition had to be withdrawn.[47] However, the poll on 8 August illustrated the risks, as this normally safe suburban seat was retained by only 503 votes. After a pause during the recess, Beaverbrook launched his campaign in earnest in October 1929, and began to have an impact in the south and in the arable farming counties. Over the following year, the pressures within the Conservative Party and from the Empire Crusade, combined with the economic situation and its effects upon public opinion, led to a series of shifts in policy towards protectionism.

In the autumn and winter of 1929, complaints from the grass-roots that the Party had no clear or constructive programme became more persistent. In October, Neville Chamberlain recorded that the mood was one of 'depression, distrust, and despair'.[48] Baldwin realized that a gesture must be made, and used his speech at the Party conference on 21 November to endorse a fairly vague resolution on Empire trade that had been passed. However, this involved no specific change, and it was not enough to hold the line as the pressures mounted during the next three months. By late January, Baldwin had accepted that 'the press agitation has made a definite fiscal policy necessary'.[49] His next major speech, at the Coliseum theatre in London on 5 February 1930, provided the opportunity, and he used firm language to disguise a limited extension of safeguarding, which was balanced by a specific pledge against food taxes. The latter caused Beaverbrook and Rothermere to form an alliance, and the Empire Crusade was transformed into the United Empire Party on 18 February. This was a much more serious challenge than a newspaper campaign: it proposed to organize branches in every constituency and to run candidates in elections. Its appeal for membership was responded to on a significant scale in many safe seats and some of the agricultural areas, and this prospect of division alarmed many local association executives and backbench MPs.[50] A further shift of policy was needed to close the dangerous rift that was opening up, and at the National Union Central Council meeting at the Hotel Cecil on 4 March 1930 Baldwin returned to the referendum policy of 1910. This time it was an advance towards tariffs rather than a retreat from them, and it led to a truce with Beaverbrook that lasted until the summer.[51]

The high point of this co-operation came in the West Fulham by-election in May, with Beaverbrook stumping the constituency in support of the official Conservative candidate. The seat was won, but not convincingly, and after this matters deteriorated again. The Party Chairman, J.C.C. Davidson, was a close member of Baldwin's inner circle, but his mistakes and unpopularity were endangering his leader, and Baldwin could not continue to defend him. In late May, Neville Chamberlain applied the decisive pressure on Davidson to resign, and in June, at Baldwin's request, took on the position himself.[52] This was a heavyweight selection that helped to restore morale, and it increased Chamberlain's influence over policy and strategy; he was already chairman of the Conservative Research Department, which had been created in November 1929. During May 1930 Baldwin was engaged upon a campaign of speeches in northern cities, in which he again emphasized the cautious aspect of his policy. Declaring that the referendum policy was being used as a shield rather than a sword, Beaverbrook gave up on co-operation and returned to the attack.[53] The press lords' inconsistency in repudiating the referendum that they had welcomed not long before gave Baldwin a tactical opening. He was able to present their attack as personal rather than political, and so isolate them from almost any support within the Party. Baldwin elevated the issue to the high constitutional grounds of attempted dictation by the press to the Party and MPs, something which neither could accept with any self-respect. Condemnation of the press magnates' 'un-English methods' and the belief that Baldwin was being unfairly hounded rallied support behind the leader.[54] Baldwin used this to summon a party meeting, held at the Caxton Hall in London on 24 June, where he easily won a vote of confidence.

Baldwin's success was based upon hostility to the press lords – an unwisely-phrased letter from Rothermere had particularly played into his hands – but there had been no change of policy.[55] For this reason, as pressure within the Party rose almost to eruption over the summer months, his victory had no lasting effect – only a few weeks later, the mood of MPs was one of 'a terrible demoralisation'.[56] The Empire Crusade was making damaging inroads, and by October 1930 the situation seemed to be sliding dangerously out of control, with the possibility of a revolt from below similar to that which had brought down the Coalition in 1922. Sir Samuel Hoare, a rising figure in the shadow cabinet, warned Neville Chamberlain that 'unless something happens quickly, everything and everybody will collapse like a pack of cards', and a senior MP, after sounding other backbenchers in the Carlton Club, wrote of 'the appalling change of feeling' since June.[57] A revision of policy had become imperative, but fortunately the most important restraining factor was diminishing, as there were signs that the rise in unemployment was at last moving opinion in the industrial regions towards protectionism. All that was needed was a pretext, as the leadership could not appear to be giving in to the press lords. In early October, as the temperature within the Party approached boiling point, Neville Chamberlain found 'a truly Heaven-sent opportunity' when the Canadian Prime Minister, attending the Imperial Conference in London, called publicly for reciprocal tariffs. Chamberlain galvanized Baldwin into a quick response, and the referendum was replaced by the 'free hand' – that the Party would ask at the next election for a mandate to introduce whatever tariffs were necessary. This was what most Conservatives wanted, and by acting decisively Baldwin took the wind of grass-roots support out of Beaverbrook's sails.

The recapturing of the policy initiative was swiftly capitalized upon by the summoning of Conservative MPs, peers and prospective candidates to a second party meeting on 30 October, also held at the Caxton Hall. The meeting gave almost unanimous support to the 'free hand' policy, before Baldwin left the hall to allow the leadership to be debated. The party leaders knew they were now on firm ground and they had not been anxious about this; they were right, although the vote – this time by secret ballot – produced a larger minority than was comfortable, with 462 for Baldwin and 116 against.[58] This was the decisive victory; although the Crusade nominee won the South Paddington by-election on the following day and Beaverbrook continued the campaign into the spring, it never again had significant support within Conservative ranks or posed a real danger.

Baldwin had two much more serious problems in the winter of 1930–31 than the continuing distraction of Beaverbrook's attacks: these were his poor performances in Parliament and the India question. The reform of the government of India, granting a larger role to the native population, emerged as a significant issue that threatened to divide the Party further, with many MPs uncomfortable about Baldwin's bipartisan support for the government's proposals. In November 1929 there had been tension over Baldwin's endorsement of the declaration by the Viceroy, Lord Irwin, that India would eventually attain dominion status.[59] The issue then receded whilst the tariff struggle dominated attention, but returned to centre stage at the beginning of 1931 as the first Round Table Conference came to an end. When its recommendations were debated in the Commons on 26 January, Churchill delivered an effective attack upon them and Baldwin in reply alarmed the Party by going too far in their favour.[60] Concern over India combined with an erosion of confidence in Baldwin's capacity amongst the shadow cabinet to produce a final brief crisis in early March.[61]

The capacity of the Empire Crusade still to damage Conservative prospects was shown in February 1931, when its intervention in the East Islington by-election led to a Labour victory. In fact, this turned Conservative opinion finally against Beaverbrook, but that was not immediately apparent.[62] The leadership crisis was triggered on 28 February when the Conservative candidate selected to fight the by-election in Westminster St George's, one of the safest seats in Britain, withdrew rather than defend Baldwin's leadership against a Crusade challenger. On the following morning, Neville Chamberlain sent Baldwin a critical and pessimistic assessment of the position that had been drawn up by the Principal Agent, Topping, a few days earlier.[63] For a few hours on Sunday, 1 March 1931, Baldwin was depressed and decided to quit, but he was soon talked out of it by his wife and closest confidants, Davidson and Bridgeman.[64] The crisis really ended at this point, for, once he recovered his energy and determination, he dealt effectively with the problems facing him. India, not tariffs, was the real concern in the Party, and Baldwin gave reassurance in a speech at Newton Abbot on 6 March in which he emphasized the safeguards that would limit any changes, and he then recaptured the confidence of both MPs and his front-bench colleagues with an outstanding performance in the Commons debate on the recently concluded Irwin–Gandhi pact on 12 March.[65] The Westminster St George's by-election was the easiest to tackle; a capable replacement candidate was quickly found in Duff Cooper, and Baldwin returned to the theme of the press lords' unconstitutional pretensions. At the Queen's Hall on 17 March, speaking in support of Cooper, Baldwin delivered his most famous attack on the press lords, condemning them for seeking 'power without responsibility – the prerogative of the harlot throughout the ages'. More important than this speech, made only two days before the poll, was Conservative impatience with Beaverbrook's increasingly reckless and personal tactics, and Cooper won easily with a majority of 5710 votes over the Crusade candidate (no other parties having stood). On 24 March, Beaverbrook negotiated a face-saving agreement with Neville Chamberlain, and the Empire Crusade was swiftly wound up.[66] More importantly, on 25 March Baldwin cleared the air with his shadow cabinet colleagues, who were allowed harmlessly to vent their frustrations.[67]

From this point onwards, the Conservatives put disunity behind them, and became a much more effective and vigorous opposition.[68] The main cause of this was the economic situation – not only the rise in unemployment, which reached 2.7 million in December 1930, but the crisis in the government's finances as its expenditure exceeded its revenue. A budget deficit was considered a serious matter – it undermined Britain's standing as a trading nation, and ultimately threatened national bankruptcy. The view of the chairman of the Bristol West constituency association was typical: 'they had never been in greater danger of national disaster than they were today'.[69] In the spring and summer of 1931 the Conservatives rallied behind another traditional position, the call for 'economy': significant cuts in government spending which would in turn make possible a reduction in the high levels of taxation.[70] Their demand was for 'equality of sacrifice', with no group being considered immune. The restoration of business confidence at home and abroad by means of 'economy' and balancing the budget was now more urgent even than tariffs, and pushed both that and the India issue into the background.[71] Conservative morale was raised by evidence that they were making an impression, and the results of by-elections from the gain at Ashton-under-Lyne in April 1931 onwards indicated that the tide had turned – and with sufficient vigour to suggest a likely Conservative landslide whenever the election came.[72] The desperation of the economic situation put the Party under some pressure, but also gave it a sense of mission and discouraged any wavering or disunity.[73] By the time Parliament rose for the summer on 30 July, the prospect of a pact with the Simonite Liberals meant that the Conservatives could realistically hope to recover power after an autumn election.

Instead, they returned to office sooner, by unexpected means.[74] The revelation on 31 July that the budget deficit was much larger than expected was followed by withdrawals of foreign reserves from London at a pace which swiftly reached crisis proportions. It was clear that only measures which included a significant cut in unemployment benefit would restore overseas confidence and secure the loan needed to avoid the collapse of sterling. A key factor in the crisis was that Parliament was not sitting, and the pace of the run on the pound left no time in which to recall it: 'the sands were rapidly running out'.[75] The Labour government needed to secure Liberal and Conservative support to show that its proposals would be approved when they did come before Parliament. Between 13 and 23 August, MacDonald and Philip Snowden (the Chancellor of the Exchequer) met the Liberal and Conservative leaders separately on several occasions. Neville Chamberlain was one of the two Conservatives at all of these meetings; Baldwin was present on the first and last days only, with Hoare accompanying Chamberlain in between. The Conservatives pressed for economies to contribute the largest part in bridging the deficit, and on 22 August they agreed with MacDonald and Snowden on a package which included a 10 per cent cut in unemployment benefit.[76] However, after lengthy debates the Labour Cabinet split over the proposal, and by the evening of Sunday 23 August it was clear that it could not continue in office, and MacDonald so informed the King.[77]

A meeting of the three party leaders was arranged with the monarch for the following morning; as Lloyd George was recovering from an operation, the Liberals were led during the crisis by his deputy, Sir Herbert Samuel. Baldwin expected MacDonald to resign and the Conservatives to form a government with Liberal support; this would deal with the crisis, after which there would be an election on normal party lines.[78] However, already influenced by Samuel in this direction, the King made a powerful appeal to MacDonald to remain as Prime Minister of an all-party emergency government, as his presence would add to its credibility and help restore foreign confidence. Having extracted promises from Samuel and Baldwin to serve under MacDonald 'for the sake of the country', the monarch withdrew, leaving the three leaders with no more to do than 'settle the details'.[79] The result was the first National Government, with an emergency cabinet of only ten – four of whom were former Labour ministers remaining in post, two were Liberals and four were Conservatives: Baldwin, Neville Chamberlain, Hoare and Sir Philip Cunliffe-Lister.

This was not an outcome that the Conservatives had ever intended or wanted, and it was not particularly helpful to them – the Cabinet had a free trade majority, and their room for manoeuvre was restricted.[80] However, the Conservatives were as swept away by the atmosphere of crisis as anyone else; rather than being cool and calculating, their actions were the best they could manage in a situation of confusion, uncertainty and near-panic.[81] On the day the government was formed, Austen Chamberlain wrote to his wife that 'it has been – perhaps still is – a question of hours between this country and the deluge'.[82] The Conservatives were also concerned that implementing the cuts could be unpopular, and the presence in the Cabinet of MacDonald and other Labour figures would make their position less exposed.[83] The key terms in the agreement to create the government reflected Conservative fears that they would lose their present advantages, and so it was affirmed that the government was only temporary for the duration of the crisis, that the economies would at least equal any additional taxation, and that after the crisis there would be a general election fought on existing party lines and programmes. With these reassurances emphasized, and equally affected by the crisis atmosphere, the Conservative Party meeting held at the Kingsway Hall on 28 August gave unanimous approval to Baldwin's actions.

The National Government did not turn out to be temporary, although the other points made on its formation were achieved, sometimes in an unexpected way. The emergency budget was passed on 10 September, but two weeks later the gold standard and parity with the dollar had to be abandoned. The pressures of the crisis pushed the government into closer unity; its continuance became in itself the main hope of restoring stability, and it was clear that a public mandate would be necessary before confidence could return and economic recovery begin. With some difficulty, the Cabinet agreed to go to the country as a National Government, but simply seeking 'a doctor's mandate' to take whatever remedies it thought necessary – under that umbrella, each party would advocate its own solutions.[84] Crucially, this left the Conservatives free to campaign for the 'free hand' on protection; at the Kingsway Hall, Baldwin had promised 'a straight fight on tariffs and against the Socialist Party', and this he delivered. Held on 27 October, the election was a massive victory for the National Government, within which the Conservatives were the overwhelming majority. In most constituencies there was a straight contest between one recognized National candidate (usually a Conservative) and Labour, and this mobilized the anti-Socialist vote to great effect. The National Government won 554 seats: there were 470 Conservatives, 35 Simonite Liberals, 32 orthodox Liberals following Samuel, and a handful of 'National Labour' supporters of MacDonald. The official Labour Party was reduced to only 52 MPs, but its vote had not collapsed – at 30.8 per cent of the poll, its share was actually fractionally higher than in 1923.

What followed was not a Conservative government, nor was it a front of dupes disguising a Conservative government. MacDonald remained Prime Minister until June 1935, when he made way for Baldwin, and the Liberal and Labour groups had a disproportionately large share of cabinet posts, including many of the most powerful. In several areas, the government followed non-Conservative policies, including interventionism in agriculture, housing and regional policy; it also continued the bipartisan policy on India, against which Churchill led a right-wing rebellion.[85] However, in key respects it delivered what Conservatives wanted: first, the preservation of economic and social stability; second, the avoidance of extremism and the containment of the Labour Party; third, the balancing of the budget and implementing of economies; fourth, at last the introduction of tariff duties and imperial preference, enacted in 1932. For these reasons, it remained acceptable to both Conservative leaders and followers for the remainder of the decade, with the successful results of the 1931 and 1935 elections proving that, despite Disraeli, if the times are troubled Britain may indeed love a coalition.[86]

Comparison and analysis

Three issues were central to both of these periods in opposition. The first was the long-standing Conservative wish to introduce protectionist tariffs, which they saw as the solution to the economic difficulties of the nation and the consequent industrial strife and class conflict. However, the introduction of duties on food imports was unpopular with working-class voters, and this produced tensions between tariff enthusiasts on the right of the Party and pragmatists and moderates in the centre and left. These problems were added to by forces outside the Party, and in particular the 'Empire Crusade' of the press lords Beaverbrook and Rothermere in 1930–31, which became a direct attack upon Baldwin's leadership. The minority position of the two Labour governments further complicated Conservative strategy, as an election could come with little warning and the Party could not risk adopting positions that were more advanced than the current public mood. Responses to the potentially destructive question of tariffs were shaped by this tactical danger and the other two issues.

The second theme was fundamental in Conservative politics between the wars, and the principal concern of Baldwin as Party leader. This was the problem of how to respond to the democratic electorate created by the 1918 Reform Act, and in particular to the rise of the Labour Party. There was considerable fear that the public would be misled by demagogues and agitators into simplistic and short-term 'soak the rich' measures of redistributing wealth. This would undermine property rights, lead to economic chaos and social anarchy, and end in revolution – the agenda of the 'Bolshevism' that many Conservatives believed lay behind the Labour Party, preparing to supplant it (hence the credibility of the 'Zinoviev letter'). Conservatives were uncertain which strategies would meet the challenges of 'Socialism' and class-based politics, but Baldwin and the leadership established after the overthrow of the Lloyd George Coalition in 1922 were convinced that simple negative 'anti-Socialism' was not enough, and that the Party must present a positive, idealistic and inspiring alternative. Part of this was the appeal of the Empire, but this raised the question of imperial economic unity and thereby revived the thorny issue of tariffs. During both periods in opposition the Conservatives sought to avoid extreme positions and match their policies to popular expectations. In 1924 Baldwin set out the agenda of the 'New Conservatism', and a new type of wide-ranging policy reappraisal produced a statement of aims and principles, *Looking Ahead*. Although this formal structure was not repeated in 1929–31, Baldwin put much effort into speaking campaigns in the industrial regions where the Conservatives had lost seats, and kept policy moderate even when this caused tension and dissent within the Party – not only over tariffs, but also in adopting a bi-partisan position over the future of India. These concerns also governed their tactics in opposition, both in reacting to Labour bills in the House of Commons and in the very limited and cautious use made of the Conservative majority in the House of Lords.[87]

The third issue was the attitude to be adopted to the third party, the Liberals. Pacts and coalitions with other parties played a major part in the Conservatives' electoral success in the inter-war period. Only twice, in 1922 and 1924, did they win a majority when standing alone, and these victories had much to do with the disarray and misfortunes of the Liberal Party. The Conservatives' success in the decade following the introduction of adult suffrage in 1918 was as much a surprise to themselves as anyone else. It did not seem to rest upon any permanent or reliable foundations, but to be contingent upon circumstances and events. The only election which the Conservatives approached with some confidence was 1929, when they had the poorest result of the whole period. The drastic reduction from 412 seats in 1924 to only 260 in 1929 underlined the unpredictability of public opinion.

In fact, the volatility was not so much in the electorate, as in the party system. In particular, it was the condition of the struggling Liberal Party which largely determined the outcome of inter-war elections. When the Liberals were in a pact with the Conservatives, as in 1918, 1931 and – partly – 1935, the concentration of the anti-Socialist vote secured large parliamentary majorities over the Labour Party. When the Liberals were divided or lacked the resources to field candidates in many seats, the Conservative Party standing alone obtained governing majorities that were comfortable (1922) or massive (1924). However, when the Liberals were united around a clear issue or programme and were able to run a large number of candidates, the Conservatives lost marginal seats – and so the 1923 and 1929 elections resulted in minority Labour governments. The Liberals were seen as the witting or unwitting aides of Labour's success, and this was confirmed by their general support of the minority Labour administrations in the House of Commons. The resentment was the greatest in 1929, partly because the Liberals were no longer seen as having a credible chance of forming a government, and therefore to Conservatives they seemed to have only a wrecking role. Thus, in considering the Conservatives' periods in opposition between the wars, it is essential to remember that they were facing two other parties, and that their relations and rivalry with the party not in office (the Liberals) were more fraught and critical than those with the government of the day (Labour).

This was an especially sensitive area because the strategy of alliance in an anti-Socialist front had been rejected by the majority of the Conservative Party in the fall of the Lloyd George Coalition in 1922. The overthrow of the pro-coalition leadership had led to the ascent of Baldwin and a new generation of Conservative leaders, and they and the mainstream of Conservative MPs were constantly suspicious of possible plots to reverse the verdict of 1922.[88] Hostility to Lloyd George and fears of a revival of coalitionism coloured the atmosphere of Conservative politics between 1922 and 1931, and were particularly acute during the spells in opposition. These uncertain periods presented a wider range of tactical alternatives and opportunities, whilst the leadership was less cohesive and co-ordinated than was the case when in government. The minority status of the two Labour governments was a key factor, as their continuation in office depended upon most Liberal MPs declining to oppose them. This led some Conservatives to consider co-operation, especially to forestall Labour taking office, or to advocate deals and pacts to detach sections of Liberals and defeat the government. However, most Conservatives blamed the Liberals more than Labour for their electoral defeat, and were more resentful of Liberal tactics and antagonistic to their continued role as a significant force. The temptation to alliance for the short-term expediency of ousting the Labour government was usually more than outweighed by reluctance to give any succour to the long-term future of the Liberal Party and the rejection of any echo of coalitionism. Even so, on both occasions the role of the Liberals was crucial in the fall of the government and the return to office of the Conservatives.

This is not to suggest that the Conservatives were complacent about the challenge posed by the rising Labour Party. They understood its potential appeal to the 'working classes' who made up the bulk of the electorate, and tended pessimistically to subscribe to the assumption that Labour had a particular attractiveness to such voters, especially the male workforce of the industrial towns. The Conservatives trod gingerly in their handling of economic and social issues, and in the tone and policies they employed in opposing the Labour Party – one of Baldwin's frequent concerns was the failure of his long-anticipated successor, Neville Chamberlain, to conceal his disregard for the parliamentary Labour Party. The Conservatives were particularly aware that a stance of reactionary resistance, dogged defence of upper-class privilege or simple negative anti-Socialism would not work in the new electoral situation, and would only be counter-productive.

On both occasions, there was controversy over the strategy that had led to defeat, but in opposite ways. In 1923, Baldwin's sudden adoption of a protectionist policy was criticized as a misinformed gamble, made worse by mistakes in its execution. The policy was unwelcome to some MPs – particularly in industrial regions such as Lancashire – and the majority were unprepared for an election so soon.[89] In 1929, Baldwin's refusal to move in the protectionist direction, by ruling out the extension of safeguarding duties to the iron and steel industry, had been opposed by the substantial section of tariff enthusiasts in the parliamentary party. The criticism in 1929 (mainly after the defeat, though in some cases beforehand) was the dullness of the Party's platform, with its negativity encapsulated in the famous poster slogan of 'Safety First'. There had been an over-reliance upon the government's record of worthy social reforms and Baldwin's personal popularity, and the flagship measure at the end of the parliament, de-rating, was seen as too technical and lacking in immediate effect to have much resonance with the voters.

In both opposition periods, the major part of the problem was that the Conservatives had lost power. A victory in 1923 would have validated Baldwin's initiative and silenced almost all free trade recalcitrance within the Party; success in 1929 would have been accepted by all wings as confirmation of the wisdom of the watered-down protectionism that was the restricted application of safeguarding duties as practised in 1924–29. There were also criticisms of the decisions that had led to the elections, and their timing. This was especially the case with 1923, when the sudden advent of a dissolution after only a year of the parliament, and the casting away of the first Conservative majority since 1900, seemed to confirm every doubt about the experience and competence of Baldwin and the 'second eleven' leadership that had come to the helm after the overthrow of Lloyd George and his supporters in 1922. The timing of the election was less of an issue in 1929 – after four and a half years, the Parliament was nearing its end – but there were some who thought that a few months earlier or later might have made a difference.

After both defeats, the desire for an inquest quickly waned, for similar reasons. In 1923, the concern that it would be a means through which the coalitionists would return to power restrained many Conservative MPs from venting their feelings in public. The advent of the Labour ministry was a further impulse to unity, as the political situation was fragile and uncertain. In both instances, the possibility that another election could come at any moment made Conservative MPs and candidates more concerned with looking outwards and to the future. Given Labour's minority position, there was the possibility that the government could be defeated in the Commons with very little warning. It was also the case that both Labour governments enjoyed some successes and appeared popular in their first few months, and so might go to the country themselves and ask for a secure majority. In 1929, after nearly five years as Prime Minister, Baldwin's personal prestige was much higher than it had been in 1923. Also greater was the almost universal recognition that he was the Conservatives' most popular figure and greatest electoral asset. He could rely upon the support of the younger MPs on the centre and progressive wings of the Party who had been drawn to his moderate and moral stance. Although many of these lost marginal seats in 1929, such as Duff Cooper and Harold Macmillan, others had safer berths and remained loyal to Baldwin during the internal strife of 1930–31, including R.A. Butler, Anthony Eden and Oliver Stanley.

What saved Baldwin after both defeats was the lack of an alternative leadership that was acceptable to the mainstream of Conservative MPs and local constituencies.[90] Given the inexperience or unimpressiveness of most of the 1922–24 cabinet, the only possible successors in 1923 would have been the return from the wilderness of the former coalitionist ministers, upon their own terms. This was unacceptable on several grounds: the reasons behind their rejection remained valid, and the last thing most Conservatives wanted was a renewed coalition – as was demonstrated by the ineffectualness of the coalitionist intrigues in December 1923 and January 1924. Their plans foundered on a simple reality: most Conservatives would rather see a weak minority Labour government in power – almost certainly not for long – than a well-placed coalition with Lloyd George pulling the strings, whether he was outside or inside the Cabinet. In addition, the sulking and sniping of the Conservative coalitionists, whilst stopping short of overt disloyalty and divisiveness, had not endeared them to the parliamentary party – Lord Birkenhead, the most public critic, was particularly resented. Finally, any invitation to return would imply that the Carlton Club vote of 1922 had been a foolish rejection of the leaders' authority, and involved more humble pie – both now and in the future – than most Conservative MPs were willing to stomach.

Two questions remain, of which the first is how effective the Conservatives were in opposition to the first and second Labour governments. For part of each period they were unable to concentrate their attention upon the opposition role, whilst they dealt with the legacy of defeat and with problems of disunity. These were resolved much more quickly in 1924 than in 1929–31; although the first opposition period was briefer, a much smaller proportion of it was affected by internal distractions, whilst in 1929–31 these lasted for nearly two years. The Conservatives also had more success as a parliamentary opposition in 1924, partly because the balance of parties gave greater tactical opportunities and partly because Labour ministers and MPs were less experienced. The Conservatives were able to block or emasculate a range of measures, but in both periods they faced little in the way of alarming legislation – though they certainly disliked Labour's line in several areas, such as coal or trade union legislation in 1930–31. Less could be achieved in 1929–31, and in both periods the Conservatives were extremely cautious about making any use of their heavy preponderance in the House of Lords, for fear that it would give the government an easy target in reviving the cry of 'peers versus people'.[91] In both periods they faced the strategic dilemma of every opposition: whether to adopt the 'active' approach of initiating new departures, or the 'reactive' stance of waiting for and exploiting the problems of the government. Changes of orientation were more necessary in 1924 than in 1929, and in the first period the Conservative leadership followed the 'active' course. In 1929–31 Baldwin favoured the 'reactive' approach, and the main developments in policy were either forced upon him or – in the case of the decisive shift to the 'free hand' in September 1930 – largely the work of others. However, the difference is less than it may seem – whatever the method, the purpose in both periods was the same: to position the Party in the most moderate position that Conservative opinion could accept.

The second question, which follows from this, is how and why the Conservatives returned to power. A time-honoured mantra in British politics has it that 'oppositions do not win elections – governments lose them'. In other words, there is comparatively little that the opposition party can do to control the situation, as it is limited to the internal arrangements of its leadership, organization, policies and general image. The Conservatives retained Baldwin as their leader after both defeats, despite grumbling and (in 1929–31) a rebellion against him. There were sound reasons for doing so: he was the best public communicator that they had and was able to project a moral appeal that no alternative leader could match, and so he had the widest appeal – especially to 'middle opinion', or former Liberal voters. As well as the advantage of incumbency, he also – whatever his failings – divided the Party least. What was more significant in both periods were changes in the composition of the front bench around Baldwin. In 1924, the debilitating rift caused by the overthrow of Lloyd George was healed, and a new unity achieved on the anti-coalitionists' terms. In 1929–31, there were signs of a change of generation at leadership level, with an 'old gang' (including the most prominent coalitionists, such as Churchill, Birkenhead and Austen Chamberlain, but some others as well) making way for those who had made their name not before 1914 but since 1922.[92]

Deficiencies in the party machine were not considered to have been a major factor in either defeat; in 1923 it performed well in difficult circumstances, and by 1929 the central and local organization had attained an unprecedented level of development and sophistication. There was comparatively little to do here, although Neville Chamberlain whilst Party Chairman in 1930–31 held a review of Central Office and made some minor changes.[93] What was vital were the changes in strategy, policy and public image. This almost entirely revolved around the issue that had separated the main parties in Britain since 1903: free trade versus protection. The 1923 defeat was mainly attributable to two self-imposed handicaps: the unpopular and vulnerable tariff policy, and the rushed election for which the Party was unprepared, thereby wasting the Conservatives' usual advantage of organizational superiority. The crucial difference was made in 1924 by shelving protection, and by the fact that the Party had time to prepare for the next election, as no one expected Labour to be in office for very long. Baldwin's 'New Conservatism' simply reinforced this, with its moderate tone and appealing content, as did the policies gathered together in the *Looking Ahead* programme. The position in 1929–31 was more complex, but here Baldwin succeeded in keeping the official policy on tariffs as closely aligned as possible with public opinion in the industrial marginals that had to be won back, even when this did not satisfy demands from the regions that contained most of the Party's safe seats. At the end of the parliament, it seems clear that the decision to act patriotically and appear to sacrifice party advantage by serving in the National Government was popular, with Party feeling and public attitudes synchronizing during the crisis.

During both oppositions, what the Conservatives did – and, perhaps still more, the dangers they avoided – helped to improve their position. When the Labour governments fell, the Conservatives were united, purposeful, possessed efficient organization, had attractive policies (moderate social measures in 1924, tariffs after the economic crisis in 1931), and followed an effective campaign strategy. Some of these things could be said for Labour in 1924, but none of them for the Liberals in either 1924 or 1931. At the end of the day, the governments did 'lose' the elections: they took place because the Labour governments were defeated (1924) or collapsed (1931), and they were fought largely on their record. However, in 1924 Labour was not thought to have performed badly, especially by its own supporters, and it was the Liberals who really lost. In 1929, Labour's failures in the key areas of unemployment and economic confidence were all too clear, and hence their heavy defeat.

Notes

1. J. Ramsden, *The Age of Balfour and Baldwin 1902–1940* (London: Longman, 1978), 183.
2. For the political developments of 1922–24, see C. Cook, *The Age of Alignment: Electoral Politics in Britain 1922–1929* (Basingstoke: Macmillan, 1975); M. Cowling, *The Impact of Labour 1920–1924: The Beginning of Modern British Politics* (Cambridge: Cambridge University Press, 1971).
3. Cook, *Age of Alignment*, 141–3.
4. Memo by Dawson, 20 Dec. 1923, Bodleian Library, Dawson MSS; Amery diary, 8 and 13 Dec. 1923, in J. Barnes and D. Nicholson (eds), *The Leo Amery Diaries, Volume 1: 1899–1929* (London: Hutchinson, 1980), 361–2 (hereafter *Amery Diaries*).
5. Derby to Birkenhead, 7 Dec. 1923, and Derby diary, 10 Dec. 1923, Liverpool Record Office, Derby MSS, 920/DER(17)/29/1.
6. Memo by Stamfordham (Private Secretary to King George V) of Baldwin's meeting with the King, 10 Dec. 1923, in R. Churchill, *Lord Derby: 'King of Lancashire'* (London: Heinemann, 1959), 552.
7. Derby diary, 11 Dec. 1924, Derby MSS, 920/DER(17)/29/1.
8. Memo by Balfour of conversation with the King on 9 Dec. 1923, written on 10 Dec. 1923, Scottish Record Office, Balfour (Whittingehame) MSS, in Cowling, *Impact of Labour*, 337.
9. Norton-Griffiths to Davidson, 12 Dec. 1923; Ormsby-Gore to Davidson, 9 Dec. 1923, Jackson to Davidson, 9 Dec. 1923, House of Lords Record Office, Davidson MSS, 168; Derby to Birkenhead, written but not sent, 11 Dec. 1923, Derby MSS, 920/DER(17)/29/1.
10. Bridgeman to Baldwin, 8 Dec. 1923, Cambridge University Library, Baldwin MSS, 35/173–4.
11. P. Williamson, *Stanley Baldwin: Conservative Leadership and National Values* (Cambridge: Cambridge University Press, 1999), 236–9; for an example of the alarmist vision of the conduct of a Labour government, see Birkenhead's views, relayed to the King's private secretary, Stamfordham memo, 10 Dec. 1923, in Churchill, *Derby*, 553.
12. Baldwin's remarks recorded by the Archbishop of Canterbury, Randall Davidson, who saw him on 12 Dec. 1923, memo by Davidson, written 12 Dec. 1923, in P. Williamson and E. Baldwin (eds), *Baldwin Papers: A Conservative Statesman 1908–1947* (Cambridge: Cambridge University Press, 2004), 137.
13. Bridgeman diary, Jan. 1924, in P. Williamson (ed.), *The Modernisation of Conservative Politics: The Diaries and Letters of William Bridgeman 1904–1935* (London: The Historians' Press, 1988), 175–6 (hereafter *Bridgeman Diaries*).

14. There remained some resistance to the return of Birkenhead, but this was swallowed as the price of securing complete and effective reunification: Salisbury to Baldwin, 26 Jan. 1924, Cecil to Baldwin, 1 Feb. 1924, Baldwin MSS, 159/258–61, 35/203–7; Neville to Hilda Chamberlain, 24 Jan. 1924, to Ida Chamberlain, 30 Jan. 1924, in R. Self (ed.), *The Neville Chamberlain Diary Letters: Volume 2, The Reform Years 1921–1927* (Aldershot: Ashgate, 2002), 204, 206 (hereafter *NCDL Vol. 2*).

15. Memo by Austen Chamberlain of meeting with Baldwin on 5 Feb. 1924, written on 7 Feb. 1924, Birmingham University Library, Austen Chamberlain MSS, AC 35/4/35; Derby diary, 7 Feb. 1924, Derby MSS, 920/DER(17)/29/1.

16. The only clear advocate of keeping the protectionist policy was Amery; he was supported by Neville Chamberlain and, less definitely, by Bridgeman: Amery diary, 7 Feb. 1924, *Amery Diaries*, 367–9.

17. In one example of the change in opinion, Wakefield Conservative Association (hereafter CA) made critical comment on the tariff policy in November 1923, but in February 1924 passed a resolution approving Baldwin's re-election as leader and promising him continued support: Wakefield CA, Exec. Ctte., 8 Nov. 1923, Council, 11 Feb. 1924, Wakefield CA office.

18. *Morning Post*, 11 Feb. 1924; Derby to Salvidge, 19 Jan. 1924, to Woodhouse, 29 Jan. 1924, Derby MSS, 920/DER(17)/17/2, 920/DER(17)/20/4.

19. Derby to Lord Stanley, 10 Jan. 1924, and Derby diary, 23 Jan. 1924, Derby MSS, 920/DER(17)/29/1, 920/DER(17)/39; Amery diary, 7 Feb. 1924, *Amery Diaries*, 367.

20. Ramsden, *Balfour and Baldwin*, 190, 207–15.

21. That Austen Chamberlain and Birkenhead would support Baldwin's re-election as leader was known by mid-January: Derby to Salvidge, 19 Jan. 1924, Derby MSS, 920/DER(17)/17/2.

22. Derby to Birkenhead, 19 Feb. 1924, Derby MSS, 920/DER(17)/33.

23. Baldwin to Joan Davidson, 20 Mar. 1924, *Baldwin Papers*, 146–7; see correspondence in Baldwin MSS, 51/60–79.

24. There were mixed feelings about Churchill still, but his return was welcomed in some quarters; see Uxbridge CA, Central Council, 27 Sep. 1924, Uxbridge CA office.

25. Bradford South CA, Joint Exec. Ctte., 3 July 1924, Bradford Central Library; Wells CA, Finance Ctte., 25 June 1924, Wells CA office.

26. Neville to Ida Chamberlain, 16 Feb. 1924, *NCDL Vol. 2*, 208.

27. It was particularly desired to avoid a dissolution over the issue of the boundary between the Irish Free State and Northern Ireland, which was soon to come before Parliament: Derby to Baldwin, 4 Sep. 1924, Derby MSS, 920/DER(17)/33.

28. Bridgeman diary, general entry '1924', *Bridgeman Diaries*, 177.

29. Neville to Ida Chamberlain, 7 June 1924, *NCDL Vol. 2*, 228; D. Dilks, *Neville Chamberlain: Volume 1, 1869–1929* (Cambridge: Cambridge University Press, 1984), 376–8.

30. Davidson to Hoare, 28 Dec. 1923, Davidson MSS, 169.

31. P. Norton, 'The parliamentary party and party committees', in A. Seldon and S. Ball (eds), *Conservative Century: The Conservative Party since 1900* (Oxford: Oxford University Press, 1994), 113.

32. S. Ball, 'The 1922 Committee: the formative years 1922–45', *Parliamentary History*, 9, no. 1 (1990), 129–57.

33. National Union Exec. Ctte., 29 Jan. 1924, Bodleian Library, Conservative Party Archive (CPA), NUA/4/1/4.

34. Headlam diary, 15 and 25 Feb. 1924, in S. Ball (ed.), *Parliament and Politics in the Age of Baldwin and MacDonald: The Headlam Diaries 1923–1935* (London: The Historians' Press, 1992), 38–9.

35. Ramsden, *Balfour and Baldwin*, 197. In one example, membership increased from 791 in May 1923 to 1792 by 31 Aug. 1924: Kincardine and West Aberdeenshire CA, Organization Ctte., 19 Sep. 1924, Kincardine and Deeside CA office.

36. Davidson to Hall, 19 Dec. 1923, Davidson MSS, 155; Norwich CA, Report to A.G.M., 2 June 1924, Norfolk Record Office; Bradford South CA, Joint Exec. Ctte., 8 Apr. 1924, Bradford Central Library.

37. Woodhouse to Derby, 9 Oct. 1924, Derby MSS, 920/DER(17)/20/2; Baldwin to his mother, 12 Oct. 1924, and comments to Lord Stamfordham, Memo by Stamfordham, 21 Oct. 1924, *Baldwin Papers*, 160–1.

38. Gwynne to Baldwin, 30 Oct. 1924, Baldwin MSS 36/26.

39. Keighley CA, Annual Report, 1924, Leeds Record Office. There was still support for a protectionist policy in agricultural areas: Lincoln CA, Exec. Ctte., 26 Sep.1924, Lincoln CA office.

40. Memo by Stamfordham, 2 June 1929, Windsor Castle, Royal Archives, RA.K.2223/30; Headlam diary, 5 and 6 June 1929.

41. Headlam diary, 10 Feb. 1928, 7 and 31 May 1929; Peterborough CA, Exec., 8 June 1929, Peterborough CA office; Accrington CA, AGM, 11 June 1929, Manchester University Library.

42. For a full account of the Conservative Party in this period, see S. Ball, *Baldwin and the Conservative Party: The Crisis of 1929–1931* (New Haven and London: Yale University Press, 1988).

43. For a typical view from the Party centre: Headlam diary, 3 July 1928.

44. Beaverbrook to Derby, 7 Mar. 1930, Derby MSS, 920/DER(17)/33; Hilton Young to his wife, 1 Mar. 1930, Cambridge University Library, Kennet MSS, 107/3.

45. Gwynne to Baldwin, 21 Feb. 1930, Bodleian Library, Gwynne MSS, 15.

46. Baldwin's comment to Sir Basil Peto, recorded in his wife's diary, 5 February 1930, Peto MSS (courtesy of Mr J. Peto, Woodbridge, Suffolk).

47. Baldwin to Ferguson, 23 July 1929, Baldwin MSS, 36/268–9.

48. Neville to Ida Chamberlain, 22 Oct. 1929, in R. Self (ed.), *The Neville Chamberlain Diary Letters: Volume 3, The Heir-Apparent 1928–1933* (Aldershot: Ashgate, 2002), 159 (hereafter *NCDL Vol. 3*); Kent Provincial Division, AGM, 15 Oct. 1929, copy in Hatfield House, Salisbury MSS, S(4)131/107.

49. Salisbury's memo of conversation with Baldwin, 28 Jan. 1930, Salisbury MSS, S(4)133/67–71.

50. See data on Empire Crusade membership figures in Ball, *Baldwin and the Conservative Party*, appendix 2, 222–3.

51. Beaverbrook to Baldwin (via Horne), 3–4 March 1930, Baldwin MSS 57/25–26; 'Lord Elibank's "Empire Free Trade" diary', Nov. 1929–May 1930, Scottish Record Office, Elibank MSS, SRO/GD/32/25/74, ff.15, 20–21.

52. Neville to Hilda Chamberlain, 25 May and 21 June 1930, *NCDL Vol. 3*, 185, 191.

53. Beaverbrook to Hoare, 15 May 1930, Cambridge University Library, Templewood MSS, VI/I; Beaverbrook to Croft, 19 May 1930, Beaverbrook MSS, C/101; Elibank diary, f.55.
54. Smithers to Salisbury, 19 Aug, 1930, Salisbury MSS, S(4)136/148.
55. Headlam diary, 24 June 1930.
56. Butler to his father, 11–14 July 1930, Trinity College, Cambridge, Butler MSS, D48/744–754.
57. Hoare to Neville Chamberlain, 8 Oct. 1930, Templewood MSS, VI/I.; Croft to Neville Chamberlain, 4 Oct. 1930, Churchill College Archives Centre, Croft MSS, 1/7/Ch34; Ormsby-Gore to Salisbury, 5 Oct. 1930, Salisbury MSS, S(4)137/44–45.
58. Bridgeman to Neville Chamberlain, 16 Oct. 1930, and Neville Chamberlain to Bridgeman, 18 Oct. 1930, Shropshire Record Office, Bridgeman MSS, SRO 3389/103 and 104.
59. Hoare to Irwin, 13 Nov. 1929, India Office Library, Halifax MSS, EUR.C. 152/18/1/298; Davidson to Irwin, 9 Nov. 1929, Davidson MSS, 188; Dawson to Irwin, 31 Oct. 1929, Dawson MSS.
60. Austen to Ivy Chamberlain, 2 Feb. 1931, Austen Chamberlain MSS, AC 6/1/785; Lady Peto diary, 24 Feb. and 6 Mar. 1931.
61. Austen to Ida Chamberlain, 28 Feb. 1931, Austen Chamberlain MSS, AC 5/1/532; Ball, *Baldwin and the Conservative Party*, 134–5.
62. Ball, *Baldwin and the Conservative Party*, 140–2.
63. Memo, Topping to Neville Chamberlain, 25 Feb. 1931, Baldwin MSS, 166/50–53.
64. Dawson diary, 1 Mar. 1931, Dawson MSS; Bridgeman diary, 28 Feb. and 1 Mar. 1931, *Bridgeman Diaries*, 243–4; Jones diary, 11 Mar. 1931, T. Jones, *A Diary With Letters 1931–1950* (London: Oxford University Press, 1954), 4–5; Ball, *Baldwin and the Conservative Party*, 137–9.
65. Amery diary, 5 Mar. 1931, in J. Barnes and D. Nicholson (eds), *The Empire at Bay: The Leo Amery Diaries, Volume 2: 1929–1945* (London: Hutchinson, 1988), 151 (hereafter *Empire at Bay*); Dawson diary, 12 Mar. 1931, Dawson MSS; Freemantle to Salisbury, 14 Mar. 1931, Salisbury MSS, S(4)140/20–21.
66. Neville Chamberlain diary, 25–31 Mar. 1931, Birmingham University Library, Neville Chamberlain MSS, NC 2/22.
67. Neville to Hilda Chamberlain, 28 Mar. 1931, *NCDL Vol. 3*, 250; Amery diary, 26 Mar. 1931, *Empire at Bay*, 158.
68. Moore to Neville Chamberlain, 31 Mar. 1931, Neville Chamberlain MSS, NC 7/11/24/24.
69. Bristol West CA, A.G.M., 20 Mar. 1931, Bristol Record Office.
70. Ball, *Baldwin and the Conservative Party*, 154–9; Baldwin at Glasgow, *The Times*, 13 Dec. 1930.
71. National Union Exec. Ctte., 19 Feb., 12 May, 16 June 1931, CPA, NUA/4/1/5; Conservative Parliamentary Party, India Ctte., *The Times*, 23 June 1931; Halifax CA, Exec., 12 Jan 1931, Halifax CA office; Dorset West CA, Exec., 30 Jan. 1931, Dorset Record Office.
72. Neville to Hilda Chamberlain, 2 May 1931, *NCDL Vol. 3*, 256–7; Hannon to Beaverbrook, 10 June 1931, House of Lords Record Office, Hannon MSS, 18/3.

73. White to Derby, 6 Feb. 1931, Derby MSS, 920/DER(17)6/33; Ipswich CA, AGM, 13 Mar. 1931, Suffolk Record Office; Reigate CA, AGM, 18 Mar. 1931, Surrey Record Office.

74. For the Conservative Party in the 1931 crisis, see Ball, *Baldwin and the Conservative Party*, ch. 9; for the crisis generally see P. Williamson, *National Crisis and National Government: British Politics, the Economy and Empire 1926–1932* (Cambridge: Cambridge University Press, 1992); A. Thorpe, *The British General Election of 1931* (Oxford: Oxford University Press, 1991).

75. Comments of Bank of England officials at a meeting with Neville Chamberlain and Hoare on 20 Aug. 1931, Neville Chamberlain diary, 22 Aug. 1931, see also Neville to Anne Chamberlain, 21 Aug, 1931, Neville Chamberlain MSS, NC 2/22, 1/26/446.

76. Neville to Anne Chamberlain, 3.00 p.m., 23 Aug. 1931, Neville Chamberlain MSS, NC/1/26/447.

77. Neville to Ida Chamberlain, 23 Aug. 1931, *NCDL Vol. 3*, 275–6; the news that the Cabinet disagreed and could not continue arrived whilst Chamberlain was writing this letter.

78. Memo by Dawson, 'Events of Sunday 23 August', 24 Aug. 1931, Dawson MSS; Baldwin to Lucy Baldwin, 23 and 24 Aug. 1931, *Baldwin Papers*, 265–6, 268; Butler to his father, 28 Aug. 1931, Butler MSS, D48/873.

79. Memo by Wigram, 'Memorandum of events surrounding the formation of the National Government, 22–24 August 1931', 27 Aug. 1931, Royal Archives, RA.GV.K.2330(2)/1.

80. See summary of shadow cabinet discussion: Steel-Maitland to Baldwin, 28 July 1931, Scottish Record Office, Steel-Maitland MSS, SRO GD193/94/2/179–81; Neville Chamberlain diary, 6 July 1931, Neville Chamberlain MSS, NC 2/22.

81. Ball, *Baldwin and the Conservative Party*, 172–86.

82. Austen to Ivy Chamberlain, 3:00 pm, 24 Aug. 1931, Austen Chamberlain MSS, AC 6/1/800.

83. Neville Chamberlain diary, 23 Aug. 1931, Neville Chamberlain MSS, NC 2/22; Cunliffe-Lister to his wife, 24 Aug. 1931, Churchill College Archives Centre, Swinton MSS, III(313)/1/5; Austen to Ivy Chamberlain, 24 Aug. 1931, Austen Chamberlain MSS, AC 6/1/800; Bridgeman to Baldwin, 16 Aug. 1931, Baldwin MSS, 44/35–38.

84. Memo by Hankey, 'Note of Events during the week ended Saturday October 3rd', and Hankey diary, 25 Sep.–6 Oct. 1931, Churchill College Archives Centre, Hankey MSS; Lord Sankey diary, 5 Oct. 1931, Bodleian Library, Sankey MSS.

85. Williamson, *National Crisis*, 528–30; D.J. Wrench, 'Cashing in: the parties and the National Government, August 1931 to September 1932', *Journal of British Studies*, 23 (1984), 152–3.

86. 'England does not love Coalitions' was the famous concluding phrase of Disraeli's defence of his first budget on 16 Dec. 1852: R. Blake, *Disraeli* (London: Eyre and Spottiswoode, 1966), 345.

87. P.A. Bromhead, *The House of Lords and Contemporary Politics 1911–1957* (London: Routledge and Kegan Paul, 1958), 151–6.

88. Davidson most of all, but he was far from alone in this; for a backbench and junior ministerial example of such suspicions, see Headlam diary, 8 Jan. 1924, 23 July 1925, 18 July 1928, 3 June 1930.
89. Cook, *Age of Alignment*, 121–2, 136–9.
90. Amery diary, 2 Mar. 1931, *Empire at Bay*, 151.
91. S. Ball, 'Failure of an opposition? The Conservative Party in Parliament 1929–1931', *Parliamentary History*, 5 (1986), 85–6, 95.
92. Ball, *Baldwin and the Conservative Party*, 159–61, 189.
93. 'Report of the Committee appointed by the Chairman of the Party to enquire into the working of the Central Office', 9 Mar. 1931, CPA, CCO/500/1/5.

8
The New Conservatism? 1945–1951

David Willetts

Reactions to defeat

> Bedevilled by years of pseudo-Conservatism, shaken in morale by the
> intellectual superiority which they had allowed the Labour Party to
> assume, ashamed of many of the things they believed in their hearts,
> the Conservatives lacked a doctrine. It was fatal that they should have
> lacked a method too.[1]

This was one observer's explanation of the Conservative Party's massive
defeat in July 1945, after the end of the Second World War in Europe.
They had dominated British politics since the fall of Lloyd George in
1922, but polled 9.4 million votes (41.5 per cent of those cast) to the
Labour Party's 11.7 million votes (49 per cent of the poll), and were
reduced from 358 seats to only 214 in the new House of Commons. Three
crucial publications captured the way in which the world had moved
against Conservatives. First, there was the belief that Conservatives
were the 'Guilty Men', the famous title of the 1940 book co-authored
by Michael Foot and others.[2] The Conservatives were held responsible
for pre-war depression and for appeasement. The most lurid caricature
was painted of the Conservatives' record in government and there was
little that they appeared to be able to do to escape from it. Secondly,
it was argued that these mistakes were not just accidental – it was
because Conservatives only represented the narrow self-interest of the
affluent. 'Simon Haxey' (a pseudonym) produced a book in 1939, *Tory
MP*, published for the Left Book Club, which argued that Baldwinism,
corporatism and reluctance to confront Hitler were directly related to

the conspicuous commercial interests and property-holdings across the Empire of many Tories.[3] Thirdly, there was the Beveridge Report of 1942, which set out an agenda for domestic reconstruction. It was massively popular and had been wholeheartedly endorsed by Labour, but many Conservatives were very wary of it. So the Conservatives were faced with a critique of their record, an attack on them for sleaze, and a shift in the political agenda to which they had no clear response.

The Conservatives identified two main reasons for their defeat: organizational weakness and a policy vacuum. Blaming organizational weakness tied in with the Conservatives' picture of themselves as the patriotic party. They had allowed their organization to decay during the war, while Labour had been busy campaigning. Ralph Assheton, the Party Chairman from 1944 to 1946, made the point very clearly: 'The Party could not make up in a few months for its six years of neglect of its organization and propaganda. We need not be ashamed of that neglect. Our Party went to the war.'[4] There was undoubtedly something in this argument, though it can be exaggerated. In 1943 Winston Churchill had made a direct appeal to the Party to keep local associations going 'in the national interest', but it did not happen. Meanwhile, the trade unions and the Labour Party had organized better. Conservatives believed that the left-influenced Army Bureau of Current Affairs had turned many of the troops 'pansy pink', and certainly the votes returned from the forces overseas ran 9 to 1 in favour of Labour. The Conservative Party was so used to possessing organizational superiority that the very thought that Labour had overtaken them in this respect seemed like a reversal of the natural order.

The Conservative Party had also lost the battle of ideas. R.A. ('Rab') Butler in particular recognized that Labour had won a propaganda victory. This was evident from comparing the stilted Conservative manifesto, *Mr Churchill's Declaration of Policy to the Electors*, with Labour's manifesto, *Let us Face the Future*. The Conservatives had been on the intellectual defensive ever since the publication of the Beveridge Report in November 1942. According to by-elections and the opinion surveys of the time, it was in that year that the Labour Party gained the lead. Churchill had set up a Post-War Problems Committee under the chairmanship of Butler and David Maxwell-Fyfe as early as July 1941. However, he steadfastly refused to give his imprimatur to any of the thoughts emerging from the Committee, because he wanted to focus exclusively on the war effort. It was thus very much like the Unionist Social Reform Committee after 1910 – experts having interesting ideas, but lacking a political strategy.

By 1945 the Party was facing a hostile intellectual climate with a weak organization and a feeble and uncertain policy agenda of its own. Yet between 1945 and 1951 the Conservative Party gained 3.7 million votes, and went on to hold office for 13 years. It was an extraordinary political revival. The seeds of the recovery are to be found in one of the most notorious incidents of the 1945 election campaign. In his first party political broadcast, Churchill had warned 'There can be no doubt that Socialism is inseparably interwoven with Totalitarianism and the abject worship of the state.'[5] He went on to claim that a Labour government would need the powers of a 'Gestapo' to implement its programme. This claim originated in the extraordinary influence on the Party leaders of F.A. Hayek's *The Road to Serfdom*, published in 1944. It is a passionate warning of the perils of collectivism and traces the links between national Socialism and Soviet Communism. (Churchill had wanted to warn of a Soviet NKVD in his speech, but decided not to because of the alliance with Soviet Russia.) The book had an immediate impact on many Conservatives. Central Office sacrificed 1.5 tons of their precious paper ration for the 1945 general election so that abridged copies could be printed as campaign literature. Churchill's speech may have damaged the Conservative campaign, by confirming to many voters how out of touch Conservatives were. But the story of the next six years is how the Conservatives learned to express their fears about collectivism in a way which chimed in with the voters' experiences and won their support.

The seeds of recovery

There was serious disagreement in the Party about how far to take their anti-collectivist approach. Many of the groups which embody intellectual tensions within Conservatism up to this day can trace their roots back to this period: both the Tory Reform Group on the left and the Progress Trust on the right were formed around this time. Assheton, the Party Chairman from 1944 to 1946, was on the right. An entry in Anthony Eden's diary records a row with Assheton in front of Churchill about whether right- or left-wing candidates were to have the pick of forthcoming by-elections:

> Told A[ssheton] in front of W[inston] that if he and his friends continued to regard our Party as close corporation for extreme right it had no future. This treatment was typical. Remained glowering all the evening, thought it necessary.[6]

Part of the newness of this New Conservatism was the emergence of right versus left disputes which are recognizable to this day. But the achievement of the leadership was to fashion from this a synthesis which was credible, endorsed by the vast bulk of the Party, and attractive to the electorate.

The Party's first steps after the landslide defeat of July 1945 were not promising. It was not sure how to respond to Labour, especially given Labour's enormous post-election popularity. The Conservatives' first approach was therefore to claim that Labour was simply carrying on with the ideas which had been developed in the wartime Coalition government. In his first speech in opposition, Churchill argued: 'Here and there, there may be differences in emphasis in view, but in the main no Parliament has ever assembled with such a mass of agreed legislation.'[7] But this line of argument left Conservatives with no distinctive voice, and intense parliamentary conflict over the government's policies soon replaced it.

The Party also tried to correct what was seen as Labour's unfair caricature of the Conservative record. Shadow ministers were frustrated that the popular conception of the 1930s was of mass unemployment in Jarrow, not of economic expansion in towns such as Coventry and Oxford. Central Office put out publications with titles such as *Labour's Lies about the 1930s*, tackling head-on what they saw as Labour's dangerous mythology, but there was no interest in the Conservative Party fighting what were seen as hopeless historical battles. After two years, the Party gave up trying to persuade people of the success of its previous record in office. Instead it shifted to the opposite approach – stressing how much it had changed, even if sometimes the change was deliberately exaggerated. Indeed the Party had looked at changing its name because its associations were so negative. Ideas were canvassed in *The Times* and *Daily Telegraph* in the autumn of 1945 with suggestions such as 'Conservative Democrats', 'Progressive Conservative', or 'National Democrats'. In July 1946, a group of Young Conservatives passed a resolution calling 'upon leaders of the Party to abandon the outworn title of Conservative and suggest that on the bridge of Unionism the conflicting armies of liberty may join forces'. Churchill went on to urge Lord Woolton, Party Chairman from 1946, to look at the idea of changing the name to the Union Party. Harold Macmillan wanted it to be called the New Democratic Party. Assheton, the outgoing Chairman, wanted it to become simply the Unionist Party. Woolton is frank about this in his own memoirs, discussing the various options for the new name for the Party:

Large numbers of Conservatives were trying to find a new name for the party because 'conserving' seemed to be out of joint with this new world that was demanding adventure and expansion and a rejection of the economic restraints of the pre-war life of this country under a Conservative administration ... The word 'Conservative' was certainly not a political asset when compared with the Socialist word 'Labour' ... I would have liked to call the Conservative Party the 'Union Party'.[8]

The idea of changing the Party's name now seems absurd. The obvious interpretation of this idea is defeatism. But changing the name was to have been part of a wider strategy, of which both Beveridge and Churchill were leading exponents, of creating a new 'united front against Socialism'. They thought that the advantage of the Unionist name was that it both suggested this union between different groups as well as harking back to the old Tory belief in Unionism.

A new structure was set in place for the Party to conduct its large-scale policy review. Four institutions were crucial. The Post-War Problems Committee, established by the wartime coalition in 1941, was succeeded in 1946 by the Advisory Committee on Policy and Political Education (ACPPE), which was chaired by Butler. The Conservative Research Department was revived, and also headed by Butler. A new parliamentary Secretariat was created, specifically aimed at helping front-benchers and servicing parliamentary groups and committees. Finally, a new Conservative Political Centre had been established in December 1945, again under Butler, to deal with political education and consultation on policy with the Party membership. This body was responsible for the 'Two-Way Movement of Ideas'. Stuart Ball claims 'this innovation greatly improved communication within the Party'.[9] This structure gained coherence and consistency through Butler's role in chairing all three of the crucial bodies that were working on the policy review.

Butler describes in his memoirs how he was consciously trying to learn from Labour's propaganda success in the run-up to 1945. He recognized that:

Socialism provided [the electors] with a vision and a doctrine to which we had no authoritative answer or articulated alternative. Herbert Morrison knew this and had taken advantage of his position on the home front to roll out pamphlets and speeches which gave a very firm impression of leading to the left. He recorded in his autobiography that I carefully examined what he had done for the Labour Party prior to and during the 1945 election and told my staff that I wanted to do the same for the Conservative Party. This information was correct. Surveying the wreckage in the summer of 1945, which I had been almost alone in predicting, I resolved to do whatever lay within my power to ensure that we did not go into another election with the propaganda victory already lost.[10]

Butler's role in renewing policy was matched by Woolton's in renewing the Party's organization. Lord Woolton was appointed as Chairman of the Party on 1 July 1946, taking up his post shortly before the party conference of October 1946, the first since the end of the war. This saw expressions of the deep unhappiness of party members at the state of the Party. Between them, Woolton and Butler played a crucial role in helping the Party to recover from defeat. We will look at Woolton's renewal of organization and Butler's renewal of policy in turn.

Reforming the party organization

Lord Woolton described the situation a year after the Party's defeat as follows:

> We had our backs to the wall: we had been heavily defeated: we had very little money: the Party was depressed. The political Press of the country was largely staffed, on its reporting sides, by members of the Labour Party, and everywhere there was a slant towards Socialism and a disbelief that in the new post-war world this old Conservative Party could ever govern the country again.[11]

Woolton was an unusual figure to appoint as Party Chairman. Born as Frederick Marquis in 1883, his previous career was in retailing. He had made his reputation at Lewis's, where he had coined the slogan 'Lewis's brings prices down', becoming managing director and then chairman of the company. He was created Baron Woolton in 1939, and served as Minister of Food from 1940 to 1943, becoming a popular figure with the nickname 'Uncle Fred'. In that post and as Minister of Reconstruction in 1943–45 he had no party affiliation, and only joined the Conservative Party on the day after its election defeat, motivated by his gratitude to Churchill and his opposition to nationalization. His appointment was widely welcomed: as a constituency association delegate remarked at the 1946 party conference, 'We are so grateful we have someone who has qualifications other than that he is a well-informed gentleman of outstanding respectability.'[12]

When Woolton arrived at his desk in Central Office in September 1946 he found a wise note left by Stephen Pierssene, himself newly appointed as Principal Agent, reminding him that the Conservative Party was:

not a chain of multiple stores, but an association of voluntary and independent bodies with an intense dislike of domination from the centre. The strength of this structure is derived not from methods or systems, nor from any driving force from above, but from personal relationships built on goodwill.[13]

Given Woolton's background, he was tempted to go for a radical change in the structure of the Party. He commissioned a report which criticized the divisions between the 'trichotomy' of professionals in Central Office, the voluntary Party and the parliamentary Party. One option was to bring all of these different parts of the organization under one governing body, with democratic input from the members. However, on reflection Woolton decided instead upon a different approach: 'I soon found that the primary need of the whole of the Conservative Party, but in particular of the Central Office, was that it should believe in itself, and in its capacity to convert the electorate to Conservatism.'[14] The best way to deliver this renewal was through modernizing media management and polling, reviving Party membership, and reforming Party funding. Woolton observed: 'In my business life I had extensive experience of the use of advertising. I decided to apply that experience to selling the Conservative policy in Britain.'[15] He instituted regional press officers, so that local newspapers could be briefed as well as the national press. John Profumo was recruited to train politicians for television performances. Central Office staffing rose above 200 in 1947, and the expenditure reached that of the 1920s in real terms. From the late 1940s, sophisticated private polling techniques were used on key regional areas and social groups, including floating voters and Liberal voters (who shared many of the same characteristics).

Party membership had fallen below 1 million when Woolton launched his first membership drive in the autumn of 1946. This was not very well organized, but still managed to put on about 250,000 new members. However, it was the second membership drive, launched at the 1947 party conference, which really saw membership rise significantly. By April 1948, party membership had increased by 1 million, and it was to rise further to a peak of 2.8 million by 1952. Most of the recruits came from the middle classes, particularly women. Woolton also tried to bring younger people in to the Party. Leo Amery had noted uncomfortably in his diary on election day in 1945: 'Most of the [Conservative] committee rooms were "manned" by dear old ladies of 80 or thereabouts and I don't think I saw a man anywhere except at the three main ones.'[16] Woolton gave a high priority to bringing younger people into the Party, and the Young Conservatives were established in July 1946, replacing the pre-war Junior Imperial League as the party's organization for youth and young adults. Over a thousand 'YC' branches had been formed by January 1947, and 40 Young Conservatives were to stand as parliamentary candidates in 1950. The organization became an important part of British social life in the post-war era; in Tony Hancock's famous radio programme 'The Blood Donor' a few years later, his reason for giving blood is that he wants to do something for his country but would not join the Young Conservatives as he did not yet want to get married and could not play table-tennis.[17]

Woolton's political insight was that a mass membership for the Conservative Party could counteract the influence of the trades unions on the factory floor. In his memoirs, he commented that there was no better polling day machine for Labour than a shop steward coming out onto the factory floor and commanding 'Come on boys: vote the ticket'.[18] Woolton's response was for the Conservative Party to mobilize the middle classes. The elections of 1950 and 1951 were the most class-partisan elections in British electoral history. The Conservatives' real gains were not amongst working-class men but amongst middle-class voters and women. Although the Conservative share never fell below about a third, the working-class male vote remained stubbornly Labour in 1950 and 1951.

At the same time as boosting membership, Woolton also needed to boost the Party's finances. The position which he inherited was dire. However, he did not significantly cut spending. Instead, he lived dangerously and reckoned that political activity by the Party, even if very expensive, would eventually generate funds from the membership. In April 1947 expenditure was running at four times income, but gradually the income began to expand. Woolton understood that he could use money-raising as a positive device to help change the image of the Party: By asking for money from as broad a range of people as possible, he would solve two problems at once – both bringing in the funds and changing the image of the Party. So, when he launched his financial appeal at the 1947 Party conference, he said:

> I want the support of every section of society – a broad democratic response from people who are prepared, according to their means, to

pay for their political beliefs ... Everyone thinks of us as a rich party, and our opponents always try to make out that we are a rich man's party. Neither is true ... In the past the Party has been shy of asking for money, and it has collected for its central fund from a few hundred people. Well, it is not so easy to do that now – and I do not want to do it.[19]

The issues of financing the Party and the selection of candidates were closely linked. For many associations, what Quintin Hogg had described in 1943 as 'the virtual sale of safe seats' had become a method of financing themselves as well as selecting candidates. Hogg described the system as 'a festering sore in the Conservative Party for years. At conference after conference the system has been pilloried and condemned, but, although the bottom has dropped out of the market since the war, no radical reform has been attempted.'[20] All this changed after the report of the committee chaired by David Maxwell-Fyfe, which was approved at the Central Council meeting of March 1949. Constituencies were to cease selecting their candidates on the basis of their capacity to meet their election expenses and make extra donations to the local party. This would both broaden the social range of candidates, and force local associations to become more active and seek subscriptions from the mass of electors. Woolton noted in his memoirs that 'the organization of the Party was weakest in those places where a wealthy candidate had made it unnecessary for the members to trouble to collect small subscriptions'.[21] In areas where expenditure continued to be financed from grandees, such as Liverpool, the Party was to collapse in the 1960s. Instead, local parties were to finance themselves out of their own membership, and to pass on part of this to help fund the Central Office through a quota scheme that was based upon the size of the Conservative vote in the constituency. This removed the stigma of Central Office being funded by vested interests, and the Party got a broader financial base and a new breed of candidates chosen by more meritocratic procedures.

Woolton described the end of the sale of safe seats as 'revolutionary' and added that it 'did more than any single factor to save the Conservative Party'.[22] The Party lost no opportunity to present the Maxwell-Fyfe reforms as changing both its financial base and its methods for selecting candidates. It recognized that changing the image of the Party meant more than simply changing its policies. Its composition and character must also change. The 1945 election had already seen a significant shift in the composition of the parliamentary Party. One MP who lost his seat, Walter Elliot said that 'the century of domination by the industrial north is over. We have now to reckon with the rule of the Home Counties.'[23] The Party's final abandonment of protectionism and shift to a greater stress on the free market than at any point in the previous 50 years partly reflected the change of its composition to being a party of south-eastern commerce as against northern industry. Iain Macleod, at this time one of the 'backroom boys' working in the Conservative Research Department, had no doubt of the significance of the Maxwell-Fyfe changes in terms of the composition of the parliamentary Party: 'I have always thought that this had a profound effect on the changed image of the Tory Party ... Maxwell-Fyfe ranked with Woolton and Butler as the architects of the post-war change.'[24]

Together, Woolton's initiatives and the Maxwell-Fyfe Report's reforms transformed the Party machine from the shrunken and enfeebled entity of 1945. Although it is tempting to see these developments as a completely new beginning for the Party, in reality much of it was renewing and restoring what had been a very successful party organization in Baldwin's time. The Party had been at the forefront of using media in the 1920s. The Young Conservatives were in many ways the successors of the inter-war Junior Imperial League. Some of the genuine innovations, such as creating a candidates' list, had been around as ideas for some time. As always with Conservatives, the origins of some of the boldest innovations can be traced far back into history.

Intellectual renewal: the *Industrial Charter* and beyond

In October 1946 the Party conference met for the first time since the election defeat. The Party activists were frustrated and unhappy. Although Churchill had agreed to the new structure for the policy review, he was still opposed to any fresh statements of Conservative philosophy or principle, let alone any policies or programme. It was pressure from the activists at the Party conference which forced him to act. Contrary to the plans of the Party managers, the following resolution was debated and passed:

> That this Conference is of the opinion that the Conservative Party, in order to counter the misleading and insidious propaganda of the socialist party, should, without further delay, prepare and issue a statement, in a concise form easily understood by the electorate, setting forth the policy for which the Conservative Party stands and simultaneously a statement giving in fuller detail the principles and programme of the Party.[25]

It was not clear exactly what these principles should be, but Churchill now had to bow to the pressure to do something. He set up an Industrial Policy Committee to draft the policy statement that became known as the *Industrial Charter*. Again, Butler was to chair this body, and it was his personal role which ensured consistency and compatibility across the range of the Party's policy activities.

Butler intended that his Committee would produce a generalized document, a new Tamworth Manifesto, to show that the Party was aware of how much politics had moved on since 1939. It was to be a statement of political principles rather than a detailed policy document. The charter was published in May 1947 at a press conference chaired by Butler (having been deliberately leaked to *The Observer* and the *Sunday Express* on the previous day). It was promoted in speeches by Eden, Butler, and Harold Macmillan, and in Research Department and Central Office pamphlets. There was a lively political battle about the charter fought through the media during the summer, which helped to generate more interest. Churchill remained detached from the whole process, and had the charter received a hostile response it could easily have been abandoned before ever becoming official Party policy.

At the October 1947 conference the charter was accepted with only three dissenters, after opposition had been marginalized to a position of extremism. The charter had been managed to create a consensus at the highest levels of the Party and amongst the rank and file. According to Reginald Maudling's memoirs, Churchill read the proffered draft of the section of his conference speech endorsing the *Industrial Charter* 'with care and then said, "But I do not agree with a word of this". "Well, Sir",' Maudling replied, '"this is what the conference has adopted." "Oh well," he said, "leave it in".'[26] Churchill then included the paragraph in his speech at the end of the conference, thereby endorsing it. With this approval from the leader, the *Industrial Charter* was thereafter indisputably an authoritative statement of official Party policy.

The *Industrial Charter* was structured in three parts. First, it analysed what it called the present crisis in industry. This focused upon how measures might be taken to increase the productivity and output of the economy. It took a broadly monetarist explanation of the problem of inflation, talking of the need to 'keep the supply of cash and credit to the size which will match the supply of goods'. Its proposal is a delectable piece of political fudge: 'We should not reverse the cheap money policy but we should pursue it with restraint.' The second section of the charter was entitled 'The Place of government in a Free Society', and put a clear emphasis on personal freedom and deregulation. It argued that:

'The tendency to rely on controls – like the habit of forming a queue – has already gone too far and is sapping dangerously the independent character of the people.' Not only were controls too onerous, but taxes were too high as well:

> The plain fact is that there is a very definite limit to the proportions of his personal income that the citizen is prepared to allow the government to spend for him in normal times of peace. We believe that government expenditure at current levels, which the Socialist government appear to contemplate with equanimity, already exceeds this limit.

There is also an explicit recognition of the obligation of government to maintain employment (though with some caveats):

> But perhaps its greatest duty is to ensure that such main priorities as the maintenance of employment and our well-developed social services are fulfilled before subsidiary objectives are sought and that the tasks set are not beyond the capacity of the resources available.

This acceptance of an obligation to maintain employment is a significant endorsement of something like Keynesian responsibility for macroeconomic policy. Today we understand the perils of the Keynesian approach. But, as Robert Skidelsky has shown, the Keynesian recognition of the role of macro-economic policy was at this time the free market alternative to the traditional Fabian model of trying to deliver objectives such as high employment and price controls through direct micro-economic intervention. The battle lines between Conservative and Labour over the next generation were to be on precisely these micro-economic issues, where the *Industrial Charter* is unambiguously in favour of deregulation, denationalization, lower public spending, and lower taxes. In all these respects, it reads like a contemporary Conservative document. The third section of the charter explicitly made it clear that Conservatives were opposed to nationalization in principle, but accepted that there were practical constraints on what could be denationalized.

The criticism which began in the smoking rooms of the House of Commons as soon as the document was published, and which has carried on ever since, was that the policy was 'semi-Socialist'. Butler tackled this head-on in his memoirs, when he defended the Charter as follows:

> Our need [was] to convince a broad spectrum of the electorate, whose minds were scarred by inter-war memories and myths, that we had an

alternative policy to Socialism which was viable, efficient and humane, which would release and reward enterprise and initiative but without abandoning social justice or reverting to mass unemployment. Until the progressive features of our thought had been fully exposed to public view, no one (to adapt Charles II's epigrammatic cynicism) was going to kill Attlee in order to make Churchill king.[27]

The *Industrial Charter* had two objectives. The first was to destroy what Butler saw as a dangerous myth about Conservatism which had formed in the voters' minds because of their experience of pre-war recession and unemployment: 'Our first purpose was to counter the charge and the fear that we were the party of industrial go-as-you-please and devil-take-the-hindmost, that full employment and the Welfare State were not safe in our hands.'[28] But this was not the whole story, as there then had to be something to distinguish Conservatism from Socialism: 'Our second purpose was to present a recognizable alternative to the reigning orthodoxies of Socialism – not to put the clock back, but to reclaim a prominent role for individual initiative and private enterprise in the mixed and managed economy.'[29]

The *Industrial Charter* marks the definitive point at which the Conservative Party became the party of freedom and the free market. It established a key set of Conservative arguments which have been deployed ever since. It is nothing less than the recognizably modern political message of the Conservative Party. The *Industrial Charter* states that 'Socialists believe in giving people orders. Conservatives believe in giving people opportunities.' That remark could have appeared in a press release from Central Office today. By contrast, pre-war Conservatism had an undeniably historical feel to it, not least because of the Party's strong leanings towards protectionism and corporatism in that period. After 1945, the Party was on an intellectual trajectory towards much greater stress on personal freedom and opportunity. This was also the central message in three powerful and thoughtful books of Conservative philosophy which appeared during this period: Quintin Hogg's brilliant book, *The Case for Conservatism*; David Clarke's wise essay, *The Conservative Faith in a Modern Age*; and Richard Law's libertarian *Return from Utopia*.[30]

The *Industrial Charter* was the intellectual underpinning for Woolton's united front against Socialism. Now specific groups threatened by the Labour government could be identified, and their particular concerns addressed. There were appeals to industrialists threatened by nationalization, and there were further charters – for example, on Imperial policy, on agriculture, and on Scotland. But there was one group of far greater significance than all the others put together: women.

The politics of austerity: creating a united front against Socialism

By 1947, the Conservative Party was modernizing its organization and its policy framework, but opinion showed that voters were still deeply suspicious of the Conservatives. Research by Ina Zweiniger-Bargielowska has shown the stringent conditions within which housewives had to operate. The calorie intake of the middle classes fell from approximately 3275 kcals per day in 1932–35 to a low point of 2307 in 1947. For the working classes the figures also fell but from 2859 in 1932–35 to 2308 in 1947; they had achieved unparalleled equality, but at a very low level. Dr Zweiniger-Bargielowska quotes *Social Survey* data from April 1948 that 55 per cent of respondents felt they were not getting enough food to keep in good health, and 59 per cent thought they would be able to work harder on a better and more varied diet. In November 1947, a Gallup poll showed that 62 per cent preferred life before the war to the present, which also must have blunted Labour's attack on the Conservative record in the 1930s. It was indeed the age of austerity. In March 1949, 75 per cent still considered their present diet worse than it had been before the war.[31]

The increasingly arduous task of running a household fell mainly on women. This was the reason for the militancy of the British Housewives' League.[32] Conservative rhetoric on rationing and control was deliberately targeted at winning the support of female voters. They were the most obvious victims of Labour's policies, and would gain most from Conservative policies to dismantle government controls. As austerity carried on through the late 1940s and even intensified, so the arguments in the *Industrial Charter* about the evil of controls came to seem ever more telling, and the Conservative message was most directly experienced by women. Douglas Jay's remark, when a minister in the Attlee government, that the civil servant in Whitehall knows best is famous, but less familiar is the previous sentence which helped to give the remark so much of its political charge at the time: 'Housewives as a whole cannot be trusted to buy the right things ... The gentleman in Whitehall really does know better what is good for the people than the people themselves.'[33] It was women above all who were on the receiving end of the most intrusive and irritating of Labour's controls, notably the rationing of food and clothes. Labour's slogan during the 1945 election campaign had been to 'ask your Dad', and now the Conservatives responded that Labour had forgotten to 'ask their Mums'. Women voters were the most important part of a wider 'united front' against Socialism. The Hayekian message which had seemed overstated and absurd in 1945, achieved a resonance with voters because of their post-war experience of austerity, rationing, and controls. If Labour was the party of male producers, the Conservatives were the party of female consumers. It was in these formative years of Margaret Thatcher, who fought her first parliamentary contest at Dartford in 1950, that the Conservative Party first linked the housewife, the consumer and the market place in a coherent political strategy.

Another important group was businesses threatened by nationalization. The initial targets for nationalization – coal, rail, and electricity – had suffered from under-investment and often the owners wished to sell. However, other more prosperous and successful targets came within the government's sights. The Conservatives developed strong links with the sugar, cement, insurance, and iron and steel industries in particular, all of which feared that they would be next on the list for nationalization.

The Liberals were another target. Again, the argument was that Labour's demand economy Socialism was a threat to fundamental Liberal beliefs in free trade. For over 40 years the Conservative Party had flirted with protection and tariff reform. Now that it was moving back towards free trade, there was the basis for a new alliance with the Liberals. Woolton summarized it very simply in May 1947: 'Our object must be to combine with moderate Liberals wherever they are organized and to attract them individually where no organization exists.'[34] The merger of the National Liberals, the wing of the party led by Sir John Simon which had been allied with the Conservatives since 1931, was arranged in the Woolton-Teviot Agreement of May 1947. However, much to Churchill's regret, the Conservatives were unable to clinch a deal with the remaining independent Liberal Party; this had been part of his wartime coalition, but had withdrawn and fought the 1945 election as a separate party. The Conservatives saw the supporters of the Liberal Party as a crucial target group, as their analysis of the electorate showed that the floating voters whom they had to win over had characteristics which strongly suggested they were Liberals.

All this added up to a 'United Front against Socialism'. Resting on a solid core of argument, this had an intellectually coherent message and appealed to key electoral groups. However, it had not yet been tested electorally. Although the Conservatives had not been performing well in local elections, they did not yet face the problem in a parliamentary test, but this was about to change.

Philosophy or programme? From by-election to general election

The first two years after the landslide defeat in 1945 saw the Party perplexed, confused, and uncertain. The two years after that, from 1947 to 1949, saw three people above all – Butler, Woolton and Maxwell-Fyfe – put in place a strategy for Conservative recovery. Conservative philosophy and principles were expounded in a sophisticated and attractive way. The Party machine was thoroughly overhauled. Membership and finances were growing. The changes in the nature of the Party's candidates and membership were linked to the fresh statements of Conservative principles from its leading thinkers. It looked as if things were going the Conservatives' direction, and both Butler and Woolton were spoken of as future leaders of the Party.

There was however one crucial gap in this record of achievement: the Conservatives had not gained a single seat at a by-election since 1945. This was the reason why the by-election in the marginal seat of Hammersmith South, caused by the death of the sitting Labour MP in February 1949, mattered so much. The Conservatives had a new model candidate in Anthony Fell, and as Woolton observed to the latter's minder: 'It is most important that we should win this by-election, not only to sustain the morale of our own supporters, but also to demonstrate to our opponents the progress which Conservatism is making in the country.'[35] However, the Labour Party fought back vigorously. There were scares that Conservatives would reduce old-age pensions, abolish food subsidies or cut back social services, and Labour held the seat although with a slightly reduced majority. The *Daily Telegraph* leader the following morning criticized the Conservative Party as follows:

> When we consider [the defeat] in conjunction with the almost unbroken failure to win back a seat in three-and-a-half years we are forced back on some explanation of a general character and this is not far to seek. The Party has not succeeded in translating its policy and intentions into terms which are acceptable or even intelligible to large numbers of the electorate.[36]

The disappointing outcome provoked a brief crisis of confidence in the Conservative ranks, especially amongst MPs. The search for a culprit exacerbated long-standing tensions between Butler and Woolton: Woolton blamed Butler for failing to come up with more policy proposals, and Butler blamed Woolton for focusing Central Office on merely 'socialist bashing' rather than publicizing the policy ideas which the Conservative Research Department had already developed.

The debate sharpened the long-standing disagreement within the Party about how detailed a programme should be put before the electorate when in opposition. Butler recalls in his memoirs how he disagreed with Churchill about this:

> 'When an Opposition spells out its policy in detail,' he lectured me, 'the government becomes the Opposition and attacks the Opposition which becomes the government. So, having failed to win the sweets of office, it fails equally to enjoy the benefits of being out of office.' There is rather more truth and tactic in this than I was always happy to allow at the time.[37]

Lord Woolton also recorded his view in his memoirs:

> It is always dangerous in politics to be committed to detail in any programme. But I concluded that it was at least as dangerous to be so vague that the nation could think that the Conservatism that we were expounding would be no different from the Conservatism of the 'thirties. We therefore decided to take the risk of defining in terms the policies we would encourage the nation to undertake.[38]

After 1949, the pressure was to move to a more hard-edged and clear programme with stronger messages on the economy. Churchill himself may have been doubtful about this approach, as he was the most consistently sceptical of the value of a detailed programme. He observed: 'It is not so much a programme we require as a theme. We are concerned with a lighthouse not a shop window.'[39] Nevertheless, the Party leadership concluded that they needed to offer more to the electorate. The statements of principles were not enough, and there was a need to offer a fuller programme. The result was *The Right Road for Britain*, published in July 1949. This document was a significant shift to the right when it came to economics and industry. There was more stress on free enterprise and the market economy, as the Conservative contrast to Labour's centralized planning. But there was also a robust defence of the welfare state to counter-balance scares that Conservatives would dismantle it. This was the distinctive Conservative post-war mixture of free enterprise with a more explicit commitment to the welfare state. The Party had moved right on the economy but slightly left on social services.

The Right Road for Britain was to be the basis for the general election manifesto, *This is the Road*, published in January 1950 as a prelude to the election a month later. It is interesting to have an assessment of that manifesto from the youngest Conservative candidate who fought in that election:

> Very heavy public spending had kept the standard rate of income tax almost at wartime levels – nine shillings in the pound. Far from being dismantled, wartime controls had, if anything, been extended – for example rationing was extended to bread in 1946 and even potatoes a year later. It was therefore possible to fight the 1950 election campaign on precisely the kind of issues which are most dangerous for a sitting government – and ones with which I personally felt most at ease – that is, a combination of high ideological themes with more down to earth 'bread and butter' matters. ... The 1950 Conservative manifesto was a cleverly crafted document which combined a devastating indictment of socialism in theory and in practice with a prudent list of specific pledges to reverse it.[40]

That was Margaret Thatcher's assessment. Lord Woolton expected the Party to win the 1950 election, but it fell short by a small margin. Labour had an absolute majority of six in the House of Commons with 315 seats; the Conservatives had 298, the Liberals 9 and the Irish Republicans had 2. The expectation was that there would have to be another election in the near future. Conservative parliamentary opposition was now very effective indeed, but the Party still needed a vivid, populist policy to catch the public imagination.

Sharpening the ideological divide 1950–51

The Conservative Party's morale was boosted by the enormous advance it had made in 1950. In Parliament it now faced an exhausted government that was not believed to be likely to last a full term. Even so, it was not inevitable that the Conservatives would win the next election. This was to be secured by three crucial developments.

First, the Party finally got to grips with what many of the polls showed to be the social policy issue that the electorate were most worried about – housing. As early as April 1946, Churchill had shown his awareness of the issue in typical style: 'I know of no more cheering spectacle than the smoke from the chimney of a British cottage home.' He then went on to criticize the limits placed on private building by the Minister of Health,

Aneurin Bevan, as 'the pedantic, irrational enforcement of socialistic prejudice'.[41] We have already seen how the rationing and austerity of the post-war years hit the housewife and reduced living conditions to a much lower standard than before 1939. Housing was also suffering: slum clearance programmes were going slowly, bomb damage was not being dealt with, and the rate of new building was paltry. Harmar Nicholls, who had just been elected as Conservative MP for Peterborough in 1950, was worried that inadequate housing was putting families under too much pressure. The biggest barriers to constructing new housing were the heavy-handed controls imposed by the Labour government, together with the requirement that many of them be built not just for the public sector but by public sector direct labour organizations. Nicholls led a rebellion at the Party conference in October 1950 to commit the Party to the target of building 300,000 new houses a year. This successfully brought together several Conservative themes. It was a measure to help families, not through Socialism but by unleashing free enterprise from Labour control. And, although no one had the tactlessness to mention the point, it harked back to Baldwin's housing boom which had helped pull Britain out of depression in the 1930s. The pledge to build 300,000 houses a year formed a crucial part of the 1951 manifesto.

The second development was the growing sense of international crisis, as Stalin's behaviour became increasingly aggressive and war in Korea loomed. In the immediate post-war years many Conservative front-benchers had been exasperated with Churchill's long absences abroad. Some were even embarrassed by his speech at Fulton, Missouri, on 5 March 1946, which used the phrase 'Iron Curtain' to describe the consolidation of Soviet control in eastern Europe. Labour depicted Churchill as a war-monger, but his warnings increasingly looked prescient. There was an ideological battle being fought between the western democracies and Communism. Once more, Churchill's judgement had been vindicated: just as in the 1930s he had pointed to the Nazi peril, so now his warnings as early as 1945 and 1946 of the Soviet threat were proved right. The Conservative stress on individual freedom was now enhanced by Churchill's position as the first international leader to warn of the danger of the Soviet expansionism. The document that was being prepared for the October 1951 conference became the Conservative manifesto when the election was called in September. Because of the outbreak of hostilities in Korea, the sense of a wider ideological clash between left and right on an international scale pervades the document: the critique of Labour was not just one of domestic policies, but also of the international situation.

The third development was a clear sharpening of the ideological divide on economic management. Far from a new cross-party consensus emerging, the ideological debate with Labour was intensifying. Some commentators wrongly assume that after Harold Wilson became president of the Board of Trade in 1947, Labour jumped on the Conservative bandwagon and began their own bonfire of controls. In fact, Wilson's initiative was deliberately restricted to a small range of consumer goods: his underlying approach remained deep-rooted in wartime planning. In June 1950 Wilson submitted a joint Cabinet Committee paper entitled *The Long-Term Arrangements for Control of Prices*, in which it was argued that price control was required permanently and should have an even wider coverage than that suggested by officials. The King's Speech in 1950 included a commitment to legislate so as to put onto a permanent basis the wartime economic controls which had been temporarily extended in 1945. As late as February 1951, the Labour government had drafted a Full Employment Bill which included powers allowing the government to place orders on a continuing basis for products of all types produced by industry, to undertake the manufacture of any goods itself and to sell any of the products it obtained. They were still, in other words, in a pre-Keynesian world in which full employment was to be achieved by direct government micro-economic intervention.

This intense ideological conflict helped to maintain Labour's support as well. Its vote increased from 13,266,176 in 1950 to 13,948,883 in 1951, and if anything it increased its support amongst organized male workers. However, it was a different story with women. Labour's women's organization reported to their Party conference in 1952 that 'the last election was lost mainly in the queue at the butcher's or the grocer's'.[42] In 1951 there was a large swing towards the Conservatives amongst women which was crucial for the outcome: if women had divided between the main parties in the same proportion as men, the Labour Party would have won every election from 1945 to 1970.

In this class-based politics, the third party vote was savaged. A group of senior Liberals in the Lords resigned from the party and took the Conservative whip in the summer of 1951. Churchill and Macmillan wished to go further and offer proportional representation in the large towns in order to attract the Liberals into a merger, but this was not a view shared by many of their colleagues. There was a dramatic reduction in the number of Liberal candidates from 475 in 1950 to only 109 in 1951. This gave a very significant electoral boost to the Conservatives, and the result of the election was Churchill's return to power with an overall majority of 17.

Assessment

There had not been an exclusively Conservative government since 1929 when the Conservatives finally returned to office in 1951. It was a triumphant recovery from the landslide defeat of 1945. Above all, it was the achievement of three crucial figures, none of whom were really conventional Conservatives. Churchill had kept an Olympian detachment from much day to day domestic politics. Instead he warned of the new Soviet threat. And given his own record of nearly 20 years as a Liberal MP he focused on the strategic objective of winning over Liberals as part of the 'united front against Socialism'. Lord Woolton came from a non-party background, with extensive experience in business and retailing. He transformed the Party organization and modernized the way in which candidates were selected so a much broader range of backgrounds were represented. R.A. Butler had appeared fatally damaged by his association with appeasement in the 1930s but he recovered to lead the intellectual renewal of the Party. He set out a framework for modern Conservatism which dominated the Party in the second half of the century. Deregulation of industry was matched by an acceptance of the main features of the welfare state. The policy programme was reinforced by vigorous political activity that identified key groups who were losing out under Labour and for whom the Tory message of freedom and deregulation really struck a chord. Industrialists, worried that their industries would be the next targets for nationalization, were a crucial group. But even more important were housewives with their grim daily experience of rationing and the queue.

This transformation of the Party was not straightforward. There were deep ideological divisions, particularly about whether to accept fixed exchange rates and the tie to the dollar in the Bretton Woods system. Some wanted the Party to go even further and dismantle Attlee's welfare state. This was the basis for media scares which ran from 1949 right through the two election campaigns. There were allegations that education spending would be reduced, that there would be more charges for the NHS, and that pensions would be cut. The 1951 victory was very close and at the time it certainly looked most unlikely that Conservatives would rule for the next 13 years. They had barely any lead in the polls until 1953 because of the electorate's fears about what they might do. But the gradual implementation of exactly what was promised in 1951, no more and no less, gradually yielded political benefits. In July 1954 Butler delivered one of his most triumphant speeches:[43]

In the last three years we have burned our identity cards, torn up our ration books, halved the number of snoopers, decimated the number of forms and said good riddance to nearly two-thirds of the remaining wartime regulations. This is the march to freedom on which we are bound. And the pace must quicken as we go forward ... our aim is freedom for every man and woman to live their own lives in their own way and not have their lives lived for them by an overweening state.

Modern Conservatism had found its voice.

Notes

1. W.L. Burn, 'The General Election in Retrospect', *The 19th Century and After* (1947), 18.
2. 'Cato', *Guilty Men* (London: Gollancz, 1940).
3. 'Simon Haxey', *Tory MP* (London: Gollancz, 1939).
4. *Conservative Agents' Journal*, Jan. 1946, in J. Ramsden, *The Age of Churchill and Eden 1940–1957* (London: Longman, 1995), 91.
5. M. Kandiah, 'The Conservative Party and the 1945 general election', *Contemporary Record*, 9, no. 1 (1995), 34.
6. Eden diary, 27 July 1945, in Ramsden, *Age of Churchill and Eden*, 100.
7. *House of Commons Debates*, vol. 413, col. 95
8. Lord Woolton, *The Memoirs of the Rt. Hon. the Earl of Woolton* (London: Cassell, 1959), 334–5.
9. S. Ball, *The Conservative Party in British Politics 1902–1951* (London: Longman, 1995), 111.
10. R.A. Butler, *The Art of the Possible* (London: Hamish Hamilton, 1971), 129.
11. Woolton, *Memoirs*, 334.
12. National Union Annual Conference, 1946, quoted in Ramsden, *Age of Churchill and Eden*, 109.
13. Memo by Pierssene, 27 May 1946, commenting on J. Ball's memo on Party reorganization, Conservative Party Archive (CPA), Bodleian Library, WHP/1/3.
14. Woolton, *Memoirs*, 334.
15. Woolton quoted in M.D. Kandiah, 'Lord Woolton's chairmanship of the Conservative Party 1946–1951', unpublished D.Phil. thesis, University of Exeter (1992), 130–40.
16. Amery diary, 5 July 1945, in J. Barnes and D. Nicholson (eds), *The Empire at Bay – The Leo Amery Diaries, Volume 2: 1929–1945* (London: Hutchinson, 1988), 1047.
17. 'The Blood Donor', Tony Hancock, BBC TV, 23 June 1961.
18. Woolton, *Memoirs*, 352.
19. National Union Annual Conference, 1947.
20. Q. Hogg, 'Problems of Parliament', *The Spectator*, 26 Nov. 1943.
21. Woolton, *Memoirs*, 345.
22. Ibid., 346.

23. C. Coote, *A Companion of Honour: The Story of Walter Elliot* (London: Collins, 1965), 248.
24. From Macleod's invitation to Selwyn Lloyd in 1963 to chair a new inquiry, CPA CCO/120/4/1, in Ramsden, *Age of Churchill and Eden*, 94.
25. National Union Annual Conference, 1946.
26. R. Maudling, *Memoirs* (London: Sidgwick and Jackson, 1978), 45–6.
27. Butler, *Art of the Possible*, 132.
28. Ibid., 146.
29. Ibid.
30. Q. Hogg, *The Case for Conservatism* (Harmondsworth: Penguin, 1947); D. Clarke, *The Conservative Faith in a Modern Age* (London: Conservative Political Centre, 1947); R. Law, *Return from Utopia* (London: Faber and Faber, 1950).
31. Ina Zweiniger-Bargielowska, *Austerity in Britain: Rationing, Controls and Consumption, 1939–1955* (Oxford: Oxford University Press, 2000), 4–5, 81–2.
32. P. Martin, 'Echoes in the wilderness: British popular Conservatism, 1945–1951', in S. Ball and I. Holliday (eds), *Mass Conservatism, The Conservatives and the Public since the 1880s* (London: Frank Cass, 2002), 124–29
33. M. Kandiah, 'Lord Woolton's chairmanship', 219.
34. Quoted from ibid., 74.
35. Woolton comment to John Baker White MP, in ibid., 147.
36. *Daily Telegraph*, 26 February 1949.
37. Butler, *Art of the Possible*, 135.
38. Woolton, *Memoirs*, 347.
39. Kandiah, 'Lord Woolton's chairmanship', 226.
40. M. Thatcher, *The Path to Power* (London: HarperCollins, 1995), 70.
41. H. Jones, '300,000 houses a year and the Tory revival after 1945', *Contemporary British History*, 14, no. 1 (2000), 102.
42. J. Hinton, 'Militant housewives: the British Housewives' League and the Attlee government', *History Workshop Journal*, 38 (1994), in Zweiniger-Bargielowska, *Austerity in Britain*, 236.
43. Butler, *Art of the Possible*, 173.

9
Planning for Power: 1964–1970

Mark Garnett

Two months after the general election of June 1970, a Conservative candidate wrote of 'a mood of euphoria in Tory ranks'.[1] His own constituency had rejected him, but his party had returned to power after six years in opposition. Labour's margin of victory in the 1964 general election had been little more than 200,000 votes, and only 13 seats. But that contest had brought to an end 13 unbroken years of Conservative government, and was preceded by a rapid succession of serious blows to party morale, notably the failure to negotiate Britain's entry into the EEC, the Profumo Affair, and Harold Macmillan's resignation in October 1963. At best, the Conservatives seemed to have run out of steam in 1964; unkinder critics could portray them as complacent custodians of a decadent social and economic system. They were beaten more soundly in a second general election, in 1966. To bounce back by 1970 – taking less time to recover office than Churchill had required after 1945 – was an impressive feat. In the process the Party carried through a crucial reform of its procedures, and conducted a far-reaching policy review. By 1970 the experienced Conservative front-bench team seemed well equipped to resume their party's 'natural' governing role, after Harold Wilson's regrettable usurpation.

Yet on closer inspection the recovery looks far more equivocal. Indeed, the Tory 'euphoria' after the 1970 election was partly the product of astonishment. Recalling the situation just before the poll, one well-informed Conservative writer claimed that 'few British political leaders in modern times can have entered into an election with such a multitude of favourable indications'.[2] However, Robert Rhodes James was not referring to his own leader, Edward Heath, but to Wilson. Indeed, the expectations of some of Heath's closest allies were so pessimistic in June 1970 that they had made contingency plans for a change of leadership in the aftermath of another defeat.[3]

Conservative gloom before the 1970 election is all the more remarkable because Labour had proved a serious disappointment to most of its supporters. The 1966 contest had been held on its own terms, and delivered a majority of 98. But even after this its record made a mockery of Harold Wilson's speeches in opposition, which had been collected under the title *Purpose in Politics*. A more apposite title would have been *Improvization under Pressure*. The government's failure was symbolized by the devaluation of the pound in November 1967, after a sustained and dogged fight to maintain its value. The Conservatives were ahead in the opinion polls even before this policy disaster, which Wilson compounded with his notorious 'pound in your pocket' broadcast. The opposition's lead had stretched to 24 per cent by April 1968. Yet by the autumn of 1969 the margin was down to single figures, and in the following May Gallup placed Labour seven points ahead. Naturally Wilson took this as a signal to call the only poll that really mattered, especially since the trend was echoed in May's local government elections. It was reported that Tory MPs had been plunged into 'black despair' by the opinion poll, and two-thirds of the voters now assumed that Labour was set for a hat-trick of general election wins.[4]

Several explanations have been advanced for the result of the June 1970 election, which defied almost all of the pollsters by giving the Conservatives an overall majority of 30. Heath had always been far more confident of victory than his closest colleagues. His optimism was shared by many candidates, who felt that the published opinion polls bore no relation to real feelings in their constituencies. Some observers argued that there had been a swing towards the Conservatives – or away from Labour – late in the campaign. Public criticisms of the government's economic record by Lord Cromer, the former Governor of the Bank of England, and the announcement, less than a week before the election, of disappointing balance of payments figures for May, could be cited as specific pieces of bad news which crystallized underlying public misgivings. Wilson's campaign tactics backfired; aiming at an impression of imperturbable competence, he merely looked complacent. On the positive side, the Conservatives had recruited several talented media advisers who helped to produce the most effective television broadcasts of the campaign, and the Party organization was in far better shape than Labour's. Admirers of Enoch Powell argued that their hero had helped to win crucial seats in the Midlands, handing the keys of Downing Street to Heath, the man who had allegedly 'betrayed' him in 1968. Finally, just three days before the election England failed to retain football's World Cup, losing 3–2 to West Germany.

Hindsight increases the temptation to search for contingent factors which might so easily have been different and swung the result the other way. Since 1979 Thatcherites have gleefully pointed to Heath's indifferent electoral record, which ended up as 'played 4, won 1, lost 3'. Perhaps, then, the 1970 victory was a fluke rather than the crowning moment of an impressive political recovery? Yet the statistics tell a different story. With 46.4 per cent of the vote, Heath's Conservatives performed far better than the Party ever did under Mrs Thatcher. Indeed, more people voted Conservative in 1970 than in 1983 – despite the fact that the electorate had grown by almost 3 million in the interim, and that in the latter year Mrs Thatcher had dissolved Parliament at the most propitious time, aided by the 'Falklands Factor'.

In June 1970 a government with an overwhelming parliamentary majority was defeated for the first time since the Second World War. Rhodes James felt that the 1970 election bore comparison with previous 'seismic' contests in 1886, 1906 and 1945.[5] The fact that the psephological effect of this particular political earthquake was relatively short-lived does concern us here, to the extent that the ensuing defeat of February 1974 can be traced to decisions taken during the opposition period. On the Conservative Party itself, the effects are still being felt. The aftermath of the two 1974 defeats, resulting in the elevation of Margaret Thatcher to the Party leadership in the following year, also owed a great deal to imperfect memories of the previous Conservative recovery. The key issues of 1964–70 – notably immigration and 'Europe' – remain problematic today, as the Conservatives struggle to shed their image as 'the nasty party'. In the years under review, by contrast, it is more plausible to argue that senior Conservatives were not nasty enough.

Parliamentary problems

Between 1964 and 1970 the Conservatives felt in full the occupational hazard of a modern opposition party. They seemed capable of making headlines only when they were in trouble. For the parliamentary Party of the time, this experience was unsettling and new. Even those MPs who had been in the Commons between 1945 and 1951 had been cushioned by the fact that their leader was a national icon who could win publicity across the world whenever he chose to make a speech. Between 1964 and

1970 the Party faced a much less deferential press and public, and there was no shortage of issues which could impair its image.

For example, the illegal Rhodesian unilateral declaration of independence (UDI) on 11 November 1965 created one of those rare situations in British politics – a crisis for the governing party which was even more dangerous to the opposition. Labour was divided about the appropriate degree of punishment for the racist Smith regime: some argued for economic sanctions and others advocated military action. But the Conservatives were split three ways. Some advocated strict sanctions, others wanted such action to be limited, and the old Imperialist right-wingers believed that the Rhodesians had done nothing wrong. The Monday Club, formed in 1961 to oppose Macmillan's colonial policy, provided the latter group with a convenient organizational base within the Party. In the month after UDI feelings on Rhodesia were far too strong for the resourceful Chief Whip, Willie Whitelaw, to manage. Eighty-one Tory MPs defied the official line of abstention on sanctions: 50 voted against them, and the remainder supported the government. Rhodesia remained a running sore for the Conservatives up to the 1970 election, along with the related issue of South African apartheid.

In 1968 the Party suffered another self-inflicted wound with even more serious repercussions outside Westminster. Immigration from the 'New Commonwealth' had caused little trouble to the Party until the 1961 Party conference, when concern at the sharp increase in numbers over the previous two years was reflected in the submission of 40 motions from the constituencies. The Macmillan government responded with the 1962 Commonwealth Immigrants Act, which brought to an end the period of unrestricted settlement rights for Commonwealth citizens. This measure was reinforced by Labour legislation in 1968, rushed through Parliament in response to predictions of a mass influx of Asians expelled from Kenya. But these restrictions were still insufficient for many Conservatives, who also rejected the compromise view that in return for stricter limits on new arrivals, those immigrants already settled in the UK should enjoy legal protection from discrimination in the fields of housing and employment.

The shadow spokesman on Defence, Enoch Powell, emerged as an eloquent mouthpiece for this constituency. Having taken a leading role in arousing opposition to the arrival of Kenyan Asians, on 20 April 1968 Powell broke through the tacit parliamentary consensus on race. Speaking to kindred spirits in Birmingham, he asserted that the nation was 'busily engaged in heaping up its own funeral pyre'; that politicians who opposed further restriction were 'mad, literally mad'; and that Labour's proposed measures against discrimination would give a licence to 'the stranger, the disgruntled and the *agent provocateur*'.[6] Although he was careful to allude to official Conservative policy, he was well aware that his colleagues in the shadow cabinet had been struggling to devise a suitable form of words for a reasoned amendment, which would allow them to vote against Labour's Race Relations Bill on second reading while making clear their principled opposition to discrimination. By accident or design, Powell's rhetoric was most offensive to his oldest political friend. He implied that Iain Macleod, and 13 other Conservative MPs, had been 'mad, literally mad' when just two months earlier they had voted against the restrictions imposed by Labour's Commonwealth Immigrants Bill.

The rights and wrongs of Powell's subsequent sacking have been vigorously debated ever since.[7] But whether or not Powell deserved his fate, his departure on this explosive issue threatened to ignite a funeral pyre for his party. Although attitudes on domestic race relations and immigration tended to reflect existing divisions over Rhodesia, the controversy over UDI was overshadowed after Powell's spectacular intervention. Another three-way split within the Party was underlined when the bogey-man of the right wing, the liberal-minded education spokesman, Sir Edward Boyle, left the front bench in the following year. This background of dissent on race relations was all the more troubling because economic stability was gradually returning under the strict management of Roy Jenkins, Labour's Chancellor since the 1967 devaluation. The only crumb of consolation after Powell's speech was an even greater sense of unity among his erstwhile front-bench colleagues, who had already exhibited an unusual degree of solidarity. But, as we shall see, this was far from being an unmixed blessing; it tended to distance the Party's senior figures from many of the rank and file, in and out of Westminster, who had grave doubts about the direction taken by the Party since 1964 on a wide range of issues.

Institutional reform

This level of internal dissent would have bad enough at any time, but in 1968 it represented an additional potent threat to the authority of a leader whose position was already vulnerable. Edward Heath was the first Conservative since Austen Chamberlain in 1921 to rise to the top of the Party without already holding the office of Prime Minister. The product of a marriage between a carpenter and a parlour maid, Heath symbolized the advent of a more 'meritocratic' society. But the decline of deference cut both ways: the change of outlook within the Party which permitted his ascent meant that there would be no reservoir of institutional respect to keep him afloat in difficult times.

The story of the Conservative recovery after 1964 is dominated by a decision which was taken in November 1964, to review the process by which the Party's leader was chosen. Although Sir Alec Douglas-Home had emerged with credit from the 1964 election campaign, the circumstances of his succession to the premiership in the previous year still rankled with some senior colleagues. The consultation process within the Party had been more thorough when Home took over from Macmillan in 1963, compared to the informal soundings six years earlier when the latter had replaced Sir Anthony Eden. But the new temper of the times was unsympathetic to the operations of the Party's secretive 'magic circle', and the process was undoubtedly rigged to the benefit of an aristocrat whose private views were even more anachronistic than his public pronouncements and his image.[8]

After defeat in the 1964 general election, Home conceded that the 'magic circle' would have to be conjured away. Although he had posed as a 'reluctant candidate' back in October 1963, Home proved even more reluctant to step down. Rather, he hoped that a new system would make his party look more democratic without the necessity of changing its leader. The revised rules, announced in February 1965, meant that in future the influence of the Party's unelected grandees would be less than that of the most obscure backbench MP. They could make their views known, but the real electorate in the Commons would be at liberty to reject their preferences. An election could be called every year, 'within twenty-eight days of the opening of each new session of parliament', but only if the leadership was vacant. Any MP wishing to stand only needed to secure the support of a proposer and a seconder, who could remain anonymous. A single ballot would be sufficient, provided that the leading candidate enjoyed an overall majority plus a minimum lead of 15 per cent over the runner-up. If no one jumped these hurdles, the slate would be cleaned for a second ballot. Prospective candidates could hold back from the initial contest, if they calculated that no outright winner would emerge and preferred not to declare themselves at the outset. An overall majority was still required, and the top three candidates would go forward to a final run-off if necessary. This third ballot would allow MPs to declare a second preference, ensuring that a clear winner would be found once the least popular candidate had been eliminated.[9]

This system would be used just once, in August 1965; Conservative leadership contests only became notorious after 1974, when the rules were revised to allow challenges to an incumbent leader. Arguably the process which created the vacancy was even less democratic than the 'magic circle'; Home gave up the leadership on 22 July, having been convinced by Whitelaw that this would be in the best interests of the Party. Three candidates were nominated for the contest to replace him, but there was only one ballot. Actually the winner, Heath, failed to satisfy the exacting requirements of the process, although he did secure an overall majority. The result was: Edward Heath 150, Reginald Maudling 133, Enoch Powell 15. Although the rules allowed him to fight on, Maudling promptly conceded. His leadership campaign, like the man himself, had been criticized for apparent complacency. To make matters worse for Maudling, as Chancellor in the Home government he had failed to deliver victory, and subsequent economic problems had left his stewardship open to criticism from detached commentators as well as Labour. By contrast, at the time of the 1964 general election Heath was seen as the real driving force behind the government. In recognition of this, Home had made him chairman of the Advisory Committee on Policy (ACP) when the Party returned to opposition; and as shadow Chancellor he had proved his mettle in co-ordinating a successful attack on Labour's first budget, in April 1965. In these circumstances even Sir Keith Joseph, who was not noted for his campaigning abilities, was able to persuade Margaret Thatcher to switch from Maudling to Heath. The latter also enjoyed the support of most Conservative-leaning newspapers, and he could entrust the running of his campaign to dynamic, well-connected MPs like Peter Walker and James Prior.

However, in spite of these crucial advantages for Heath, the public favoured Maudling by a wide margin, and many MPs had good reasons of their own for hesitation. It was possible to be impressed by Heath's determined championship of a bill to abolish Resale Price Maintenance (RPM) in the last few months of the Home government, while retaining strong misgivings about the measure itself and deploring its divisive effect on the parliamentary Party.[10] Heath had been a great success as Chief Whip in the difficult period between 1955 and 1959. But once he had moved on from this task he seemed aloof and insensitive, entirely lacking the gift for trivial personal attentions which cement the loyalties of backbench MPs. Thus a system which had been designed to give every opportunity to the candidate with the fewest enemies – i.e. someone very much like Home himself – had presented the Party with a man who was described by one senior Conservative as 'a rough rider'. After Maudling stepped aside, commentators rationalized the result by saying that the Party had chosen an abrasive debater who had risen through his own abilities. In reality, under the rules it had voted in vain for a second ballot.[11]

In hindsight, the relatively bloodless transition is of more than academic interest. In retirement Heath took pride in the fact that the 1965 leadership contest had been conducted without a demeaning round of television interviews, and he refrained from canvassing in person.[12] But on this occasion it really might have helped if the Party had conducted a more prolonged, public and searching inquiry into the qualities of a wider range of plausible candidates. Heath's personality and beliefs would dominate his party for the next decade, but this was no guarantee of personal popularity at any time, either in the Party or the country. If the Conservatives had lost in June 1970, few outside the leader's immediate circle would have regretted his departure. Heath's resolution during the 1970 campaign meant that the result apparently transformed him from potential scapegoat to conquering hero overnight: 'it was not a Party but a man who won this election', wrote one unsuccessful candidate. Others were left with a mixture of gratitude and guilt, and Heath lacked the kind of social skills which could have resolved this unstable combination to his advantage.[13]

Some MPs began to wonder if they had made a mistake within weeks of the 1965 leadership election, when Heath was worsted in his early parliamentary exchanges with Wilson. Evidence of his tendency to ruffle feathers on his own side came at the 1966 Party conference, when officers of the National Union gave vocal support to the Party Chairman, Edward du Cann. This demonstration was a successful attempt to head off rumours that du Cann was about to be sacked by Heath. It proved to be no more than a temporary stay of execution; Anthony Barber became Party Chairman the following summer. Whatever the quality of du Cann's work at Central Office, from the outset Heath seemed determined to find fault with it. Du Cann had voted for Maudling; more importantly, he had also failed to offer consistent backing to Heath over RPM when both men were at the Board of Trade. The impression, whether accurate or not, was that Heath nursed personal grudges.[14]

Du Cann's reputation as a dynamic businessman had made him seem like an ideal appointment when Home made him Chairman after the 1964 general election. But whatever the leadership might have hoped, the Party's traditional practices and ethos offered limited scope for reform from the top, even after Heath became leader. For example, an initiative to make urban constituencies more responsive to central direction was firmly resisted, and 'Project '67', an attempt to cajole local parties into examining the social make-up of their constituencies, was quietly dropped because few members were willing to undertake the work. An effort was made to revise the candidates' list, with mixed results. But steps had been taken to control expenditure – an initiative continued by Barber – and a partial reorganization at Central Office was carried out.[15] To improve co-ordination Sir Michael Fraser, who enjoyed a remarkable degree of confidence among the Party's professional workers, was made Deputy Chairman and Secretary to the shadow cabinet in 1964. Although he relinquished the chairmanship of the Conservative Research Department (CRD), Fraser's influence continued to be felt after his move across Westminster from Old Queen Street to Smith Square.[16]

Undoubtedly the Party became a more effective campaigning organization between 1964 and 1970, while Labour's 'penny farthing' machine stagnated. An appeal for funds launched by Lord Carrington at the 1967 conference comfortably exceeded its £2 million target within 15 months, at a time when the government's economic policies were particularly vulnerable to criticism from within the business community; but the constituency parties contributed more than £900,000, a reflection of high morale among the grass-roots membership at this time. The money allowed the Party to improve the pay of its agents in the run up to the 1970 election. Many of the best-paid agents were assigned to seats which had been identified as 'critical' after the 1966 election. These were Labour- or Liberal-held constituencies (68 in all by 1970), which the Party needed to win in order to secure a working majority. Advertising was focused on these seats, which were visited by the best-known Conservative speakers. Campaigning was informed by intensive and relatively sophisticated opinion surveys, identifying key target groups within the electorate.[17]

The search for a philosophy

Although the Conservative organization was reformed and refreshed after 1964, none of that would have helped if the Party had failed to convince the electorate that it could address the country's problems. In this respect there was a serious setback in January 1966, when the Conservative MP Angus Maude complained that his Party had become 'a meaningless irrelevance' in the eyes of voters. During difficult times in the past, he argued, its 'instinct for survival' had inspired it to reconnect with the real wishes of ordinary people. But it seemed to have lost this happy knack. While the country was increasingly frustrated by a bureaucracy which was over-centralized and increasingly remote, the opposition continued to 'talk like technocrats'. This, Maude felt, 'would get them nowhere'.[18]

At the time, Maude was the Party's spokesman on Commonwealth Affairs. Had he been a politician with the usual ambitions, his article would have been inexplicable. But his personal idiosyncrasies had already been demonstrated through a temporary withdrawal from politics after the Suez crisis of 1956–57. Whatever the merits of talking 'like a technocrat', Heath could hardly be expected to tolerate a front-bencher who talked like a traitor. Although the leader was not mentioned by name, he was clearly the target of the article, having been responsible for policy-making for more than a year by the time Maude launched his attack. The Party's alleged loss of direction could only have originated with Heath's elevation; no one could have discerned 'technocratic' tendencies in Alec Home. Considering the timing, the most surprising thing is that Heath hesitated before sacking Maude. The article appeared during a key by-election campaign in Hull North. When Labour duly retained that seat, increasing its majority despite an intensive effort from the Conservatives, Wilson decided to call the 1966 general election with a strong wind behind him.

Maude had chosen to speak out because he genuinely felt that the Party could only present a united front on a foundation of policies which arose from a clearly defined philosophical position. In short, he was arguing for the kind of 'first order' ideological underpinning which Socialism allegedly provided for Labour. Heath could have retorted that far from unifying the Party, Socialism was actually the major source of Labour's factional disputes. More importantly, it was not the case that Heath lacked a philosophy. Despite appearances, he did not merely believe that 'whate'er is best administered is best'. Although he had been a fairly inactive member of the 'One Nation' group of Conservative MPs when he had joined Maude, Powell and Macleod as a founder-member back in 1950, Heath's outlook remained consistent with the position outlined in the group's eponymous pamphlet. For him the state was at least potentially a valuable instrument in the battle to promote prosperity and prevent social dissolution. But, in the words of the 1965 policy document *Putting Britain Right Ahead*, 'the State should serve the people not dominate them'. The document emphasized that progress depended on 'those who succeed in rising above the average'. Innovators, and dynamic industrialists, would be given greater freedom to produce wealth which would benefit everyone in society. Welfare spending would be better targeted, and thus more generous to those in genuine need. Finally, it was affirmed that 'modern Conservatism is firmly on the side of those who wish Britain to excel in the world'; contrary to the fears of Heath's critics, membership of the European Economic Community (EEC) was perfectly compatible with patriotism.[19]

In short, Heath's ideas satisfied the requirements laid down by Lord Coleraine, another critic who detected and attacked a lack of 'philosophy': 'Any political association which exists to further by parliamentary action the ends which its members combine to promote, must have a coherent and generally consistent body of principle on which to base itself.'[20] But Maude and Coleraine were really objecting to the *nature* of Heath's thinking, rather than any lack of ideas. They regarded Heath's position as merely the latest instalment in a post-war quest to reach an accommodation with Socialism. This is not the place to examine in detail the conflicting claims which have been advanced in the long-running dispute over the 'true' nature of British Conservatism.[21] But it was hardly likely that the conservative outlook, which had developed in the era of aristocratic society, could be transplanted unchanged into an emerging consumerist democracy heavily influenced by distinctively liberal assumptions. For a Conservative Party facing a moderate Labour leader, the problem was particularly acute; as the authors of the 1966 Nuffield election study noted, it was ironic 'that the final emphasis of the Conservative leader was on the need for radical change, and of the Labour Party on the need for patriotism and stability'. Two years later Samuel Brittan spoke for many detached observers when he characterized the clash between left and right in British politics as a 'bogus dilemma'.[22] Yet this kind of talk was anathema to purists like Maude and Coleraine, and even Conservative supporters who could live with the 'technocratic' approach had some sympathy with their strictures. From this perspective it was misleading that Maudling and Heath, both of whom accepted the broad outlines of the post-war 'consensus', should have taken together almost 95 per cent of the vote in the 1965 leadership election – and that the conventions of the time prevented Powell from backing his candida-ture with an elaborated and fully-publicized critique which would have given the Party an opportunity for a debate on its future direction.[23]

All one can say is that in the 1960s, at least, Heath's approach commanded widespread support among the Party's most thoughtful and dynamic members. Some of Heath's key allies, like David Howell and John MacGregor, had served as chairmen of the Bow Group, the ginger group favoured by most young Conservative intellectuals. Its membership increased by 50 per cent between 1966 and 1968, topping 1000 for the first time in the latter year. Although some prominent Bow Groupers, like Geoffrey Howe, Michael Howard and Norman Lamont, later participated in the radical Thatcherite attack on the post-war 'consensus', in the mid-to late 1960s the Group was broadly united behind Heath's reformist, 'technocratic' position. Howe, Howell and MacGregor all contributed to a book of essays published in 1965, advancing ideas based on intensive research over a wide range of policy areas.[24]

Howell, who became MP for Guildford in 1966 at the age of 30, can be regarded as the Party's 'technocrat in chief'. He had worked in the Treasury and started writing leading articles for the *Daily Telegraph* before becoming chairman of the Bow Group in 1961. From 1964 to 1966 he was director of the Conservative Political Centre (CPC), with responsibility for disseminating new ideas and stimulating discussion among the Party membership. He took the leading role in the production of the 1966 manifesto, and before the 1970 election produced *A New Style of Government*, a CPC pamphlet which argued for radical change in a bureaucratic machine which was in danger of being overloaded. The pamphlet's title became a central theme in Heath's speeches before the 1970 general election, and preparations were made to bring dynamic businessmen into government to prosecute the strategy in office. Wherever possible, administrative tasks would be 'hived off' from Whitehall to semi-autonomous agencies.

Howell epitomized the Party's problem of presentation, since his distinctive ideological argument for a slimmed-down state was couched in the vocabulary of a management consultant. But those who demanded 'clear blue water' between the Conservatives and Labour might also have been disconcerted by the fact that Howell applied his principles impartially. For example, a characteristic Bow Group argument was that the state should be used to break up monopolistic practices on both sides of industry. Heath's abolition of RPM had been the most dramatic concrete example of this approach, to the outrage of the Party's traditional supporters in the retail sector. After he became leader, the Group hoped for further measures of this kind – whatever their effect on opinion in the business community – to complement radical reform of the trade unions. From this perspective Sir Keith Joseph, later to be acclaimed as the intellectual architect of Thatcherism, privately conceded in 1969 that 'free market' competition was actually 'an artificial state which depended upon government'.[25]

Finally, although he was a 'One Nation' politician through commitment rather than calculation, Heath could provide a sound electoral rationale for his approach at a time when Party research underlined the demographic advantage enjoyed by Labour. Lord Coleraine criticized the Conservative leader for courting 'floating voters', arguing that the Party would win if it mobilized its natural supporters.[26] But the success of this strategy depended on widespread apathy in the Labour ranks. By 1966 Labour enjoyed an 11 per cent lead when voters were asked to identify the party which was 'best for people like yourself'.[27] Without a drive to update the Conservative ethos and image which extended its appeal beyond its traditional bedrock of support, this trend looked very likely to continue. Even if 'technocratic' language was unlikely to win the hearts of those who were predisposed to vote Labour anyway, it promised to connect the Conservatives with young managers – a group whose influence was out of proportion to its numbers. In the 'meritocratic' climate of the time it was natural to portray these ambitious apparatchiks as the next generation of social 'pacesetters', whose ideas would be transmitted through the workplace and the media, eventually permeating the whole electorate. This was an effective riposte to Fleet Street commentators like Samuel Brittan, who complained in 1968 that the opposition was making no attempt to influence the 'climate of opinion'. And even if Heath and his colleagues had accepted the full 'Powellite' economic prospectus, they were surely right to think that any suggestion of a hard-line *laissez-faire* approach would alienate uncommitted voters as well as disrupting the fragile unity of the Party.[28]

In hindsight, Heath's detractors were able to claim that the Party won in 1970 despite obvious philosophical shortcomings, and that these undermined its performance when back in office. Fittingly, it was Enoch Powell who encapsulated this critique in a vivid soundbite, alleging that Heath 'would immediately become angry and go red in the face' when confronted with an idea.[29] This view was echoed by Brendon Sewill, the CRD director, who complained in 1968 that the Party seemed reluctant to tell the public 'where the car was going rather than what we were going to do inside the engine'.[30] Too much can be made even of this contemporary remark; after all, an official like Sewill is paid to issue counsels of perfection. In fact, as early as 1965 Sewill had drawn up a paper which suggested a coherent narrative for the Party, tying in the themes of modernization and EEC entry. This coincided perfectly with Heath's own thinking.[31]

The most cogent criticism of the 'technocratic' approach was voiced by William Deedes, who reflected on 'the sense of estrangement many Conservatives outside Westminster feel about their leaders and their representatives. It is plain enough to them', Deedes continued, 'that the old world *has* come to an end, and far from regretting it their elected representatives seem to be making a good thing of it'. The promise of more efficient administration could not begin to touch the fears of people who were repelled by consumerism and the 'permissive society'. At least in part, this undercurrent of unease explains (although it scarcely condones) the rapturous response in some quarters to Powell's 1968 speech. Maude himself tried to address deeper social problems in a lengthy treatise which appeared in 1969. But his broodings, like those published by Coleraine in the following year, came too early to inform a coherent public debate. Deedes only reported the mutterings among Conservative supporters in the autumn of 1973, when the Heath government was being engulfed by problems on all sides. And even if Heath and his colleagues had tried to articulate the half-conscious fears of the late 1960s, it is difficult to see what practical difference they could have made to contemporary trends. For all the talk of 'Victorian Values', even the Thatcher governments made no concerted attempt to restore the 'old world'.[32]

The policy exercise

Whether or not Heath disliked political philosophizing, no one could accuse the Conservatives of lacking policies under his leadership. Indeed, the shadow Chancellor Iain Macleod identified 131 'distinct specific promises' in the 1966 manifesto.[33] The document, *Action not Words*, incorporated the findings of policy groups established after Heath became chairman of the ACP in October 1964. Originally there were about 20 of these, but by the spring of 1965 their ranks had swollen to 36. The typical group included outside experts, from business and academia, as well as interested MPs and the official Party spokesperson. After the 1966 election many of the groups reconvened, and others were added in response to changes in the policy agenda. Ironically, at the very time that Maude launched his attack on the inadequacy of his party's thinking, a Philosophy Group was being put together (although Heath's critics would not have been surprised to discover that it was stillborn).

The 1964–70 policy exercise is often seen as the hallmark of the Heath leadership as a whole. It was bound to be identified with him, given his central position within the policy-making process even before he became leader. But the nature of the exercise can also be advanced in support of Maude's critique, and it is certainly true that the emphasis on empirical research, rather than theoretical disquisitions, was highly congenial to Heath's outlook. However, had he been leader even Maude would have found it difficult to proceed on very different lines in the circumstances of 1964. If Labour had secured a comfortable majority in that year's election, Conservatives could have indulged themselves in the luxury of a systematic and prolonged rethink. As it was, the policy-makers knew that Wilson would call another poll whenever it seemed most likely to improve his parliamentary position; and the misadventures of the last Conservative government were always likely to furnish him with his leading campaign theme. It would be impossible for the Party to launch a convincing defence of that record while advocating an entirely new approach to policy problems.

At the same time, though, the Conservatives did have to persuade voters that Labour's 1964 victory had been based on a confidence trick. Thus there would have to be a few fresh policies, but not so many as to expose the Party to the obvious criticism that it could have implemented these ideas while it had the chance. As Sir Michael Fraser put it years later, these circumstances explained both 'the scale ... and the shallowness of the operation'.[34] Ironically, a very similar dilemma would be revisited on Heath after the narrow defeat of February 1974, while his successor Margaret Thatcher ended up with more than four years to reflect, in opposition to a government which had already asked the electorate for an improved mandate.

The urgency of the situation when Heath took over responsibility for policy making was reflected in an instruction that the groups should report back within six months. This demanding timetable was particularly onerous for the CRD, which had to continue its routine briefing work while servicing the groups. Since the process brought in outsiders with conflicting commitments, it was difficult for the groups to follow a regular schedule of meetings. Often several groups would meet on the same day, and even at the same time; the enthusiasm of some had to be curbed, others had to be coaxed, and several (notably the group studying Europe) existed purely for form's sake, because the policy goals were already established beyond dispute. Despite these problems, the policy document *Putting Britain Right Ahead* was ready for the 1965 Party conference.[35]

John Ramsden has rightly described *Putting Britain Right Ahead*, rather than the election manifestos of the period, as 'the key document of 1964–70'.[36] It certainly established a template for the main policy themes of the opposition years. On the face of it, this could be interpreted as an indictment of the leadership, which fought the 1970 general election on roughly the same policies which had been assembled in haste and decisively rejected by the electorate four years earlier. Yet, unlike Mrs Thatcher between 1975 and 1979, Heath was entirely responsible for the programme of his party throughout the opposition period. At no time could he shelter behind the alibi that his personal views were opposed by a majority of his front-bench colleagues; and having stood on a platform which he fully endorsed in 1966 it would not have been easy for him to present a much-changed programme four years later. Furthermore, for understandable reasons he considered that the 1966 general election had been something of a swindle practised on the public by Labour. Four months after its re-election the government was announcing spending cuts to prop up the pound, validating Heath's campaign warnings that this would turn out to be a 'vote now, pay later' election.

If the electorate had not listened first time round, the only way to get the Conservative message through was by means of patient repetition, and, where necessary, refinement. Although the Party's polls indicated as late as autumn 1968 that less than a third of the electorate knew what the Conservatives stood for – almost the same figure as in 1966 – this could be taken as a reason to keep plugging away, instead of rushing back to the drawing board.[37] By the winter of 1969, Heath was confident enough of victory to establish a committee on future legislation – an unprecedented step for any opposition. The CRD produced a legislative timetable in March 1970.[38] All this began to look rather hubristic when the Party's polling lead evaporated over the following weeks. But the important point is that thanks to the work of the policy groups Heath felt able to turn his thoughts towards timing, rather than content.

With Europe established as the unarguable centrepiece of the strategy, the strengths and frailties of the Party's preparations for government are far better illustrated by trade union policy. Reform of the unions was seen as a key element in Heath's drive for 'modernization'. Along with Europe, it was a piece of unfinished business which lent credence to the jibe that the Tories had presided over 'thirteen wasted years'. Belatedly, at the 1964 election the Conservatives had promised to hold an inquiry. Six months later Labour established a Royal Commission, headed by Lord Donovan, to investigate industrial relations.

Donovan was one of Wilson's less explicable initiatives. The Commission only went ahead after the TUC had secured the inclusion of George Woodcock, their General Secretary. After this, Donovan was most unlikely to report in favour of radical reform. In anticipation of a whitewash, the Conservatives got their own blow in early, publishing their proposals in *A Fair Deal at Work* in April 1968. The Party could scarcely be convicted of opportunism, because the main policy lines had been established early on in the review. Initially headed by Lord Amory (and in later years by Keith Joseph and Robert Carr), the group took only four months to compile a 25-page document recommending a comprehensive revision of union law, which aimed to restore some order to Britain's increasingly anarchic industrial relations. For some Conservatives – including Joseph – the prospect of trade union legislation offered the chance of launching a strike of their own, against the political levy which provided Labour with most of its funding.[39] This option was rejected as unnecessarily provocative. After that decision, the policy group was left to chew over details – notably whether the onus for bringing prosecutions should fall on the government or employers. Tinkering with the policy continued even after the publication of *A Fair Deal at Work*; in November 1969 Carr compared the reform to the process of renovating an old house, with new problems being uncovered as the work went along.[40]

In its final form, the policy was a determined attempt to avoid alienating the unions, while redressing the balance of power in the work-place. Unions and employers could apply to a Registrar, who would decide if their constitutional procedures were fair. Once registered, a union would enjoy certain privileges – or at least, would not be subjected to the additional penalties, including unlimited fines, which could be meted out to unregistered unions. Everyone would have the right to belong (or not) to a union, and employers would have to recognize those organizations which were approved by a majority in the work-place. Legally binding agreements would be drawn up between unions and employers, and these would be enforced by a new industrial relations court. In disputes which were deemed to endanger the national interest, there would be a compulsory 'cooling-off' period of 60 days and a pre-strike ballot.

Despite the Labour government's capitulation on its own proposals in 1969, the Conservatives remained convinced that their far-reaching bill would succeed. In their most optimistic moments they hoped that the legal machinery would not have to be used at all, as if rationality would suddenly dawn on both sides of industry when they were faced with such a sensible and balanced package. Private soundings with union leaders suggested that they would make a terrific fuss until the legislation was enacted, at which time they would tell their members that further resistance would be futile. While Carr and his team thought that this piece of intelligence gave them a trump-card, in fact it ensured that they embarked on the game playing 'blind'; when the clamour against the bill duly began shortly after the 1970 election, they persisted in thinking of the union opposition as no more than an elaborate bluff. Over-confidence about their own proposals had helped to ensure that the Conservatives missed a trick in 1969, voting against the White Paper *In Place of Strife* when, as James Prior later pointed out, a warm welcome to the government's proposals could have helped to solve the problem without doing anything to resolve Labour's internal divisions.[41] As a well-planned failure, the 1971 Industrial Relations Act rivals even Margaret Thatcher's poll tax; immersed as they were in legalistic minutiae, the policy-makers quite forgot to bear in mind political realities, and the rudiments of human psychology.

The lavish preparation of the Party's policy on industrial relations was in marked contrast to the treatment of prices and incomes. In part, this was because of the intimate link between the two policies; most senior Conservatives assumed that a successful attack on militant trade unionism would in itself reduce much of the inflationary pressure from wage increases, thus avoiding the need for tough deflationary measures which might increase unemployment. Yet in the late 1960s the country was experiencing the new phenomenon of 'stagflation', in which inflation and unemployment were edging up simultaneously, contrary to Keynesian expectations. With good reason, Samuel Brittan warned against any assumption that union reform on its own would 'prevent wages from rising faster than productivity'.[42] If his caution was heeded at all, it was not taken seriously enough by shadow ministers.

On prices and incomes, it is certainly possible to accuse the Conservative leadership of refusing to countenance radical thinking because it was wedded to what had become economic orthodoxy. Iain Macleod clearly spotted the danger of stirring up an ideological debate. In April 1968, during a typically desultory discussion, he argued that 'the Party should forget the metaphysics on this subject' and concentrate on the practical fact that Labour's compulsory policy was not working. Later, according to his shadow cabinet colleague Peter Walker, he argued that it would be 'crazy' to say in advance that the Party would adopt such a policy, even if in the last resort it had to enact one. It could be ruled out before an election, in the hope that the leadership could explain any enforced changes afterwards.[43]

This was a high-risk strategy, and it will never be known whether Macleod could have pulled it off when the policy was duly adopted in November 1972. But Heath had already cramped his own room for manoeuvre, in a major speech at Carshalton in July 1967. Although he conceded that the government should relate prices and incomes to productivity when it was the employer, and that the provision of advice and information to the public could serve a useful educative purpose, a compulsory policy was roundly condemned as 'not only impracticable, but unfair, undesirable and an unjustifiable infringement on the freedom of the individual'. In the 1970 manifesto, this language was echoed by the blunt statement that 'We utterly reject the philosophy of compulsory wage control.'[44]

Like most of his shadow cabinet colleagues, Heath was actually no more than agnostic on the subject of prices and incomes policy. The only explanation for the harsh rhetorical line adopted at Carshalton is that he had decided to appease the right wing of his party – those who bemoaned the lack of a philosophical edge to the Party's programme – on a subject where he saw no danger of his words coming back to haunt him. Yet his dogmatic posture meant that he was placing all his bets on the industrial relations policy as a weapon against inflation. Prices were bound to play a central role in any election campaign, and the 1970 manifesto contained the promise that 'In implementing all our policies, the need to curb inflation will come first.' Deeply troubled by the lack of contingency planning, Brendon Sewill produced a paper for the Selsdon Park conference in January 1970, but discussion of prices did not get far beyond Reginald Maudling's acknowledgement that 'the subject was going to be a very big gap to fill in our policy'.[45] A sub-committee was set up afterwards, but only met once (and inconclusively).

As it turned out, opinion surveys on economic attitudes provide the best explanation of a late surge in support for the Conservatives during the 1970 election campaign. On 8 June a clear majority of voters (44 per cent to 35 per cent) accepted opposition assertions of a looming crisis, but Labour was seen as the best party to deal with it by a margin of 5 per cent. Eight days later, this deficit had been transformed into a Conservative lead of 4 per cent.[46] Confidence had been draining away from the government on this subject even before the adverse trade figures of 15 June, which strongly suggests that the Conservative decision to campaign on 'shopping basket' issues had paid off handsomely. Yet this was precisely the area in which the policy exercise had proved least helpful.

As Sewill reflected years later, far from having a convincing strategy to control inflation, 'most of our policies were designed to put it up!' – at least in the short term.[47] Most notably, the Party's decision to introduce Value Added Tax (VAT), which would switch part of the tax burden from incomes to consumption, was sure to increase prices. The policy group which dealt with taxation – a sub-committee of the Policy Group on Future Economic Policy – was held to be one of the success stories of the review, developing ideas which led to Anthony Barber's reforming budget of 1971. Yet there had been serious difficulties even in this key area. Before the 1966 general election the Taxation Group had produced detailed proposals for a graduated 'wealth tax', an additional burden for 'owners' which would leave room to lighten the load on high earners. As well as helping to balance the budget, the idea also promised to thwart any attempt by Labour to portray the Conservatives as unthinking friends of the rich, whatever the source of their wealth. For this very reason, the wealth tax was too radical for the parliamentary Party to swallow. Despite the eloquent advocacy of Arthur Cockfield and persistent support from Joseph, the policy was dropped in 1968.

State ownership of industry was another area in which the Party drew back from radical proposals. In this case, though, Heath's caution was due only in part to ideological considerations. It was prompted by what he held to be inadequate policy work, by a group set up late in 1967 with Nicholas Ridley in the chair. Discussing the group's first report in 1968, Iain Macleod noted that it was 'politically important to denationalise something. The question was what?'[48] By contrast, then as later Ridley saw the issue of state ownership as an ideological litmus-test. Whatever the practical difficulties, there should be a presumption in favour of exploring ways of returning state industries to the private sector. Even 'natural monopolies' – utilities like electricity provision – should be sold off. From Ridley's perspective, these huge, bureaucratic concerns offended against the laws of the free market whether they were owned by taxpayers or by shareholders; it was unlikely that they would ever be subject to competition in either case, but the chances would be improved if they were in private hands. This was too naive even for Joseph and Margaret Thatcher, who criticized Ridley's approach at a meeting of the Economic Policy Group held in the absence of Heath and Macleod. The 1970 manifesto merely contained a characteristic pledge to make the nationalized industries more efficient, and an unequivocal rejection of any further encroachment from the state.[49]

Selsdon Park

In retirement, Ridley claimed that the shadow cabinet approved his policy 'with one or two deletions and additions', and that it was included in the 1970 manifesto, albeit 'suitably disguised'. After the election, Ridley was given a junior post in what became (in October 1970) the Department of Trade and Industry. However, he lamented that his ambitious proposals were 'quietly dropped'; in practice, the denationalization programme only embraced the travel agent Thomas Cook, and a chain of pubs in the north-west of England which had been taken over by the state during the First World War. From this perspective, it was unsurprising that Ridley should choose to resign from the government in April 1972.[50]

Few ministers manage to write their memoirs without committing factual errors, and most of them deliberately distort the past in a misguided attempt to set the record straight. But as a model of inaccuracy Ridley's account cannot be bettered. Far from being 'quietly dropped', his plans were never accepted; and instead of resigning in 1972 as a matter of principle, he was sacked. He even tampers with his chronology, implying that he was asked to head the ill-fated policy group after becoming 'enthusiastic' about his party's developing election platform at some point in 1969. In reality, he was asked to lead the group in 1967, and two years later he was well aware that his plans had proved too radical even for sympathizers like Thatcher and Joseph to swallow. It is hardly surprising that he fails to mention the sequel to this phase of the story. Somehow the report of his abortive policy group found its way to Tony Benn, who leaked it to the press in order to damage the Heath government two months after Ridley's dismissal.[51]

In a perceptive forensic analysis of trends within the Conservative Party published in 1974, Andrew Gamble argued that despite the support from the Bow Groupers, in opposition Heath had been too weak to resist 'ideological pressure from the Right'. Two years previously, the Labour convert Humphry Berkeley had claimed that the leader had 'wrenched the Conservative party so far to the right that it is no longer recognizable as the party which I represented in parliament only six years ago'. But although we have seen that Heath did make rhetorical concessions to the right when he felt he could afford to do so, there was never any question that the Conservatives under his leadership would move outside the broad outlines of the post-war 'consensus'. Thus, although Berkeley was rightly exercised by the decision to resume (defensive) arms sales to South Africa, this can be seen as an attempt by the Party leadership to buy off the Monday Club at an acceptable price, rather than a capitulation to either the 'traditional' or 'New' Right.[52]

This is the proper context in which to evaluate the shadow cabinet meeting at Selsdon Park Hotel at the end of January 1970 (not 1969, as Ridley wrongly remembered). When Heath and his colleagues assembled at that fateful venue, they could hardly have imagined that their deliberations would still be controversial three decades later. The meeting had been planned by Sewill and James Douglas of the CRD, as a way of getting front-benchers to concentrate their minds on the likely contents of the Party manifesto, to thrash out any outstanding points and to develop coherent themes for presentation to the electorate. These hopes were only partially realized. Much of the discussion revealed how much work still needed to be done, and it also uncovered new sources of disagreement.

In 1995, Margaret Thatcher admitted that 'The idea that Selsdon Park was the scene of debate which resulted in a radical rightward shift in Party policy is false.'[53] In this context, at least, the source is unimpeachable, and Thatcher's verdict should finally have put an end to the myth of Selsdon

Park, which had already served its purpose for her wing of the Party. For Heath to have performed a 'U-turn' after 1970, as his critics maintained, he had to have charted a clear direction before shifting to a new one. As we have seen, Heath did indeed have a relatively coherent philosophy, but it was not the one favoured by the right. In order to discredit him when he was down, the Thatcherites had to foist on him the very ideas which, at the relevant time, they had criticized him for rejecting.

This strategy only worked because of a cynical soundbite delivered by a politician who, in right-wing eyes, had even less credibility than Heath. At the press conference after the Selsdon meeting a tougher line on law and order was mentioned, in an attempt to win some headlines. Normally, this rhetoric would have been a one-day wonder. But in Nottingham less than a week later, Harold Wilson decided to rally his party by launching an hysterical attack on the opposition, claiming that its policies marked 'an atavistic desire to reverse the course of twenty-five years of social revolution. What they are planning is a wanton, calculated and deliberate return to greater inequality.'[54]

No well-informed observer could take this tirade seriously, and Conservative supporters who knew that Wilson was talking nonsense could still happily vote for their party. Yet the Prime Minister had inadvertently succeeded where the shadow cabinet had signally failed, by enticing people who would not normally have been interested to look at the Conservative programme. Some, like the lukewarm Labour supporter David (later Lord) Young, became so enthusiastic that they later imagined Heath to have 'paraded Selsdon Man'. Others, like Ridley, wished that Wilson's allegation had been true after all, and in later years made their wishes seem like the reality. Even those who half-admitted the truth could not resist joining in this game. In retirement Keith Joseph claimed that 'there were in that Selsdon document the seeds of much of what we still wanted to do and more or less carried out after 1979'. Actually rather more of those 'seeds' had been sown at the little-publicized Sundridge Park meeting. Joseph has some excuse for his misleading remark, because his own speeches at the time, on economic competition, did indeed run ahead of his party's official thinking; but this only ensured that Heath denied him any role in economic policy-making when he formed his government. Others have no such alibi, even if they were not actually at the meeting. Alan Clark, for example, was generous enough to accept that Selsdon Man was a myth; but he argued nevertheless that Heath had brought his problems on himself by 'foolishly and opportunistically' suggesting law and order as the theme for the press conference. By claiming that his policies on privatization went into the manifesto in a 'disguised' form, Ridley suggested yet another gambit for the Thatcherites. On this view, Heath might not have appeared very right wing after all, but only because he was frightened of alienating floating voters. It was as if Lord Coleraine had been right all along; despite Heath's flirtation with the floaters he had owed his victory to the right-wing Party faithful, who had turned out in droves because they saw through the flimsy veil of moderation in Heath's programme. The outright winner in this contest of contorted logic, though, is Norman Tebbit, who recalled that by 1971 he 'began to wonder whether Ted Heath had any real understanding of what lay under the Selsdon manifesto'.[55] At least Ridley had taken some part in the policy review; Tebbit was only adopted as a Conservative candidate in 1968.

Conclusion

Douglas Hurd has argued that the work of the 1965–70 policy review 'was greater in quantity and higher in quality than any which a political party had previously attempted in opposition'.[56] Yet one suspects that the emphasis on the policy review, then and since, reflects more than anything the lack of any other concrete achievements. At least policies and Party institutions were under Conservative control, and developments in these spheres could be trumpeted to maintain morale. But in reality the initiative between 1964 and 1970 always rested with Wilson. Before the 1970 election the shadow cabinet was made the subject of some flattering pen-portraits in a book called *Here Come the Tories*.[57] That breathless title was half-conscious testimony to the inability of the front-bench team to quicken the political pulses without external assistance. It would still be inaccurate to describe the 1970 result as a 'fluke', and it was more than just a rejection of Wilson. But Stuart Ball is surely right to rank the overall performance of Heath's party fifth out of the six periods of Conservative opposition in the twentieth century.[58]

When one assesses the lasting legacy of those years, all the painstaking preparations for government count for nothing, compared to one of the crudest and most tenacious of all post-war political myths. Ewen Green has argued that the success of the Selsdon Park myth makes it 'just as "real" as any "objective" assessment of the events of 1970'.[59] But even within the Conservative Party the myth only gained ground *after* 1970. It is part of the 'real' and 'objective' story of Heath's downfall, perhaps, but it can only play an important part in explaining the 1970 victory for those who have accepted the Thatcherite case.

The continuing debate might be infuriating for historians who are still battling to restore a sense of perspective to the period, but 'Selsdon Man' does give rise to other pertinent reflections. The Heath government was consistently unlucky. Despite its travails the Party came within a whisker of re-election, and given the doom-laden demographic predictions of the 1960s it was remarkable that it ran Labour reasonably close in the October 1974 renewal which could easily have been a repeat of 1966. But much of its bad luck arose from a fundamental mistake, embedded in both the format and the content of the policy review and Heath's general approach to the politics of opposition.

The usual criticism of Heath as an opposition leader is that he ran his shadow cabinet as if it were in government already.[60] While this does explain much of the dissatisfaction with the Party's performance between 1964 and 1970, there ought to have been a pay-off in a seamless transition once the election had been won. In fact the tendencies which made the Conservatives ineffective in opposition continued to hamper them when they had recovered power. The real problem was not that shadow ministers had spent too much time rehearsing; rather, they soon discovered that they had mistaken the nature of the task ahead of them. Faced with a Prime Minister who governed through gimmicks and gestures, the Conservative leader and his colleagues had constructed a programme based on a rational consideration of the national interest, overlooking the possibility that shifty tactics might have been forced on Wilson by the unrealistic demands of what had become a fickle electorate. Insulated from the pressures of office, they consistently over-estimated the rationality of the average voter, and in particular of the unions and employers who were being asked to respond to a 'modernized' framework of policy. In short, despite the wise counsel of Harold Macmillan behind the scenes, they were prepared for everything except 'events'. The popularity and persistence of the Selsdon myth might be irrational; but as such it is a product of the same tendencies which made ordinary union members confront Heath as if he were a new Hitler, and convinced industrialists to pick up easy profits during the property bubble of the early 1970s rather than searching for constructive long-term investments.

Once the voice of healthy cynicism within the Cabinet had been silenced by Iain Macleod's early death, ministers were left with no protection against the consequences of their fundamental mistake. Whatever Heath himself might have thought, he had not won the 1970 election on policy preparation or personal integrity. Apart from Wilson's tactical errors and the fact that his period in office had been barren of achievement, the main factor was a Conservative advertising campaign which played upon fears within the electorate, particularly on the subject of inflation where, as subsequent events were to demonstrate, the Party was under-prepared.[61] Far from being the prelude to 'a new style of government', for the opposition the 1964–70 period was much like the usual mixture of false dawns and unintended consequences. On balance, the Party's leaders were more honest and well-intentioned than the norm: but in the modern democratic era that only explains why their ultimate failure was so complete.

Notes

1. E. Wright, 'The future of the Conservative Party', *Political Quarterly*, 41 (1970), 387.
2. R. Rhodes James, *Ambitions and Realities: British Politics 1964–70* (London: Weidenfeld and Nicolson, 1972), 235.
3. See M. Garnett and I. Aitken, *Splendid! Splendid! The Authorised Biography of Willie Whitelaw* (London: Jonathan Cape, 2002), 85.
4. James Margach in *Sunday Times*, 17 May 1970, quoted in T.F Lindsay and M. Harrington, *The Conservative Party 1918–1970* (London: Macmillan, 1974), 259.
5. Rhodes James, *Ambitions and Realities*, 267.
6. The text of the speech is reproduced in H. Berkeley, *The Odyssey of Enoch: A Political Memoir* (London: Hamish Hamilton, 1977), 129–37.
7. For contrasting views see Berkeley, *Odyssey of Enoch*, and S. Heffer, *Like the Roman: The Life of Enoch Powell* (London: Weidenfeld and Nicolson, 1998).
8. For a recent analysis of the 1963 leadership saga, see I. Gilmour and M. Garnett, *Whatever Happened to the Tories? The Conservatives since 1945* (London: Fourth Estate, 1997), 186–203. For Home's social views, see his private 'confession' to Sir Michael Fraser, 19 December 1963, National Archives, Public Record Office (PRO), PREM 11/5006.
9. The 1964 rules are reprinted in N. Fisher, *The Tory Leaders* (London: Weidenfeld and Nicolson, 1977), 194–7.
10. See the blunt criticisms of RPM and its prime mover in the letter from John Morrison, Chairman of the backbench '1922 Committee' to Home, 15 April 1963, in PRO, PREM 11/5/54.
11. A. Roth, *Heath and the Heathmen* (London: Routledge and Kegan Paul, 1972), 186.
12. Interview with Sir Edward Heath, March 1998.
13. Wright, 'Future of the Conservative Party', 388.
14. J. Ramsden, *The Winds of Change: Macmillan to Heath, 1957–1975* (Harlow: Longman, 1996), 268–9.
15. See Heath's curt criticism in E. Heath, *The Course of My Life: My Autobiography* (London: Hodder and Stoughton, 1998), 290.
16. J. Ramsden, *The Making of Conservative Party Policy: The Conservative Research Department since 1929* (Harlow: Longman, 1980), 237; interview with James Douglas, July 2004.
17. D. Butler and M. Pinto-Duschinsky, *The British General Election of 1970* (London: Macmillan, 1971), 102, 283, 288–9.

18. 'Winter of Tory discontent', *Spectator*, 14 January 1966.
19. 'Conservatism 1965', in *Putting Britain Right Ahead* (Conservative Central Office, 1965).
20. Lord Coleraine, *For Conservatives Only* (London: Tom Stacey, 1970), 20.
21. For a thought-provoking recent contribution, see E.H.H Green, *Ideologies of Conservatism: Conservative Political Ideas in the Twentieth Century* (Oxford: Oxford University Press, 2002).
22. D. Butler and A. King, *The British General Election of 1966* (London: Macmillan, 1966), 124; S. Brittan, *Left or Right: The Bogus Dilemma* (London: Secker and Warburg, 1968).
23. Although the analogy should not be taken too far, it is interesting to compare Powell's fate with that of the equally intellectual John Redwood in 1995. In contrast to Powell, his problem was *too much* exposure for his ideas. Even so, he won 89 votes against a sitting Prime Minister, whereas in 1965 Powell did not even secure the support of his old friend Maude.
24. *The Conservative Opportunity: Fifteen Bow Group Essays on Tomorrow's Toryism* (London: Batsford, 1965).
25. See J. Barr, *The Bow Group: A History* (London: Politico's, 2001), 88–115; Joseph quoted in minutes of a seminar held at Sundridge Park, September 1969, Bodleian Library, Carr MSS, uncatalogued.
26. Coleraine, *For Conservatives Only*, 68.
27. Figures from Gallup Polls, cited in L. Johnman, 'The Conservative Party in opposition 1964–70', in R. Coopey, S. Fielding and N. Tiratsoo (eds), *The Wilson Governments* (London: Pinter Publishers, 1993), 192.
28. S. Brittan, 'Some thoughts on the Conservative opposition', *Political Quarterly*, 39 (1968), 145–55. As a participant in the policy-making process, Brittan was well placed to comment; but his contribution was really yet another appeal for the Party to say something different, rather than saying the same thing differently.
29. 'Symposium on Conservative Party policy making, 1965–70', *Contemporary Record*, 3 (1990), 37.
30. Quoted in Ramsden, *Conservative Party Policy*, 272.
31. Ramsden, *Winds of Change*, 257–8.
32. W. Deedes, 'Conflicts within the Conservative Party', *Political Quarterly*, 44 (1973), 393; A. Maude, *The Common Problem: A Policy for the Future* (London: Constable, 1969).
33. Ramsden, *Winds of Change*, 263.
34. 'Conservative Party policy making', 36.
35. See Conservative Research Department files, Bodleian Library, Conservative Party Archive (CPA), CRD 3/24/9–10.
36. Ramsden, *Making of Conservative Party Policy*, 257.
37. Poll findings in CPA, PS/68/9.
38. For Future Legislation Committee see CPA, CRD 3/13/2.
39. See A. Denham and M. Garnett, *Keith Joseph: A Life* (Teddington: Acumen, 2001), 151–8.
40. Carr to Maudling, 24 November 1969, Carr MSS. For an excellent discussion of the policy preparations on industrial relations, see R. Taylor, 'The Heath government and industrial relations: myth and reality', in S. Ball and A.

Seldon (eds), *The Heath Government 1970–74: A Reappraisal* (Harlow: Longman, 1996), 164–9.

41. J. Prior, *A Balance of Power* (London: Hamish Hamilton, 1986), 48–9; Gilmour and Garnett, *Whatever Happened to the Tories?*, 240.
42. Brittan, 'Conservative opposition', 152.
43. Steering Committee minutes, 3 April 1968, CPA, SC/68/5; R. Shepherd, *Iain Macleod* (London: Hutchinson, 1994), 519.
44. E. Heath, text of speech at Carshalton, 8 July 1967, Conservative Central Office (CCO) handout; *A Better Tomorrow*, 6.
45. Selsdon Park meeting minutes, 1 February 1970, seventh session, 7, CPA, CRD 3/9/93.
46. Johnman, 'Conservative Party in opposition', 201.
47. Ibid.; 'Conservative Party policy making', 38.
48. Shadow cabinet minutes, 24 July 1968, CPA, Leader's Consultative Committee (LCC), (68)254.
49. Economic Policy Group meeting minutes, 8 February 1968, CPA, EPG/66/70; *A Better Tomorrow*, 13–14.
50. N. Ridley, *My Style of Government: The Thatcher Years* (London: Hutchinson, 1991), 4.
51. T. Benn, *Office without Power: Diaries 1968–72* (London: Arrow edition, 1988), 349.
52. A. Gamble, *The Conservative Nation* (London: Routledge and Kegan Paul, 1974), 102; H. Berkeley, *Crossing the Floor* (London: Allen and Unwin, 1972), 102.
53. M. Thatcher, *The Path to Power* (London: HarperCollins, 1995), 160.
54. Quoted in J. Campbell, *Edward Heath: A Life* (London: Jonathan Cape, 1993), 265.
55. Lord Young, *The Enterprise Years: A Businessman in the Cabinet* (London: Headline, 1990), 15; A. Clark, *The Tories: Conservatives and the Nation State 1922–1997* (London: Weidenfeld and Nicolson, 1998), 412; Denham and Garnett, *Keith Joseph*, 193; N. Tebbit, *Upwardly Mobile* (London: Futura edition, 1989), 134.
56. D. Hurd, *An End to Promises: Sketch of a Government 1970–74* (London: Collins, 1979), 12–13.
57. T. Stacey and R. St Oswald (eds), *Here Come the Tories* (London: Tom Stacey, 1970).
58. S. Ball, 'The Conservatives in opposition, 1906–79: a comparative analysis', in M. Garnett and P. Lynch (eds), *The Conservatives in Crisis: The Tories after 1997* (Manchester: Manchester University Press, 2003), 23.
59. E.H.H. Green, 'Thatcherism: an historical perspective', *Transactions of the Royal Historical Society*, Sixth Series, 9, 38.
60. The overall record is cogently assessed in J. Ramsden, 'The Prime Minister and the making of policy', in Seldon and Ball (eds), *The Heath Government*.
61. It was typical of Heath's luck that a phrase in a press handout, promising that Conservative policies 'would, at a stroke, reduce the rise in prices', was later garbled by his opponents as an irresponsible promise to cut prices outright. But a regular theme of campaign broadcasts was that the cost of living had been allowed to rise too far under Labour, strongly implying that prices would be cut rather than merely curbed by the Conservatives.

10
The Making of Thatcherism: 1974–1979

Dennis Kavanagh

During the period from March 1974 to May 1979 the Conservative Party experienced the familiar dilemmas of opposition: a leadership crisis, factionalism and striking out in a new direction while trying to mollify supporters of the previous regime. These problems took on an extra dimension because it was the first time in the Party's history that a party leader, Edward Heath, had been ousted in a competitive election. He also took his defeat badly and for a time seemed to regard his successor, Margaret Thatcher, as a usurper. Yet, as a result of the May 1979 general election Margaret Thatcher began her term as the longest and most dominant peacetime Prime Minister in the twentieth century. The Party made the biggest post-war election swing between the two parties and remained in office for the next 18 years. It proved to be a significant turning point in the modern party system and in the political agenda. Since 1979 there have been no more incomes policies or social contracts with the unions, Keynesian demand management has been abandoned and trade union power, which helped to destroy two governments in the 1970s, has been tamed.

But to what extent were the Conservative preparations for office in the years 1974–79 responsible for this major change in the Party's fortunes? There is something of a triumphalist version, retailed by Lady Thatcher and her supporters, or those who denigrate the Heath and Major records in comparison with hers, or critics – on Labour's left and right – of the Wilson and Callaghan governments. Some also claim that the 1974–79 period was a model of successful opposition because:

a) The Party established an electoral ascendancy over Labour
b) Margaret Thatcher broke through in terms of gaining public approval for herself and her ideas
c) Conservative policies were reshaped, presaging what became Thatcherism in the 1980s.

Not surprisingly, Tony Blair in 1994–97, William Hague in 1997–2001 and Iain Duncan Smith in 2001–03 all looked back to the 1974–79 period as a model of how to be a successful opposition.

This chapter, however, challenges all the three of the above claims. As late as October 1978, some opinion polls reported a small lead for Labour. The big shift to the Conservative Party followed a few months later in response to an outside event, the 'Winter of Discontent'. Until then there was still much criticism about the Party's failure to make more electoral progress. Surveys also showed a lack of electoral enthusiasm for Thatcher personally and for many of her ideas, particularly about prioritizing tax cuts ahead of spending on core public services. Finally, the Conservative policies in the 1979 manifesto (even more than in October 1978) on such issues as privatization, tax cuts and, until late in the day, industrial relations were actually quite modest. The radicalism came later, in government.

The Heath interregnum

Edward Heath's decision, when faced by the coalminers' strike, to call a general election on 28 February 1974 – and his defeat – came as a double shock to most of his ministers. They had been ill-prepared to fight an election only three and a half years into the life of the government, with a parliamentary majority still intact, and in defence of a statutory incomes policy that was contrary to the manifesto on which they were elected in 1970. They were also not clear how an election victory would get the miners to go back to work.

After a second general election defeat, in October 1974, some Conservatives became aware of a larger and more daunting picture. The Party had now lost four of the five last general elections, although three of these (1964 and two in 1974) had been lost narrowly; the Liberals were making inroads in Conservative support in the south-east and among the middle class, and the Party seemed to have lost the battle of ideas among opinion-formers to the advocates of collectivism. In particular, the Conservatives appeared to have no electorally persuasive answer to the politically-linked problems of rising prices, a workable incomes policy and trade union power. An apparent lesson of the loss of office in February 1974 was that a Conservative government was not strong enough to take on strikers in key industries but that if it sought co-operation it would be a second best to Labour, which had a 'social contract' with the unions.

There were three phases in Conservative reactions to life in opposition. After the February election defeat, there was agreement that not much could be done immediately about the leadership or policies; Harold Wilson's government lacked a parliamentary majority and it was expected to call a fresh election within months. The Conservative Party was inhibited from quickly adopting radically different policies because it would call into question the policies it had just fought on. Moreover, Heath strongly believed that they were the right policies. Sir Keith Joseph, a member of the shadow cabinet, infuriated Heath with his public repudiation of incomes policies and his conversion to monetarism. He was, in effect, saying: 'We were all wrong' (see below). For the general election in October 1974, the Party adopted a 'softer' line to appeal to those Conservatives who had defected to the Liberals, and had a positive policy on housing. The manifesto promised to end household rates, sell off council houses at a third below the market value to tenants of at least three years standing, and peg mortgage rates to 9.5 per cent or less; the main, and initially reluctant, party spokesman for these attempts to 'buck the market' was Margaret Thatcher. Heath also held out the prospect of forming a government of national unity to cope with the urgent economic crisis – an international recession, high inflation and rising unemployment – in contrast to the appeal for strong party government in February. Much of this thinking was shaped by the BMRB survey panel, which showed how and why the Conservative Party had lost ground between 1970 and 1974.[1]

During the second phase, following the October 1974 election defeat, rethinking on policy and strategy was again suspended, largely because of the widespread assumption that the leadership question had first to be resolved. Was Heath staying or going and, if he went, who would replace him? For the 12 months after the February defeat, therefore, the Party had severe problems in positioning itself on the two central issues in British politics at the time: (a) incomes policy, widely seen as the only politically-possible instrument for tackling inflation, and (b) the trade unions – whose co-operation was regarded as essential to achieve (a).

The third phase began when Thatcher was elected Party leader in February 1975.

Leadership

Heath's position as opposition leader after the February election defeat was precarious. Some of his friends urged him to step down at once after the October 1974 election defeat, on the grounds that it would improve the election chances of a supporter of his policies, probably William Whitelaw, or at least to offer himself for re-election immediately and catch his party critics off guard. He did neither, fearing that a right-winger (probably Sir Keith Joseph) would benefit. His inaction meant that his opponents were free to campaign for a leadership election.

Eventually Heath agreed to offer himself for re-election. New rules had to be drawn up, as the existing rules provided for an election only in the event of a vacancy. The new arrangements provided for Conservative MPs to hold an annual leadership election, the winning candidate now needed an overall majority of all MPs eligible to vote (as opposed to the previous arrangement, which covered only those MPs voting) and the winner had to have a lead of 15 per cent over the runner-up. The new rules also allowed fresh candidates to enter on the second ballot. This last provision meant that a stalking-horse candidate could enter and test the strength of Heath's support on the first ballot. Each of these new provisions had the effect of increasing Heath's vulnerability to a challenge and that of his successors as well. Heath was aware of this.[2] He may not have been aware that Lord Home, overseeing the drafting of the new arrangements, instructed the official who was drafting them to make a change of leader easier, because 'the Party will not have Ted'.[3]

Sir Keith Joseph and Edward du Cann, the chairman of the '1922 Committee', soon ruled themselves out as challengers. Other likely figures also refused to stand; they felt committed to Heath because they had served in his cabinet and among them the spirit of collective responsibility persisted. An exception was Thatcher, who had been Education Secretary in Heath's government. When Sir Keith withdrew, she decided to stand.

Heath enjoyed the support of most of the shadow cabinet, senior party figures and the Conservative press. If his support was largely among senior colleagues, Thatcher's was among backbenchers. He had built up resentment among those to whom he had not given office, those who objected to his economic and European policies, those disappointed at not receiving political honours (as Prime Minister he was particularly niggardly in this regard), and those who would not forgive his coldness or lack of diplomacy in his dealings with them. The first ballot on 4 February 1975 showed that he had exhausted too much of his political credit and MPs, for various reasons, rallied to Thatcher. She finished top with 130 votes to Heath's 119. 'We got it wrong', he said to an aide, and resigned immediately. On the second ballot other candidates, including Whitelaw, entered, but Thatcher had momentum and went on to win outright. The first Conservative leader to be chosen in a competitive election (in 1965), Heath was also the first to be defeated in one. Although his refusal to resign or hold an election earlier was motivated by his fear of a right-wing takeover, it can plausibly be argued that his tactics actually led to the outcome he wished to avoid.

The contest and the outcome decided the leadership but it did not calm Conservative nerves. Heath took a long time to be reconciled to defeat and his sense of injustice increased as Margaret Thatcher and Sir Keith Joseph distanced themselves from his government's record; in his view, they were rewriting history. For a time the election caused nearly as much bad blood in the Party as did Thatcher's own ousting from the leadership in 1990.

But what did the leadership contest mean for the Conservative Party? The accepted view is that MPs had voted primarily to get rid of Heath, rather than to elect Thatcher. Although Thatcher did not campaign as a radical right-winger, recent research suggests that there was an ideological element to the vote. Some 80 per cent of Conservative MPs on the left of the Party voted for Heath on the first ballot and a similar proportion of the right voted for Thatcher.[4] There was also a top–bottom split, as most of those who had held office under Heath voted for him or for Whitelaw, respectively, on the first and second ballots.

Sir Keith Joseph's closeness to Thatcher lent an ideological element to the contest. In a series of speeches and writings, he was setting out a fundamental critique of the economic policies of the Heath government – of which he had been a member – and calling for free market policies. He confessed the error of his ways – and by implication of his colleagues –with his confession: 'It was only in April 1974 that I was converted to Conservatism.' In a much-publicized speech in Preston in September 1974, he advanced the monetarist analysis of the causes of inflation.[5] But Heath and his supporters feared that critics could portray Sir Keith as an advocate of increasing unemployment as a method of curbing a greater evil, inflation. As long as Thatcher did not disown Sir Keith, she was associated with him – attracting the support of MPs on the right and alienating many on the Heath wing of the Party. Indeed, she was Vice Chairman of Joseph's new think-tank, the Centre for Policy Studies. Moreover, MPs knew that Thatcher, more clearly than Heath, stood for lower taxes and less state intervention in the economy. In a pre-election article in the *Daily Telegraph* on 30 January 1975, she had signalled her determination to change the Party's direction when she wrote: 'One of the many reasons for our electoral failure is that people believe too many Conservatives have become Socialists already.'

Thatcher as leader

Margaret Thatcher wore the crown uneasily for much of the period in opposition. She knew that many of the senior figures in the Party had not supported her on the first ballot. Of the shadow cabinet, perhaps only Sir Keith had done so. Her political caution was clearly seen in her appointments. She immediately made Whitelaw her deputy and a year later he was also given the Home Affairs portfolio. She did not appoint Sir Keith shadow Chancellor of the Exchequer. Airey Neave was given Northern Ireland and, as her chief of staff, warded off more right-wing suggestions,[6] as did other senior figures like Lord Carrington, Francis Pym, Lord Hailsham and Peter Thorneycroft. Although she did not appoint Robert Carr or Peter Walker, both former cabinet ministers and Heathites, she was slow to promote her supporters like Norman Tebbit, John Nott, Nicholas Ridley, Cecil Parkinson or Nigel Lawson. When Norman St John Stevas was moved from Education in November 1978 (to become shadow Leader of the Commons) he was not replaced by Rhodes Boyson, his right-wing deputy, but by the more centrist Mark Carlisle.

James Prior occupied the key post of shadow Employment Secretary. Her supporters correctly regarded him as the main obstacle to taking tough measures against the unions. She did not feel strong enough to move him, or wholeheartedly implement the 'Stepping Stones' policies (see below) or – until the 'Winter of Discontent' of 1978–79 – to strengthen the Party's policies. She was opposed in principle to the closed shop, but reluctantly accepted it – she did not want to get too far ahead of public opinion or the views of colleagues.[7] Around the shadow cabinet table she was also faced by Michael Heseltine (shadowing the Department of Trade and Industry until 1976, and then Environment), a man of interventionist if not corporatist inclinations; Ian Gilmour (shadowing Home Affairs for a year and then Defence), a Keynesian; and, until his dismissal in November 1976, Reginald Maudling (shadowing Foreign Affairs) a former Chancellor of the Exchequer and strongly identified with Keynesians and incomes policy. She acquiesced in, rather than welcomed, what she regarded as a 'fudge' about pay policy in *The Right Approach to the Economy*.[8]

It was therefore not surprising that Thatcher sometimes made policy 'on the hoof', making comments in interviews which surprised and sometimes annoyed colleagues who were responsible for the particular policy area and had not been consulted. This was so with her remarks on people feeling 'swamped' in response to a question on levels of immigration (see below), on Soviet expansionist designs, and the case for referendums on strikes in essential services. When challenged, she would often forcefully articulate her right-wing views on a variety of topics. But there was ample evidence of caution. Her shadow cabinet was broad-based, indeed Heathite, she allowed debate and she took advice from different people. Many shadow spokesmen did not enthuse about what a good Prime Minister she would be. Douglas Hurd, a future member of her cabinet, reflected: 'If she becomes Prime Minister she would have to listen a great deal and this would prevent her doing the right-wing and foolish things that she now sometimes does.'[9]

She was also aware that she was not regarded as an electoral asset for the Party.[10] She regularly trailed the Labour Prime Minister, James Callaghan, in the opinion polls on questions about who would make the best Premier, and some surveys even showed that the Party would gain more support with Heath as leader. Her image was that of a strong leader, one who spoke her mind, but who was also out of touch, snobbish and divisive. In the 1979 general election a MORI poll found that the Conservatives were preferred on policies over Labour by 40 to 35 per cent, but trailed on leadership by 41 to 35 per cent. There is, however, no evidence that this had much independent effect on votes in the general election.[11]

Central Office

Since 1951, Conservative Central Office had acquired a reputation as a formidable election-winning machine. The Party had been a pacesetter in fund-raising, use of private polling, employing an advertising agency and taking a professional approach to television broadcasts.[12] Although its standing was poor in the wake of the Party's election defeat in February 1974, it was Heath who had overruled Central Office advice over election timing. Any electoral consequences of organizational shortcomings, such as the failure to deliver party literature on time or relying more on the findings of opinion polls than the views of party workers, were insignificant when set beside the bigger problems from the government's record on rising prices.[13]

During the first year of opposition, Central Office still bore the heavy imprint of the Party leader. William Whitelaw succeeded Carrington as Party Chairman, and both were strongly identified with Heath. Chris

Patten, who had served as Carrington's personal assistant, replaced the politically like-minded James Douglas as Director of the Conservative Research Department, with Sir Ian Gilmour as its chairman. The Department was therefore in the hands of people steeped in the 'one nation' values of R.A. Butler. Heath had appointed Michael Wolff, his special adviser and speechwriter, to a new post of Director-General, effectively chief of staff, at Central Office in April 1974. Wolff had no background in the organization structure and his appointment upset the voluntary side of the Party, who looked to Sir Richard Webster, the Director of Organization, to protect their interests even though there was some expectation that he would be retiring soon. Sir Michael Fraser, the long-serving chairman of the Research Department and a Deputy Chairman of the Party, retired. Heath's appointments reflected his belief that the Party had to pursue 'moderate' policies. As in his choice of shadow cabinet colleagues, Heath did not reach out to his critics on making appointments to Central Office.

However, Central Office responds to the demands of a new Party leader, and Thatcher relied on her surprise choice as Party Chairman, Lord Thorneycroft, to mould it to her wishes. Thorneycroft, aged 65 when appointed, had served in Sir Alec Douglas-Home's government in 1963–64 and previously had been Chancellor of the Exchequer in 1956–57 under Macmillan. In the interim, he had become a City figure and as Party Chairman managed to retain a number of his City posts. He was a dominant player in Central Office, forceful in strategy discussions, close to Thatcher and an important influence on the election manifesto.

He soon made his mark by dismissing Wolff within weeks, a step that infuriated some ministers, including Jim Prior. Thatcher later defended the action: 'The right concept, but the wrong man.'[14] Once Heath had departed, Wolff's position was always vulnerable. He was not replaced and Sir Richard Webster was seen in some quarters as the gainer, but Webster himself was summarily dismissed in January 1976 and replaced from within the organizational structure by Anthony Garner. Patten remained but Sir Angus Maude, another who had fallen foul of Heath, replaced Ian Gilmour as chairman of the Research Department.

Perhaps no appointment gave the new leader more satisfaction than that of Gordon Reece as Director of Publicity in March 1978. He had advised her informally when she ran for the leadership in early 1975. He influenced how she approached the media and how she presented herself, encouraging her to soften her voice, dispense with hats ('too redolent of middle class Conservative women') and avoid as far as possible interviews with forceful broadcasters, who tended to make her more abrasive. He was struck by Thatcher's innocence of the media. Her famous 'swamping' remark about immigration followed a deliberate leak of a party document on the topic. Reece said: 'She did not realise that (the question) had been deliberately set up by a leak.'[15] After each broadcast, he commissioned research to gauge audience reactions. The target audience was not the readers of broadsheets but of tabloids, and viewers not of late-night current affairs programmes but of early-evening magazines, largely watched by women. He also cultivated newspaper editors, particularly of the *Daily Mail* and the *Sun*, and was a key figure in the Party's decision to appoint Saatchi & Saatchi as its advertising agency (see below).

Alistair McAlpine, aged 32, was appointed Treasurer in 1975, and under his direction income was substantially increased. The Party was in debt after fighting two general elections in 1974. He managed to double the quota payments from the constituency associations and was successful with smaller businesses, whose contributions (an average of £250) were channelled through the Industrial Councils. McAlpine was no master of the details of policy and when meeting potential business donors, the ex-Conservative MP and *Daily Telegraph* journalist, Jock Bruce-Gardyne, accompanied him. The latter was a source of useful political gossip as well as good political ammunition. He would handle such questions from company chairmen as: 'Why should I give money to a party that does this or that?' or 'What is the Conservative policy on this or that?'.[16] McAlpine also found it useful to have Reece with him; potential donors were reluctant to provide money for the general running of the Party, but could be tempted to finance an advertisement. He would point to Reece and say: 'This is the tip of the lance that will kill the dragon of socialism. He is our St George.' Reece would then outline an idea for a party broadcast or poster and, prompted by McAlpine, would suggest what it would cost.[17] Central Office cut back on private polling until late in the parliament, and in 1976 the scheme for the central employment of local constituency agents was abandoned. Instead, it concentrated on providing resources for the 97 so-called 'critical' seats, and by 1979 each one had the services of a full-time agent.

Publicity and public relations

The key step in preparing for the election was the appointment of Saatchi & Saatchi as the Party's advertising agency in March 1978. Reece's background in religious broadcasting convinced him of the need to appoint an agency with political commitment; he did not believe in 'hired guns' in political advertising.[18] The Saatchi brothers founded the agency in 1970 and since then had gained a reputation for their aggressive and creative work. The advertisements were certainly eye-catching, perhaps none more so than the 'Labour Isn't Working' poster in the summer of 1978. The agency sought to overturn the popular view that Labour had a better record on unemployment and prices than the Conservatives. Researchers found that the average record of each post-war Labour government was actually worse than that of its Conservative predecessor. The press adverts (aimed at skilled working-class voters and placed mainly in the *Daily Mirror* and the *Sun*) and the election broadcasts were designed to correct this perception.

The agency took negative campaigning to a new level in British politics. To Gordon Reece, the object of the advertising was 'To make the voters dissatisfied with the government'.[19] Other posters used simple slogans: 'Educashun Isn't Working'; 'Britain Isn't Getting Any Better'; 'Labour Still Isn't Working' and 'Cheer Up. They Can't Last Forever'. Much of the negativism was reinforced by the press onslaughts on the Labour government.

It is likely that the Saatchi effect during the general election was greatly exaggerated. The damage to Labour had been done in the previous summer, stemming the usual summer swing back to the government of the day. Thereafter, Lord Thorneycroft pressed the agency to be less jokey and less adversarial in its broadcasts and advertisements. Tim Bell was the link between Central Office and Thatcher and the agency. Reece and Bell took the 1974 Conservative vote for granted and concentrated on capturing the soft or dissatisfied Liberal and Labour voters. They also concentrated on housewives in skilled working-class homes and first-time voters. They wanted to exploit the mood for change and Reece, who believed that voters decided on impressions, said that his object was to 'make them think Conservatives are good for you'.[20] All this was in contrast to the appalling relations between Labour politicians, officials and publicists.[21]

In November 1978, the agency submitted a draft strategy document for a 1979 election campaign. It sought to exploit the mood of hopelessness and cynicism and provide a message of hope. Its key message, in upper case in the original document, was:

IT IS A MESSAGE OF ATTITUDE AND PHILOSOPHY NOT SPECIFIC POLICIES WHICH CREATE THE CLIMATE IN WHICH TO WIN THE COMING ELECTION.

MESSAGE. A VOTE FOR CONSERVATIVES [*sic*] IS A VOTE FOR OPPORTUNITY, FREEDOM, CHOICE AND SELF-RESPECT.

OBJECTIVE. TO ENSURE THAT THE ELECTORATE IS DISSATISFIED
WITH THE GOVERNMENT AND CONSIDERS A REAL ALTERNATIVE
EXISTS VIZ.: OPPOSE AND PROPOSE.

The electorate

Surveys suggest that in the late 1970s there was an erosion of Labour
values among the voters, rather than a Conservative breakthrough. For
the first year of the Parliament, the opinion polls showed that Thatcher
struggled to make an impact and there was little improvement in party
fortunes. A strategy note from the Research Department director, Chris
Patten, observed: 'An inflation rate in excess of 20 per cent, and a level of
unemployment above 1 million, have not taken the political toll of the
government that one might have expected.'[22] The Conservatives moved
into a substantial lead in the opinion polls for a year from the autumn
of 1976, in the wake of the IMF intervention and high – though falling
– inflation. The lead was reduced in 1978 as inflation fell to single figures
and voters' economic confidence improved. However, even before the
'Winter of Discontent', skilled workers were attracted to Conservative
appeals on taxes, council house sales and welfare benefits.

What might have happened had Callaghan called an election in
October 1978 is one of the great 'if only's of modern British politics.
When Callaghan was making his decision in August, the Conservatives
had leads in published opinion polls of 2 per cent and 7 per cent. But
other surveys, conducted before the announcement but published after
it, reported Labour leads of 6 per cent (MORI) and 7 per cent (Gallup).
On 26 October, Labour held Berwick and East Lothian in a by-election
with an increased majority. Callaghan seems to have calculated that at
best he would not gain a majority and the Conservatives, although they
might be denied a majority, might form a minority government and then
dissolve at a favourable time.[23]

Conservative leaders discussed electoral strategy at length. Before the
'Winter of Discontent', the Party trailed Labour on the salient issues of
prices, trade unions and strikes, and unemployment. But it did have an
advantage on immigration and law and order, although these issues were
less salient than the economic ones. Some argued that the Party should
therefore campaign to raise the salience of these issues and create a so-
called populist authoritarian agenda.[24] They seized on the improvement
in the Party's standing in the opinion polls after Thatcher remarked
during a television interview in February 1978 that people felt 'swamped'

by a sudden influx of immigrants. But Patten's memo, 'Further Thoughts on Strategy', argued that it would be a mistake to concentrate only on raising the salience of the non-economic issues and that economic issues mattered more to the Party's target voters. Concerned at the slow pace of the Conservative electoral recovery, he doubted that the Party was seen as a credible alternative government in the media, City or industry, and that it needed to express its policies 'in a convincing tone of voice and in sufficient intellectual depth'.[25]

However, the 'Winter of Discontent' of 1978–79 changed the electoral fortunes of the parties significantly. It damaged Labour in the areas that mattered to voters and where it had been strong: handling the trade unions and strikes, and keeping prices down. Although Labour made some electoral recovery between the beginning of the disruption and 3 May, when the election was held, it never regained its former level of support. The main voting study of the election unsurprisingly showed that immigration, race and law and order all helped the Conservatives. But when it examined the voters' positive and negative comments, it found that the issues of handling trade unions and strikes gave Conservatives their biggest advantage over Labour.[26]

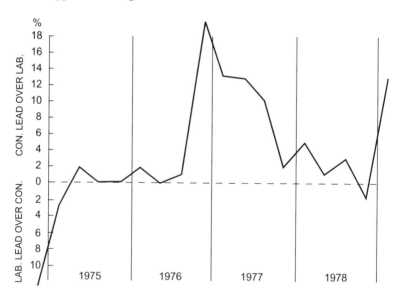

Figure 10.1:   Party Support 1974–79

Source: Taken from D. Butler and D. Kavanagh, *The British General Election of 1979* (Macmillan Press, now Palgrave Macmillan, 1980), p. 29.

The climate of opinion

When she became Party leader, Margaret Thatcher believed that the Conservatives had lost the initiative among opinion formers in schools, universities and the churches to advocates of collectivist, egalitarian and anti-capitalist values. She suggested that the left had captured the vocabulary of political and social debate and there was no authoritative Conservative response. Conservatives, she complained, were 'rather too non-political, whereas Socialists regarded politics as the most important thing in life'.[27] To be effective, politicians, should have 'a clear philosophy and a coherent set of beliefs from which the Party's arguments and policies should follow'. As she wrote in her memoirs: 'And in Opposition argument is everything'.[28]

The dominant figure in trying to reverse the tide was Sir Keith Joseph, partly from his outpost at the Centre for Policy Studies and partly from his responsibility in the Party for research and policy development. In speeches, pamphlets and newspaper articles, he excoriated the evils of collectivism, prices and incomes controls, excessive taxation and public spending, trade union power and state ownership, because: 'We must fight the battle of ideas in every school, university, publication committee [and] television studio.'[29] He expounded the merits of the social market economy, the case for entrepreneurial capitalism, the bankruptcy of much of the conventional wisdom, and the importance of controlling the money supply to curb inflation – even if in the short run it cost jobs. Many of the speeches were published, including *Monetarism Is Not Enough*, *Conditions For Full Employment*, *Why Britain Needs a Social Market Economy* and *Reversing the Trend*. Above all, he refuted so-called Keynesianism with its reliance on greater public spending as a way of reducing unemployment, and tried to reclaim the great economist as a spokesman for sound finance. Governments, he urged, should abandon something that they could not deliver.

Sir Keith also distinguished between the *common ground*, an area on which there was general agreement between the parties and which the voters accepted, and the *middle ground*, a point midway between the policies of Labour and Conservatives. He complained that Labour gave a turn of the ratchet to Socialism each time it was in office and that this was then accepted, in the interest of continuity, by the next Conservative government. The trouble was that each Labour move to the left was forcing the Conservatives to adjust to a more left-wing middle ground. The analysis impressed Thatcher and reinforced her detestation of so-called consensus politics.

Thus was born the idea of 'Josephism', soon known as 'Thatcherism'.[30] In speeches and interviews, the leader praised the free market and its indispensable links with a free society, warned against expecting too much of the state, called for the withdrawal of the trade unions' legal privileges, and expressed her scepticism about the pursuit of equality. Complaining that too many of her upper-class predecessors (and colleagues) had felt inhibited from taking necessary decisions because of guilt over the mass unemployment of the 1930s, she insisted in a speech that she would not be intimidated by what she called 'bourgeois guilt'.[31]

The Institute of Economic Affairs, Friedrich Hayek and Milton Friedman had propounded such ideas for a number of years. However, now that major politicians were speaking out and the existing stock of policies were clearly failing, there was a more receptive audience. The ideas were supported by sections of the press, particularly the *Telegraph* papers, *The Times* and the *Daily Mail*, and such weeklies as the *Spectator* and *The Economist*. They provided a platform for prolific commentators like Paul Johnson, Roger Scruton, T.E. Utley, John Vaizey, George Gale and Frank Johnson. In *The Times* and the *Financial Times*, the influential economic commentators Peter Jay and Samuel Brittan respectively, and the editor of *The Times*, William Rees-Mogg, advanced the case for monetarism and cast doubt on incomes policies. In addition, right-wing academics and intellectuals participated in seminars at think-tanks such as the Centre for Policy Studies, the Institute of Economic Affairs and the Adam Smith Institute. Labour and the left could not match the range of this activity.

Thatcher, however, knew that a number of her colleagues did not share her values or the need to fight a battle of ideas. Shadow colleagues savaged Sir Keith's paper on political strategy, 'Notes towards the definition of policy', at a meeting on 11 April 1975. Lord Hailsham's notes of the meeting include the following:[32]

> RM (Reginald Maudling) 'I do not agree with ONE little bit'
> IG (Ian Gilmour) spoke in defence a Conservative consensus, thought the paper too critical of past Conservative policy
> TR (Tim Raison) 'too much misery in Keith's paper' and there are matters on which 'we have got to operate a consensus'
> FP (Francis Pym) 'The Keith paper is a recipe for disaster' and there is a 'need for a broad measure of agreement'

Prior disliked what he regarded as her absolutism and habit of talking in terms of black and white:

It is wrong to speak of winning an intellectual argument, because that implied you had a body of doctrine by which your views should be judged. I hope the Conservatives will never have such a body of doctrine or dogma. There is a continuing worry whether Margaret really understands the political process, the limits of the possible.[33]

In the same interview, he expressed his support for proportional representation on the grounds that it was conducive to the stability of government and 'it is more important to have continuity than to have big-C Conservatism'. To Joseph's credit, the tide began to turn. By 1979 ideas about money supply, more controls on trade unions, greater selectivity in welfare and raising educational standards were more widely accepted among the policy community. In his famous 1976 party conference speech, the Labour Prime Minister, James Callaghan, had signalled the end of Keynesian ideas of spending one's way out of unemployment. Among voters there was a similar shift to the right on many issues between October 1974 and May 1979, although there was still strong support for the welfare state and a willingness to see it expanded by means of higher taxes.[34]

Policy

As ever, Conservative policy-making in opposition had to strike a balance between immediate responses to government initiatives, answering national problems and foreshadowing policies which the Party in government would adopt in some four to five years' time. The process under Margaret Thatcher was less harmonious than during the Heath exercise of 1965–70, particularly on the key issues of industrial relations and pay policy. Another contrast with the Heath exercise was that there had been a fissure in the Party and the overthrow of a leader. Thatcher was always conscious that while she had to present a new direction for the Party, she could not make too sharp a disjunction from the 1970–74 Heath government. Her task was eased, however, by the widespread agreement that, after the experience of the Industrial Relations Act, the Party should avoid too much detail too early in the Parliament. She thought it was far better to state broad policy objectives and principles from which policies could be developed. Indeed her Party Chairman wrote to her on 5 May 1978 stating that he and Gordon Reece favoured a one-page manifesto – although the Research Department did not – so that they could 'enter government unencumbered by costly pledges and free, guided by our declared principles, to develop and apply policies according to circumstances'.[35]

Labour leaders could look with some envy at how the senior politicians and the leader dominated the making of Conservative policy. There was little or no effective outside pressure from the party conference or National Union. As usual, policy groups were chaired by the appropriate shadow minister and reported to the Advisory Committee on Policy, which was chaired by Sir Keith Joseph. The Research Department provided secretarial support for each policy group, and the Steering Committee and the full shadow cabinet took the final decisions. After 1974, the Research Department had a rival in the Centre for Policy Studies. Three of the most influential figures on the front bench, Thatcher, Sir Keith Joseph and Sir Geoffrey Howe, were associated with the Centre. It had a more free market outlook than the Research Department, was a support for Sir Keith and provided a home for the authors of the controversial 'Stepping Stones' programme in 1978 (see below). Outside the Party, think-tanks like the Institute for Economic Affairs and Adam Smith Institute also canvassed a range of free market policies.

Thatcher had to compromise on the two long-running and divisive areas of pay policy and industrial relations, and their shadow hung over the deliberations of the shadow cabinet for most of the Parliament. The Party sought to detach itself from Heath's statutory pay policy but also to take account of Labour's voluntary policy, which had the acquiescence of the trade unions and the support of the public. Sir Geoffrey Howe chaired the Economic Reconstruction Group, which also included Joseph, Nigel Lawson and John Nott, as well as other shadow ministers whose remits impinged on economic policy. The team worked out detailed proposals for tax reform and supply-side measures. On inflation, Howe favoured monetary targets backed by a social partners approach, as in West Germany, and the idea of a forum in which the major interests could regularly meet and 'concert' economic policies. The idea was taken up in the mid-term policy documents, *The Right Approach* (1976) and *The Right Approach to the Economy* (1977). The last document was drafted by the MP David Howell and drew on the reports of policy groups on taxation, industrial relations, public expenditure and industry.

Howe's group insisted on 'responsible' pay bargaining and opposed a free-for-all. For the public sector it would seek a voluntary pay policy, rely on cash limits where it was the paymaster, and not pay more than could be afforded. It would also not bail out companies in the private sector that made excessive pay settlements. Thatcher, however, was opposed to ideas of tripartism and incomes policy, and was unhappy with the work of this committee.[36] She ensured that it was published under the names of the principal authors (Howe, Joseph, Prior, Howell and Maude), and not formally endorsed by the shadow cabinet.

There was a similar caution over privatization, a flagship policy of Thatcherism in the 1980s. Nicholas Ridley's report on the nationalized industries made modest proposals for tightening financial discipline, selling off shares in the electricity grid and ending the telephone monopoly. An appendix recommended that the government should try and avert a coal strike by paying the miners above average increases and, in case this failed, build up coal stocks. When it was leaked to *The Economist* on 27 May 1978 and provoked Labour and union attacks, it was disowned. Some work was done on privatization but the final manifesto proposals covered only the recently nationalized aircraft and shipbuilding industries and the National Freight Corporation.

Once the Labour government had passed up the opportunity of calling a general election in October 1978, an immediate Conservative problem was how to react to the government's 5 per cent pay policy. Some critics portrayed Thatcher's opposition to it as approval for a wages free-for-all, and Heath called for Conservatives to support the government in the battle against inflation. The divisions were played out against the Party's failure to recapture the marginal Berwick and East Lothian seat at a by-election. The shadow cabinet eventually reunited around the policy earlier announced in *The Right Approach to the Economy*, and its endorsement of 'responsible' pay bargaining which should take into account government monetary, fiscal and spending policies and consultation about the economy with the Trades Union Congress and the Confederation of British Industry.[37]

Thinking on the constitution was driven by the need to respond to events and Labour initiatives. Although some Conservatives supported electoral reform, Thatcher's resistance was only strengthened by the Lib-Lab pact in March 1977; proportional representation, she feared, would only benefit an anti-Conservative party. She also rejected it for the direct European elections because it could be a lever for extending the principle to Westminster. In the free vote on direct elections with a regional list system of proportional representation for the European Parliament, held in November 1977, 16 Conservatives voted for the change and 30 abstained.[38]

On devolution, the Party moved from its pro-devolution stance under Heath. In December 1976 the decision to impose a three-line whip against Labour proposals led to bitter debate and the resignation as Party spokesmen of Alick Buchanan-Smith and Malcolm Rifkind, and the replacement of the former by the anti-devolutionist Teddy Taylor. Twenty-seven Conservatives abstained and five voted with the government. The

Party's new position was to oppose an elected assembly and call for a constitutional conference.

Nicholas Edwards, the shadow minister for Wales, headed a committee on referendums. Thatcher had earlier raised the possibility of referendums on anti-government strikes in the public services. She was impressed with the report's reference to the number of previous Conservative leaders, going back to A.J. Balfour, who had approved the use of the device for considering proposed changes to the constitution. Lord Home's committee on the reform of the House of Lords reported in January 1978 and, faced with a Labour threat of abolishing the upper chamber, proposed that a majority of members be elected, with the rest nominated. Some Conservatives complained that the constitution was now unbalanced and facilitated an elective dictatorship. Lord Hailsham canvassed a bill of rights (as did Sir Keith Joseph), and a stronger House of Lords elected by proportional representation.

The Conservatives had long been seen as more restrictive on immigration than Labour. Although the major parties had sought to keep the issue above politics, the personality of Enoch Powell (although no longer a Conservative MP) identified the Party with a less liberal position. Advocates of a tough line were encouraged by the rise in party support in the opinion polls following Thatcher's 'swamping' remarks in January 1978. By April 1978, the shadow Home Secretary, Whitelaw, had worked out a policy to control the rate of immigration but not to end it. The new policy provided for a Conservative government to introduce a quota system for immigrants and a compulsory registration of dependants of immigrants who were already ordinarily resident.

As shadow minister for Employment, Prior was determined to avoid a repeat of the Heath government's Industrial Relations Act (1971) and any policies which might lead to another confrontational 'who governs' election. He wanted to keep in touch with moderate trade union leaders and gain their support for an incomes policy. But he was surrounded by more hawkish voices in the shadow cabinet, particularly from those who wished to end the closed shop and introduce union ballots. Both Sir Keith Joseph and Sir Geoffrey Howe spoke forcefully on industrial relations matters, but at the end of the day Thatcher, however reluctantly, usually sided with Prior. His presence in the shadow cabinet was a symbol of moderate Conservatism. The draft manifesto for an October 1978 election was something of a setback for Thatcher, as colleagues backed Prior's 'softly-softly' approach.

Thatcher, prompted by Joseph, seized on the thinking provided by two outsiders, John Hoskyns and Norman Strauss, who had been brought to her attention by Sir Keith Joseph and by Alfred Sherman at the Centre for Policy Studies. The first was a computer software entrepreneur who had sold his business for a large sum in 1974 and the latter a corporate planner at Unilever. They argued that Britain's economic decline was caused by the inter-linked problems of inflation, over-manned nationalized industries, weakening economic competitiveness and worsening public finances. They called for a strategic approach to tackling the problem and asserted that trade union reform was a crucial first step; unless that was done the unions would be able to block 'Turn-Around' policies. To be able to take decisive action when they were in government, the Conservatives should be trying to win the argument before the election. She liked the programme but also realized that it would be difficult to get colleagues to accept it. The idea of social contracts was still in the air and Prior and Patten did not accept the analysis, believing that it was still important not to offend moderate union leaders.

Hoskyns and Strauss continued to work up the 'Stepping Stones' strategy (so-called because it was a step-by-step approach), and first presented it to the Steering Committee on 30 January 1978.[39] It was a communications strategy designed to convince the country of the need for change. The presentation distinguished between four categories of policies to reverse economic decline. The first was *good housekeeping*, prudent policies which should have been implemented a long time ago. Secondly was *turnaround*, which was a set of policies to get the country out of its mess. Third was *outflanking*, the actions which would make it difficult for trade unions to oppose the turnaround policies. Fourth were *symbolic measures*, which were to show that the policies were not prompted by anti-trade union prejudice.

The 'Winter of Discontent' greatly advanced the case for more radical action on the unions. Until then, Thatcher had been circumspect in dealing with Prior and little progress was made with 'Stepping Stones'. She was now emboldened. It was in this area that the manifesto changed significantly between that drafted for a possible October 1978 election and one published in May 1979. By the beginning of 1979, the government's pay policy had collapsed and the trade unions were no longer partners of the government. In her party political broadcast on 17 January 1979, the combined efforts of Thorneycroft and Patten persuaded Thatcher to scrap her original plans and seize the high ground by offering support for government action to bring the disruption to an end. She offered to back the government on a programme of no-strike agreements in key services, taxing the supplementary benefits of strikers, secret ballots for union elections and a code of practice for secondary picketing. Only the first two proposals were new. The government's predictable refusal to accept the proposals left her free to attack abuses of trade union power and call for legislation, something that even Prior now accepted. The shadow cabinet also agreed that it would provide more safeguards and improve compensation for workers who had lost their jobs because of the closed shop.[40]

Thatcher had commissioned Chris Patten to prepare a draft manifesto for an October election, based on the reports from the shadow spokesmen. She was unimpressed with the draft she received in July, complaining about its list of costly promises. In the margin of a draft in August she wrote: '??? This paragraph is pathetic.'[41] In her memoirs, she commented: 'In truth, I was disagreeably reminded what little progress we had made in opposition in the last three years. If we continued thinking in these terms, how would we ever manage to turn the country round?'[42] Although Sir Geoffrey Howe was pleased with the work his group had done on economic policy, he felt that something was still lacking. In summer 1978 he reflected: 'Well, what puzzles me is that when we are so obviously right we have had such limited success in getting our case across. We are puzzled by our failure to do better in such circumstances.'[43]

Yet, on the eve of the 1979 election what was striking was the moderation of Conservative policies. There was no suggestion that a Conservative government would provide a major reversal in many policy areas. It was a relatively short and thematic manifesto. She reminded colleagues of mistakes made by Hugh Gaitskell – in her view 'the best leader Labour ever had' – when he went into the 1959 general election with too many detailed policies.[44] Proposals for privatization were strictly limited and the proposals to sell back shares in the recently nationalized aerospace, shipbuilding and national freight operations followed the practice of previous Conservative manifestos with regard to recent Labour nationalizations. On taxation, the Party would cut the top rate of tax to the European average (60 per cent) and switch from direct to indirect taxation. Recent Labour budgets, however, had been moving in this direction, and again it was consistent with previous Conservative policies. Comprehensive schools would be retained, although the mandatory ending of selection under the 1976 Act would be repealed. A Parents' Charter, an assisted places scheme (to compensate for the government's abolition of the direct grant school scheme), and the introduction of national standards in key subjects presaged future developments. The closed shop would be retained, although compensation for victims would be improved. On pay, wage bargaining in the private sector would be left to employers and workers – although it warned that they would have to abide by the consequences of the agreements they made. In the public sector, pay settlements would be governed by what each sector could afford (although the Conservatives promised to honour the future recommendations of the Clegg Comparability Commission, which the government had established in January to head off further strikes in the public services). This last commitment made nonsense of the policy of cash limits in the public sector. It is not surprising that in his biography of Margaret Thatcher, John Campbell's chapter on Conservative policy-making is entitled 'Thatcherism Under Wraps'.

There was clearly a change of direction, both from the Conservative position in 1974 and from some of the policies of the Labour government. But it was not a radical free market platform. Thatcherism was to emerge over time, when Thatcher was in Number 10. She had decided views and they were expressed forcefully. In opposition, however, they were not entirely reflected in the fine print of policies. This was largely because the key arena for deciding policy was the shadow cabinet, and this was a politically moderate body.

Conclusion

Timing is crucial, in history as well as in politics. The past may look very different, depending on when it is viewed. The verdict on the Party's record to October 1978 is different from that offered when the period is extended to May 1979. In October 1978, the Conservatives were level-pegging with Labour in the polls. The success of the government's agreement with the TUC over pay policy reinforced Labour's boast that only it could work with the unions and that the policy would be put at risk under a Conservative government. In view of Labour's poor economic record, its lack of a working parliamentary majority and of press support, the unpopularity of the unions and the slight improvement in living standards, this was a discouraging verdict on the Conservative performance in opposition. On the policy front, the Party was offering change that was modest; as long as Labour followed IMF-approved policies, it was difficult to attack the government. Faced with a shadow cabinet that was less than enthusiastic about her views on pay and the trade unions, Thatcher was cautious.

The upsurge of industrial unrest and the collapse of the government's pay policy in the 'Winter of Discontent' of 1978–79 changed the political scene dramatically. The Labour government was visibly unable to control events and trade union leaders could not negotiate with any authority on behalf of their members with the government. The government had depended so much on its special relationship with the trade unions to deliver industrial peace and low inflation that it was now left reeling. Thatcher's warnings about the unworkability of pay policy and social contracts were spectacularly vindicated. Her warrior-like qualities now appeared to be more appropriate than Callaghan's more conciliatory stance. She was, as we have seen, able to toughen up party policy on industrial relations. The electoral standing of the main parties on key issues was decisively altered and so was their support (see Figure 10.1). But there was no ringing endorsement of the Conservative Party. To quote the British Election Study:[45]

> the Conservative Party benefited considerably from the decline in the electorate's confidence in Labour's ability to manage the economy that had occurred since 1974. ... It was not that the electorate in 1979 had much more confidence in the Conservatives than Labour, when it came to dealing with such problems in the economy as strikes, unemployment and inflation ... the balance [of likes and dislikes data] was unfavourable to Labour more because of expressions of dissatisfaction with Labour's performance than because of positive support for the Conservatives.

It is the argument of this chapter that the 'Winter of Discontent' and the virtual collapse of the Labour government did more than anything else to win the election for the Conservative Party. It is a classic case of a government losing an election rather than an opposition winning it. What an opposition can do, and Thatcher did, is to prepare for office, present itself as a credible alternative to the government, and exploit the opportunities that are presented. The events of the winter of 1978–79 created a powerful image of a Britain under siege, teetering on the edge of bankruptcy and ungovernability – an image eagerly exploited by Conservatives and their press supporters, and one that was to repay rich electoral dividends for the Party in the 1980s and beyond. But what if Callaghan had called the general election in October and lost it? Surely a new Conservative government that tried to maintain a version of his pay policy and imposed wage restraint in the public sector, would have faced at least the same level of disruption? In that case, the images of the two parties would have been reversed. Labour's warnings about a return to chaos under the Conservatives would have been vindicated and it would have been able to replay the images of rubbish piling up in the streets and the dead remaining unburied under the 'confrontational' Conservatives. October 1978 would have been a good election to lose.

Even in May 1979, the expectations of many new Conservative ministers were rather modest; some anticipated that in government Thatcher would face practical problems and be corralled by the advice of senior colleagues and civil servants. On the basis of the Conservative manifesto, the existing thrust of Labour government policies and the views of many of Thatcher's senior colleagues, there was no reason to expect a dramatic departure. On the eve of the 1979 election, Peregrine Worsthorne commented in the *Sunday Telegraph*: 'Whatever happens in the election is not going to make much difference. There will be neither revolution nor counter-revolution', and change would be measured 'in inches not miles'.[46]

Notes

1. J. Alt, I. Crewe, and B. Sarlvik, 'Partisanship and policy choice', *British Journal of Political Science*, 6 (1976), 273–90.
2. E. Heath, *The Course of My Life* (London: Hodder Headline,1998), 530–1.
3. See obituary of James Douglas, *The Times*, 28 Oct. 2004.
4. P. Cowley and M. Bailey, 'Peasants' uprising or religious war? Re-examining the 1975 Conservative leadership contest', *British Journal of Political Science*, 30 (2000), 599–629.
5. Sir Keith Joseph, 'Inflation is caused by governments', Preston, 5 Sep. 1974.
6. Airey Neave, interview, 22 Aug. 1978.
7. Margaret Thatcher, interview, 9 Aug. 1978.
8. M. Thatcher, *The Path to Power* (London: HarperCollins, 1995), 404.
9. Douglas Hurd, interview, 28 June 1978.
10. D. Butler and D. Kavanagh, *The British General Election of 1979* (Basingstoke: Macmillan, 1980), 75–9; J. Campbell, *Margaret Thatcher: Volume 1, The Grocer's Daughter* (London: Jonathan Cape, 2000), 317.
11. B. Sarlvik and I. Crewe, *Decade of Dealignment: The Conservative Victory of 1979 and Electoral Trends in the 1970s* (Cambridge: Cambridge University Press, 1983), 130–1.
12. A. Seldon and S. Ball (eds), *Conservative Century: The Conservative Party since 1900* (Oxford: Oxford University Press, 1994), 188, 194, 300, 564–72.
13. D. Kavanagh, '1970–1974', in A. Seldon (ed.), *How Tory Governments Fall* (London: Fontana, 1996), 359–86.
14. Margaret Thatcher, interview, 9 Aug. 1978.
15. Gordon Reece, interview, 9 Mar. 1993.
16. J. Bruce-Gardyne, interview, 21 Sep. 1978.
17. Alistair McAlpine, interview, 17 Sep. 1978.
18. Gordon Reece, interview, 9 Mar. 1993.
19. Gordon Reece, interview, 19 Sep. 1978.
20. Gordon Reece, interview, 19 Aug. 1978.
21. Butler and Kavanagh, *General Election of 1979*, 132–6.
22. Patten memo, Feb. 1976, Conservative Party Archive (CPA), Bodleian Library, LCC/76/98.

23. K. Morgan, *Callaghan: A Life* (Oxford: Oxford University Press, 1997), 636–42.
24. I. Crewe and B. Sarlvik, 'Popular attitudes and electoral strategy', in Z. Layton-Henry (ed.), *Conservative Party Politics* (London: Macmillan, 1980), 272.
25. Memo by Patten, 'Further Thoughts on Strategy', 27 Feb. 1978, CPA, LCC/78/65.
26. Sarlvik and Crewe, *Decade of Dealignment*, 134–6.
27. Margaret Thatcher, interview, 9 Aug. 1978.
28. Thatcher, *The Path to Power*, 240.
29. B. Harrison, 'Mrs Thatcher and the intellectuals', *20th Century British History*, 5 (1994), 211.
30. On this see A. Denham and M. Garnett, *Keith Joseph* (Chesham: Acumen, 2001).
31. Thatcher's speech at Institute of Economic Studies, New York, 15 Sep. 1975.
32. Hailsham's notes of meeting of 11 Apr. 1975, Churchill College Archives Centre, Hailsham MSS, HSLM/1/1.
33. James Prior, interview, 28 June 1978.
34. Sarlvik and Crewe, *Decade of Dealignment*, 130–1; D. Robertson, 'Public opinion and electoral cleavages', in D. Kavanagh and G. Peele (eds), *Comparative Government and Politics* (London: Heinemann, 1984), 214–41.
35. Thorneycroft to Thatcher, 5 May 1978, Churchill College Archives Centre, Thatcher MSS, THCR/2/7/1/15.
36. Thatcher, *The Path to Power*, 404: Campbell, *Thatcher: Volume 1*, 403–5 and 438.
37. A paper by Lord Thorneycroft, entitled 'Pay Policy' and dated 21 November 1978, was influential. It opened: 'We are politicians. We should not forget this', and it urged colleagues not to talk much about pay policy for they were divided, the government's 5 per cent limit on pay settlements enjoyed broad public support, and the Party would suffer if it was perceived as favouring a wage free-for-all. The Party should stick with the policies of the *Right Approach to the Economy* and consult with both sides of industry. Thatcher MSS, THCR/2/6/1/242.
38. Proposals that she should think about an accommodation with the Liberals annoyed Thatcher. Chris Patten wrote to her on 20 January 1978 that 'it might be useful to find out if the Liberals, in the event of a hung Parliament, had thought about the price they would exact for offering support'. She wrote in the margin 'No negotiations at all'. Thatcher MSS, THRC/2/7/1/56. Also see Campbell, *Thatcher: Volume 1*, 401, 419.
39. Steering Ctte., 30 Jan. 1978, Thatcher MSS, THCR/2/6/1/249.
40. J. Hoskyns, *Just in Time* (London: Aurum Press, 2000), 55. Also see A. Taylor, 'The "Stepping Stones" programme: Conservative Party thinking on trade unions, 1975–79', *Historical Studies in Industrial Relations*, 11 (2001), 107–33.
41. Conservative Party draft manifesto, 30 Aug. 1978, LCC(78)186.
42. Thatcher, *The Path to Power*, 410.
43. Sir Geoffrey Howe, interview, 19 July 1978.
44. Margaret Thatcher, interview, 9 Aug. 1978.
45. Sarlvik and Crewe, *Decade of Dealignment*, 165–6.
46. *Sunday Telegraph*, 29 Apr. 1979.

11
The Barren Years: 1997–2005

Anthony Seldon and Peter Snowdon

Introduction: the natural party of government

The Conservative Party throughout its history has resented defeat in general elections. Since the late nineteenth century, the Party has seen itself as the 'natural' party of government, with periods of opposition the exception, and office the norm. With a broad appeal to all sections and parts of the country, its character has chimed with the heartbeat of the nation. Its longest period in the wilderness was between 1846 and 1866, but even during this, there were brief tenures of power in 1852 and 1858–59. Apart from this, periods out of office between 1783 and 1997 only twice exceeded nine years, in 1830–41 and 1905–15; the remaining opposition periods were often much shorter.

However, the Party learnt to be phlegmatic about losing power because experience taught it that the pendulum always swung back, sometimes within a single parliament. When recovery took longer, exceptional factors were at play. Return to office after 1830 was delayed due to deep divisions over Catholic Emancipation and franchise reform. After 1906, despite the problems of the tariff reform policy, the Conservatives drew almost level with the ruling Liberals in little over four years. The most prolonged period of opposition, from 1846 to 1866, was the result not only of the profound split over the repeal of the Corn Laws, but also of facing a formidable opponent. The Liberal leader, Lord Palmerston, positioned his party in the centre ground of British politics, wrapping it in the cloak of nationalism with a robust foreign policy. Combined with his cautiously reformist domestic policy, this left the Conservative Party with little opportunity to make a broad national case to the electorate.

The Conservatives also suffered from a dearth of strong leaders, and had to wait for Palmerston's death in 1865 and Disraeli's rise to the leadership in 1866–68 before they could regain confidence and power.

In its periods in opposition, the Conservative Party has traditionally avoided recrimination, has changed the leader, rejuvenated the Party organization to reconnect with its supporters, and adapted its policies to appeal again to the middle ground. Only once did the Party return to office under the same leader after it had been out of power for more than five years, with Churchill in 1951. However he had promoted himself as a national leader in the war, and only became a partisan Conservative leader after the war. The formula of the three mantras of refreshed leadership, policies and organization has failed only once before 1997, in 1846–66. Is the period since 1997 witnessing the first such breakdown of the *status quo* for 150 years?

We argue that the Conservatives are indeed now in the same predicament as they were in the mid-nineteenth century. As after the repeal of the Corn Laws in 1846, the Conservative party has become deeply divided over Europe and domestic policy. In the mid-nineteenth century, the main non-Conservative party, the Liberals, were led by a leader who stole the Conservatives' clothes; since 1997, the main alternative party has been headed by a leader, Tony Blair, who has stolen not only the Conservatives' clothes, but, far worse for the Party, its two 'secret weapons', or keys to its hegemony: its hunger for office and adaptability.

Since its formation in 1900, Labour has been the ideological and sectional party in British politics. It has been the party of the working class and trade unions, and committed, in doctrine at least, to the principles of democratic Socialism and public ownership at home, and internationalism abroad. Debate over the degree of nationalization, taxation and spending, and non-belligerence abroad, split the Labour Party regularly throughout the twentieth century. The Party's pragmatists wanted it to be flexible, while the dogmatists desired ideological purity and accused the pragmatists of 'selling out'. With Labour thus defined, it was comparatively easy for the Conservatives to appeal to all sections of the nation, while their 'dogma-light' approach allowed a continual updating of policies to keep in step with the preferences of a changing electorate. The Conservative Party in the twentieth century thus learnt to champion the welfare state and to lead the jettisoning of the Empire. It was the 'focus group' party long before anyone had ever heard of the phenomenon.

From the 1980s, the traditional profiles of the Conservative and Labour Parties began to reverse. It was the Conservatives who first under Thatcher became the ideological and dogmatic party, and, in exhibiting a willingness to rebel against the leadership, lost their seemingly unquenchable hunger for office. This all-pervasive appetite had ensured discipline and loyalty to the leadership, allowing it relatively speedily to overcome its splits in the past. However, under the Blair–Brown–Mandelson *coup d'état*, from the late 1980s 'New Labour' was becoming the non-ideological party, ejecting any positions (even public ownership in Clause IV of the Party's constitution) which might alienate middle-ground voters. After four successive defeats from 1979 to 1992, the new masters of Labour were all the more able to insist on obedience to the leadership at all costs by means of a central *diktat* that the Party would have tolerated at no previous time in its history.

The keys are lost: 1979–97

We now examine exactly how the Conservative Party allowed itself to lose the two keys – hunger for power and adaptability – which explained its electoral hegemony. Conservatives have generally seen 'Black Wednesday', the day in September 1992 when Britain was ejected from the European Exchange Rate Mechanism, as the moment the Party's popularity was lost. Since that point, the Party has barely risen above 35 per cent in opinion polls. Many right-wing commentators and figures in the Party scapegoated John Major, Prime Minister from 1990–97, as the culprit for the Conservatives' woes. They characterized him as unsound on policy, weak on party management and incapable of giving a clear lead. To many in the Party, Mrs Thatcher was the greatest peacetime Conservative leader of the century, and for years after her fall in 1990 she was looked back on as the standard all future Conservative leaders must meet.

Mrs Thatcher did indeed achieve much of lasting benefit for Britain during her premiership, above all liberalizing the economy and thus sowing the seeds for the ensuing economic prosperity, taming the over-mighty trade unions, and restoring Britain's standing on the world stage. She was the most successful Conservative leader electorally since Lord Liverpool in the very different circumstances of the early nineteenth century, winning elections in 1979, 1983 and 1987. However she also damaged the Party. Its appeal became less to the whole nation, and it became more of an English party. Her uncompromising espousal of market economics made the Party more of a right-wing, ideological force than it had traditionally been. Conservative leaders in the past had almost all been inclusive, not polarizing. The electorate as a whole moreover never became convinced of Thatcherite values: her three general election victories were achieved with only 42–44 per cent of the popular vote, with the non-Conservative vote split between Labour and the alliance of Liberals and the new Social Democratic Party. Her strident tone on many issues created disharmony in the Party, but it was her unrelenting hostility to the European Union and fanning of the flames of Euroscepticism that did the most enduring damage. Her lack of sympathy for local government, or indeed time for the Conservative Party in the country, contributed further to a decline of the Party at the local level. Mrs Thatcher was thus the author of many of the woes of the Party in the 15 years after her fall in 1990. That seminal event brought to a head not just divisions over policy but, even more damagingly, over personalities, with many in the Party in the country and in the right-wing press, and some of the parliamentary Party, wanting the blood of the 'regicides' who had brought down their hero. To many, Major was not a legitimate successor.

It was thus a divided and uncertain party which Major inherited in November 1990, lagging behind Labour in the polls, unpopular at home above all over the Thatcherite poll tax, with a deteriorating economy, and split over Europe. In April 1992, Major took the Party to a victory which had long looked in doubt, winning more votes (over 14 million) than the Conservative Party (or any other) had ever won in history. Subsequently, although he did not himself destroy the Party's twin keys of pragmatism and hunger for office, he did little to reverse trends already in train. While doing much to complete the Thatcher legacy in privatization and public services, Major worked to bring party policy more onto the centre ground. Like Balfour, but unlike Peel, he tried to reconcile a split party. Major knew that to come down too decisively on one side or the other of the European divide would cause greater disruption and risk splitting the Party. However his attempt to find a middle position, with his 'opt outs' on the Social Chapter and the single currency negotiated at the Maastricht Conference in 1991, and later with his 'wait and see' policy on the single currency, was scorned by the Eurosceptic right, and deemed weak by the Europhile left.

Increasingly from 1993, many Conservative MPs concluded that the Party was unelectable under Major, and open shows of defiance became common. Never in the last century had the leader been treated with so little respect by some ministers, MPs and by the Conservative press at large. Never in the Party's history had a leader been so undermined by the machinations of his immediate predecessor. Mrs Thatcher's Eurosceptical voices 'off' and her palpable derision for Major fortified his critics to more open displays of defiance. Major had to resort to votes of confidence to ensure that key legislation passed through Parliament. In November 1994, the gravity of his position was underlined when he resorted to withdrawing the whip from eight Eurosceptic rebels. The initial 1992 majority of 21 meanwhile began to ebb away and, with dissent rife, Major decided in June 1995 that the Party must 'put up or shut up'. He thus put himself through the unprecedented step for a Conservative leader of seeking to be re-elected leader by his own MPs to give him a fresh mandate. His victory was less than convincing and dissent was barely stifled in the final two years of his premiership, while in December 1996, the government lost its majority in Parliament altogether. By the end, even some of the Cabinet were being openly contemptuous of Major's leadership. The tight-knit party of loyalty and unity had become a pack of angry, disillusioned and disputatious individuals. Recrimination, which the Party had mostly avoided throughout history, thus began whilst they were still in office. When the general election was called for 1 May 1997, not even Major in his heart of hearts expected to win.

Understanding and misunderstanding the 1997 general election

Major himself admitted that a fifth successive term in office would 'stretch the elastic of democracy too far'.[1] In electoral terms, that elastic recoiled sharply on 1 May 1997, with the Conservative Party being reduced to a rump of 165 MPs. The last general election of the 'Conservative Century' had produced the heaviest defeat for the Party since the birth of mass democratic politics in 1918. Not since 1906 were so few Conservative MPs returned to Parliament, and the share of the vote in 1997 (30.7 per cent) was the lowest since 1832. New Labour's remarkable achievement was to lure so many dispossessed Conservatives (over 2 million) into its electoral big tent, while tactical voting and a resurgent third party further damaged the Conservatives.[2]

The Party trailed Labour in every age and occupational group, except the over 65s and the AB professional classes.[3] Left without any representation in Scotland, Wales and most of England's large cities and metropolitan areas, the parliamentary Party was halved in size, while a third of its survivors (who mostly represented rural and suburban seats in southern England) only won with precariously small majorities.[4] The heaviest losses were in Greater London, the Midlands and south-east England, areas that had underpinned the Party's strength in the 1980s and early 1990s.[5] Peter Kellner suggests that were it not for the economic recovery under Major in the mid-1990s, the Party could have faced electoral annihilation (as happened to the Canadian Progressive Conservative Party in 1993), threatening its very existence as the main opposition party.[6]

After 18 years in office, many Party officials and MPs were ill-prepared for the harsh realities of life in the wilderness. Central Office was left with morale and energy at low ebbs after one of the longest-ever election campaigns. The voluntary party in the country had become a shadow of its former self, following more than a decade of declining membership and activism and a shrinking base in local government. A quarter of the parliamentary Party elected in 1997 were new entrants to the House of Commons, while only 36 of those re-elected had previous experience of opposition from before 1979.[7] Philip Cowley and Mark Stuart called it 'one of the smallest and least-experienced groups of parliamentarians ever to constitute Her Majesty's Opposition'.[8]

Failure to come to terms with the nature of the rout and the causes behind it exacerbated the Party's predicament in the new political landscape. After nearly two decades of Conservative rule, the needs, anxieties, priorities and aspirations of the electorate had become harder for the Party to decipher and comprehend. Many simply failed to acknowledge how British society had changed in the 1990s. Complacency and ignorance were ubiquitous at all levels of the Party. While some ignored the nature of the threat posed by New Labour, others dismissed the rise of Blair's party as a temporary phenomenon, believing that the pendulum would again soon swing back in the Conservatives' direction as it had in the past. The Party had no clear idea how to handle Blair and the New Labour phenomenon – any more than they had known how to respond to Blair before 1997. One of Major's failures was not providing a convincing Conservative case against New Labour. Under the influence of Maurice Saatchi from 1996, the Party opted for a 'New Labour, New Danger' strategy and tried to demonize Blair personally, when clearly the key element in New Labour was its moderation and lack of threat. Throughout the period 1997–2005, the Conservatives were to continue to fail to find a convincing line of attack on New Labour.

In his booklet *After the Landslide*, the MP and former minister David Willetts was a rarity in making a serious effort to look to history for instruction.[9] Willetts argued that 'modernizing' the Conservative Party 'is just what the Party has always had to do after a defeat on the scale of the one it suffered in 1997'.[10] This would neither require 'jettisoning essential Conservative principles' nor aping New Labour. However, there was little time given to reflective voices. In so far as there was a conventional wisdom, it was that Major had been to blame, and that the Party had gone 'mad' in 1990 and paid the price for abandoning Thatcher and Thatcherism. Major was scapegoated personally, and this was a substitute for serious discussion. No proper *post mortem* was undertaken of the 1997 defeat, while sympathetic historians like John Ramsden, who could have taught the leadership much, were wantonly ignored.[11] What might the leadership have learnt from wise voices about the experience of New Labour and the 1997 landslide defeat? That as long as Labour was able to remain in the centre ground, life would be very difficult and there would be no sudden swing back of the pendulum. That there should be a prolonged and sympathetic overhaul of the Party's policy and organization, whilst continually reminding the electorate that the policies the government was espousing were not authentically Labour's but emanated from Conservative principles. Steadiness and moderation would be key to heal the Party, and regain the public trust that had been lost in the splits and sleaze of the mid-1990s. Governments lose power far more than oppositions win it, and so the most that could be expected would be to establish a reputation as a competent and principled opposition party with a clear-cut identity and policies of its own which were widely understood by the electorate. If this is the 'minimum requirement' of an opposition party, then how far did the Conservatives achieve this between 1997 and 2005?

Hague, 1997–2001

William Hague's four years were to prove one of the most troubled and ineffectual opposition periods the Party has experienced. For comparison, one has to look to 1906–10, when the Party was led by Balfour and bitterly divided over the issue of tariff reform. Even then, there was some progress under Balfour on policy renewal accompanied by very significant electoral recovery in the 1910 elections. Under Hague's leadership there would be no such progress.

Leadership: the search for authority

Few would have expected such a junior cabinet minister, who had only entered Parliament at a by-election in 1989, to succeed Major in June 1997. However, in 'skipping a generation' and finding a leader even younger (36) than Blair (44), this appointment had sound logic behind it. He would face the unenviable task of healing the Party's wounds over Europe as well as forging a united platform. Revitalizing its moribund structures and organization would also be a priority. Such an undertaking would require a leader who carried clear authority, could draw on a wealth of political experience and who was capable of putting in place adroit strategic thinking. Despite his strengths and confidence, Hague possessed none of these three requirements to a sufficient degree.

The very fact that Hague emerged as Major's successor during the seven-week leadership contest was indicative of the divided state of the Party. The two most likely successors were already ruled out: Michael Heseltine, who had been Major's able deputy, saw his long-held leadership ambitions come to an abrupt end due to an attack of angina a few days after the election, whilst Michael Portillo, who had the advantage of youth combined with experience as a senior minister in the Major Cabinet, had lost his seat and so was ineligible to stand. The surviving 'big beasts of the jungle' entered the race: Kenneth Clarke made his bid with support mainly from the pro-European left and Michael Howard, Peter Lilley and John Redwood split their support among the Eurosceptic right. Initially hesitant, Hague entered the race when he realized that his preferred candidate, Howard, would not win. Hague launched his bid with the slogan 'A Fresh Start', marking himself out as the candidate who could appeal to the centre-right without being overly identified with the recent 'murky' past.[12] Although Clarke remained the favourite, winning the first two ballots of Conservative MPs, and enjoying the support of the majority of constituency chairmen, his pro-European stance and his surprise last-minute pact with Redwood counted against him in the final round.[13] Hague's 92 to 70 vote victory was testament to the professionalism of his campaign (aided by Thatcher's ringing endorsement), but it did not conceal the fact that he was elected as demonstrably the least offensive and ideologically charged candidate on offer (rather like John Major in 1990). There were few among his parliamentary colleagues 'who wanted Hague because of what he could deliver'.[14] His accession to the leadership therefore did not rest on his personal authority, and this he now had to earn from the parliamentary Party, the voluntary party and – most importantly – public opinion.

Organizational reform

Hague decided that a strategic priority in the first half of the new Parliament was a radical overhaul of the Party's structures as well as its leadership election rules. Unity, decentralization, democracy, integrity and openness were the guiding principles set out in his first keynote speech as leader in July 1997. Indeed, in an effort to outflank New Labour's success as a mass membership party, he promised nothing less than a 'democratic revolution'. He first proposed the reforms at the 1997 Party conference as *Blueprint for Change*, and repackaged them for approval by the Party membership in 1998 as *The Fresh Future*.

The organizational reforms were handicapped by an impatient desire to achieve quick results, and ill-considered proposals were rushed through without proper consultation.[15] Hague turned to his former colleague at the McKinsey management consultancy, the newly-elected MP Archie Norman, to act as his key advisor on the reforms. Norman, the saviour of the ailing supermarket chain Asda, was charged with rebuilding the Party's structures on business management principles. The 'Conservative Mandelson', as Norman was feted, enjoyed much greater influence over the reorganization package than Hague's first Party Chairman, Lord Parkinson, who found the Chairmanship on his return carried much less authority than he had enjoyed in the same post fifteen years earlier.[16] At the heart of the *Fresh Future* reforms was the creation of a new 'Party Board' to take overall control over both the professional and voluntary wings of the Party. The composition of the Board was weighted heavily against the rank and file, with only five of the 17 members representing the grass-roots. Despite Hague's proclaimed desire for decentralization, the Board and its assorted sub-bodies were to centralize power within the Party, extending the power of national officials over local parties.[17]

The Hague–Norman package was endorsed by an all-party ballot in February 1998 – with the undemocratic elements of the changes to the Party's structure overshadowed by the appeal of a new voting system for the leader.[18] Pressure had been mounting from activists for selection by a ballot of MPs alone to be replaced by a 'one member, one vote' system, paralleling one of Blair's reforms of the Labour Party. Hague believed that the selection of leader should not be restricted to the 'rump of MPs from the south-east of England', but many of his parliamentary colleagues jealously guarded what they saw as their traditional rights of determining the leader (even though Conservative MPs had only held that power since 1965).[19] A new 'hybrid' system ensured that the membership in the country had the final say in a run-off of two candidates pre-selected by Conservative MPs. Its first test-run in 2001 received widespread criticism; not least because the membership had little say on the wider selection of candidates by MPs (476 Conservative associations did not have a sitting Conservative MP through whom to express their opinion), and the winner of the membership ballot, Iain Duncan Smith, did not enjoy the support of the majority of his parliamentary colleagues – a major factor in the diminishing of his authority as leader. Yet another criticism of the new electoral system was the power it gave to the Conservative press, and especially the two *Telegraph* titles, to influence heavily what the Party in the country thought, which it did with its traditional Eurosceptic, right-wing voice.

The Party's professional organization was another target of Hague's reform. However, in closing many regional offices and dismissing respected officials, Norman's 'rationalization' did little to improve morale.[20] He created a network of new Party sections and agencies, replacing (and in some cases duplicating) the fund-raising, membership recruitment and marketing activities conducted at a local level. A campaign 'war-room' was set up, emulating Labour's open-plan Millbank headquarters, incorporating press, policy and research. The media and communications operation was enhanced with the appointments of the experienced Amanda Platell and Nick Wood. Many of the reforms were sensible, and dictated by the need to make economies, but their combined effect was to produce a confused chain of command at Central Office. Initiatives to arrest the long-term erosion of membership also came to little, and Hague's ambitious target of a million members within five years remained a dream.[21] The Party's finances did improve, largely due to the generosity of 'high value' donors such as the Party's new treasurer, Michael Ashcroft, who bankrolled it to the tune of £1 million a year between 1997 and 2001.[22]

Very little progress was made in opening up candidate selection for the Westminster, European and new devolved Assembly elections. The leadership pulled back from implementing radical proposals, such as all-women short-lists, to show how much the Party had changed, in order not to offend traditionalists and associations. The parliamentary Party thus remained predominantly a white, male and middle-class clique.[23] Despite the gloss of the 2001 campaign machine, there were fewer members, activists and agents on the ground even than in 1997, a depleted army of area campaign directors, and an almost non-existent organization in major cities other than London. Richard Kelly had argued that Hague merely 'managed to replace one ineffective organization with another', adding that this was an 'indefensible mistake given the time and resources devoted to the reform and the hype it later received'.[24] As one senior shadow cabinet member observed, the reorganization initiative 'not only damaged Hague; it also badly damaged the party'.[25]

Policy renewal

Policy renewal saw Hague's Party encounter even more profound problems. Again, the leadership moved hastily, taking too little time to reflect on the nature of the Party's ideological uncertainties. In 1997 Conservatism was suffering from a crisis, battered by years of uncertainty about the

Party's identity, that was further compounded by the ambiguities of the post-Cold War world and a seemingly ever more federal-inclined European Union (EU). The slaying of the demons of the 1980s, with the defeat of communism and militant trade unionism, had deprived the Conservatives of clear targets in the 1990s.[26] Much effort was expended trying to find a 'narrative' to explain why the electorate should vote Conservative, but none could be found. The centre ground of British politics had shifted away from tax cuts and privatization on to the new territory of improving public services and the quality of life. New Labour was moving into this fertile ground, equipped with policies shorn of the Conservatives' ideological baggage. Initially, if hesitantly, Hague steered the Party towards the centre ground, but he failed to commit with any confidence to a coherent policy agenda based upon it. He told his shadow cabinet that they had to stop thinking as if they were in government and think like an opposition, which encouraged them to be reactive and confrontational, to the detriment of long-term coherence. In the absence of progress in the polls mid-way through the Parliament, the leadership retreated into a rightward direction, abandoning the centrist approach which he had initially lauded.

Traditionally in opposition, the leader and shadow cabinet steer policy formulation. The way Hague managed his shadow cabinet reveals much about how the process broke down. His initial team reflected a balanced cross-section of the parliamentary Party, including many of his more experienced colleagues from Major's Cabinet (with the notable absence of the pro-European Clarke, who preferred to pursue his business interests). Hague determined to lance the boil of the single currency by ruling out membership for the ensuing Parliament. In the short-term this strategy appeased the Eurosceptics without forcing the Europhiles, now a small but vocal minority on the Conservative benches, to consider defection. However, Hague's continuing abandonment of Major's equi-distance on Europe later provoked senior pro-Europeans to resign from the shadow cabinet.[27] Hague returned to an uncompromising stance on the single currency in the run up to the 2001 general election – only to reopen old wounds and highlight the Party's obsession with the subject, to Labour's glee.

So Hague gave out confusing signals to his followers. He insisted shadow ministers display contrition over past policy failures, such as the ERM ejection, while also encouraging them to be reactive and chip away at Labour.[28] Preoccupied with his organizational reforms, Hague did not give as much attention to policy renewal until 1998. So he asked his deputy and shadow Chancellor, Peter Lilley, to launch a large-scale consultation exercise. So poor was collective memory that it was forgotten that Major had himself launched the largest 'consultation exercise' in the Party's history but two years before. 'Listening to Britain' was set up by Lilley with the aim of reconnecting with groups in society alienated from the Party after 18 years in office. Aside from his emphatic rejection of replacing the pound with the euro, Hague claimed that every policy was subject to review and potential revision, although Conservative principles – in particular the low-tax, free market economy – were not. The process attracted a modest 40,000 people in over 150 meetings throughout the country. Although shadow ministers took the time to listen and speak to 'ordinary' voters, the exercise failed to produce a convincing debate about the Party's *raison d'être* at the turn of the century. The resulting document, published in 1999, showed little fresh thinking about the Party's purpose in the years ahead.

'The Common Sense Revolution' was the slogan assigned to the new set of policy proposals. This ranged from a 'tax guarantee' (pledging that tax would decline in the next Parliament as a percentage of GDP) to populist law and order measures, and was still skewed towards the Party's traditional strengths rather than striking into new territory, notably reform of the public services. A series of further slogans were floated by the leadership in an attempt to capture the public imagination: 'Compassionate Conservatism' and 'kitchen table Conservatism' suggested a softer and more socially-liberal agenda, designed to appeal to the modernizing wing of the Party. Hague's early speeches talked of 'a broad and tolerant party in the mainstream', but like George W. Bush's 'Compassionate Conservatism' in the USA, the flirtation with the centre proved to be less about substance and more about rebranding and slogans.[29] Meanwhile, Lilley and several other shadow ministers, including Willetts, continued to develop policy in a genuinely more 'modernizing' direction. They were assisted by Daniel Finklestein and Andrew Cooper, Directors of Research and Strategy at Central Office, two of the Party's more imaginative thinkers.

Lilley's Butler Memorial Lecture in the spring of 1999, coinciding with the twentieth anniversary of Mrs Thatcher's first election victory, could have been the moment for a bold move forward. Lilley hit a fresh note in arguing that there were limits to Thatcherism, and that the Party needed to move on. Conservatives, he said, had 'always believed that the public services are intrinsically unsuited to replacement by universal delivery through the free market'. However, the full implications of Lilley's provocative speech had, in a lapse of communication indicative of his leadership, apparently not been properly digested by Hague.[30] He and his acolytes were not yet ready to see Thatcherism questioned. Lilley's speech was seminal, not least because it was delivered by one of the chief cheerleaders of the Thatcher era. Rather than inaugurating a serious debate on the merits or otherwise of extending the Thatcherite revolution into the public services, it provoked a backlash. In the absence of a strong lead from Hague, it raised the 'no entry sign over again examining various Party taboos'.[31] As one shadow minister recalled, the episode, and Hague's failure to support Lilley, made it 'much harder subsequently to make sensible policy changes'.[32] Within two months of the speech, Lilley had left the shadow cabinet along with other heavyweights including Howard, Norman Fowler and Gillian Shepherd.[33]

Between 1999 and the 2001 election campaign, Conservative policy changed direction to focus on bolstering the Party's 'core' support. Frustrated by the lack of progress in the opinion polls, and concerned by unease on the right of the Party, the leadership appeared increasingly to shape policy in response to the latest headlines in the *Daily Telegraph* and *Daily Mail*.[34] Tony Martin, the Norfolk farmer who shot dead a burglar in his home, received support from the leadership, while the repeal of Section 28 (which prohibited the 'promotion of homosexuality' in schools) and the increase in bogus asylum seekers provoked defensive policy pronouncements. The Party's success in the European Parliament elections of June 1999 further encouraged Hague and his advisers (such as Andrew Lansley) to amplify their Euroscepticism.[35] Bashing the EU might have gratified those who were already opposed to it; but it did little to win new support among the voters at large.

The Party was all too easily lampooned by its critics for peddling 'bandwagon politics'. As Simon Walters argued in *Tory Wars*, his exposé of the personality-riven Hague years, the social authoritarianism of Ann Widdecombe, the shadow Home Secretary, and others like Liam Fox and Duncan Smith antagonized the modernizers and social liberals inside the shadow cabinet. Foremost among the latter were Portillo and Francis Maude, who wanted the Party to adopt a much more liberal line on 'lifestyle issues', such as gay marriage and multiculturalism.[36] The toxic mix of personality and policy differences at the top remained deeply harmful, and proved to be as much a hallmark of Hague's leadership as it had been of Major's. Hague began to see plots everywhere, and was suspicious in particular of Maude and Portillo, who had returned to the front line, against the grain of policy, as shadow Chancellor in February 2000. In this climate, by the spring of 2001 Hague relied almost exclusively on a small group of trusted and ultra-loyal advisers. Unlike Blair in opposition, Hague had not been able to assemble a Private

Office of outstanding quality, and he was increasingly suspicious of the motives of modernizing voices from within and outside the shadow cabinet.[37] As the polls failed to improve, senior Party figures increasingly looked to salvation in a post-Hague era. The policy agenda had become so narrowly defined that the 2001 election campaign was fought on £8 billion of tax cuts, saving the pound and cracking down on crime and illegal immigration. Hague had at last found a coherent platform to accompany the Party's manifesto *Time for Common Sense*, but this populist 'core vote' platform did not find an echo with the moderate mass of public opinion.[38]

External factors: outmanoeuvred and outclassed

Several years after the 2001 defeat, Hague admitted that 'what went wrong was the amount of switching in our policy direction'.[39] He was frustrated at the lack of attention that some of his earlier initiatives, such as 'Listening to Britain', received in the national media.[40] Other than Hague's robust performances at Prime Minister's Question Time, the task of opposition made few headlines in the face of an all-conquering – and for a long period apparently flawless – Labour government. Gordon Brown's decision to grant partial independence to the Bank of England, and the forging of a stable economic policy framework, reassured many former Conservative voters. Labour captured the Conservatives' mantle as the prudent managers of the nation's finances, while Conservative warnings of 'stealth tax rises' and downturns after 1997 fell utterly flat as the economy continued to grow. Labour moved further into Conservative heartland policy areas with its strong stance on crime. Not only did New Labour continue to hold the Conservatives' two keys of pragmatism and hunger for office; they also remained united and able to please the Conservative press. Hague's Conservative Party was cornered, outclassed and outgunned. The continuing revival of the Liberal Democrats confounded the Conservatives' efforts to recapture lost ground. A bitter reminder of the Conservatives' vulnerability came in 2000, when the Liberal Democrats scored a spectacular by-election victory at Romsey, a formerly safe Conservative seat in southern England.

Only once during Blair's first term did William Hague manage to capitalize on a domestic crisis. In September 2000 the Conservatives launched a concerted attack on the excessive levels of fuel duty and managed to achieve a brief lead in the opinion polls as the government struggled to resolve the dispute with the road hauliers. However, once Blair regained control of the crisis, the Party was unable to mount a more damaging offensive and make political capital. Foreign missions in Iraq in 1998, Kosovo in 1999 and Sierra Leone in 2000 further highlighted Blair's presence as a strong-armed leader on the world stage, while his shrewd pulling back from Britain entering the single currency further appeased the right-wing press. Blair's personal superiority over Hague in understanding the national mood was never seen more clearly than in his conduct in the week after the death of Princess Diana, which contrasted starkly with Hague's arch performance. In the face of such competition, Hague was never able to present himself as a credible alternative Prime Minister. Hague's youth, which might have counted for him, quickly came to be seen as a drawback: compared to Blair, he always seemed ineffectual, uncharismatic and unconvincing, a boy up against a man.

Understanding and misunderstanding the 2001 general election

On 7 June 2001 the British electorate's verdict on the Conservative performance in opposition was resoundingly clear. The turnout fell from 71.5 per cent to just 59.4 per cent, and Labour's historic second 'landslide' victory was achieved on a popular vote (10.7 million) which was lower than all but two of the eight post-war general elections it lost. Conservative support fell to a new low, with only 8.3 million people choosing to vote Conservative (1.4 million fewer than in 1997).[41] With a mere 1 per cent increase in the Party's share of the vote, producing a net gain of one seat, Hague's defeat ranks as one of the poorest electoral performances in the Party's history. It was the lowest popular vote for either main party since the 1931 general election, when the Labour Party was split by the formation of the National government.[42] What made matters worse for the Conservatives was that Labour and the Liberal Democrats continued to advance in the seats that mattered the most – particularly in 'Middle England'.[43] The Conservatives improved their standing in the majority of the seats retained in 1997, but Hague's Eurosceptic campaign failed to make the inroads planned in the south-west, while the populist offensive on crime and asylum did nothing to regain marginal seats in London and the south-east. While a recovery in Scotland and Wales remained elusive (apart from a solitary gain in south-west Scotland), the Party failed even to come second in any of the Manchester or Liverpool constituencies. Progress made in the mid-term elections in the previous four years, particularly in the European and local elections in 1999, had failed to be built on to produce anything like the 11.6 per cent swing the Party required to regain an overall majority in 2001.[44]

It was now vital that the Party learnt from its mistakes after 1997 and took the time to reflect on the lessons of two successive defeats.

However, Hague's immediate resignation catapulted the Party into yet another protracted leadership election, denying it the opportunity to regroup, calm its nerves and undertake a thorough *post mortem*. Some senior Conservatives were wary of making the Party appear divided by openly debating the causes of defeat.[45] As one such figure observed, there was 'absolutely no collective understanding of what had gone wrong', while 'the personality and policies of the three main leadership candidates [Portillo, Clarke and Duncan Smith] squeezed out any serious analysis'.[46] Once again, the issue of Europe and figure of Mrs Thatcher returned to haunt the leadership contest. This time Clarke's campaign, which gained momentum after Portillo's leadership bid unravelled, failed to impress the grass-roots, who now determined the final result. To them, his unpopular pro-European views were more significant than his stature as a national figure with the experience and weight to take on Blair and New Labour. Portillo's precipitous journey towards a social liberal agenda had proved too much for many of his parliamentary colleagues, who were also troubled by his involvement in plotting during the Hague years. After he fell, the 'modernizers' were left with no option but to support Clarke against Duncan Smith, whose record as a Maastricht rebel in the Major years inspired anxiety in some but excited the Thatcherite right. Duncan Smith's campaign was well-organized, but the acrimonious contest, which was drawn out over three months, thwarted any hopes for concealing engrained divisions – particularly over Europe. The Party was arguably in an even weaker state in the months following June 2001 than it had been after May 1997. It would now need an inspired leader to lift it out of the gloom.

Duncan Smith, 2001–03

When Iain Duncan Smith was forced from his position as Party leader in October 2003, commentators were swift to condemn his leadership as even more ineffective than Hague's. This verdict was unduly hasty and perhaps unfair, given the modest strides made in policy renewal, and the impact of circumstances beyond Duncan Smith's control. He shared many of the problems which had faced Hague after 1997: a defeated and demoralized party unable to come to terms with its predicament, seemingly incapable of undertaking real thinking into the reasons for its unpopularity and still deeply riven by personality clashes. Duncan Smith, eager to learn the lessons of Hague's vacillations on policy, favoured a strategic approach to recovery. However, it did not take long for the underlying weakness of his position, and still more the inadequacies of his leadership style, to bring his short tenure to an end.

Leadership: underlying weakness

Duncan Smith's triumph in the final round of the 2001 leadership election, winning by a margin of three to two over Clarke, settled the debate over Europe but was otherwise a hollow victory. Like Hague four years earlier, he began as the underdog but, unlike his predecessor, he critically failed to win support from a majority of his colleagues in the parliamentary Party; indeed, in no ballot did he win more than a third of their votes. Securing the second place in the final round of the MPs' ballot by only one vote revealed all too visibly that Duncan Smith had not received the acclamation of the Party in Westminster. Popularity with the rank and file in the country was no compensation. Many on the Conservative benches, including former whips and ministers from the Major government, questioned why they should demonstrate loyalty to a man whose Eurosceptic behaviour had threatened the very survival of the Party in office in the mid-1990s. Here was also a figure, who, having declined to serve in the Major administration because of his opposition to its European policy, had never held even the most junior ministerial office.[47] As shadow Social Security Secretary and shadow Defence Secretary under Hague, Duncan Smith had raised his profile, but his personality, and views on anything other than Europe, remained a little-known quantity outside the precincts of Westminster.

Duncan Smith's first shadow cabinet leaned heavily towards the Eurosceptic right, and notably included figures like arch fellow Maastricht rebel, Bill Cash; there were few counterbalancing voices from the centre left and pro-European wing of the Party. When Portillo and Clarke refused to serve, some Conservative MPs were reported in the press as saying that 'the lunatics have taken over the asylum'.[48] Though his appointments did not attract favourable comment outside the right-wing press, Duncan Smith's team included some rising stars, such as Oliver Letwin, who was promoted to shadow Home Secretary, and he brought back experienced heavyweights like Howard. Duncan Smith also appointed 'modernizers' from outside the parliamentary Party to key positions of influence at Smith Square. Dominic Cummings, Director of Strategy, and Mark MacGregor, Chief Executive, promised policy freshness at Central Office, and some stability after the Hague–Norman upheavals.

Policy renewal: signs of progress

One of Duncan Smith's first acts as Party leader was to announce a thorough review of policy. Aiming to restore the Conservatives as the 'party of ideas', he declared that the process would be conducted with 'urgency and energy'. He instigated a reorganization of the Conservative

Research Department, appointing Greg Clark as Director of Policy in charge of a new Policy Unit, modelled on Thatcher's Number 10 Policy Unit, and commissioned sophisticated polling and market research. A wider range of outside advice was drawn on from businesses to think-tanks and professional organizations. All this suggested a more thoughtful and inclusive approach to policy renewal than had occurred under Hague. Duncan Smith sought to focus on the salient issues of the 2001 election, moving beyond the narrower 'core vote' focus under Hague. He demonstrated decisive leadership in calling on the Party to close down its discussion of Europe completely and to examine health, education, transport as well as crime.[49] Reforming the public services and helping 'the vulnerable' in society were to become his mission, striking a very different tone from that of his predecessor, or indeed from the kind of policies those on the centre and left of the Party feared he might espouse.

Policy-making was to be developed over three stages: identifying problems in the key policy areas while learning from experience overseas, bringing forward specific proposals through consultation documents, and elaborating the proposals long in advance of the next manifesto. Over the next 18 months, significant work was undertaken, particularly on health policy, where consultation documents such *The Wrong Prescription*, *Alternative Prescriptions* and *Setting the NHS Free* brought a focus to public service reform which had been lacking for several years. However, although the process benefited from more considered analysis, policy proposals such as the 'Patients' passport' and greater choice for patients still left questions unanswered and did not curry favour with many within the health profession. Duncan Smith's vision of 'Compassionate Conservatism' (first espoused from a Glasgow housing estate) stemmed in part from his Christianity and sense of social justice, but it still did not convince the political world that he had yet found a coherent agenda. His case was also weakened because key figures in his shadow cabinet were never convinced about his 'Compassionate Conservatism'.

The policy review process culminated in *Leadership with a Purpose: A Better Society*, a broad-ranging document published for the 2002 Party conference. Duncan Smith had earlier spoken of the 'five giants' that the next Conservative government had to defeat – failing schools, crime, substandard healthcare, child poverty and insecurity in old age – deliberately echoing the language of the Beveridge Report some 60 years earlier. Letwin's fresh thinking, particularly on examining the causes of crime, stirred debate within the Party and its associated think-tanks. His articulation of the 'conveyor belt to crime' and the 'neighbourly society' heralded fertile policy development, and received favourable comment in contrast to some of David Blunkett's more populist measures as Home Secretary. Howard proved an effective shadow Chancellor, the first since 1997 to challenge Gordon Brown's mastery of detail and prowess at the Dispatch Box. By making reform of the public services a priority over tax cuts, Howard sought to neutralize Labour's attacks on 'Conservative cuts', which had been so damaging in the 2001 election. Yet the Party's position on how to reduce the tax burden remained unclear – a problem that was later to afflict Howard's leadership as well. The post-2001 policy review still lacked an over-arching coherence, and offered nothing like the intellectual nor political grasp of Butler's stewardship of policy formulation after the 1945 landslide defeat.

Progress on policy was damaged by the leadership's handling of internal divisions. The government's Adoption and Children Bill in 2002, which had been amended to allow for adoption by unmarried couples (making no distinction between heterosexual and homosexual couples) received the support of some Conservatives MPs on the socially liberal wing, contrary to the Party's official opposition. The rebellion, which included Clarke, Portillo and other 'modernizers', was small but provoked what was seen as a panicked response from Duncan Smith, who imposed a three-line whip over an 'issue of conscience' that would normally demand a free vote, and then issued the disproportionate injunction (for such a minor issue) that the Party had to 'unite or die'.[50] The episode highlighted Duncan Smith's uncertain leadership skills, as well as the rift in the Party over social policy, with modernizers/liberals unable to reconcile their differences with conservatives in either private or public. Modernizers became increasingly frustrated with Duncan Smith, feeling he was also becoming too populist, as in his opposition to the government's policy on university tuition fees. On another important matter, the Commons vote on action in Iraq in March 2003, 16 Conservative MPs defied the leadership to vote against the government.

With hindsight, this was a key moment when Duncan Smith could have exercised real leadership by probing the government's motives for war, Blair's decision-making process prior to hostilities, and Britain's apparently slavish following of America in defiance of international opinion. However, he lacked the cast of mind to strike out on such an independent line, and so failed to give the Party its opportunity to attack the government on the most vulnerable policy of its second term. He then failed to give a clear lead when Blair was at his most vulnerable following the death of David Kelly in the summer of 2003. Duncan Smith opted for what one colleague described as an 'almost invisible' stance over that summer, allowing the Liberal Democrats to seize the initiative in attacking Blair, but then launched a disproportionate attack on the Prime Minister at the Conservative Party conference in October 2003.

Organization and marketing: confusion and chaos

Duncan Smith decided to steer clear of further organizational reform and instead focused on the need to give the Party a better public image. A marketing director and marketing department were thus established within party headquarters.[51] Under the chairmanship of David Davis and then Theresa May, Central Office tried to encourage more women and ethnic minority candidates to apply and be included on the centrally approved candidates list, but hardly any progress was made in this key area where the Conservatives very visibly lagged behind Labour. Local associations continued to assert their autonomy, often choosing candidates that conformed to the white, male, middle-class stereotype, though openly gay and ethnic minority candidates were selected in a handful of seats. Membership continued to decline after the 2001 election, but the Party's revitalized youth wing, Conservative Future, saw its membership increase to over 10,000 by mid-2003.[52] Party finances showed little sign of improving, with corporate and individual donations remaining at relatively low levels, whereas the number of individual donations made to the Liberal Democrats increased dramatically after the 2001 general election and Labour's cash tills continued to ring. Worryingly for Duncan Smith, some former donors chose to withhold support from the Party unless it changed its leader.

It was Duncan Smith's tactical errors, including his mismanagement of personnel at Central Office, that finally precipitated his downfall in the autumn of 2003. His dismissal of Research Director Rick Nye and Campaigns Director Stephen Gilbert, who had served the Party for several years, and appointment of Paul Baverstock as 'Strategy and Communications Planner', upset many staff in late 2002. In early 2003 he summarily dismissed Mark MacGregor, the modernizing Chief Executive, replacing him with an old confidant and former Maastricht rebel, Barry Legg.[53] Legg lasted only two months, resigning after the Party Board registered its formal objection to his appointment. Duncan Smith's failure to consult the Board about the appointment further undermined his authority, which had already been damaged by the departure of other respected figures, including his chief of staff, Jenny Unglass, and Director of Strategy, Cummings. Allegations of impropriety in the financing of Duncan Smith's Private Office in the House of Commons (the so-called 'Betsygate' saga), although subsequently shown to be unfounded, added to the impression of confusion at the top of the Party. By the end, the Conservative whips concluded he would never acquire legitimacy as leader.

External factors: struggling to be heard

In a claim that came to be seen as naive and hubristic, Duncan Smith had announced that people would be able to form a judgement on his leadership after only three or four months. Only two days before his election as leader, the al-Qaeda attacks on New York and Washington heralded the beginning of the 'war on terror'. The world after 11 September 2001 offered Blair opportunities to ensure his international statesmanship would come even more to the fore, leaving Duncan Smith's Conservative Party in the shadows. The latter's immediate pledge of unqualified support for military action against Iraq brought him short-term approval from Washington and plaudits from the right-wing press, but no long-term political gain.

Continuing prosperity during Labour's second term ensured that Conservative efforts to dent the government's record made little impact. However, cracks in the New Labour edifice began to appear after 2001. Its divisions and policy difficulties, including university tuition fees and foundation hospitals as well as over Iraq, offered Duncan Smith opportunities for making political capital that had never been available to Hague. Yet his stock had fallen so low with the press, with the exception of the *Daily Telegraph*, that his voice struggled to be heard.[54] His 'quiet man' image (launched at the 2002 Conservative Party conference) failed to excite the electorate, as opinion polls continued to show Blair and Kennedy as more popular leaders. The Liberal Democrats capitalized electorally on the government's discomfiture, winning a series of safe Labour seats at by-elections. By contrast, the Conservatives' poor performances, particularly at Brent East in September 2003, were the final straw for many Conservative MPs who lost whatever confidence they may have once had in their fledgling leader. As with Hague, he suffered from the fatal perception that no one saw him as a convincing Prime Minister-in-waiting. Despite exhibiting many promising instincts, such as trying to make the Party again an inclusive, centrist force in politics, his fundamental weakness of personality counted too heavily against him.

Howard, 2003–

Michael Howard began his leadership in November 2003 with advantages enjoyed by neither of his immediate predecessors. He had political experience at a high level (notably as Major's Home Secretary) having first become a minister under Thatcher. No Conservative leader since Heath in 1965 came to the post with so much experience. Unlike Hague and Duncan Smith, he had the great benefit of being elected unopposed, and was clearly seen as the man most likely to unite the Party after years of quarrelling. The Party had absorbed the disappointing leaderships of Hague and Duncan Smith, and now had a vested interest in seeing Howard (who had come bottom in the 1997 leadership election) succeed. Although clearly a man on the Eurosceptic centre-right of the Party, his personal friendship with the 'big beasts' on the left of the Party – Clarke, Heseltine, Malcolm Rifkind and Chris Patten – resulted in them holding their fire. Howard claimed he had never briefed against anyone, expected no one else to do so, and said he was determined to restore discipline to the Party – and, unlike Duncan Smith, he could do so with credibility. The media were in agreement that at last the Conservatives had a heavyweight figure and, crucially, a potential Prime Minister, as their leader. As significant, by late 2003, Blair and New Labour had further lost their sheen and some of their popularity with the electorate and the press. The war on Iraq and its aftermath, party divisions (notably over tuition fees) and personal fatigue, were dragging Blair downwards. Howard had an extraordinary opportunity. He had sparred with Blair very effectively in the Commons ten years before, and was considered at least Blair's equal as a debater. The political world held its breath in expectation at the first sustained Conservative onslaught on Blair since he became Labour leader in 1994.

Most optimistic of all probably for Howard was that there were realistic expectations of his leadership. Few expected him to overturn Labour's majority of nearly 160 in a single parliament, let alone in the 18 months that he was likely to have before the next general election. He began promisingly: on the day he declared his candidacy for the leadership, he delivered a speech (drafted by Francis Maude) at the Saatchi Gallery in which he declared 'when the government gets things right I won't oppose for opposition's sake'. The speech appeared statesmanlike, suggesting that he wanted to reclaim the moral high ground, almost unknown territory to the Conservatives for several years. It also suggested that he understood the 'minimum requirement' of the principal opposition party, to look and sound like a government-in-waiting. However, as one colleague commented, 'the problem was that Michael didn't really connect with the words he uttered. He kind of did, but not fully. Before long, day to day pressures intervened.'[55]

Howard certainly changed his tone in the first three months of 2004. It was partly that the more consensual line he articulated in the Saatchi Gallery speech did not chime with the sympathies of those two assertive voices of Conservatism, the *Daily Telegraph* and *Daily Mail*. However, it was also not in Howard's personality to be a consensual figure: he is by nature combative, and by profession a forensic lawyer, and these facts combined to make him want to be on the front foot against Labour. In the first quarter of 2004 he was determined to establish his credibility as a Prime Minister-in-waiting, and to convey his own personality and mission to the electorate. He set out to achieve this in a variety of ways, including his 'I believe' statement, which listed his personal credo, initially in a double page spread in *The Times* in January 2004. He developed his theme in a series of speeches. At Burnley he attacked the far-right British National Party, which revealed his passionate, as well as profoundly anti-racist, side. In Berlin he delivered a speech outlining his pragmatic Eurosceptic line towards the European Union, and at home he delivered another powerful 'British Dream' speech in which again he expounded on his vision for the country. In January 2004, one poll showed the Conservatives with 40 per cent support, the highest since Black Wednesday, and ahead of Labour. Howard and his team hoped to build on this momentum when the Hutton Report was published, and expected it to be far more damning of Blair than it was. Instead of opting for a measured response, Howard acted as if he was the prosecuting counsel and was portrayed as opportunistic: it was his first serious miscalculation as leader.

From March to June 2004, under the influence of his new joint Party Chairmen, Maurice Saatchi and Liam Fox, he moved into a new phase which was a prolonged attack on Labour on the lines that it had 'let down' the electorate. The view was taken that the June local government, European and London Assembly elections should be viewed as a referendum on the performance of the government and that the Conservatives would be seen to be failing if they did not lay bare the government's weaknesses, as they saw them. Progress was made in some municipal areas in local government elections, especially in the West Midlands and North West, and Labour was pushed into third place in the share of the vote. However, overall, the Party's platform did not make more than a modest impression on the electorate. Particularly worrying for the Conservatives was being out-performed by the United Kingdom Independence Party (UKIP) in the European elections.

The summer of 2004 saw yet another new phase, which was positive campaigning on the Conservatives' new policies on public services.

Private party polling suggested that health and education were seen as two negative issues for the Conservatives, so Howard determined that he should put forward fresh policies to counteract the criticisms that Conservative policies were out of touch or unrealistic. By late summer, polls were indeed suggesting that the Party was slightly ahead of Labour on education. The leadership also commissioned a far-reaching review of public spending under City troubleshooter, David James. The review would identity public sector 'waste' and propose savings to fund the Party's fiscal commitments before the general election. However, again it was Iraq where the Conservatives failed to win the argument. In an interview in the *Sunday Times*, Michael Howard had suggested that he would have voted with the Labour rebels in March 2003 (while still supporting the war) if he had known the full facts about weapons of mass destruction at the time. This troubled the parliamentary Party so that, when it came to the debate in the Commons on the Butler Report, it was not fully behind the leader, and his performance was felt to lack credibility and stature. Howard's biggest mistake was not to have better prepared the ground, which was highly fertile. Blair's conduct of the Iraq war remained his greatest weakness, but Howard failed to push home his case. Then, just before the summer recess in 2004, the Party performed disastrously in by-elections in Leicester South and Birmingham Hodge Hill, beaten into third place by a resurgent Liberal Democratic Party. Howard bounced back from criticism over the summer with strong speeches on crime and immigration, and a shadow cabinet reshuffle in early September in which Redwood returned. This was seen as an attempt to woo back potential defectors to UKIP, and some modernizers like John Bercow read the signs and resigned. Howard's authority was further undermined when the Conservatives were beaten into fourth place that month in the Hartlepool by-election.

From the autumn, the final phase of Howard's leadership before the general election began: the so-called 'timetable for action'. His office had decided that it would be 'inconceivable that the general election would be on any other date than in May 2005'.[56] This phase was thus all about preparing for the election. Based on focus group research undertaken over the summer, Saatchi in particular argued that the electorate was disillusioned with the failure of Labour to deliver on its promises. The Conservatives thus needed to give not only specific policy pledges but also a clear timetable for delivery if they were to gain any credibility. Howard's speech to the Conservative conference, a masterpiece of inoffensiveness, set out the Party's stall for the general election, which was more centrist than the Party had produced in 2001, with an emphasis on health and education. Howard's personal qualities as a potential Prime Minister were also highlighted in contrast to what his team saw as an increasingly vulnerable Tony Blair. 'We want the general election to be a presidential contest between the two leaders', one aide said.[57] However, his team also realized that still, by early 2005, they had yet to find an 'over-arching narrative' to explain what the Howard Conservative Party was all about, and why people should vote for it rather than for Labour or Liberal Democrats. Despite announcing costed spending proposals, which would match (and in some areas exceed) the government's own plans for the public services, the Party struggled to produce a distinctive and bold policy platform in early 2005. The James Review recommended £35 billion of savings, of which £23 billion Howard and Letwin pledged towards re-investment in 'frontline' public services, while £8 billion would help to reduce government borrowing. The remaining £4 billion would finance 'targeted tax cuts', without specifying whom they would benefit. The announcements in January 2005 produced mixed messages about the Party's priorities on taxation and spending, leaving many commentators to conclude that Howard and his team were trying to please everyone, while satisfying none.

Howard chose to model his opposition leadership team on the tight-knit group around Blair in 1994–97. His decision-making has thus been very top down, which he justified partly because there was comparatively little time before the general election and there was so much work to be done. 'We all knew in November 2003 that we would have only eighteen months to do everything', one aide said.[58] The shadow cabinet, the parliamentary Party and the Central Office have all been consulted regularly but have, for the most part, been only bit players in the strategic decisions of his leadership. His initial decision to have a small shadow cabinet to enhance co-ordination and communication was jettisoned in July 2004 when he brought in extra figures.

The key figure in Howard's team has been his political secretary, Rachel Whetstone. This is partly because she has known him for over ten years (she was his special adviser in government) and partly because he finds her advice sympathetic and shrewd, though he does not always follow it. For example, she strongly urged him to ditch the Party's opposition to the government's policy on tuition fees, but he chose not to follow her view, which was shared by modernizers. Nor did he follow her advice on identity cards. One of Whetstone's roles is to keep Howard in touch with the output of 'think-tanks' like Policy Exchange. She has played a similar role of sounding board, networker and 'groomer' as Anji Hunter did for Blair, although she is more involved in policy. The second key figure has been Stephen Sherbourne, his chief of staff, who was an adviser in Number 10 to Thatcher and Major, and who possesses a wisdom, steadiness and experience offered by no other in the team. Sherbourne echoes the role of Jonathan Powell in Blair's court and is primarily a fixer who is not particularly concerned with policy. The third key figure is Guy Black, the press secretary, another fixer, who works with, and is trusted by, journalists. However, he is not a strategic media figure like Alastair Campbell nor Peter Mandelson, partly because Howard does not want such a figure and views Campbell in particular as a deeply corrupt and corrosive force. The final key figure in Howard's team, albeit less significant than the first three, has been Lynton Crosby who was charged in November 2004 with bringing together the organization and strategy for the general election campaign. Crosby had helped to mastermind four successive general election victories for Australian Prime Minister, John Howard. Ruthless targeting of key marginal seats has been one of his hallmarks. None of these four had worked for the Party under its previous two leaders, which gave the benefit of freshness, but the inevitable drawback of lack of institutional familiarity.

Within Central Office, the most influential voice on policy has been former Major adviser and director of the Research Department, George Bridges. He was particularly responsible for putting in place many of the policies on the public services since the summer of 2004. Saatchi and Fox have not been as central as many initially expected, and the former in particular is thought by some in the Party, notably the modernizers, to be fighting the battles of the 1980s and 1990s rather than of the early twenty-first century. The modernizers disliked Howard's flirtation in late 2004 with tax cuts and populism, and feared a retreat to a 'core vote' strategy. They groaned at Howard's decision to bring back the arch-Thatcherite and Eurosceptic, Redwood, believing it to be a gift horse to Labour in the general election campaign. Divisions also came to the fore in late 2004 and early 2005 over identity cards, but the proximity of the general election and fear of damage from open displays of disunity will keep such divisions at bay until after the election. Proposals for tougher controls on immigration, albeit more detailed than the Party's plans before 2001, provoked criticism from some quarters that Howard had retreated into 'core vote' territory.

Howard's task would have been made much easier had opinion polls suggested that his strategy was denting Labour. However, poll after poll since March 2004 has shown little change in the Conservatives' low levels of support at little over 30 per cent – no higher than under Hague and Duncan Smith. The *Economist*, which in January 2004 had praised

Howard for creating 'a resurgent and reinvigorated' party which was again 'a disciplined fighting force', concluded in November that 'the once impressive Mr Howard has shrunk in the job'.[59] Some in the Party are already positioning themselves for the post-election (and possibly post-Howard) world. There was much journalistic talk in the months leading up to the general election of the 'Notting Hill' set (David Cameron, George Osborne and Michael Gove) as the new hope for the Party. Howard himself has always maintained in public and in private that he believes he will win the general election and that the opinion polls are inaccurate. While the official line of his team remains that the election is there to be won, soberer voices believe that a gain of some 40 seats to just 200 MPs would be more than sufficient to show the success of Howard's leadership and ensure that he would stay on as leader. The Liberal Democrats remained a concern, with their performance against Labour worrying those who thought it was only at the expense of the Conservatives.

Howard's age (62) was not his only personal drawback, and he did not look or sound sufficiently appealing on television. His image still suffered from the killer comment of his one-time junior minister at the Home Office, Ann Widdecombe, that there was 'something of the night' about him. Like Blair, he is a barrister who excels at oratory and debating, but not in thinking strategically about policy. Howard said he was 'going to put in place a clear strategy which was designed to win the election and I won't be blown off course by opinion polls or newspaper headlines'. However, no more than Hague nor Duncan Smith did he analyse correctly how to make the most of the opportunities before him, nor did he plot a consistent course and stick to it. Yet, of the three, Howard had the easiest task, with Blair vulnerable for much of 2004 until he rallied towards the end of the year. The defection of former higher education minister, Robert Jackson, in January 2005 was a poignant reminder that New Labour could still appeal to disaffected Conservatives, however long their service to the Party.

2005: a pre-election audit

After nearly eight years out of office, is the Conservative Party about to mount a serious challenge for power? The Party is in some ways better positioned for the 2005 general election than for the previous two. Membership may not be at the levels of 1997, but Party activists are better mobilized and have benefited from an injection of younger recruits from Conservative Future. They have been swelled by more than 7500 Conservative councillors, although the Party has yet to recover its local government strength to 1979 levels, when potentially 12,000 councillors were able to campaign for Mrs Thatcher's first election victory. The results of the local government and London Assembly elections confirmed some revival of grass-root activism. However, as one commentator has observed, the Party's electoral progress at a local level does not match that achieved by Labour in the mid-1990s (especially at parliamentary by-elections) and the recovery is 'not sufficient to suggest any chance of winning the next general election'.[60]

Conservative Central Office was renamed Conservative Campaign Headquarters, and in July 2004 moved to modern premises in Victoria Street, close to the Palace of Westminster. 'Hit Squads' have been dispatched to galvanize local parties in key marginal seats, while Liam Fox has imposed a disciplined regime for candidates as well as organizing 'compulsory campaign fitness training programmes'.[61] The appointment of Lynton Crosby promised a more professional and better organized campaign than that of 2001. An influx of donations since Howard became leader has enabled the Party to invest in sophisticated computer software and equipment.[62] The 'Voter Vault' system, successfully pioneered by Karl Rove and the Republicans in the United States, was procured by Fox in mid-2004 – heralding a new era of targeted campaigning in marginal seats. The Party's new machinery has concentrated resources on 900,000 swing voters, and has been helped by a number of regional call centres, with the largest based near Birmingham.[63] Despite the hopes for the Party's new hi-tech campaigning tools, the majority of full-time agents continue to be employed in safe rather than marginal seats. As Justin Fisher has observed, the Party still lags behind Labour and the Liberal Democrats in channelling resources and manpower into target seats.[64]

Howard's advisers and strategists privately expressed concern about the lack of a breakthrough in the polls so close to the general election.[65] Most troubling for Howard's bid for power have been the idiosyncrasies of the electoral system, which heavily favour the incumbent government. Even if the Conservatives lead in the popular vote by 2 per cent at the election, Labour could still win a majority of seats. The Party requires a lead in votes of 11.5 per cent vote over Labour to achieve a bare overall majority.[66] It is expected that turnout will fall further, particularly in safe Labour seats, but Labour candidates still require a lower threshold of support than their Conservative rivals to secure election as a result of distribution of votes.[67] The prospects of a major electoral breakthrough are not good.

In the event of defeat, there will be three kinds of explanation given by the Party. The right wing will say it lost because 'we were insufficiently

Conservative and Eurosceptic'. Another faction will try to steady nerves and argue (as it did after 1997 and 2001) that it will take 'one more heave' to displace Labour, which will become a much easier task with the certainty that Blair will go before the next election. A third group will say the Party lost because it failed to modernize its policies and organization in a sufficiently thorough-going fashion. Some siren voices will also predict the break-up of the Conservative Party. The three explanations mirror precisely those offered for Labour's woes in the 1980s and 1990s, with Michael Foot epitomizing the first thesis, John Smith the second, and Blair the third. What will matter for the Conservatives will be finding a leader who will be able to redefine the Party for the new era, as successful Conservative 'epoch-making' leaders have always done in the past.[68] Making the Conservative Party again a convincing and credible government-in-waiting will be the first requirement.

Conclusion: internal and external factors

There are two main verdicts on the Conservative Party in opposition from 1997 to 2005. The first says that there was little or nothing more that could have been done by the three leaders, given the 'external' factors of the scale of Labour's landslide and the discredited state of the Conservatives in 1997. This view is upheld by most Conservative insiders. The second blames the decisions and characters of the three successive leaders, and says that much more could have been done to dent Labour's lead and credibility. We will examine these 'external' and 'internal' arguments, before offering our own 'third' way.

As we argued in our introduction, Blair is no ordinary leader of the principal non-Conservative party. He is a phenomenon which has not occurred since Palmerston in the mid-nineteenth century. Palmerston led the Liberal Party into a dominant position in the centre ground, making it almost impossible for the Conservative Party to do much. Then, as now, the government ran an assertive foreign policy and was bolstered by a strong economy. Then, as now, there was a dearth of men of real leadership calibre. Only Palmertson's death in 1865 and Disraeli's emergence paved the way for a Conservative recovery. Now it may only be Blair's departure and a refortified Howard (or his successor) that will enable the Conservative Party to become an effective fighting force once again. In this analysis, there was little more that any of the three leaders could have done after 1997.

However, this interpretation is unduly fatalistic. Balfour's party was more deeply split after 1906 and Churchill faced an effective Prime

Minister in Attlee after 1945, but both recovered enough seats at the next election to come close to matching the governing party. Hague, Duncan Smith and Howard barely dented Labour's popularity. Mistakes were certainly made by each leader: changes of direction under Hague, tactical unsteadiness under Duncan Smith and failure to exploit Blair's vulnerability and offer a clear platform under Howard. The last had the most experience and faced a weakened opponent, but lost too many opportunities. Therefore, none of the three leaders can escape culpability for the failure to make more progress.

The most convincing verdict on 1997–2005 combines both analyses. The external circumstances were unusually unfavourable, but they were unnecessarily compounded by internal factors. These were the failures of the leadership to provide a steady platform based on adapting Conservative principles for the new era, and the failure to study history and do more to recover the Conservatives' two no-longer 'secret weapons' – adaptability and hunger for office. Finally, far too little was done to achieve the 'minimum requirement' of opposition, providing a clear alternative government with widely understood and credible policies. Had the Conservative Party done so, Labour's increasingly divided, uncertain and modest record in government could have been far more convincingly exposed. Therein lies the greatest failure of the Conservatives' barren years of 1997–2005.

Notes

1. Interview with John Major in A. Seldon, *Major: A Political Life* (London: Weidenfeld and Nicolson, 1997), 287.
2. The 1997 ICM exit poll data and the British Election Panel survey show that about 2.2 million of those who voted Conservative in 1992 switched directly to Labour, with 1.4 million switching to the Liberal Democrats and about 750,000 to the Referendum Party and UKIP. Fewer than 1 million who voted Conservative in 1992 stayed at home. Also see T. Hames and N. Sparrow, *Left Home: The Myth of Conservative Abstentions in the General Election of 1997* (London: Centre for Policy Studies, 1997).
3. See D. Butler and D. Kavanagh, *The British General Election of 1997* (London: Macmillan, 1997), 244–6.
4. The Conservatives lost a total of 178 seats, one short of Labour's winning overall majority: P. Norris, 'Anatomy of a Labour landslide', *Parliamentary Affairs*, 50 (1997), 1–2.
5. The Conservative share of the vote fell by 14.1 per cent (loss of 30 seats) in Greater London and 13.2 per cent (39 losses) in south-east England. The average national swing from Conservative to Labour was 10 per cent: Butler and Kavanagh, *General Election of 1997*, 256.

6. P. Kellner, 'Why the Conservatives were trounced', in P. Norris and N.T. Gavin (eds), *Britain Votes 1997* (Oxford: Oxford University Press, 1997), 120–2.
7. B. Criddle, 'MPs and candidates', in Butler and Kavanagh, *General Election of 1997*, 202.
8. P. Cowley and M. Stuart, 'The Conservative parliamentary Party', in M. Garnett and P. Lynch (eds), *The Conservatives in Crisis* (Manchester: Manchester University Press, 2003).
9. See D. Willetts and R. Forsdyke, *After the Landslide: Learning the Lessons of 1906 and 1945* (London: Centre for Policy Studies, 1999).
10. Ibid., 1–2.
11. See John Ramsden, *An Appetite for Power* (London: HarperCollins, 1998).
12. According to his biographer, Hague was supremely confident of his chances. Knowing that Heseltine and Portillo were out of the race, he calculated that he would win if he stood. See J-A. Nadler, *William Hague: In His Own Right* (London: Politico's, 2000), 8.
13. The irony is that if party members voted in the 1997 leadership election, as they did in 2001, Clarke might have won, due to his popularity in the country: G. Peele, 'Towards "New Conservatives"? Organizational reform and the Conservative Party', *Political Quarterly*, 69 (1998).
14. They point to the fact that Hague only attracted a quarter of the parliamentary Party's support in the first ballot of the leadership election, many of whom would have preferred Portillo if he had been available. See Cowley and Stuart, 'The Conservative parliamentary Party', 68.
15. Conservative Central Office did organize 'road shows' in the autumn of 1997 to open *Our Party: A Blueprint for Change* to consultation, but only 3000 members attended and it became clear that the leadership's proposals were not open to revision: Garnett and Lynch, *Conservatives in Crisis*, 88.
16. Private interview, 21 Nov. 2004.
17. The Party Board was also given the power to enforce compulsory audits and 'efficiency criteria' governing the everyday conduct of local associations, and the financial independence of local associations was also discreetly weakened: R. Kelly, 'The Party didn't work: Conservative reorganization and electoral failure', *Political Quarterly*, 73 (2002), 40–2.
18. Although 96 per cent of members supported the *Fresh Future* package, only 33 per cent of the estimated membership took part. It was also a take-it-or-leave-it package, denying members the opportunity to approve some of the reforms and not others. Ibid.
19. Private information.
20. The 'rationalization' of Central Office involved a £3 million cut in spending and the redundancy of 40 per cent of the staff: see Garnett and Lynch, *The Conservatives in Crisis*, 91.
21. Official estimates of party membership were 756,000 in 1992, 400,000 in 1997 and 300,000 in 2001, but recent research indicates that these figures are too high. Richard Kelly estimates that the total membership may have fallen to fewer than 260,000 in 2001 (on the basis of ballot returns in the 2001 leadership election): Kelly, 'The Party didn't work', 43.
22. By 2000, the Party's £8 million deficit from 1997 had been converted into a surplus of £2000: Garnett and Lynch, *Conservatives in Crisis*, 93.
23. Private information.

24. Kelly, 'The Party didn't work', 39.
25. Private interview, 21 Nov. 2004.
26. M. d'Ancona, paper given to a Demos seminar, 12 July 2001.
27. Ian Taylor, David Curry and Stephen Dorrell resigned from the shadow cabinet in 1998. Two Conservative MPs defected in the 1997–2001 parliament: Peter Temple-Morris joined the Liberal Democrats over the issue of Europe in June 1998, while Shaun Woodward crossed the floor to Labour over the leadership's policy on 'Section 28' in December 1999.
28. Private interview, 21 Nov. 2004.
29. E. Ashbee, 'The US Republicans: lessons for the Conservatives?', in Garnett and Lynch, *Conservatives in Crisis*, 41–6.
30. Private interview, 21 Nov. 2004.
31. Ibid.
32. Ibid.
33. Ibid.
34. Ibid.
35. Although the Conservatives topped the poll with 36 per cent and 36 MEPs, turnout for the European elections was only 24 per cent.
36. S. Walters, *Tory Wars: The Conservatives in Crisis* (London: Politico's, 2001).
37. Private interview, 21 Nov. 2004.
38. P. Norris (ed.), *Britain Votes 2001* (Oxford: Oxford University Press, 2001), 66–71.
39. A. Seldon and P. Snowdon, *The Conservative Party: An Illustrated History* (Stroud: Sutton Publishing, 2004), 131.
40. Ibid.
41. Butler and Kavanagh, *General Election of 1997*, 260–1.
42. The Conservatives polled even fewer votes in 2001 than Labour's electoral nadir in 1983, when it polled 8.4 million votes.
43. Labour held 23 of its 30 most marginal seats and increased its majorities in many of the leafy, suburban seats, such as Enfield Southgate, Wimbledon and Bristol West: Norris, *Britain Votes 2001*, 13.
44. The national swing from Labour to Conservative was 1.8 per cent: ibid., 8.
45. Interviews, David Willetts and Francis Maude.
46. Ibid.
47. Duncan Smith was the first leader of the Conservative Party not to have served as a cabinet minister before becoming leader: P. Snowdon and D. Collings, 'Déjà vu? Conservative problems in historical perspective', *Political Quarterly*, 75 (2004).
48. *Guardian*, 19 Sep. 2001.
49. G. Clark and S. Kelly, 'Echoes of Butler? The Conservative Research Department and the making of Conservative policy', *Political Quarterly*, 75 (2004).
50. Peter Riddell described Duncan Smith's decision as 'both wrong and tactically inept', *The Times*, 5 Nov. 2003.
51. See J. Lees-Marshment, 'Mis-marketing the Conservatives: the limitations of style over substance', *Political Quarterly*, 75 (2004).
52. *Sunday Times*, 29 June 2003 and 2 Nov. 2003.
53. R. Kelly, 'The extra parliamentary Conservative Party: McKenzie revisited', *Political Quarterly*, 75 (2004).

54. Even the normally loyal Conservative commentator, Bruce Anderson, called on Iain Duncan Smith to resign, arguing that he did not possess the 'judgement, the personality, the intellect, the leadership skills or the self-confidence to lead his party anywhere near victory': *Spectator*, 5 May 2003.
55. Private interview, 21 Nov. 2004
56. Private interview, 19 Nov. 2004.
57. Private information.
58. Private interview, 19 Nov. 2004.
59. *Economist*, 10 Jan. and 6 Nov. 2004.
60. D. Broughton, 'Doomed to defeat? Electoral support and the Conservative Party', *Political Quarterly*, 75 (2004).
61. *Daily Telegraph*, 6 Mar. 2004, 29 Apr. 2004.
62. J. Fisher, 'Money matters: the financing of the Conservative Party', *Political Quarterly*, 75 (2004).
63. P. Oborne, 'The mean machine', *Spectator*, 20 Nov. 2004.
64. Fisher, 'Money matters'.
65. Private interview, 19 Nov. 2004
66. Broughton, 'Doomed to defeat?'.
67. Snowdon and Collings, 'Déjà vu?'.
68. This is the general argument in Seldon and Snowdon, *Conservative Party*, 23–133.

Appendix
The Conservative Party in General Elections 1868–2001

Before 1918 constituencies polled on different days, and the date shown for general elections up to 1910 is that of the first polls: with the exception of Orkney & Shetlands and the university seats, constituencies polled in the course of the following 14–16 days. In the 1918 and 1945 elections the count was delayed until 28 December and 26 July respectively to allow for the collection of the postal ballots from the forces serving overseas.

The figures for 1886 to 1910 include Liberal Unionists. Those for 1918, 1931 and 1935 are for the Conservatives alone and do *not* include the other groups with which they were in coalition. However, by 1945 the distinction between Conservative candidates and the remaining National Liberals was of local significance only, and they and the small number of purely 'National' candidates are included in the figures for 1945 to 1951.

Date of election	Candidates nominated	Unopposed returns	MPs elected	Total votes received	% share of vote
17 Nov. 1868	436	91	271	903,318	38.4
31 Jan. 1874	507	125	350	1,091,708	43.9
31 Mar. 1880	521	58	237	1,426,351	42.0
24 Nov. 1885	602	10	249	2,020,927	43.5
1 July 1886	563	118	393	1,520,886	51.4
4 July 1892	606	40	313	2,159,150	47.0
13 July 1895	588	132	411	1,894,772	49.1
1 Oct. 1900	569	163	402	1,767,958	50.3
12 Jan. 1906	556	13	156	2,422,071	43.4
15 Jan. 1910	594	19	272	3,104,407	46.8

Date of election	Candidates nominated	Unopposed returns	MPs elected	Total votes received	% share of vote
3 Dec. 1910	548	72	272	2,420,169	46.6
14 Dec. 1918	445	41	382	4,144,192	38.6
15 Nov. 1922	482	42	344	5,502,298	38.5
6 Dec. 1923	536	35	258	5,514,541	38.0
29 Oct. 1924	534	16	412	7,854,523	46.8
30 May 1929	590	4	260	8,656,225	38.1
27 Oct. 1931	518	49	470	11,905,925	55.0
14 Nov. 1935	515	23	387	10,496,300	47.8
5 July 1945	618	1	210	9,972,010	39.6
23 Feb. 1950	619	2	298	12,492,404	43.5
25 Oct. 1951	617	4	321	13,718,199	48.0
26 May 1955	624	–	345	13,310,891	49.7
8 Oct. 1959	625	–	365	13,750,876	49.3
15 Oct. 1964	630	–	304	12,002,642	43.4
31 Mar. 1966	629	–	253	11,418,455	41.0
18 June 1970	628	–	330	13,145,123	46.4
28 Feb. 1974	623	–	297	11,872,180	37.9
10 Oct. 1974	622	–	277	10,462,565	35.8
3 May 1979	622	–	339	13,697,923	43.9
9 June 1983	633	–	397	13,012,316	42.4
11 June 1987	633	–	376	13,760,583	42.3
9 Apr. 1992	645	–	336	14,092,891	41.9
1 May 1997	648	–	165	9,602,989	31.4
7 June 2001	643	–	166	8,357,292	31.8

Index